Quest For A Meaningful Life

Through
Christianity, Judaism, Islam, Hinduism, and Buddhism

By Ivan Beggs

For forty years Ivan Beggs listened to hundreds of people about suffering, forgiveness, faith, hope, love, sex, afterlife, and how they turned to their faiths for comfort. He explored how Christianity, Judaism, Islam, Buddhism, and Hinduism addressed their concerns. In this book he tells the story and gives suggestions for a Meaningful Life.

This book is useful for interesting and lively group study and a comparative religion course.

Full Color Illustrations

Copyright © 2020 by Ivan Beggs

All rights reserved. No part of this publication may be reproduced, distributed, or transmitted in any form or by any means, including photocopying, recording, or other electronic or mechanical methods, without the prior written permission of the publisher, except in the case of brief quotations embodied in critical reviews and certain other noncommercial uses permitted by copyright law.

For permission requests, write to the publisher: quest4a@protonmail.com

"Quest For A Meaningful Life" by Ivan Beggs.

Editor: Jim Nelson, Hendersonville, NC
Book Designer: Phyllis Barnard, Candler, NC
Cover background picture: GCShutter @iStock by Getty Images
Cover creation: Ivan Beggs – All rights reserved

ISBN: 978-1-7341167-0-0 Soft cover – full color illustrations

REL017000 RELIGION / Comparative Religion
BIO018000 BIOGRAPHY & AUTOBIOGRAPHY / Religious
SEL031000 SELF-HELP / Personal Growth / General

First Edition

14 13 12 11 10 / 10 9 8 7 6 5 4 3 2 1

Dedication

Many thanks to Marlene, my wife for fifty years, for her patience and especially my children. Thank you to the many people listed in the Acknowledgments who helped form and create this study, even though they didn't realize they were contributing. And many thanks to people who have struggled with faith and doubt. We are not alone. It was tempting to title the book, "We Are Not Alone."

Please send comments for discussion and to improve the book to:

quest4a@protonmail.com

Please remember in your comments that we are guests in each other's lives.

Enjoy the reading and your quest.

CONTENTS

Part I

Childhood to Seminary

Chapter 1 - In the Beginning 1

Chapter 2 - The Children's Home 17

Chapter 3 - A New Start 41

Chapter 4 - The Army 59

Chapter 5 - Seminary – The Questions 75

Chapter 6 - Seminary – The Responses 83

Part II

14 Themes of 5 Religions

Chapter 7 - Pain, Suffering, and Evil 101

Chapter 8 - Sin and Karma 125

Chapter 9 - Forgiveness 135

Chapter 10 - Faith 163

Chapter 11 - Hope 183

Chapter 12 - Joy 189

Chapter 13 - Love 197

Chapter 14 - Sex 207

Chapter 15 - God's Character 223

Chapter 16 - Experiencing God 239

Chapter 17 - Afterlife 249

CONTENTS

Chapter 18 - Scriptures 265

Chapter 19 - Authority 291

Chapter 20 - A Meaningful Life 325

Part III

Creating a Meaningful Life

Chapter 21 - Love and Work 347

Chapter 22 - Happy, Healthy, Wealthy, and Wise 351

Chapter 23 - Maslow's Hierarchy 353

Chapter 24 - Finance, Economics, And Psychology 363

Chapter 25 - Freewill - Creative or Reactive life 367

Chapter 26 - Guests in Our Lives 369

Chapter 27 - Sex 379

Chapter 28 - Might not Happen 385

Chapter 29 - Create Your Own Meaningful Life 393

Bibliography 397

Figure and Cover Permissions 415

Figure List 422

Acknowledgments 426

Recommendations 429

About the Author 431

Introduction

Your quest for a meaningful life will probably be different from mine. However, the themes, issues, questions, and problems will probably be similar. Hopefully this writing gives you some helpful ideas for your journey. Enjoy the reading.

After graduating from seminary, I listened to people's concerns for forty years. I listened to neighbors, friends, co-workers, strangers in airports, in airplanes, on a ship, in coffee shops, bars, and places I have forgotten. I listened to people in the US, England, Germany, Romania, France, China, India, Vietnam, South Korea, and in South America.

For whatever reasons, they felt comfortable talking, chatting, and wondering with me. Sometimes, their stories were brief. Occasionally, they told their stories for hours. At first, they related easy parts of their lives. Then quietly transitioned to their concerns and finally their issues with a meaningful life.

Most people just enjoyed their lives and what they were doing. Whatever their circumstances were, most accepted them. Though many had concerns about pain, suffering, evil, love, sex, afterlife, forgiveness, experiencing God, and more.

I took those concerns and explored how Christianity, Judaism, Islam, Buddhism, Hinduism, and several other faiths did and did not address those issues. The vastness of the project and the realization that one or many people could spend lifetimes on such an exploration forced me to limit the writing part of the project to the five major faiths, which is 77% of the world's population.

To clarify my thinking for myself, I first wrote about what prompted me to start the Quest for a meaningful life. So, Part I describes the events in my life from birth, a children's home, the Army, and seminary that propelled me on the forty-year Quest which became Part II. It explains what each of the five faiths said about people's questions and concerns about their faith and a meaningful life. Which naturally led to how can people create a meaning life with or without religion, which is Part III.

Thus, the book is readable in or out of sequence as Parts I, II, and III. Or delve into any chapter you wish. Each Part and each chapter can stand alone.

Hopefully a few souls will find this book helpful. Or, if nothing else, at least interesting and simulating. My guess is that reading it by yourself will be helpful and that reading it as part of a discussion group will be interesting, lively, and provide the most benefit to you and to your group.

Part II of the book is excellent for a comparative religion class. The views of the five major religions followed by a discussion are presented on each of fourteen topics of great concern to many people.

Best of wishes and thoughts to you on your quest for a meaningful life. Please feel free to let me know where you are at in your personal or group journey, search, quest, or whatever you choose to call it and how to improve the book. This book is meant to be part of a respectful conversation between you, me, and many others.

>   Ivan Beggs
>   quest4a@protonmail.com

Part I – Childhood to Seminary

Chapter 1

In the Beginning

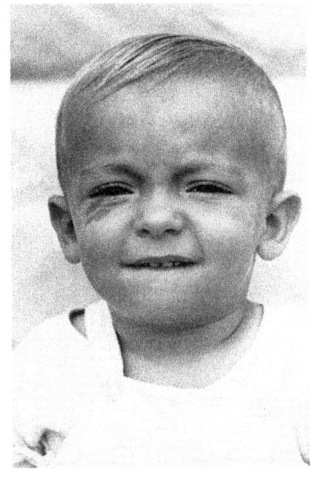

Figure 1.1 Ivan as a one-year-old in Peru.

In late 1940, Dad told my grandmother he would go to sea for only one year. Then he would stay home and become a New York harbor pilot. However, events beyond his control changed his life and in turn eventually created me.

Dad was on a cargo ship, Steel Seafarer, on the Red Sea on September 5, 1941. At eleven o'clock at night he had just finished taking a shower. Put his shorts on. Lit a pipe, when suddenly there was a loud explosion which shook the ship. It started listing.

He said, "I said, Oh sugar." Well not actually. I was a child when he told me the story. So, he winked and continued.

"Everyone on the crew ran up on deck. Sparks, the radio operator, instantly sent off a distress signal that the ship was sinking. It continued to list. So, we jumped into the sea. Swam away. In less than ten minutes the ship sank. In the morning a British destroyer picked us up. I spent several weeks in Egypt courtesy of the British Army." [1]

Two postcards addressed to my grandmother say that Dad will be home by the middle of December 1941.

A local New York newspaper tells of Dad's story about a torpedo sinking the ship and his promise to my grandmother to return home in a year. It implies that he will stay home and become a New York Harbor pilot. The article concluded, "Beggs of course, may stick to his promise never to take another trip. But he'll have to use all his will power to keep away from the fresh salt air for the rest of his life"[2] The warning was right. Dad spent the rest of WWII working on Merchant Marine ships, taking cargo from the US to England, and for the invasion of Africa, the invasion of Italy, and for D-Day in Europe.

Meanwhile, before the war between Germany and the US started, Mom and her husband-to-be hurriedly left Germany for Switzerland. Mom said that her future husband had fears of being on the wrong political side of Hitler; so, he had to leave. Mom said, "At the train station, I happily waved goodbye to my parents and family. They knew I was leaving for good; but, no one told me." Later, in Switzerland, they were married. Eventually, they bribed their way into Spain, then Portugal, and finally on to a ship to the US.

When they arrived in New York, a US Customs Agent wanted to take Mom's Horner Accordion apart to check for contraband. She said, "If I can play music with the accordion, will that be enough to prove there is no contraband and no need to take the accordion apart?" They agreed.

---

1 (Pratt 1941) Ralph S. Pratt's account differs a bit from what my father told me some fifteen years after the incident. Pratt said that no radio signal was sent and that they scrambled onto two lifeboats and rowed to shore. They arrived around 11 AM. The Egyptians were nice and British Navy picked them up.

2 A torn page from a scrap book tells the story. Because of the tears there was no date of the article nor the newspaper. Most likely the paper was the local paper, "The Staten Island Advance" sometime in September 1941.

She played polkas. A crowd of several hundred gathered around her and began to clap and dance while waiting for customs agents. The agents yelled to stop playing and get on through the process. Mom and her husband quietly melted into the German American community. Because there were issues of his not being able to father a baby, they later divorced.

During World War II, Mom and Dad met each other at a party in New York City. After the war, he changed jobs from working in the Merchant Marines to working for the American Embassy in Peru. There I popped into the world in a home birth. My handwritten birth certificate is in Spanish. A year later, Dad changed jobs to a US company in Venezuela shipping freight by sea.

Oil

Venezuela was "oil country." It was everywhere. Sometimes I would go with dad to Maracaibo, usually late at night. I would fall asleep on the backseat of the car. When we came near the oil fields, the deep hum of oil derricks going up and down and burning off the methane would wake me up. The fires burning against an inky blanket air seemed like destruction and hell. The smell, dad said, "Was the smell of money being made." The first few times the fires scared me. Later they became fascinating.

At first, we lived in Puerta La Cruz, Venezuela. A Coca-Cola truck made a sharp left turn near our home. The truck flipped over spilling thousands of Coke bottles over the road and into a small oil pond. The villagers came running. While they were grabbing cases of Coke, the driver was running around waving his arms screaming at everyone to stop stealing the Coke. No one listened. They just laughed at him and kept taking the Coke; even eventually taking the bottles that fell into the oil pond.

The babysitter was nice. But she didn't pay close attention to me. She liked to be with her boyfriend. She told me not to say anything to my mom. So, I kept quiet. I went off to play with some other children. One time, while she was with her boyfriend, the other children and I had great fun playing in one of the many pools of oil by the oil field. We were all covered from head to toe with sun warmed crude oil. It was in our hair, on our faces, torso, legs and bare feet. It was great fun.

However, when I got home, mom was beyond furious. Outside, she poured gasoline on me to get most of the oil off. Then she took a hose and soap and washed me off. Then she took me inside and washed me again. Never did see that nice babysitter again. Did she ever marry her boyfriend and have a family?

The Docks

As a five-year-old, I enjoyed going with Dad to the docks in Puerto La Cruz, La Guairá (Caracas) and Maracaibo, Venezuela. His job was to make sure that ships for Grace Line had a berth, stevedores, customs paperwork, and space for unloading and loading cargo. While he did that, I wandered around, watching the dock activities.

In those days, ships carried goods on pallets and had a few passengers. The ships had booms and cranes to load and unload individual pallets and cars. Forklifts zoomed around carrying the pallets. Men yelled and cursed at each other, 'Get out of the way." "Move that s...t over there." "Your mother is a ..." And so on.

The stevedores often played the game of 'spill the pallet.' They started yelling and cursing that they wanted more money for that type of work. The dock foreman yelled obscenities back at them. The yelling and cursing would go on for a while. Then the stevedores stopped a pallet in midair. Silently the pallet swung back and forth. Time stopped. All eyes looked at the foreman.

He became irate. The stevedores yelled that they wanted more money. Suddenly, there was 'an accident.' The pallet tipped, and the cargo fell into the space between the ship and the dock. There was more yelling and cursing. The foreman came to Dad and they huddled, waving their arms at each other. Meanwhile all the loading or unloading stopped. The stevedores silently grinned and looked at Dad and the foreman. Then the foreman yelled at the stevedores the new price. Everyone was happy, except Dad. He walked by me with an angry face. The loading and unloading continued.

Afterwards, I ran around the docks with other older kids. Sometimes, we tried to sneak on one of the freighters. But someone was always paying attention to whoever tried to get on or off the ship. He had a stick about as long as a broom handle. He mildly swung it up and down at us. We knew he would smack us. It was fun teasing the guard. We all knew we would not get on the ship.

We had to be careful with all the activity of forklifts, stacks of pallets that might fall over, drunks sleeping or waddling around, pallets moving up and down, the loading and unloading of trucks and the ships. We had to pay close attention. For the life of me I don't remember the games we played besides trying to sneak on the freighters. Hide and seek between pallets? Whatever it was, it was fun.

Figure 1.2 Afterwards, I ran around the docks with other older kids Typical scene where I would play and run while the cargo was loaded and unloaded from ships. Great fun.

When senoritas would walk along the docks, the stevedores would whistle and call out, expressions like, "Hey beautiful. How are you? See you tonight?" The senoritas laughed, waved, and continued. The men did not whistle or call out when foreign women got off or on the ships. A few times a stevedore whistled and said words the women didn't understand. The women made a fuss and other stevedores slapped the guy and told him to stop.

Afterwards, I would go with Dad to one of the bars. Dad had one of the senoritas entertain me at a pool table while he disappeared. However, I could barely see over the table and reach a ball. So, I just pushed the balls. A woman would bend over to explain the game and show where to push the ball. Her blouse would hang down and instead of paying attention to what she said, I always became mesmerized by what was jiggling back and forth several inches away. The men at the bar would approvingly laugh and murmur something inaudible. She would smile and giggle. I was confused and enjoyed the mesmerizing view.

A while later Dad came back quite happy, buy drinks for the dockhands, the foremen, the managers, and the senoritas, tell a few jokes, everyone would laugh, and then we left. He always said, "Now, don't tell your Mom what we just did."

At home, when Dad wasn't around, Mom would ask what Dad and I did. I told her about the ships, the cargo, the weather, the other kids, and said nothing about the bar and playing pool. However, after a while something about her asking began to seem strange.

Sitting on the Windowsill

After Christmas, 1951, in Caracas, I was sitting on the broad windowsill watching the heavy rain. It was pleasant looking through the wooden bars of the big window at the houses below and the cemetery across the street. The windows were only wooden bars for decoration and to keep people out. The weather was so nice, there was no need to have glass or screens. I liked hearing the strong summer rain and feeling the moist breeze.

Suddenly, brown stuff came out of the front door of the house below. The lady screamed, "The toilet is overflowing. The toilet is overflowing." I thought it was so funny for someone's toilet to overflow that much. I giggled and called Mom to see the funny sight.

Then I wondered, "How can the toilet-over-flow go out the front door of the house, while brown toilet stuff comes in through their backdoor? Huh? How can that be?"

Suddenly, brown-toilet stuff came in the backdoor of my house. It rushed through the open screenless kitchen door, flowed through the living room, and took my toys out the open front door. I thought, "There is no toilet by the backdoor."

Mom grabbed me and placed me firmly on the stairs and screamed, "Go up!"

After the rains and the mudslide stopped, I looked out. Mud covered the street. Mud pushed cars down the street towards the bay. Mud covered the cemetery, knocked over gravestones, pushed mausoleums over. Mud tossed caskets into piles.

Immediately, Mom got a shovel and a hose. Somehow, by herself she shoveled the mud out of the house. Then she sprayed the mud off the stone floor and walls. Several days later, the servants came back to clean the stone walls, the stone floors, clothing and furniture. But Mom energetically did the major cleaning before the warm air dried the mud solid inside the house.

A few days later it was entertaining watching the front loaders put mud into dump trucks and the men waving their arms pointing in different directions, yelling and cursing at each other. After the warmth hardened the mud on the street, the men yelled and cursed more.

Parties

Because of Dad's job they had a lot of parties at our home near Caracas. The ship officers, Venezuelan men, and other visitors from around the world, told stories about the adventure, fun, sorrow, the recent war, and most importantly about the world. They told jokes, laughed, ate and drank. It was great fun.

Towards the end of the parties, I collected the plates and glasses and took them to the kitchen. Then I got the idea it was a waste to throw out the liquids. So, I cleaned the glasses by drinking the ice-diluted hard drinks, which gave me a pleasant feeling. One time, several times I fell asleep in the living room. The laughter of the ship officers and Venezuelans woke me up. I stumbled off to bed.

When Dad and I went to the docks, he pointed out the drunks that were sleeping on the streets, alleys, and near the docks. He said, "That is what happens when they drink too much. Drinking too much will kill them." He never told me not to drink. He just emphasized that drinking can be fun but can also hurt and kill. Decades later he died from drinking too much.

My eager ears loved the Venezuelan men. They really enjoyed telling me in Spanish their jokes, their stories, and their sayings. They often said in Spanish, "Americans are like bulls in a china shop."

I said, "Huh? What does a bull do in a china shop?"

They said, "They shit all over, wreck the place and then they go home."

Hearing these stories, I felt that I and people living all over the world were ONE people living in one big town. Years later in high school, I made the connection of the world as one big town while reading the delightfully warm play, "Our Town."

However, my mother was not happy with my view….

The Bear Who Wasn't a Bear

A sweet and caring Venezuelan babysitter read a Spanish children's book to me. My favorite book was, "El Oso Que No Era Oso" (The Bear Who Wasn't a Bear). Perhaps at one point I had it memorized.

It was a story about a bear who goes to sleep in the woods for the winter. When he wakes up in the springtime, he was in the middle of a factory. A foreman sees him and yells, "Get back to work."

The bear says, "But I am a bear. I don't work here."

They go to the manager, the manager's boss, the manager of the manager's boss, and eventually to the president of the company. The foreman has one secretary, one trash can and one telephone. The manager has one more of those than the foreman. And so on. The president has five trash cans, five secretaries, and five telephones.

The president says, "Let's go to the zoo and the circus."

At the zoo, a little bear says, "If you were a bear you would be in here, not out there."

At the circus, a little bear says, "If you were a bear, you would be in here, not out there."

So, the president, the manager's manager, the manager, the foreman and the bear go back to the factory. The bear stands in front of a machine and works.

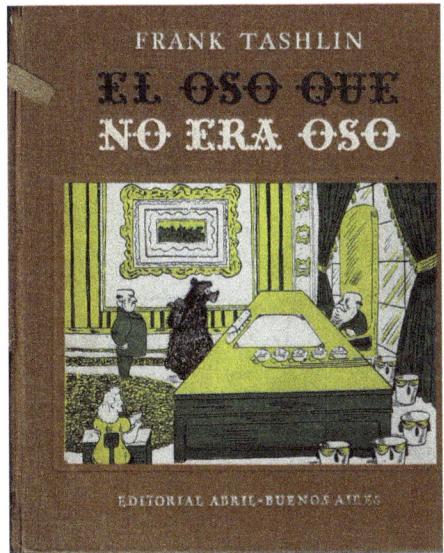

Figure 1.3 Cover of my favorite book the baby sitter would read to me.

The factory closed, and people lost jobs. The babysitter always said, "Americans do that a lot."

Then the bear goes back to the woods. He sits in the falling snow outside of his den. He thinks, "Am I a bear or not a bear?"

After pondering the events, he concludes, "I am a bear."

He goes into his den and goes to sleep.

After reading the story, the babysitter always said to me, "You are who you are."

Figure 1.4. The bear thinking about who he is.

Sometime later,

Mom pointed at me,

While screaming at Dad, "He thinks he is a South American. He is becoming a South American." He needs to know HE IS an American.

Mom and Dad were quiet people who never fought. But that day was different. Sixty-eight years later, I remember that morning like it was a few minutes ago. I was five-years old living in Caracas, Venezuela playing in the living room with little trucks, cars and boats. A nice warm pleasant breeze gently drifted inside.

Figure 1.5 He knows he is a bear.

Mom continued screaming, "He (meaning me) thinks HE is a South American. HE must know he is an American. We must go to the States!" In vain Dad tried to persuade her that life was nice. There was a big house with a gardener and a maid. The weather was beautiful year-round. The Caribbean was a block away.

I thought, "Why did Mom want to go live where bulls shit all over the place and ruin things? Why would Mom want to live where bulls made a smelly mess in homes, streets and business? Anyway, what are bulls doing in a china shop? They don't belong there. They belong in the bull ring with a matador. Anyway, why do Americans come here and make a mess?"

But Mom was determined.

She won.

Since Dad worked for a company that had ships, Mom and I left Maracaibo, Venezuela by a freight ship. In the evening, from the stern of the ship, I sadly looked at the receding harbor lights and the black, thick, warm, pleasant darkness enveloping the ship. The ship's propeller made such a pleasant rhythmic ka-thump, ka-thump, ka-thump sound that I wanted the warm water to caress me so that I could more keenly feel the propeller's rhythm. I was depressed leaving nice Venezuela to go live where bulls made messes in china shops and people's homes.

Then a sailor came by and said, "Time for dinner." My arms and legs moved like heavy wet sandbags.

After a week at sea watching the flying fish, porpoises, sea gulls, beautiful fluffy clouds in the warm blue skies, and the gentle waves, I was bored. So, leaving Mom sunbathing, I explored the ship. Eventually, I went up to the bridge and opened the door. This was the place to be. The power. The thrill. I would make the ship go zoom, zoom, zoom like I did with my toys!

Figure 1.6. Alone in the wheelhouse, I steered the freighter all by myself hoping it would go like a speedboat.

Holding on to the wheel, I made noises like a speed boat, "Rrrrrrrr rrrrrrrr." I spun the wheel to the left, to the right, to the left, to the right. I wanted the ship to move like a speed boat that would go zoom, zoom, zoom! Instead, the freighter slowly, ever so slowly -

sloooower than a snail – drifted to the left, then drifted to the right…. then the left…. then the right. That was boring. Boorrring.

But on my right-side was a nice bright shiny brass handle with a pointer to words that I could not read. I pulled the handle back. It went, ding-ding. I pushed it all the way forward. Ding-ding. Backward – ding-ding – and forward – ding-ding. Over and over I pushed the handle. That was boring.

So, I left the bridge, went down the stairs to where Mom was sunbathing. I played with my toy boats, zooming them right and then left.

Suddenly….

The door on the bridge flew open. The ship's captain stormed out. He looked down at me. Screamed words that I don't remember and probably shouldn't repeat. Instead of calmly walking down the stairs, he put his hands on the railing and slid down the stairs. He was running straight at me. Mom, dressed only in her bathing suit, jumped up, and put out her arms like a defensive football player. The Captain stopped. But he kept screaming.

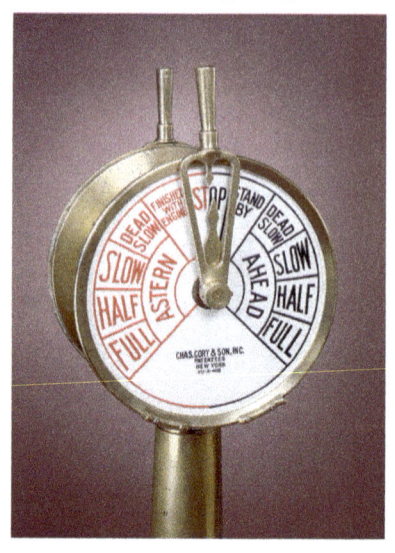

Then I moved the handle to full astern, then to full ahead, then full astern, then full ahead, then left the wheelhouse.

Meanwhile, unknown to me, all the changes I was making with the helm and the ship's speed were visible in the engine room. An engineer contacted the bridge to find out what was happening. But there was no response. He did not know what was going on. So, he notified the crew to get on deck and prepare to abandon the ship.

The crew ran up on deck and gathered where Mom and the ship's captain were 'communicating.'

Mom said to the Captain, "You must tell him why what he did was wrong." So, he starts.

But then she says, "You have to get down to his eye level."

So, he kneels. Looks at me eyeball to eyeball. He said, "What you did was wrong. The ship is off course. I am going to spend a lot of time figuring out where we are and make course corrections. This is going to cost a lot of money for the fuel."

I thought, "I don't have an allowance nor a job. How am I going to pay for this?"

Then he said, "Besides, it was extremely dangerous. We could have had an accident."

In a child's simple mindedness, I squeaked in a high-pitched voice, "If it was so dangerous, how come no one was there?" The ship's crew tried to stop giggling. They bit their lips. Sucked on their thumbs. They smirked. They looked at each other trying to stop giggling.

I was confused.

The Captain stood up like a killer whale breaching the ocean surface. Clinched his fists besides his legs. Screamed, "Grrrrrrrrrrrr." Stormed back up to the bridge and slammed the door.

A while later – was it several hours? – I was watching the sea gulls, flying fish, and porpoises. A seaman came next to me. He said, "You made the captain terribly angry and sad. During World War II…"

I thought, "World War II?" I pictured little men standing on one of those globes some people have in their living rooms. They were hitting each other with baseball bats. I thought, "That's silly. It makes no sense. The entire world could not have been at war."

He continued, "During World War II, the Captain was the Director for all Merchant Marine Maritime Operations in the North Atlantic...."

I thought, "A director?" I pictured him on a buoy with flags in the middle of the ocean. Waving ships to go straight, right, left just like a policeman would direct traffic. I thought, "But where would the buoy be? The Atlantic is so big." That made no sense.

The seaman continued, "Now he is just a ship's captain waiting to collect his retirement." I thought, "What is a retirement?"

"And now, he has been embarrassed by a five-year-old. He is feeling very sad. You made him very sad."

Decades later, an old salt (a guy who has been to sea longer than anyone can remember) said to me, "What really bothered the captain was that seamen in the bars around the world would tell the story. And all the accomplishments that he did, particularly in WWII, will be eclipsed by a five-year-old embarrassing him." The seamen around the world would laugh at him. I felt sorry for the captain. But I didn't feel guilty.

Eventually, we arrived in the New York harbor. Dad had flown to New York City by plane. He got on the launch with the harbor pilot and met us on board the ship. They told me to go outside of the cabin and to see the Statue of Liberty. I just wanted to play with my toys.

Figure 1.8 My first memory of the US.

They became insistent. So, I went outside. There was the dumb green statue holding an arm up to the beautiful blue sky with a big middle finger sticking up. Boring.

Suddenly, the deck filled up with people – and – children. Lots of children. I thought, "Where were all these kids? We could have been playing together."

A seaman came on deck. He screamed, "Get down below deck!" He swung his arms hitting people in the crowd like the paddle wheel on a river boat churning water at full speed. People ran. I ran too. The seaman grabbed the back of my shirt; hauled me up to his face. He screamed, "Not you!"

Suddenly, everyone vanished.

Gone. The deck was quiet. Empty. The silly statue just stood there looking at me and I at it with its' big finger in the air.

I went inside to tell mom and dad. They said, "Oh you were imagining things."

I persisted. They repeated, "Oh you were imagining things. You were at sea so long you were lonely and are making this up."

I persisted. They said, "You want to cause trouble?"

I squeaked out, "No."

They said, "Shut up!"

Sometime later dad explained what was going on. He said, "When the ships come into the docks, all the cargo goes through the customs agent at the beginning of the dock. If we want to take something off and not pay customs duties, we leave a present for the guy. He swivels his chair around, holds up a big newspaper and reads it. Meanwhile, the stowaways scurry off the ship and disappear into Brooklyn. They will probably do that around two in the morning when it is dark, and no one is around."

I thought, "What will they think when they meet American bulls in china shops and on the streets? I hope the children don't step into bullshit. How can I warn them to watch where they step? Why would their parents want to come where there are such bulls? This place is confusing."

Mom found an apartment in Brooklyn. I found some 'friends.' Although my English with adults was ok; however, with children, my English accent was wrong, and my vocabulary was a mixture of English and Spanish. So, whenever I spoke, funny sounds came out. After several fights, I came home and said, "I am not speaking that stupid language again!"

Mom, a German immigrant, was happy and proud.

She murmured, "He is becoming an American."

The Marshmallow Test

I don't remember when in the dimness of early childhood, nor do I remember where. Only that someone took me to a dark large basement lit only with one or two light bulbs. Adults were standing around a table. The children and adults seemed happy looking forward to a fun time. A strange guy took my hand and walked me down a dimly lit corridor. We went into a room. There was a round dusty wooden table with chairs around it. Shelves filled with boxes lined the walls. The janitor mops and buckets were against one of the walls.

The strange guy led me into a dreary room. He said, "If you don't eat the marshmallow, I will give you another one." The left the room. Feeling that was strange, I nervously opened the door, turned right, and walked away from the people. The guy at the other end of the hallway yelled, "Hey what are you doing? You are ruining the experiment." My whole body quivered. I ran outside pretending to blend into the city.

Chapter 2

The Children's Home

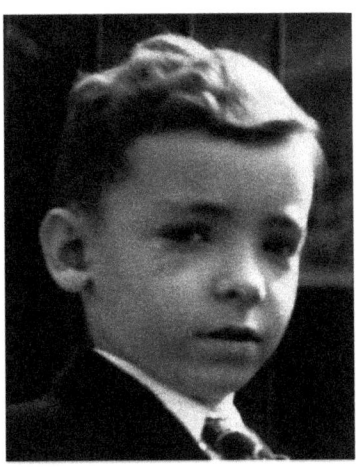

Figure 2.1 Ivan as seven-year-old.

When I was six years old, Grandma very purposefully showed me something interesting. What it was I have long forgotten; but I do remember to this very day, hour, and minute, her strong emotional focus to keep my attention on her. Meanwhile I barely noticed Mom and Dad quietly moving a suitcase to the car. So, I pretended not to notice.

After several hours of driving, we stopped. They said, "Go play with the children outside." While I was playing, I noticed dad trying to hide my suitcase as he walked into the home. At some point Mom and Dad vanished.

At the dinner table, I cheerfully said, "When will Mom and Dad pick me up?" The children erupted in laughter, pointing at me. Some had trouble keeping food in their mouths. "You are not going home! This is your home! That is funny. Ha, ha, ha! Ha, ha, ha!" Uncontrollable tears flowed. The lady who ran the home screamed, "Stop that! Stop the crying!" The more she screamed, the more I cried. The tears flowed, and muscles convulsed. No words came out

The lady firmly grabbed my right arm and pulled me upstairs into a bedroom. She pushed me on to a bed. Happy sounds filtered through the floor and hallway. In the darkness, occasionally a car would come by. I would run to the window expecting Mom and Dad to come. Another car would drive by. I would run to the window. Tears uncontrollably flowed. My little nose pressed against the glass. Hope built up with each passing car. The cars disappeared into the shadows of the trees lining the street. The engine sounds faded away into the darkness. Eventually, I just stood on the bed and watched occasional cars come and continue as engine sounds faded away.

Later, utterly alone, I just lay on the bed looking at the ceiling and watching the lights and shadows move from one side to the other side of the room as the engine sounds faded away. Crying myself to sleep, a dim realization pierced my head, eyes, heart, and stomach. No one cared. I was utterly alone. There was no one. No one. The lights of another passing car cast shadows of trees across the ceiling. Its' engine fading in the distance like my consciousness.

In the morning the hum of the children dressing, eating, dishes clanging, and getting ready to go to school sounded like a happy beehive. At school, the teacher introduced me to the class as the new student. Some days later during recess, some boys pushed me around as being "one of those." I was as tall as their chests.

They pushed, shoved, and pushed me to the ground next to a baseball bat. I grabbed it. Jumped up, aimed the bat at the taller kid's head, and swung with all my might. Because he was much taller than me, the bat clipped his shoulder which forced the bat to clip his head instead of walloping his head. They were all stunned. I was ready to hit others. They walked away muttering something. But after that no one bothered me. A teacher watching, shriveled her face like the Wicked Witch of the West in the Wizard of Oz. She was disgusted with me. I was, "One of those."

One day, a girl said, "I am not supposed to talk to you. You are one of those kids from the home. You are probably ok; but still, I can't talk to you."

Without emotion I responded, "OK. Thank you for telling me." No one cared. There was no one. No one.

Over the next few years teachers would check homework assignments by walking around the classroom. They made glowing encouraging comments to others. But they would glance at me giving despairing dismissive looks and then, like a hummingbird at a feeding station, quickly dart away.

After a while, I wondered, "How did these kids do their homework?" So, I asked several, "How do you get your homework done?" A few talked down to me saying with great pride in being better than me, that their parents helped. It felt like a dentist's lead blanket fell on my entire body. None of the kids in the home were able to help me. Heck we couldn't help each other except to play and have fun. My place in life was becoming clear. There would be no one to help me with anything. There was no way to learn in school. Why bother?

So, at school, I took bathroom breaks to wander around the hallways. They were peaceful, quiet, accepting, and lonely. The classrooms had windows in the doors; so, I could look inside each classroom. I could see what was on the blackboards, the wall, but what the teachers said was completely unintelligible. Everyone was bubbly, growing, and learning while I was being left behind with no one to help or care. My heart ached to be able to do what they were doing. To be like them. I knew in my bones that would never happen.

In those moments the halls said, "You will never learn and understand what is on the walls and what the teacher is saying. There is no one to help you with homework. The teacher does not care if you learn or not." It felt again like a heavy dentist lead blanket descended upon me. Why stay in school? Why try? Upon returning the pass to the teacher she gave an annoyed, indifferent look.

Gloves on Their Heads

One Sunday, we children from the home were sitting together in the Catholic

Church. People were walking in, genuflecting, and sitting down. Four or maybe six women came in together genuflected and sat down across the aisle, a couple of rows down. In those days in church, the women wore hats that had veils down to their noses and wore gloves. It seemed silly. What were those veils for? Keep mosquitos out? Were the gloves to keep from getting their hands dirty?

However, these women didn't have hats on. The usher came over and said that they must have their heads covered. The women said no. I thought, "Why can men come into the church without hats on and the women have to have hats on? Is God displeased with women's hair? Maybe they should get haircuts like men."

The usher became insistent. So, the women got up and left. The usher was pleased.

A few minutes later, the women came back in and sat down in the same pew. They had gloves on top of their heads. The usher was furious and said that they are insulting. To me whatever it was they were insulting seemed to be quite sensitive and worried about nonsense like women wearing or not wearing hats. The women refused to leave.

The usher left in a rage.

A few minutes later, a young priest came. He looked young because I thought the women looked old enough to be his mother. But, if he was so young, why did the women call him Father? Anyway, he politely said, "You must have your heads covered."

The women said, "Our heads are covered."

I became nervous. The women were making the priest upset. He was God. One doesn't make the priest upset. I worried that lightning would strike. The church would fall. After all, one doesn't argue with the priest who is God. One does what the priest says. I started to hide underneath the pew until someone slapped me and said to sit up straight.

Yet, the women refused to leave.

I don't remember if they took the gloves off their heads or not.

The Age of Reason – "You are Special!"

Turning seven years old, some adult proudly said to me that I had reached the age of reason, was able to understand sin, had sinned, must confess sins, and shouldn't sin from now on.. I thought, "Now I am going to learn that I shouldn't sin? Before this moment all those sins I committed and worried about didn't matter? Adults told me that all my sins were written on my heart and that God wipes the heart clean with communion. But I had been too young to have communion. God must write pretty small because as a child I had a small heart and made a lot of sins."

But now, that I reached the age of reason and could understand what my sins are, so I could be forgiven. I asked, "What happens to the sins I committed before?"

"Oh, you were too young. They don't matter, and God already forgave you."

I thought, "Fine time to find out. I could have done more sins that don't matter. Now, I sin, and it matters." I was deceived and felt angry about being deceived – again.

The first assignment was to prepare for being eco-light. "What is an eco-light? Carry a light that echoes?" That made no sense.

A child explained, "It is acolyte dummy! Just carry a stick to light candles and wear a dress." The kids giggled.

I thought, "Wear a dress? Take off my pants?" I crossed my legs.

The lady said, "Don't worry. The priest will instruct you. Just do what he says." The priest, who was GOD, was going to instruct ME! My bones trembled with fear.

A couple of days later after supper, someone dropped me off at the church. The priest who was God greeted me at the door and took me inside. We went into a dimly lit room that had a huge flat table with many draws underneath it. There were cabinets and drawers along the walls. Standing on my tippy toes it was possible to see the top of the counter. The priest said, "I will inspect you to make sure you are pure enough. So, stand by the door. Take off your clothes. I will turn around; so, you won't feel embarrassed."

Suddenly, it was darker than inky black. My arms, chest and legs were chilly and shaking. Instantly my clothes were on me. Shaking in panic, I ran past the priest down the hallway. There were doors, doors, doors, doors, and more doors. Which one went outside? Which one? Which one? Fear that the priest was chasing me gripped every molecule in my shivering body. I couldn't breathe. There was some sort of sign that I couldn't read hanging above a door.

Not knowing what to do I pushed that door open. Ran into the evening darkness and across the street. While standing under a streetlight, I couldn't breathe. I thought, "Think! Think! Think! No! Breathe first! Think later! If you can't breathe you can't think. Breathe! Breathe! Breathe!"

Slowly, I began to rhythmically breathe. A total calm awareness of everything around me settled into my bones and muscles. I became aware of the streetlight, the street, the trees, the other streetlights and sounds of occasional passing cars.

A cool indifferent breeze touched my cheeks and began to chill me. Indifferent streetlights cast shadows and illuminated the street. Indifferent cars whizzed by on an adjacent road. "I want to go home. But I don't have a home. Grandma is home. But where? It is chilly. How do I get to the children's home?"

So, I thought and thought, "Which way to go? I did not cross the big road behind me on the way here. So, don't cross it. Go that way."

I walked for a while in the darkness occasionally illuminated by a streetlight. "The road to the right looks like a dead-end. Keep going straight." At every crossing, "Right, left or straight?" Somehow, eventually the children's home appeared.

Upon entering someone said, "Oh, you are home. We don't have to get you." The phone rang. All my muscles tensed. It was the priest calling to complain that I 'had horribly disappointed him. I was a bad boy. I had displeased God. I was no good. I had failed.' Instead, the lady began happily chatting with a friend. Quickly I walked through the living room to the bathroom. Afterwards, every time the phone rang, muscles tensed, breathing stopped. Then relief, it was not the priest.

For several days or weeks, I wet the bed. Waking up trying to stop didn't help. Frequently we slept two and sometimes three to a bed. So, I would silently get up and move the sheets to dry by the time to get up. Then I would quickly make the bed pretending that nothing had happened.

It was difficult to stay awake at school. It was hard to understand what the teacher was saying. A deep sense of weakness, failure, of being no good, and futility settled in me. I couldn't do anything right. I had grievously disappointed the priest who was God. Unable to please the teachers, slapped by the lady who ran the home, and I was unable to understand school.

While walking to and from school I worried about displeasing the priest. When the phone rang, I worried the priest was complaining of my displeasing him. In school, adults looked at me knowing that I displeased the priest. The kids wouldn't play with me because I displeased the priest. Listening to every sound, I waited for the voice of God to yell from the clouds, "YOU displeased the priest!"

You Are by Nature Sinful and Unclean

During mass, a priest said, "Humans are by nature sinful and unclean. Your very essence is sinful and evil. Evil flows in your blood. Evil is in your bones." While looking down at my thin arms, there were bluish vessels of sin and evil flowing through me. A voice within said, "Get rid of the blood. Get rid of the sin and evil." At the home, I repeatedly took a table knife to get rid of the sin and evil. But the table knives were too dull to even cut the skin. So, I repeatedly took a very sharp butcher knife; but the perceived pain of cutting was too much, and I never cut the skin. Because of my sinfulness, I failed again. I failed to get rid the blood which carried my sin.

The autumn leaves were falling on the lawns and streets. I loved the smell of burning leaves and the crisp air. It filled me with delight and wonder.

The old man in the home gave me some money to run an errand to the store. On the way back, I saw an elderly man raking leaves inside his fenced-in yard. So, I started a conversation with him. At first, he was warm and friendly. Then he said, "I shouldn't be talking with you. We really don't want you people in the neighborhood. You are probably a nice kid; but you aren't wanted here." It was more proof that I was by nature sinful by thought, word and deed.

About Thanksgiving time, the fire station had a party. Children explored the firehouse and the huge red engines. It was a lot of fun. The firemen played with the children. Lifting them up on the different engines. People were extremely excited and happy.

A fireman on top of a pumper truck was helping children up. A child would climb up and the fireman reached down and pulled the child up. As I climbed up, he reached down and held my right hand and pulled. A man on the ground began yelling, "He can't get in that truck! He doesn't belong here. He doesn't pay taxes!" He grabbed my left arm and began pulling me down. The fireman pulled me up. The man on the ground kept pulling me down.

They both pulled hard in opposite directions. Hanging in space thoughts appeared, "What are taxes? Maybe I should pay taxes. How do I pay taxes?" Adults just stared mesmerized by the spectacle.

Eventually, the man let go. The pumper truck had bench seats on each side filled with children. The fireman squeezed me into the seat at the end of the truck. Children pulled away from me squeezing each other more. They must have thought I had cooties.

I was about to say, "Hey, there is more room here. We can get more in." But I thought, "Heck, this is more room for me. So, I put a leg on the bench and enjoyed the ride in the crisp autumn air. I had lots of room high above the traffic. It was fun watching the cars below, the homes and trees float by and seeing the puffy white clouds in the blue sky.

Every once in while in the home we had to line up. Some crotchety ancient heavy lady checked us. She looked in our hair, ears, noses, and mouths. She pinched our cheeks, tummy, and rump. It was annoying. At the end of the line, she mumbled comments to the lady and disappeared.

Sometimes a man and woman came and did the same as the crotchety old lady. Then they said, "We'll take this one." The girl or boy was gone like a melting snowflake. Just vanished. Every time that happened, it was the little blonde boy or girl who disappeared. My heart ached. "Take me! Take me!" No one did.

After a few times, it was clear that would never happen. The priest was right, "You are by nature sinful and unclean. You have sinned against God by thought, word and deed." He was right, my blood and bones were sinful, unlovable, and worthless.

Just before a Christmas the neighborhood ladies came over to the home. We lined up one side and the women lined up on the other side. We sang happy songs. Wrapped presents were handed out to us. One by one, from our right to left, each of us opened a present the ladies had brought. Everyone eagerly watched.

My turn! With great excitement I pulled the wrapping paper off. I slowly pulled out of the box a red and black checkered flannel shirt. The shirt froze in space just hanging, suspended by nothing. It was just a shirt. A new shirt. A new shirt that meant it would disappear. New clothes were only for special occasions that never happened. They were clothes that we never wore. We only wore old hand me downs.

A lady dejectedly said, "He doesn't like the present I gave him." Desperately I wanted a toy. MY toy. My toy to play with. Instead there was a flannel shirt. I felt bad for the lady. She meant well. She wasn't pleased the way I acted.

The priest's voice whispered, "You are by nature sinful."

The ladies said very excitedly, "It is nice that we are here. Please let the children come to our homes and play with our children." So, the next day I toddled over to one of the homes. Rang the doorbell. A child opened the door and asked what I wanted.

"Your mom said, I could come over and play with you."

Her mother called out, "What does he want?"

The girl ran to her and said, "He said you said that he could come over and play with me."

Her mom whispered, "We didn't mean that! We just said those things. Tell him to go away."

So, the child came back. She said something like, "I can't play with you today. Don't come back."

The priest whispered, "You are by nature sinful."

At the home, the lady explained why they said those things. "People say white lies to make life easier for everyone."

"So, if there are white lies, then are there black lies? Gray lies? So, white people lie to make life easier; then black people tell lies that make life harder? So black people are bad? What do gray people do? Are there gray people?"

The poor lady sighed. She must have thought, "What am I going to do with this child?"

One of the chores in the home was walking the dog. No one had an interest. So, I quietly took on the chore. After supper, I walked the dog farther and farther from the home, which took longer and longer. No one cared. In the twilight, and later in the dark, the dog and I enjoyed the fresh air, the trees and being with each other. We walked by happy, strong, and solid homes. Indoor lights cast a warm glow onto the dark streets. Perfect families were inside. Every night I fantasized living in one of those delightful homes. I resolved that I too would have a happy home, wife, and children. I would have as many children as eggs in an egg carton and lots of pets. Though, I couldn't count to twelve – let alone count.

Night after night sharing a bed with one or two children, I silently cried myself to sleep imagining a happy house, wife, and children. But it was a mirage, as in the movies, where a thirsty cowboy on a hot, dry desert sees in the distance an undulating waterhole. Then he reaches out for a drink, collapses and dies. Reality set in. I was unloved, unlovable, incompetent, failing at school, unwanted by the school kids, unwanted by mom and dad, and most of all I had displeased the priest who was God on earth.

The priest whispered, "You are by nature sinful."

On TV, there were cowboy shows. They would hang a bad guy. "That's it! Make a noose and hang myself! But how to make the noose?" After carefully watching those fleeting scenes and trying over and over to make a noose, I succeeded.

In the damp dingy basement, I stepped on a dusty black trunk. Tied the noose to a nail and slipped the rope around my neck. I jumped off the trunk. My feet landed on the floor. Got back on the trunk. Took off the noose and raised the rope higher. Then one of the children came into the basement and asked, "What are you doing?"

"Playing." We both went outside and played with the other children.

News went through the school like a whirlwind. Children had been playing hide-and-seek. A child had hidden in the leaves by the school curb. A person parking a car drove over the child. I thought, "that is a way to be dead."

After school I laid down in the school gutter, put my head firmly against the rear wheel of a car and covered myself with leaves. It was peaceful.

Peace. Rest. Calmness. Oneness with all. The gentle leaves caressed my face.

The engine started. "It will be over." The muffler made a puff, puff, puff sound. The car went forward and drove away. Sunlight cascaded through the leaves. Disappointedly, I got up and shook the leaves off. Three teachers in long grey coats looked at me and turned away in disgust. I dragged myself back to the home.

On the way, the priest's words echoed:

You are by nature sinful and unclean, by thought, word and deed.

Your very nature is sinful. Your blood and body are sinful.

You are by nature sinful.

You are by nature sinful.

You are by nature sinful.

I asked the lady, "How do you know that our blood and body is sinful?"

She responded, "The Bible says so."

"How do you know?"

"The priest and the Church say so!"

"How do they know?"

She screamed, "You doubting Thomas!" and slugged me.

Laying on the floor, a thought occurred, "Who is Thomas? Where is he?" Looking up at her massive hulk, I thought, "She didn't hurt me. She hit. It didn't hurt. She can't hurt me." Yet, it did hurt; but it didn't hurt. It was confusing.

It was more confusing to be told that I was by nature sinful. That God didn't make me sinful I made myself sinful; yet, I was born sinful. Further to know that I displeased the priest, who was God on earth. That the neighbors didn't want me around. That some strange lady would poke and prod my body to see if I was OK. This all made no sense. It was very bewildering. "How can I be OK when I am failing?" Also, my questioning the Church angered adults; so, they hit and yelled at me. My teeth deteriorated. I was utterly failing.

My eyesight weakened. The school nurse carefully examined my eyes. She told me to read the chart. I didn't know the alphabet let alone being able to see them. The nurse mumbled something about needing glasses. Uncontrollably, I cried. I ran to the chart screaming, "I can see the letters. I can see the letters." She shrugged and sent me back to the classroom.

The teacher moved me to the front of the classroom, so I could see the blackboard. But then all the kids could see how dumb I was. All confirmation that I was weak and sinful. Unloved by God.

Unloved because I displeased the priest.

One Saturday during chore time, I was raking leaves with the ancient tall grounds' keeper. It was fun. The smell of the leaves. Making rows and piles. Jumping into the rows. Running around, throwing leaves at other kids. Smelling the fresh crisp autumn air. I wanted those moments to never end. To be endlessly raking leaves, throwing them around, and having fun.

But the priest's voice kept bothering me. So, I told the grounds' keeper how I had displeased the priest and wanted to know how to make him happy.

He said, "God damn it. We'll have to go over there again and tell those guys to stop doing that stuff!!"

"You mean, I am not special? I am not the only one?"

He said, "Look son, nobody gives a shit about you! That is why you are here." He and the trees grew taller and taller. They scrapped the clouds. I shrunk smaller than a tiny bug in tall grass.

Just then a car drove by. A thought appeared, "Well, if no one cares, I will do what I want. I'll leave."

Running Away

No idea where to go. Just run away. I figured that the best time to leave was when everyone was asleep; so, leaving was easy. Unfortunately, the police always found me wandering the dimly lit streets. They shoved me into the patrol car and brought me back to the home. The woman would slap me a couple of times. Hurriedly, perhaps I was able to get breakfast. Though sometimes there just wasn't time because it was time to walk to school.

It was difficult concentrating at school. It was impossible to stay awake. The other kids shunned me.

The words, "No one gives a shit about you," echoed in the classroom like a huge gonging bell. But no one else noticed.

"You are by nature sinful and unclean" repeated over and over and over. It wouldn't stop. The words just kept coming. Take a knife and cut out the words. But the pain of putting a knife into the ears was more than the pain of hearing over and over, "You are by nature sinful and unclean. Sinful and unclean. Sinful and unclean." So, I never used the knife.

"Was this all a dream? What was real? Are thoughts real? Is the classroom real? Am I real? What is real? What is true?"

The next morning long before the sun rose, I walked along dark streets to the railroad station. The platform was dark, quiet, damp, and chilly. A couple of dim ghostly figures were waiting for a train. A giant dressed in a dark trench coat came over. "Where are you going?"

"To my Grandmother's."

"Where is that?"

Thinking, "That is a stupid question." But instead I said, "My Grandmother lives where my Grandmother lives!"

He asked, "Which platform does the train come on?"

There were two tracks. There were two platforms. One on this side and one the other side. "Which way? Which way?" There were people on this side and not the other side. So, the response was, "This side."

He then asked, "Which way does the train come to go to her place?"

"Huh?" The annoying goon walked away. I thought, "Soon the train would come, and it would be nice at Grandma's. But where does Grandma live?"

A few minutes later to the right at the end of the platform two policeman walked up the dimly lit stairs towards me. One moaned, "You again!"

At the police station there was a desk reaching to the ceiling. A ceiling light in a cage indifferently beamed down. It was difficult to see where a voice from above came from. The voice yelled, "You again! You see that room?" An arm, not connected to anything, floated above my head and pointed to the right. There was an open door to a dark room. "You know what that is? That is a jail. If you come back here again, I am going to throw you into that jail!"

A voice deep within me sternly thought, "Go ahead!"

He said to the officers, "Take him to the home. Get him out of here! I am not going to write this up."

As the cruiser drove up to the home, the windows filled with little faces. The officers banged on the front door. The lady opened it and began sobbing, "I am going to lose my license. I am going to lose my license!" She embraced me like a python squeezing its next meal.

It was clear she would start hitting me once the officers left. Thoughts pinged like a submarine's sonar searching for a target. "Is it better to be slammed against the edges of the stairs or against the flat wall? The stairs have sharp edges. The walls are flat and maybe not as painful. Yet, she can't hurt me. Or, can she hurt me?"[3] Scooching to a safer position was impossible in her ever-tightening death grip.

The officers said, "Send him to reform school."

That seemed appealing. "Reform school. That would be nice. It would be better than being here."

Once they left, she began hitting me but became distracted with getting the other children ready for school.

That afternoon, I ran away again. Unknown to me, she crowded six children into the car and began searching the streets and told the children to find me. With car windows open, I heard one of them yell, "There he is! There he is!" She grabbed me. Once again, back to the home.

This time something changed. She knelt to my height. Face to face. Eyeball to eyeball. She said with warmth and concern, "Why do you keep running

---

3 I still don't know the answer to that question.

away?"

"You keep hitting me."

"If I stop hitting you, will you stop running away?"

Dumbfounded. Frozen. Not understanding what was happening, I squeaked, "OK."

She said, "You promise?"

A weak, "Yes."

She stopped hitting me from then on.

I stopped running away.

Reading Out Loud

One day the second or third-grade class was reading out loud - again. The book had a colorful happy painting of a mother, father, and a girl and boy. I just stared at the picture, tried to withhold tears while clenching my teeth. Kept my head down, while staring at the picture. In the drawing, the cheerful father, mother, girl and boy moved around. I merged into the picture and joined them. I laughed with them. Had breakfast with them. Talked happily without carefully considering my words. It was fun. I wanted to stay and never leave.

Then like a lightning bolt striking on a warm pleasant day, the teacher called on me to read. I kept my head down. The kids giggled. She shushed them. Disapproving of me, she asked another child to read. The picture was no longer alive. I was not with the happy family in the yellow, brown, warm room, merrily chatting. My heart ached to join them, to crawl into the painting. To be frozen forever in that happiness.

Instead, the picture was slipping inside an ice-cold refrigerator freezer with the door slowly closing and their happy voices fading away. There was no way to go into the picture that was teasing and mocking me.

I heard the priest whispering, "All the children have families like this. You won't be allowed. Because you are sinful and unclean."

It was obvious. Everyone else could say what the black things (letters) on the white pages meant. I couldn't. There was nothing I could do. Nothing. It was just more proof that I was by nature sinful and unclean. My body, my thoughts, my blood and my bones were sinful and unclean. They were displeasing the priest.

Somewhere, when and how I don't remember. Some of us children from the home were by fishing boats. Happy, screeching seagulls flew around, and a small river flowed by. Little hungry sharks gobbled unwanted fish. It was appealing for the sharks to eat me. I let myself slide off the dock towards them. Towards a bit of pain and then peace. Peace. Someone grabbed me. Others said, "Ignore him. He is one of those kids. We don't want them here."

Suicidal impulses and attempts became a daily comfort. A knife. A rope. Drowning. Electrocution. Run over by a car or a train. But someone always interrupted, or it didn't work.

Then…

Science

It was difficult figuring out all the lying. Adults told lies to children and to each other. Children told lies to each other and to adults. Adults and children would seem to say one thing and then do another. The adults would lie to get us to do something.

It was frustrating me to perceive the world differently than others. Many times, I thought, "People lie. Do they know they lie? Lies. Lies. Lies. But it only bothers me."

I doubted everything. I distrusted my sight, my hearing, my taste, my smell, and my thoughts. What was true? Was this a dream? What is reality? Was I in a room? Was I eating a sandwich? Was it a just a dream or a nightmare? The

Figure 2.2 I loved my friends at the children's home. I am on the left.

only reality was physically feeling pain. Pain let me know that I was not living a dream or a nightmare. It was all confusing. Does God lie? Is reality a lie?

To ask these questions was to get slapped. Adults called me Judas. People would say, "Judas Christ!"

I thought, "Who is Judas? Judas is Christ? Christ is Judas? Or is that a different person?"

So, I stopped asking people and kids questions. I shut up. I listened more intently. Maybe if I listened better, I would understand. Maybe my confusions were because I was, "…by nature sinful in my very blood and bones."

One day a second-grade teacher explained something called science. It was something about finding out what was true. My whole body perked up. I sat up straight. Focused my blurry eyes on the teacher dressed in a white blouse and gray skirt. My ears listened carefully. My heart pounded. My body tensed. "Here would be the way to know truth!"

She explained that a long time ago people thought about what was true. Because they thought of it, they believed it must be true. Along came some guy with a funny name. I thought, "Who gives children funny names like that?" She said that he discovered that the way to find truth was by testing. She talked about a group of scholars debating about how many teeth were in the mouth of a horse. They debated and debated and couldn't agree. Some laborer heard the conversation and said, "Go out and count the teeth in the horses!"

The scholars looked at each other, thought the dirty worker was dumb. They shrugged and went back to debating.

The teacher said, "One way of finding out the truth is testing. That was a revolution in people's thinking."

I thought, "A revolution in thinking? People's brains go around and around inside their head like a spinning top? How fast does my brain spin? I don't feel it. Tops wobble when they are about to fall. Maybe because I have a bad brain and am sinful, I will wobble and fall-down. I just don't feel the wobble yet."

I pictured adults and children walking around with their unseen brains twirling. "Which way did they twirl? Right to left or left to right? Horizontally or vertically? But lies didn't bother them. They weren't interested in knowing the truth. Anyway, how can a brain turn? Isn't it connected to something? Is there a pole in the head that the brain revolves around? So, when people say that that person is off kilter, they really mean that their brain isn't going around and around correctly inside their head. Their brain is about to fall. How do people know this stuff? Can I cut out a head and watch the brain go around?"

She said that people long ago figured out the earth was round. "They watched sailing ships disappear over the horizon. The ship was visible. The body of the ship would disappear. Then the mast would slowly disappear. So, they knew the earth was round."

So, I resolved to test that. But the ocean was far away. It was an impossible test.[4]

The teacher described gravity. It holds everything together. Gravity holds everyone to the earth. But, what did it look like? How could I test it?

Then she said, "The earth is round and that because of gravity people on the other side of the earth don't stand on their heads, nor do people on the equator move on their stomachs." The children giggled." She continued, "Instead, because of gravity, everyone on earth walks on their legs."

So, I said, "That is silly! Someone in Australia must be upside down. So, they must walk on their hands. Australian girls must walk on their hands. Their dresses fall over they faces showing their underwear." Children giggled. "But the girls would not let that happen. So, they must all wear pants in Australia."

Since the teacher said to test, I momentarily tried to figure out how I could test if people in Australia walk on their hands and girls' dresses fall over their faces. Or test that gravity pulls them down they walk on their legs like people here. How can I test that?"

She continued by describing inertia. "A ball that is pushed will keep going. That is inertia. But the ball keeps rolling, then slows and stops. That is friction."

I thought, "Where does the inertia go? What is inertia? How to find inertia and see what it looks like? How do I test inertia?"

She said. "Fill a pail with water. Imagine holding a pail. It feels heavy. Gravity pulls the water to the earth. Now imagine swinging the pail of water over your head like this." She swung her arm up over her head and down.

---

4   Even as an adolescent and then as an adult, I repeatedly failed to replicate that test. I would watch a ship going out to sea. It would get smaller and smaller. Then suddenly it disappeared. The top of the bottom of the ship didn't disappear first and then the smokestack. The whole thing just vanished. But I didn't have the equipment to watch the ship. So, how did people long ago do it before there were telescopes?

Continuing she said, "But inertia keeps the water in the pail. The water stays in the pail. It doesn't fall to the earth because of gravity."

That really made no sense. "What was inertia? Heck. What was gravity? But I can do the pail of water experiment."

Everybody in class understood gravity and inertia except me. Once again, I was the stupid one. The one who didn't get it. The one who was sinful. The incompetent one. I was alone and not sure of anything; while everyone else was sure of everything. They are good and happy.

Later that day, at the children's home I decided to test inertia or gravity or whatever those things were. I got a pail and a water hose from the garage. The kids asked, "What are you doing?"

"Making a test. The teacher said that swinging a pail of water over one's head, the water won't fall out."

They laughed and giggled. They said, "She lied. She just made that up."

They all watched giggling and smirking, waiting for the water to fall out and wet my clothes. They were waiting to see me in trouble again with the lady.

I picked the pail up full of water. It was heavy. Nervously and just like the teacher showed, I swung the pail from the ground to over my head, back to towards the ground and then up over my head. Over my head and back to the ground. No water came out!

They said, "You are going to get we-et! You are going to get we-et! You are going to get we-et! Ha, ha, ha, ha!"

Then the realization hit me. How to stop swinging the pail without getting wet? The teacher never said anything about that. Swinging the pail of water was tiring. My arms tired as the pail circled slower.

Somehow, I let the pail, my arm, and my legs go gently forward. I chased my arm and the pail as I gently arced the pail downward to the ground.

The kids looked. They were silent. There was no amusing show of wet clothes and a screaming lady. They went away to play. The pail and I were alone.

What had happened? Wasn't that proof the teacher was right? Yet, no one agreed. Was I wrong? No one laughed. Their reaction was puzzling. How come they just didn't agree with what they saw? That made no sense. It was bewildering – again.

(This was a pattern that continues for me until this day: I would prove something by experiment or logic. Then people would ignore, dismiss and discount the results. Over six decades later, I still don't understand why.)

Digging to China

One day the teacher said, "China is on the opposite of the world." She described how beautiful the country and the people were. They wore different clothes. Their civilization was thousands of years old. They seemed so interesting.

So, after school, I decided to go to China by digging a tunnel behind the garage. I persuaded the other children to visit China. We all took turns digging the hole. After a while the hole was up to my chin. What made it harder was the deeper we dug the more the dirt collapsed in. So, I made the hole wider.

Just about supper time, the lady who ran the home became curious about what we were doing. She saw me in the hole up to my chin. At first her face flushed white. Then she screamed, "Get out of there. What are you doing?"

Still in the hole, I said, "The teacher said China is on the opposite side of the world. So, I am digging a tunnel to get there."

She looked at the hole almost deeper than me, screamed, "Get out of the there."

Disappointed I climbed out of the hole.

Then she commanded, "Go get supper."

She picked up the shovel and began to fill in the hole. So, I said, "I will do that."

Almost crying, she murmured, "Go get dinner."

Sadly, I walked across the yard to get dinner.

The Best Christmas Present Ever

There was some sort of party at the church. There were decorations, happy chatter, food and drink. It was a fun time.

A group of us first graders(?) were with a fifth-grade girl. She read some Bible stories. Then she handed out small gift-wrapped Christmas presents. Disheartingly, I pulled off the wrapping paper expecting another piece of clothing that the home would take away. Instead, the box had a picture of an airplane. It was a small plastic model airplane. There were three or four pieces to put together. Someone helped me snap the pieces together. Holding the plane high in the air, I and the plane flew between the mountains of tall people. Soaring freely around the basement. Up so high. Down so low. The deafening roar of the engine as the plane soared higher and higher. Effortlessly, gliding past tables, chairs, and people. Zooming back to the small group of children.

Still to this day, over sixty-five years later, it was the best Christmas present ever!!

Every year since then I send an imaginary thank you to the unknown fifth grader. She had and probably still has a warm loving heart.

Life began to happily change…

Chapter 3

A New Start

Figure 3.1 Back with mother in our new home.

In third grade, late one afternoon between Thanksgiving and Christmas, suddenly Grandma, and Grandpa came with Mom. They briefly chatted with the lady who ran the home. Then Grandpa silently put a small grocery bag of my clothing into his car. I got into the backseat next to Mom. It was strange sitting with Mom in the car with them in the late afternoon. As the car moved away, Grandma said, "That is a nice place. Are you going to miss it?"

As the yard and trees passed by, I thought, "No. The children were my friends. The lady meant well." The priest whispered, "You are sinful." I ignored him hoping he would go away.

So, instead of responding to Grandma, there was numb silence trying not to disappoint her, Grandpa, and Mom. But I just couldn't utter any words. I silently cried to myself trying to please them and not get them angry.

Grandpa drove for several hours through the evening darkness. Grandma, Grandpa, and Mom happily talked among themselves. It was a blur of passing cars, streetlights, buildings, and honking horns. I don't remember if we stopped for supper. Didn't seem like we did. I just don't remember.

Eventually, the car stopped beside a Cape Cod home. It was like the one in the movie, "Miracle on 34th Street."

In the living room was a Christmas tree with pretty lights. Underneath laid wrapped packages just like, "Miracle on 34th Street." Someone said, "You can open just one present." I sensed they wanted me to be jumping with joy at the presents. To happily run around giggling and laughing.

But instead, I was numb. My only desire was sleep, sleep, and more sleep. I was too tired to make them happy by faking joy. Everyone silently knew I had failed them. Then Grandma and Grandpa said goodbye and left.

The house was quiet. Mom showed me a room. A room - just to myself. A bed just to myself. It felt strange. As I quickly fell asleep, I missed my friends in the home. They would be happy, chattering, and playing. There would be several of us bubbly in one bedroom perhaps sleeping in one bed. We would be chattering ourselves to sleep. But now I was lucky to have a room and a Mom who cares. But it was lonely and quiet.

In the morning, Mom took me to school. There were happy noisy kids on the playground. In the classroom, the third-grade teacher introduced me to the class. She was nice. She liked me! There were big windows so tall that children used a pole to open and close the top part. The twenty-foot windows let lots of sunshine into the room. Puffy white clouds floated by. The children were warm, happy, and friendly. No one said, "You don't belong here." The children invited me to play with them at recess and after school.

It was an odd feeling to be safe and accepted. No one was going to punch me, hit me, or tell me I didn't belong. Life was nice.

Fourth Grade – "I am Special!"

Early in fourth grade, the teacher invited Mom and me to an after school meeting. I thought, "This will be special. The teacher was going to say wonderful things about me."

Then she said, "He should be put back to third grade." But the more she talked the more worried I became. She said, "He doesn't know how to read. Doesn't know how to write. Doesn't know his arithmetic. He is a nice boy. He really needs to go back to second grade."

Mom was furious. She said, "If I can get him to the fourth-grade level, can he stay in the fourth grade?"

After much heated discussion, Mom wore the teacher down. Reluctantly the teacher said, "OK. You won't be able to do it. He is too far behind. Alright, go ahead and try. I don't think it will work. You are just wasting time."

Stunned to the core of my heart, my bones, and my stomach, I felt totally powerless, helpless, and incompetent. Once again, I was sinful in my blood and bones. There were three fourth grade classes. I wasn't good enough to be in any of them.

Again, I heard the priest's words, "You are by nature sinful and unclean. You have sinned against God. Your very blood and bones are sinful." The words echoed and echoed for days.

But bless Mom's heart and determination. She became what people now call a Tiger Mom.

She made flash cards for math. Hour after hour, day after day, for weeks she drilled me in addition, subtraction, multiplication, and division. She did the same with spelling lists. Mom would say a word and then I spelled the word out loud. Eventually, after learning to write the alphabet, I had to write out the words. Over and over and over. Then I had to read little booklets with big pictures of cats, dogs, fish, people, and I don't remember what else. I had to read them to her.

Without mercy, but with a lot of determination and love, she worked and worked with me. There would be no excuses of being too tired, not wanting to, boring, or whatever else I said. No. It was time to do the work.

Ever so slowly the mastery came. My confidence grew. "I can do this. I can do this. I can do this." As fast as she could turn the math flash cards over, I gave the right answers. As quickly as she said a spelling word, I would spell out loud and write down the words. She handed me the little booklets and without hesitation or reservation, I read the sentences. I could even write simple sentences.

I felt it in my blood and bones. "I can do this!"

Figure 3.2 My first book - it is till precious to me. After reading it, I knew in my bones that I could read.

From that I learned the power and strength of discipline, focus, and work.

Then she gave me a thick book as a present. I thought, "How can I possibly read this? It is too big!" The cover had a warm happy drawing of a brown dog like the one in the children's home. The boy was me. The book was, "Paddy Points the Way." [5]

Then she left me alone for the afternoon. Page by page, the engrossing, captivating words formed a warm loving story about a boy and his dog. It was thrilling. I could read! I could read! I could read! A strange comfortable and exhilarating feeling circulated through me. A deep assurance that finally I could do something.

For the first time, I had confidence that I could read.

I could read.

I could read.

---

5   (Grew 1950)

Figure 3.3 Like Father Don Camillo, I imagined conversations with Jesus.

Much too soon, the book ended. It ended. Finished. Now what? She gave me another book, "The Little World of Don Camillo."[6] It was a comedy book about a priest in Italy and his conversations with God. There were so many chuckles. It was difficult to stop reading. Impossible to not laugh out loud. The priest seemed so happy. He had funny conversations with God and some communist – whatever that was. Sometimes he was in the church talking with God about something. Somehow, God talked to him. Don Camillo was lovable, nice, warm, and approachable. Not like – well, that other priest.

Reading books became a thrill. A favorite of mine were ten books about explorers. They roamed the earth discovering new things. They had adventures. They were brave. They had struggles and they conquered. Yes! I would explore the world and have adventures. See new sights. Go where no one had gone before. Life became fun. For the second time, I fantasized about the future.

By the end of fourth grade I went from barely second grade level to almost the top of the three fourth grade classes. No longer was there a desire to feel special. Rather, I had confidence that I could do the work and anything else. There was no need to be special in anything. Instead I had confidence in my reading, math, science, and physical strength. Truly my mother was loving

---

6 (Guareschi 1950)

and determined!

Astronomy

Around this time the TV, newspapers, school, and people were talking about the space race. Who would be first, the Americans or the Russians? The thrill of being in space captured my imagination. Then one day a friend of my mother and her husband visited. He was a rocket scientist from Huntsville, Alabama. He explained how a rocket worked and gave me some of his pre-published engineering papers. It had all kinds of strange symbols explaining how the rocket worked. He knew that I would not understand any of it. Yet it was fascinating to turn the pages of math symbols that explained how a rocket worked. For some reason, I thought, "I can do this. If math can explain how to launch a rocket into space, then it can be useful to explain everything." So, math became increasingly important to me.

Figure 3.4 Looking through a telescope for the first time and seeing Saturn. "There are other worlds out there!"

One day, the whole neighborhood turned out to watch Sputnik(?) pass overhead. A little dot moved faster than an airplane crossed the sky. People pointed to it. The thrill of the moment went to my very bones. Yet, some people mumbled that it was a mirage and government trick. That was puzzling. Why do people reject evidence right in front of them? That still is puzzling.

Although my Mom and Dad divorced, dad gave me a small telescope. Without any instruction and much fumbling, I assembled the telescope. The local newspaper said where the planets were in the evening sky. The stars were points of light. A few much brighter than other stars. Looking through the scope, stars not visible to the naked eye came into view. There were fuzzy patches that were clusters of stars and galaxies. The most unforgettable view was my first-time view of Saturn. The rings boldly circled Saturn. The thrill flowed into my bones. Looking up the scope there was only a point of light. Looking back into the scope, and there were the rings of Saturn. I had to keep adjusting the position of the telescope because Saturn kept drifting out of sight. It was then that I sensed the rotation of the earth. It was the earth turning and not the movement of Saturn that caused Saturn to move. It felt like being on a ball that was turning. It was another thrill down to my very bones. Yes, the earth turns.

Facts and experimentation make the world understandable. It was fun to understand the world. Understanding gave strength to survive.

So, I went to the library to understand astronomy better. Eventually, I devoured every amateur astronomy book in the local library. Books on Mars explained how the straight lines were canals and thus creatures lived there. But how did the author know those straight lines meant there are creatures there? Martians? Suddenly, I realized that people get a few facts and then make wild claims that might or might not match reality. They could, but they didn't declare suppositions that needed verification.

At school there was a medicine ball. It was up to my chest. It was huge. I decided that the medicine ball would be the sun. A basketball would be the earth rotating around the sun. Then crouching down on the ground, I pretended to be living on the basketball. Keeping the ball pressed on the left of my face, I slowly rotated the ball. First, I saw the sun – the medicine ball. Then I kept rotating the basketball – the earth. Then the sun disappeared.

At the same time while keeping the basketball firm against my face, I slowly moved it around the sun – the medicine ball. The sun rose, set, and rose again. For half an hour, the basketball and I circled the sun. As the sun rose and set, the medicine ball cast a shadow from the sunlight outside on the basketball.

Then a nearby small ball became the moon, circling the basketball earth and myself. The earth, the moon and my face pressed against the basketball skootched around the sun. The gym, the trees, and buildings became the fixed universe.

I felt the movements of the earth and the moon in my bones.

But this wasn't the way the Bible described the world. But the Bible mentioned…

The Slingshot

Some neighborhood boys were picking on me. It was some silly minor thing long since forgotten. But, in anger, I vowed to stop them.

TV showed Medieval armies attacking a castle. Huge catapults hurled stones, dead bodies, and fire into the castle. Walls came tumbling down. The army was victorious! So, the catapult was the weapon to use. After gathering wood, wheels, and ropes, I made a three-foot-long and two-foot-wide catapult. With practice the catapult could throw a stone fifty and occasionally a hundred feet.

Suddenly I thought, "How to pull it along the sidewalks and to school? If I needed it, there would be no time to get it ready to hit the boys before they grabbed me. I must figure out something else."

On TV, brave men ran up to tanks, threw a bottle filled with gasoline, called a Molotov cocktail, on to a tank. The tanks exploded in huge fireballs. Victory after victory! So, I collected wine, beer bottles, cloths, and matches from fields, garbage cans and other places. I practiced putting gasoline and rags that I stole from various places and stuffed them in the bottles. Then I practiced lighting the soaked rags and threw the lighted bottles against rocks, buildings, and trees. The bottles slithered to the ground. The gasoline flowed out of the bottle, putting out the small flame at the top of the bottle. Or the bottle would break and extinguish the flame. Or, the bottle would just break spilling gasoline on the ground with a flame quietly dancing and going out.

After many tries and failures, a thought occurred, "How will I carry two bottles? Put bottles loaded with gasoline and rags in my front two pockets? Then walk to school? That makes no sense." In church I heard the story about David and Goliath. Little David defeated huge Goliath with a slingshot[7]. "Well, if he did that, then I will make a slingshot!"

After making a slingshot with rubber bands, I thought, "Were there rubber bands in David's time? Was there rubber in David's time? When was rubber invented or does it grow on trees? Do rubber tires grow on trees? Do people pick tires from trees?"

Becoming a bit of a geek, I figured that the library could show me what David's slingshot looked like. A mummified friendly librarian helped me find information about slingshots. A sketch showed a man swinging a slingshot. But except for saying that he swung the slingshot above his head it didn't say how to use it. But the picture gave a general idea. Though it showed him naked. I wasn't going to use the sling shot and be naked. No.

After much trial and error, I made a slingshot from cloth and string. After many attempts of swinging the slingshot in circles around my head, the rocks kept flying to the left, right, up, down, and even backwards. Occasionally, the rocks hit me. Nothing worked.

In despair, a thought occurred, "Make the slingshot like a catapult." Then the stone made a high arc hitting a telephone pole a hundred feet away. It worked! It worked! It worked! After much practice and using "… smooth round stones…" I could hit bottles three quarters of a football field away. So, the slingshot and several smooth round stones were always with me, con-

---

7   Technically David used a sling, not a slingshot. A human puts a stone in a leather sling. He twirls it above his head and releases the stone which flies to hit the target. A slingshot is a modern version using rubber bands or some mechanical power source to do the same. In order to keep the sense of a child, the term slingshot is used here instead of sling, because not many people would understand what is meant by sling in this context.

cealed in pockets.

Late fall, just as dusk was turning to darkness, about five boys three-fourths of a football field away yelled, "There he is, get him!" Calmly I pulled out the sling shot. Looped one end to my right hand and laid the other end across my right palm. Gently I placed a smooth round stone into the slingshot. With the outstretched left arm aimed at the center of the boys, I steadied the sling shot on my right hand stretched out behind me. With all my force and focused intently on the center of the boys, my arm and the sling shot rose. At the top of the arc, I released the golf ball sized stone. It hit a boy in the chest, flattening him like a bowling pin.

The others gathered around him. A boy screeched, "He's dead!"

Uncontrollably my body wouldn't stop quivering. A thought appeared, "Well, if I killed one, I may as well kill another." After pulling out of the jacket pocket another golf ball size smooth round stone, I aimed with the left arm, steadied the sling and carefully focused on the boys. At that instant, the flattened boy struggled to get up. They left. No one ever bullied me again.

If I had been that young me today, with what is on TV and in the movies now, I wouldn't have made the catapult, nor the Molotov Cocktails, nor the sling shot.... I would have gotten a gun...

Playing Chicken with the Oil Tanker Ships

One summer day when I was about twelve years old, one of my friends said, "Let's swim out to the lighthouse." It was about a half a mile out on some rocks in the Raritan Bay between Staten Island, New York City and New Jersey. Three of us enjoyed the saltwater, the sunshine, and the waves. When we were within fifty feet of the rocks, one of my friends wanted to climb onto the rocks, and then the lighthouse. But we realized the rocks were bigger than we were, and that there would be a variety of sea life like eels, barnacles, crabs, and the ever-present sharks. So, we chickened out and swam back to the beach.

Some days later we spotted an oil tanker coming around the southern tip of Staten Island heading out to sea. One of us said, "Let's play chicken with the oil tanker!"

So, we swam out to the shipping channel just beyond the unmanned lighthouse. We waited. We could hear the tanker's engines picking up speed as it headed towards – towards where? Saudi Arabia? Libya? Venezuela? Suddenly a loud

Figure 3.5 I alone or with others would swim in front of the oil tankers. The thrill was hearing the propeller and feeling the undertow pulling us backwards. Great fun.

deep horn sounded. "Baa-ahhh. Baa-ahhh. Baa-ahhh." We rapidly swam out of the way towards shore. As the tanker passed us, we could hear the propeller blades churning the water, "Ka-thump. Ka-thump. Ka-thump." Some men were running along the deck of the ship. It was thrilling as we swam as fast as we could, and the water sucking us back to the ship. We swam harder and then were free of the undertow. Twenty minutes later we were ashore. A few minutes later a Coast Guard helicopter flew around. We lay on the beach and happily waved. It left.

For the next several days, I saw oil tankers come around the bend and head out to sea. So, I swam out by myself to the shipping channel to feel the power of the tanker, the water, the horn, and the thrill of the undertow pulling me backwards while I valiantly swam against the current. The mighty ship's horn rapidly sounded, "Baa-ahhh. Baa-ahhh. Baa-ahhh." It was thrilling. The water sucked me back toward the ship. The propellers churned, "Ka-thump. Ka-thump. Ka-thump." Then all was calm. What fun. Realizing that the Coast Guard would come, I quickly swam to shore. Just as I got to my towel on the abandoned beach, the Coast Guard helicopter flew around. I looked up and waved.

After several more times of playing chicken with the oil tankers, I realized, "Grandpa is a harbor pilot. He might be on one of those tankers and see me. He might cause some real trouble. I had better stop." But it was fun.

Sexual Awakening

Dad loved the ocean, the salt, the freedom of going from country to country. So, he went back to his love of the ocean. His route was mostly the eastern seacoast of North and South America. One day, he told Mom that he married an American woman in Brazil. So, Mom very graciously divorced dad.

After the divorce, Mom and I went to some church and neighborhood parties. I noticed that the men liked to pinch her and run their hands up and down on her butt and legs.[8] She firmly but graciously pushed them off. Their wives noticed too. They made faces at her. It was confusing. There was something that men did that Mom did not like and for some reason made women angry at her. What did she do? She didn't do anything! She would come home furious.

So, she became a, recluse not socializing in the community. Though she did have friends several hours away and two friends in the neighborhood. They would visit us, or she would visit them on weekends.

At some point, I really don't know when, different men and loud-mouthed 'experienced' boys explained the facts-of-life to me. "If a girl says no, she means maybe. If she says maybe, she means yes. If she says yes, she is a slut; you can do what you want with her."

That bothered me. It was difficult to put into words. But it made no sense. I vowed not to do what they said. What surprised me was that there were a

---

8   Years later, looking at photographs, I noticed that Mom was extremely attractive and stylish then.

group of guys that would just push and push on girls. They bragged about their activities. Yet, there was a larger group of guys that wouldn't push on the girls. But they were silent. They just wanted to be with the gals and enjoy their company. If a girl wanted to go further, that was ok. If the girl didn't want to, that bothered them a bit; but that too was ok.

Then the church said that to even think of sex outside of marriage is a sin. How could I stop thinking about sex? Girls were attractive. Why was the attraction to girls a sin? Why did God make me attracted to girls when that attraction was a sin?

What happened to my mother was confusing. What boys and men said was confusing. What the church said was confusing. It was all very confusing.

Name Calling

It seemed as if everyone had to be labeled: spic, wop, guinea, chink, queer, Jew boy, dog, douche bag, dego, slope head, monkey, nigger, slut, Irish, Catholic, Protestant, and names I have forgotten. These were not nice labels.

Around twelve years of age, I stayed for several weeks with Mom's friend in Virginia. They along with their friends took me on an evening river cruise. They all had a lot to drink and became merrily blitzed by the time the sun set. I couldn't tell where the river met the shore on either side of the small boat. Suddenly, one of the men ran to the left side of the boat yelling, "Here comes the African Queen. Here comes the African Queen!!!" All the men ran next to him.

I thought, "An African Queen. What does she look like? Royalty. I must see what she looks like."

The men threw empty beer, wine, and other bottles at the passing ship. Dimly it became evident that the ship had five or more decks of benches filled with African Americans. I became scared that several thousand of them would throw bottles and rocks down on us. I frantically looked for a place to hide.

The women said, "Oh come on guys. We want to have a fun time. Leave them alone, they want a fun time too." But the guys became angrier while yelling more and throwing more items.

Suddenly, a voice from the ship started to sing:

>We shall overcome
>
>We shall overcome
>
>We shall overcome some day

The rest of the African Americans joined in singing:

>We shall overcome
>
>We shall overcome
>
>We shall overcome some day
>
>Deep in my heart
>
>I do believe
>
>We shall overcome some day.

It became a crescendo. Strong, vibrant, united. The ship passed us. The strong voices and the dark ship fading in the distance. It felt like an alien space craft had hovered near for a few moments and then passed on to more interesting life forms.

All that labeling, name calling, and hatred made no sense. I knew people from all these groups. They were nice people. I liked them. Yet, everyone was labeling everyone else and hating. I didn't like it and resolved not to label nor hate; and I further resolved to meet all kinds of people and hate no one.

Religion

The women teachers in grammar school developed an affinity for Mom. Perhaps because she was divorced and raising a child. Bless her heart she did the best she could by working full time with as much overtime as possible, keeping a household, raising a child, and going to school functions. The teachers were encouraging. They said, "You will do well. You can do it."

Finally, someone had faith in me. For the first time, I felt a deeply growing sense of confidence. They loved teaching and those that eagerly learned.

Poor Mom, she faced the constant threat of layoffs, financial instability, and worry about money. Would dad supply alimony? It was a constant worry. On the one hand, the checks came but instead of coming at the beginning of the month, the checks would always come a few days later than the earlier checks. So, that in a year only ten checks would arrive. Mom said that was a way for him to prove he was sending the checks and she was miscalculating. So, the financial tension was present every day for years. Nevertheless, she handled it and managed to have fun with her friends.

However, for her and me, the church services supplied peace and security that, no matter what happened, all would be well. The pastor gave interesting and understandable sermons. On the one hand, the various rituals, songs, and classes all said that life now and, in the afterlife, would be good. Things will work out with God in charge. God was the solid rock for security, stability, and confidence. We love to sing, "On Christ, the solid rock I stand. All other ground is sinking sand."

But on the other hand, there was the ever present, "You are by nature sinful and unclean" mantra. More than enough times, I was aware that I didn't do enough work.

By high school, the Bible and then other religions didn't make sense. There were inconsistencies:

How could the earth be just 6,000 years old when science estimated that the earth and the universe were billions of years old?

In Genesis, there was mention of other people. Where did they come from? Who were they? Adams' sons went to some land to find wives. Where did the women come from? Who were the giants in the land?

Why would an all-knowing and loving God tempt Adam and Eve with The

Tree of Knowledge of Good and Evil? Wouldn't God know that Adam and Eve would be tempted? Wouldn't God know that God would punish all humanity for two people not obeying? Why was God so worried about Adam and Eve learning? Wasn't learning good?

Why were the Israelis slaves for four hundred years before God freed them? If they were God's chosen people to be a light to the world, then why wait four hundred years to be a light to the world? Why not skip all that time and wandering around the desert, conquering a land, fighting to keep the land, exiled to Babylon, and finally returning to the land?

Why were so many people butchered when conquering Palestine? Why does that continue to today? Why didn't God just magically make the Palestinians happy to have strange people in their land? God could just do it, and everyone would be joyous and have a huge festival.

Since Jesus had such great power, why did he heal only a few people and not masses and masses of people? Why not eradicate disease from the world? What was he thinking? Though,

> Jesus went throughout Galilee, teaching in their synagogues and proclaiming the good news of the kingdom and curing every disease and every sickness among the people. So, his fame spread throughout all Syria, and they brought to him all the sick, those who were afflicted with various diseases and pains, demoniacs, epileptics, and paralytics, and he cured them. Matt 4:23-25

However, he appears to heal only those near him. He did not heal all lands far and wide. Apparently, he was only interested in healing those who were in contact with him, or perhaps followed or believed in him. For the rest, he did nothing.

Why did God require sacrifices of lambs and then of Jesus? Did He change his mind? Does God have a mind like humans?

How can I test the Bible?

One day while wrestling with these and similar issues, a way to find answers was to ask the all-knowing all wise grownup in churches. So instead of going to school, I spent a day visiting churches. One minister looking like a fragile skeleton listened. He merely responded with a kind smile, "Just remember that God loves you." Then left. He didn't answer the questions. Why?

Another minister briefly listened and walked away.

At a Catholic Church an emaciated sad elderly lady kept the place. She uncaringly opened a door to a quiet small room. Later a fat guy dressed in a brown cassock came in. After asking several questions. He asked me, "What religion are you?"

"Lutheran."

He said, "That is your problem. If you were Catholic, you wouldn't have those problems. Now get out of here!"

The elderly lady came in. She said, "You made Father terribly angry. You should be ashamed of yourself. Now leave!"

The priests or pastors in the other churches gave similar responses. Some with love and most with a touch of hostility and hidden anger. That was puzzling. Why not answer the questions? The day made no sense.

In college the local Lutheran Church was wonderful with a warm happy social program for college kids, and a service that was bright, breezy, and uplifting. The girls were sweet, charming, and delightful; I was in love with all of them. Everyone was happy, warm, and gracious. The pastors said, "Questions and doubts about faith are normal. Don't worry about it. Just remember, God loves you."

For some reason despite my questions and doubts, the call of the ministry became stronger.

In college, the ROTC instructors encouraged people to go to a military convention in Washington, D.C. There an officer listened to career plans and answered questions. For me, he found a chaplain who listened very thoughtfully. His advice was, "The Vietnam War is going on. If you want to be a chaplain, you will be a better chaplain if you go on to active duty before seminary. Then if you still want to be a minister then go to seminary. That way you will have more experience that will help people, you will also have the GI Bill, and you can be part of the Reserves."

His advice made sense. So, instead of going into seminary after graduation I went into active duty with the Army.

Chapter 4

The Army

Figure 4.1 Engineer units built roads, bridges, and airfields in support of these operations.

Figure 4.2 The result of operations in which I did not participate but my unit indirectly supported.

Figure 4.3 I became oblivious to seeing the dead along roads or fields.

My experience in the military was building roads, bridges, airfields, and rear area buildings in support of the operations shown in the above photos. I was not involved with the direct combat; instead, came across the aftermath. Usually just one or two dead. Once in a while many more dead. This though was what my company's efforts were in support of.

For me, the Army was a broadening experience. There were people from all economic levels, races, morals, and ideas. Most of the guys were delightful and full of life. Most were draftees and didn't want to be in Germany or the Vietnam War. Yet, they had spunk, were willing to work, have fun, and longed to go home. The Army reduced my naïve view of life. The whites hated the blacks and the blacks hated the whites. The juicers (guys who drank a lot of alcohol) hated those that didn't drink and particularly hated the potheads (those that took drugs.) The potheads hated the juicers. Criminals stole and figured out ways to create minor errors and havoc. They were good people caught up in something larger than themselves. It was a valuable experience. So, my utter failure in my first assignment as a platoon leader trying to come to grips with these new situations. I became determined to master each and every situation with respect for everyone, learning from the soldiers, NCO's, officers, books, Army leadership principles, and combining my intuition and reasoning. Gradually, I became more skilled and a better officer. So in a sense, that first assignment was not a failure; rather, it was an excellent learning experience. I was down, but not out.

You Might Do Something Stupid

During the Vietnam War era, Fort Belvoir, Virginia was the Army base to train engineer officers. Halfway through the course, several hundred of us reported for a mandatory class with our future assignment orders. A charismatic officer told us to look at the orders to see where our next assignment was. Mine was to a combat engineer battalion on the DMZ in Korea. Arrival was to be just before Thanksgiving. Shivers. That will be cold and in the middle of nowhere. Yuk.

The officer then said, "If you sign up for just one more year, you can go anywhere you want in the world." While he repeated that over and over while showing slides of cars, wine, and girls. Cars, wine, and girls. Cars, wine, and girls. (The Army keeps things simple.) Finally, the proverbial light came on.

I thought, "So, I can go anywhere I want. Germany sounds nice. The Army guarantees me 21 months in Germany and then I get a short tour of twelve months. Heck, by then the Vietnam War will be over." So, I signed up for Germany.

On Thanksgiving eve, I arrived on an Army base in southern Germany. The officers had a small welcoming party for me. Two schoolteachers of the Army dependents heard that a new lieutenant had arrived. So, on their way out to dinner, they decided to check out the new guy – me. At the open doorway, they peeked their heads around the opening. I looked across the room and thought, "That is the girl I am going to marry." Then they disappeared.

The next day was a Thanksgiving holiday for everyone. So, I thought, "If I am going to marry her, then I must find her. Not knowing where her quarters were, I walked around the bachelor officers' quarters reading the names on doors. But I didn't know her name. No problem. Since I will marry her, I will find out her name. If the names were male, then it wasn't her quarters. Eventually, I came to an open door. There she was. It felt as if the heavens opened and angelic music played. I invited myself in while discretely trying to read her name on the door.

Thirteen months later Marlene and I were married. Five months after that, my orders to Vietnam arrived. She remained in Germany teaching the children of the Army soldiers and wives; while I left for Vietnam.

Upon completion of a one-week orientation training for Vietnam at Fort Lewis, Washington, a clerk handed me an airplane ticket to Vietnam along with promotion orders to Captain. Immediately I purchased the Captain rank and at the Officers Club bought a round of drinks. Quickly I said goodbye and headed for the plane.

But there was a plane delay which allowed time to explore a bookstore in the terminal. A couple of guys looking for a fight started pushing and shoving. But I just looked at them, shrugged my shoulders, and walked away.

Getting off the airplane in Vietnam, it felt as though a boiling hot freshly filled wet baby's diaper hit me in the face. As we processed in, I needed to use the men's room. There were women bathing their children in the toilets. Wash the child. Flush the toilet. Wash the child. Flush the toilet. Continue washing. Flush the toilet. I lost the desire to use the men's room.

During in-processing, it seemed as if the first and most important thing to learn was counting the days till going home. The tour of duty was 365 days – not twelve months. Many soldiers had calendars where they counted down the days until it was time to go home. Sadly, it made the soldiers more interested in getting through the days to go home as compared to winning a war. Their only interest in winning was getting on the Freedom Bird, which would fly us home. No one cared. There was no enthusiasm to win the war.

Welcome to Vietnam.

The Army allowed one Rest and Relaxation (R&R): Seven days and six nights at a choice of Hawaii, Australia, Bangkok, and perhaps some other places I forgot about. The flight was free; with the soldiers paying the remaining expenses. Soldiers could take the R&R anytime between the third and ninth month of the tour. Experienced soldiers suggested to take the R&R around the eighth month. If one took R&R at the fourth month then, when R&R was over, the remaining eight months would feel like a prison sentence. If he took R&R in the eighth month, there would be three months until it was time to go home. One could do that standing one one's head.

Since Marlene was in Germany, choosing Bangkok as a place to meet was convenient, and a place we had not been. Also, there was a school break during the seventh month of my tour. So, we easily agreed on Bangkok.

Well, relatively easy. In those days we communicated by an ancient method of letter writing. From the time I left to go to Vietnam until I was back with

Marlene, we wrote each other a letter a day. That is a total of 378 letters from each of us. My letters were postage free.

Nearly half a century later, we still have them. They are somewhere in some dusty box. Perhaps the mice or tiny bugs read them as they made homes or digested the prose. Some day we might get around to reading them. Nothing much in them. Just love notes to each other and chatter about day to day things long since forgotten, except for the ammunition dump less than one thousand feet away that blew up one night. Soldiers hunkered down for nearly three days until the thousands of pallets of 105 howitzer ammunition stopped cooking off. The first blast made a loud ringing noise.

It would take two to three weeks for a letter to go from me to her and then from Marlene back to me. There was no pattern. There would be days when no letters arrived and then suddenly a batch of four or five arrived. Marlene might be responding to something that I had asked four weeks earlier. Marlene having my letter in front of her would write a cryptic response. When it arrived a month after I wrote it, I sometimes would puzzle as to why she wrote what she did. So, I have no idea how we agreed to meet, let alone where and when to meet in a huge city like Bangkok. Was it the benevolent Army that made all the arrangements?

All I remember is getting to the airport to catch the flight to Bangkok. There was some sort of briefing. The Army always has a briefing. A briefing in the morning, a briefing at night. A briefing before crossing the street. It was no different here. Some guy had a script to read to us. Be careful of crooks and prostitutes; the war might be there too, etc. He mentioned something like, "You might do something stupid. If so, contact blah blah blah." No one cared. We were going to have fun.

One of the clerks decided to give me a tough time. I think he didn't like the war, his job, officers, or maybe was having a bad hair day. He gave some reason that I couldn't get on the plane. That caught my attention. At that moment, Marlene was arriving in Bangkok just when my flight from Vietnam would be leaving. I wanted to meet my wife and there was limited time. If I had to stuff myself in a wheel well of the plane, I was going to be on THAT flight. After much discussion and meeting with his upper food chain, I was on board. Strongly controlling my emotions, I told myself, "Careful, you might do something stupid." Eventually, the clerk handed me the boarding pass with a satisfied look. He inconvenienced a captain and got away with it. On the other hand, I too was satisfied. I almost did something stupid.

Happy exuberant soldiers were on the flight to Bangkok. It was party time!! The six nights and seven days were pure bliss. The memory of what we did is vague. Buying a skirt for Marlene and a suit for myself. We toured the city with sanctioned tours and ventured out on our own. Saw the reclining Buddha, covered with gold or gold paint. The smiling Buddha laid on its back occupying a city block. The river cruise was delightful with happy Thai people and other foreigners.

It was especially fun to partake in the water festival. The city erupted in celebration of the coming monsoon. Almost all the Thai people poured water on everyone especially foreigners. Children would run after people in the street and douse them with buckets of water. Or they would use toy water pistols. Adults would use hoses to squirt each other. Bangkok was giggling, happy, and great fun. It was a land of smiles and joy. They seemed like the happiest people in the world; unlike the people in Vietnam.

On the last day in the hotel room, Marlene's silence eerily echoed off the walls.

Then she cried.

I asked, "What's wrong?"

More silence. An ominous feeling descended over me like a dentist's lead blanket used on patients when doing X-rays. The weight was unbearable.

I asked her to explain. She then said, "I can't tell you."

The sickening feeling for some silly reason morphed into a thought. "She wants a divorce! Now, she tells me on her way to the airport."

In silence we headed to the airport. On the one hand, my heart was heavy with parting from her; on the other hand, I irrationally thought she wanted a divorce. Where that idea came from, I will never know. It had no basis. But I felt it. The flight from Bangkok to Vietnam was heavy with the silence of soldiers. None were hooting, hollering, and getting drinks. None were smiling. We just sat in the seats and stared ahead.

In a few hours I reassumed command of the company. However, I did not focus on my commander responsibilities. I didn't care. I really didn't care about anything. What was the point of doing anything? The one love of my life was leaving and there was nothing I could do. I was on the other side of the European-Asian Continent. She was on the other side. It was useless and pointless. The only gift I could give her was my life insurance policy. So, with an honorable death she would get the entire amount.

Occasionally, someone would spot some activity outside of a worksite perimeter. It was boring to guard those perimeters. The platoon or squad would do work while one or two soldiers sat or walked in the hot sun looking for a possible attack. We 'all knew' that wouldn't happen. At least we believed that. We 'knew' that the North Vietnamese and the Viet Cong 'knew' they were going to win the war; and felt that all the work the US engineers were doing was really for them. Therefore, they would leave us engineers alone. It made sense. It was comforting to think that. But, then why do the work? Why not go and directly fight them? It was confusing to think of those strategic questions while running the day to day operations of a 180-man engineer company.

But, from time to time one of the sentries would notice something. The procedure was to send a patrol to investigate. But being depressed, if I was on the site, I said, "Keep working. I will check it out myself." There was some argument about my going alone. But I hoped by going alone the VC or NVA[9] would kill me.

After a few instances, the First Sergeant said to me, "Sir! If something happens to you, the other men must go out and find you. They might get hurt or killed. Remember, you have a responsibility to the men. You keep doing this, you might do something stupid."

"Duh. That is right." So, my focus became maintenance, discipline, race relations, drug issues, alcohol issues, and the work needed by the 101st Air Mobile Division. We were in support of and not part of the 101st.

Race relations were by far the biggest issue. In one highly emotional incident, an African American soldier assaulted a white soldier with a lead pipe cracking his skull. The reason why has long been forgotten. Because of the injuries the soldier was hospitalized in Japan. As a result, a lot of the white guys wanted to 'get the n----s.' The African American soldiers were quiet and getting ready for something. Later that night, everything calmed down.

Or rather, everyone was just too tired to care anymore. As I lay down to enjoy a peaceful sleep, my field phone rang. (Oh, yeah, just to explain what a field phone was. It was a clumsy, bulky phone the size of a quart milk container. To make a call one turned the crank. It sent an electrical signal through a landline to the switch board operator who would make a connection to whomever I wanted to talk to.) When the phone rang, I was nearly asleep in peace. Groggily, I picked up the receiver.

A desperate voice squeaked, "Sir! You got to get down here now!! There is going to be a problem."

I thought, "Shit. Enough. I just want to sleep. When does this end?" After putting on my boots, I toddled like a drunk; except I hadn't drunk any alcohol, but I was wishing I had had a few drinks. I lumbered to the orderly room. There was one light on. I thought, "Maybe that light shouldn't be on.

---

9   Viet Cong. North Vietnamese Army.

Or is it too bright? I am just too tired to care right now."

The clerk said, "Sorry, Sir. I thought something was going to happen. It is all quiet now. It seemed like there would be trouble. Really, Sir, I am sorry."

"That is ok. You did the right thing. Better to do that than not call and then there is trouble. You did the right thing. Thank you."

With a profound sense of relief, I walked outside into the mild pleasant air. What a relief. I looked up at the black sky filled with jewels. In a moment of reverie, I pondered, "Are there creatures out there fighting a war like this? Might they do something stupid?"

In that instant, in less time than it takes an electron to whiz around a nucleus, ten or fifteen angry white southern soldiers came charging out of the blackness like a defensive football team rushing the quarterback. I thought, "Ah shit. Now what?"

They had clubs, sticks, and perhaps iron bars. They yelled, "We are going to get those g-d damn f'n n…. s." Their faces flushed red with anger and drinks.

I yelled, "Stop!"

They screamed at me, "We are going to get those …." How many times did they say that? They yelled other things long forgotten.

I sensed something behind me. Keeping an eye on the white soldiers, I turned my head (like an owl turns its head?) to see what was behind me. In the thick coal-like darkness something was there. Vaguely, I perceived ten or fifteen black soldiers who blended into the darkness. They were ready to do Taekwondo. It is a form of martial arts using just one's hands, legs, and body. They were ready to fight the tanked-up southern boys. They were quiet. They were ready and sober. They were intent and focused.

Suddenly, I psychologically split into three parts. One part of me was outside, calmly, coolly hovering above the whole scene, describing what was going on. There were drunk guys in front of me with sticks and clubs. There were black guys behind me ready to do Taekwondo. I was in the middle arguing with the drunks while thinking, "How does one argue with drunks? I am glad their weapons were taken away."

The second part of me continued arguing with the intoxicated soldiers.

The third part of me felt like a little imp was sitting on my right shoulder. Giggling, he crossed his leprechaun legs and whispered, "You aren't paid enough for this! Hee. Hee. Hee."

The white drunks yelled, "Get out of our way. You don't get out of our way; we will kill you."

The little imp on my right shoulder continued giggling and said to me, "Act like Barney Fife when the two big goons were going to beat him up."

So, acting life Barney Fife (but without the squeaky shaky voice) I said to the drunks, "If you kill me, you know what's going to happen. The entire world will collapse on you. One of you will rat on the rest of you and you will be in jail for the rest of your life. If you hurt me, I know EVERY ONE of your names. The world will collapse on you. Don't do anything that might be stupid."

Then the cool hovering part of me observed, "Where the hell is anyone to help?"

Suddenly, two big sergeants appeared. At that moment, they felt like two King Kongs. The white sergeant came from behind the white guys. Flaying his huge arms and hitting the soldiers. He yelled at them, "You g-d damn f..rs. Get the fuck out of here! Get out of here."

The black sergeant came from behind the black guys. He too was flaying his massive muscular arms yelling, "You goddam fucking nig..rs get the hell out of here."

As though the imp waved a magic wand, the drunk white soldiers and the Taekwondo black soldiers vanished. I stood alone in the silence. The stars twinkled above as though nothing had happened. A soft gentle cool breezed flowed.

I thought, "I might have done something stupid. We might have done something stupid."

In Vietnam, there were many events where I and others might have done something stupid; so, I never had time to think about what Marlene said to me in the hotel room. There was also no energy to ponder her parting words, "I can't tell you."

Perhaps

My tour of duty in the Vietnam War was almost over. Several days earlier and a two-hour jeep drive away, my official responsibilities had ended with the company change of command ceremony. So, I was light heartedly walking in the compound of the battalion headquarters next to the South China Sea. The relief from responsibilities, issues to work on, and the freedom to do nothing was strange. Part of me wanted to do something useful. Yet another part of me was just too mentally and physically tired. All I wanted was to be home with Marlene, enjoy her company, and get on with my life. For the first time I noticed and enjoyed the blue sky, the smell of fresh sea air, a gentle breeze caressing my cheeks, the delightful temperature, the shade of the palm trees, and the soothing sound of the ocean swells. Two hundred feet away, the gleaming enticing ocean was beckoning me to swim in prohibited waters.

Suddenly, the crack of an ear-splitting loud thunder bolt directly above me at tree top level snapped my reverie and my head upwards. A Chinook helicopter with two rotor blades was splitting like an egg into two parts as it continued forward into the South China Sea.

A soldier new to the battalion was near me. I sharply said, "Come on. Let's go." Several more soldiers also ran into the water to help guys out of the chopper.

Figure 4.4 Type of Chinook Helicopter that broke apart above me.

Moments later, a few disoriented passengers and crew stumbled out. One soldier was face down in the water. I lifted him up. But it was only his top half. One of the rotors had sliced him apart at the waist. I passed the top half to the newbie on my left. I said, "Here. You take him." His face turned paper white. I tiredly thought, "Don't faint. Where is his other half? Welcome to Vietnam."

By then two guys had climbed onto the Chopper cockpit windows. They slammed their fists against the glass trying break the windshield and get the pilots out. (We didn't know there was an emergency release lever outside right next to them. Just reach over and pull.) A wave lifted me up. I grabbed something. Looked into the cockpit. The pilots strapped into their seats were peacefully sleeping as the surf felt like a mother gently washing vomit off her babies.

I slid back into the water leaving the guys pounding on the windows with their fists and went around the left side towards where the chopper split open. I swam and walked inside. The waves repeatedly slammed my head against the roof and then let me down. The roar of the waves muffled the yells of soldiers outside. The closer I got to the pilots, the darker the cabin became. As the surf relentlessly dragged the chopper out to sea, the water level rose. The breathing room decreased from waist high to the cabin roof to less than chest high to the roof. The cabin visibility became like the end of evening twilight.

Wires, ropes, and debris tangled my legs. The water washed away my regulation booney hat I had wanted to take home. Fortunately, the jungle boots and uniform prevented cuts and punctures. I should have pulled the rolled-up sleeves of the jungle fatigues down to prevent arm injury. In the haste I didn't. Instead I just charged into the cabin while swallowing saltwater mixed with jet fuel. In the intermittent darkness, the water pushed me up, down, and sideways. I became disoriented and confused.

Figure 4.5 Lt William Hatcher with M79 Grenade Launcher and wearing a boonie hat.

Just about reaching the cockpit where the pilots were, an involuntary vomiting reflex started. Without thinking, I turned around, headed for the dim sunlight to where the chopper had split open. Somehow repeatedly untangling myself while swimming, walking, stumbling, swallowing more fuel-tasting saltwater, and banging my head against the ceiling, I tumbled out drinking more saltwater and fuel. A wave lifted me up towards the jagged sheet metal as though the ocean was welcoming me to join the pilots. Frantically, I swam away from metal razor edges, breathing hard, and spitting out fluid but not quite vomiting.

More soldiers came to help. Some brought a long thick rope to prevent the surf from dragging the chopper further out to sea. Someone was yelling to get the 50 caliber machine guns and other armaments out of the chopper to prevent the VC from using them against us.

For some reason I became focused on not having my boonie hat. That bothered me. I like that hat. I wanted that hat. But it was washed away by waves.

Why with all that happened did I focus upon a hat? There was no thought about the two guys who perished. No thought about the dozens of other people that helped prevent the waves from dragging the chopper and the two dead pilots out to sea. I walked up the beach, showered, changed my clothes, and forgot about the hat and the pilots - until writing this story..

Forty-eight years later, I still see the pilots peacefully strapped into their seats with the ocean caressingly welcoming them. Their skin tone was normal. Not like that of the greyish corpses dumped along a road waiting for retrieval. Those two were the only ones who had died that bothered me. The rest of the dead were like dead rabbits, squirrels, or birds lying along the side of an American road. Don't even notice them nor care. Yet, strangely, I still care about my boonie hat and those two pilots.

Sometimes, I wonder if I had pushed harder maybe they could have lived, had families, and enjoyed life. But most likely I would have drowned in the cockpit trying to release a complicated harness I knew nothing about and trying to punch the windows out not knowing that there was an emergency latch inches from their heads. Or perhaps I could have dragged the two pilots through the cabin towards the ripped open chopper, through the entangling wires as more contaminated water filled the cabin and our lungs. Then perhaps others could have lugged the unconscious and probably dead pilots to shore and performed CPR.

Still, I could have done more. Perhaps.

Though not really. Perhaps.

One of those things.

Who cares…?

Vietnam.

"You Might Do Something Stupid" continued

When I completed my part of the Vietnam War, Officer Personnel assigned me to a base in Germany where Marlene was teaching the military dependents' children. Not remembering her last words to me, I was bubbling with excitement to see her. Excitement to blithely chat with her, to lay with her, just to be fully with her. The first night was sheer bliss. Then, unexpectedly she said, "You remember when I said, 'I can't tell you'?"

Again, the ominous feeling of the dentist lead blanket settled over me and I thought, "She wants a divorce. Now, she tells me!"

She said, "After you left for Vietnam, Officer Personnel called and said, 'Ivan doesn't have to go to Vietnam.' So, I said to the officer, 'He already left and is on the way. I think he is in Fort Lewis, Washington.'

The officer said, 'Ok. Since he already left, we will un-cancel his cancellation orders and cancel someone else's orders who hasn't left.'

I said nothing to you in Bangkok; because, I thought you would be upset, and you might do something stupid."[10]

An Army Chaplain

On the base in Germany, one of the chaplains learned that I was interested in becoming a minister. So, he used discussions to "save" me for Jesus. While asking questions and chatting with him, he would have the Bible open on his lap. He would flip to some verse as to what the Bible said. He answered the questions and yet didn't answer them. He only answered with what the Bible said. He never replied with logic except the Bible said this is the answer. Though it seemed that there were other verses that didn't agree; but I wasn't able to point that out. After several months of weekly discussions, the quest

---

10 (In case you are wondering, fifty years later we are still married to each other. The thought, "You might do something stupid" never occurred to me when signing up for Germany and deciding on marrying the unknown girl peeking her head in the open door. Not a chance.)

for logic faded away like water slowly leaking from a kitchen sink. By then, the literal inerrant Truth of the Bible was self-evident. I 'saw the light' and on Nov 15, 1974 at 4:30 PM, I accepted Jesus Christ as my personal Lord and Savior and finally decided to become a minister. As I walked out of his office into the darkening twilight, everything seemed right with world. It felt secure, warm, and wonderful. It was a feeling of pure bliss. An unforgettable moment.

So, I bought an eight-volume set of systematic theology from the leading US conservative seminary. It was easy to read and understand. The Bible was literal and inerrant. One reads the Bible just like one reads a newspaper. Therefore, it was simple to accept the premillennial, dispensational, and evangelical interpretation of the Bible. The world made sense and no matter what would happen, Jesus was there to comfort, guide, and then greet me in the afterlife. It was very reassuring. So, much better than that priest of my childhood.

So, I applied to two very conservative seminaries and the three denominational seminaries. They all accepted me. While visiting one of the denominational seminaries, an elderly chaplain said, "If you are going to be a pastor in the denomination, then it is easier and probably better to go to one of the denomination's seminaries."

After considering his comment for two seconds, I thought, "A seminary is a seminary. They are all the same." So, I chose the denominational one instead of one of the two nationally ranked conservative ones.

Chapter 5

Seminary – The Questions

Figure 5.1 I talked individually with almost every student and faculty member of the seminary about faith and God questions.

Seminary was exhilarating and challenging. In summer school I memorized Greek vocabulary, grammar, and read simple passages. In the fall semester, the shock came when the basic teaching was not premillennial, dispensational, and evangelical. That the Bible was not inerrant and literal, nor does one read it like reading a newspaper.

So, I reasoned, if the seminary's teaching is correct, then I will change my beliefs. So, assiduously I studied in detail each point the professors made. I memorized all the various creedal variations and statements. I memorized the outlines of the various texts and was able to say what the author wrote. I pondered, thought, and evaluated the accuracy of each statement in class and in the textbooks. But it was exceedingly difficult. The issue was, "how do they know that the statements the textbook authors, professors, and students made are true?" What was the basis? It just seemed like they just plopped it out there and took it as self-evident. That was frustrating.

The theology and biblical interpretation courses were most troubling. For two years I studied each and every statement attributed to Jesus. What did He mean? Why make statements that were not clear? A sense developed that Jesus' view was radically different from that of Paul, the influence of the Emperor Constantine, and the later Church. It felt as though they corrupted His teachings.

The seminary taught that various authors who lived in cultures thousands of years ago formed the Bible. Each had their point of view. Some, like Jeremiah, were more like today's political commentators who interpret events as if God was rewarding or punishing people. The Psalms were a compilation of hymns and liturgies. Genesis was an attempt to explain faith in God by nomadic people who believed in heaven above, hell below, and life on earth. It was not meant to be a literal story of creation and the Fall of Mankind. Fallible humans wrote The Old and New Testaments. The Holy Spirit did not guide every stroke of the authors' pens.

Troubled to my very bones and essence of my being, I thought, "Oh, oh! I have come to the den of iniquity and false teachings! How can these people be saying these things? Well, if it is true then it is. If it is not true, then figure something out."

So, I spent more intellectual, physical, and emotional effort to understand where the professors, students, and authors were coming from. For over two years, in addition to normal studying, I spent an added ten hours per week studying a different New Testament passage. I devoured the resources of the seminary's commentaries. I made crude translations from Greek to English. Futile attempts to understand how an Aramaic speaking people would understand the passages. After all, the crowds that Jesus spoke to, spoke Aramaic and not Greek. The more literate people and the trades people spoke Koine Greek which was the language of the New Testament but not the language of most of Jesus' followers and audiences.

I intensely studied the parallel version of the four Gospels in both English and Greek. The four Gospels of Matthew, Mark, Luke, and John were in columns next to each other. In parallel to each other. That is why it is call the parallel version.

So, when a text appears in Mark and it also appears in another Gospel then those texts appear in columns next to each other. To make that clearer, I highlighted texts that appeared in only two Gospels in one color, texts in three Gospels in another color and texts in all four Gospels in another color. It became exceptionally clear that there was copying. The authors copied texts from each other and from a common source. That stunning realization shook my bones.

Fundamentalists say 'that is not copying; rather, the Holy Spirit dictated the texts word for word, letter for letter. This is proof of the Holy Spirit's divine guidance.' But how does one know that? There is no proof. There is only a leap of faith.

There are Bibles with Jesus' statements in red letters. Thus, the name of those Bibles is, "Red Letter Bibles." Since Jesus is important, what he said is important. So, instead of studying the New Testament from the Church's point of view, I placed myself in the very shoes of Jesus' followers. I put myself into the crowds following Jesus around for three years. Neither people nor I knew that he would die for the sins of the world. They did not have priests and a church hierarchy interpreting his talks. What would those people and I have understood? What were Jesus' main themes?

Eventually, it became clear that Jesus was teaching about the Kingdom of Heaven here and now. He taught that the apocalypse was about to happen. That people should prepare – now. That people are free now. That the teachings of the Sanhedrin and Pharisees were not liberating; rather, they were suffocating. Thus, Jesus' teaching struck at the core of the Sanhedrin and the Pharisees. So, they killed him to preserve their power structure. Jesus didn't die for the sins of humanity. He wasn't a substitutionary propitiatory sacrifice to God. He died because political forces wanted him dead and out of the way.

But that conclusion created a stunning dilemma. If those conclusions are true, then why were the church doctrines such as the Nicene Creed developed? Why did the Church focus on who Jesus was instead of focusing on what he taught?

The Nicene Creed for example says nothing about what Jesus spent years preaching. It focuses solely on who he is and not on his three years of teaching. Here is a brief outline of the Nicene Creed:

I believe in… all things visible and invisible.

Jesus will judge the living and the dead.

There is …one baptism for the remission of sins….

I look for the resurrection of the dead, and the life of the world to come.

The full version of the Nicene Creed says:

I believe in one God, the Father Almighty, Maker of heaven and earth, and of all things visible and invisible.

And in one Lord Jesus Christ, the only-begotten Son of God, begotten of the Father before all worlds, God of God, Light of Light, very God of very God, begotten, not made, being of one substance with the Father; by whom all things were made; who for us men, and for our salvation, came down from heaven, and was incarnate by the Holy Ghost of the Virgin Mary, and was made man, and was crucified also for us under Pontius Pilate; He suffered and was buried; and the third day He rose again according to the Scriptures; and ascended into heaven, and sitteth on the right hand of the Father; and He shall come again with glory to judge the quick and the dead; whose kingdom shall have no end.

And I believe in the Holy Ghost, the Lord and Giver of life, who proceedeth from the Father and the Son; who with the Father and the Son together is worshiped and glorified; who spake by the Prophets. And I believe in one holy catholic and apostolic Church. I acknowledge one Baptism for the remission of sins; and I look for the resurrection of the dead, and the life of the world to come. Amen.

Notice something. Jesus advocated living here and now and loving your neighbor. Neither the Nicene Creed nor other creeds say anything about love your neighbor. But Jesus said that was the greatest commandment. Paul said faith, hope, love and charity of these love is the greatest.[11] The creeds say nothing about living in the here and now except to accept the authority of the church and who God and Jesus is. Absolutely nothing about love. Nothing about the Sermon on the Mount. It says nothing about the imminent apocalypse nearly 2,000 years ago. Why?

That "Why?" struck like a lightning bolt to the core of my being. How can I be in such error? Something in the logic must be missing. What was missing? To understand why the Church doctrines are true became a quest. How does one prove that they are true? If they are so important, then why didn't Jesus just come out and clearly say that? Why didn't the Church also teach what he said as doctrine? Why instead, Sunday after Sunday do many churches repeat the Creed or some variations of the Nicene Creed? Why not have the Beatitudes repeated Sunday after Sunday? Aren't those more important than the Creed?

The typical response was that if Jesus revealed who he really was, the Romans would have killed him. Then the world would not have his teachings. So, he kept his God feature hidden till the end of his life. But, if he was God incarnate, then why not clearly say what was important? As a God he could have easily fluffed off armies of Romans or anyone else that would try to kill him. That would have been a real miracle. As they attacked him, he could

---
11 1 Corinthians 13:13.

have uttered a few words and made the multiple Roman Legions just lay down their arms and confess Jesus as Lord. But he didn't do that. Why? Why be so secretive and leave such confusion behind for close to two thousand years. How does one know that Jesus kept his nature hidden from the masses? One doesn't know that.

The texts say he performed miracles. Lots of miracles. But in those days so did other itinerant preachers. Just like today, there are evangelists that claim to perform miracles. As important as the miracles were back then, I noticed that very few Christian ministers performed miracles. Though I met many Fundamentalist lay people who claimed to have experienced miracles and the presence of Jesus.

So, the Church opted to proclaim who Jesus was, and is, and that the next life is more important than life now. Life was something to get through with the reward in the next life. Confess one's miserable sins now, so that in the next life all will be well. The Church quietly minimized what He taught. Why?

But the Christians I listened to said that eternity is more important than living now. So, even if one is wretched, then one will have the good life after death. Just believe the church doctrines and give money. Some churches teach the prosperity gospel where one can have the good life now and then in eternity. It was a focus on oneself with some notion about the community. It was very self-centered.

This was all very perplexing. Throughout these studies I had discussions with anyone and everyone about how they knew what they believed was correct or matches reality. I politely tried to discuss these issues with every student and faculty member at the seminary. Example topics were:

How does one know what is true?

Can one test the statements?

How does one know that the bread or wafer and the wine or grape juice is the real body and blood of Jesus? How does one know it is a symbol? How do you know that by taking the wine and bread that God forgives your sins? Do you have to mentally think of each sin? Otherwise God will not forgive each sin? Or just admit being a sinner? In any case take the wine or grape juice and bread or wafer in sincerity; then all will be well. But how do you know?

Did people believe because of the miracles? Then why not have miracles today to convince people? But apparently Jesus wanted to minimize the miracles. Yet, Paul emphasized that Jesus performed miracles. Why?

When did people come to understand Jesus was a God? There are a few people that have such great charisma that, to be in their presence, it feels like being in the presence of a god. On the other hand, there are people that felt that they were gods and others thought they were gods. How does one tell if they are functioning in reality?

Interpret the Bible liberally or literally? That it is with or without error?

If the Bible is not literal, then how does one know that the various doctrines of the different churches are true? That perhaps all the doctrines and creeds are not correct?

Chapter 6

Seminary – The Responses

Figure 6.1 I was shunned, but unlike Adam and Eve who were kicked out of the Garden of Eden, I was not kicked out of seminary.

The responses were disheartening. One professor said: "...the driving force behind all of my enthusiasm, and the reason that the seminary and the church exist, is in what God did on Easter, raising our Lord Jesus Christ from the dead. This driving force is what called me to seminary. It is my default setting through all adversity I have ever faced..."

My response was: "If God had not resurrected Jesus, wouldn't you believe His teachings and be a follower of him? Skip the resurrection and salvation. If he rose, he rose. If he didn't, he didn't. If there is salvation, then there is. If there isn't salvation, then there isn't. Before he died many believed what he taught. What he taught is different from what Paul, the later church fathers, and Constantine advocated." The professor walked away.

The other professors communicated differently. A theology professor said that the students were not interested in real theological discussion, he seemed quite frustrated with them, and annoyed with my attempts at discussions. He said in class, "You guys want to have a nice easy life by being a pastor. You really don't want to work and think about the issues."

Another theology professor kept pushing my attempted discussions off. Then he said in a class, "You know this is exactly the sort of discussion that we need." Then he charged off to a meeting. Later, in a private discussion he tried to answer all my questions in 15 minutes and became nearly irate when the answers were not immediately accepted. He then charged off like a black, ferocious tornado.

One professor said in a superior tone, "Perhaps you are being hit with too many pieces of information. You are just getting overwhelmed." He implied I was stupid and incapable of learning.

The president of the seminary said in response to some questions, "The Bible is inspired because it inspires us!" Then rushed to a meeting.

Other professors said:

> "You science and engineering guys always have trouble with this area."

> "What is your real problem?"

> "Just accept it and you'll find that it is a good life."

> "Just love the people and they will love you!"

> "Don't worry about the doctrines. That is just once a week. Love the people! That is where you will spend most of your time."

> One listened politely and giggled.

> "You are having a crisis of faith; it will make you stronger."

"The devil has you!"

"Just make 'a leap of faith' and you'll see that it all works out."

"Well, join the UCC. They believe anything."

Several avoided me.

At first students were polite and made feeble attempts at discussions. Eventually, they shunned me. Upon approaching them standing at coffee break, they would turn their backs to me. Some might be in a circle chatting with each other and wouldn't open the circle a bit to let me in. Someone else would come and they would let that person in. They avoided eye contact, or any greeting, let alone a warm greeting.

However, it became clear that most of the students unconsciously leaned towards a literal interpretation of the Bible and did not agree with the basic teaching of the seminary.

They had a vague notion about what they believed. Many said the theology and biblical interpretation was just bookish stuff and theoretical.

Many giggled that they just prattled back whatever the professors said so that they could get a good grade and endorsement.

A fair number seemed concerned about the hidden lists the seminary had about recommending students for the ministry. So, to be on the right list, they carefully engaged with the professors telling them what they wanted to hear. They couldn't wait to graduate and do their thing.

Finally, one kind soul met me alone in a classroom and said, "You are a threat to people here. No one wants to think about their beliefs which you are concerned about. That is your issue. They just want to jump over the hurdles, go through the hoops to get their degree, and then go do the pastor stuff. No one wants to talk with you. Leave them alone."

Another student at seminary had comparable questions and responses from other students and faculty. We chatted several times. One time after dinner at his apartment, our wives stayed in the kitchen, while he and I stepped out into the hallway. We discussed several topics. Then casually, barely noticeable, like a child eying a sweet candy, he looked out the window and down eight stories. Warmly, pleasantly, longingly and with a sense of relief, he casually and softly barely whispered, "That is a long way down." I barely picked up on his fleeting feeling and statement. But he quickly moved onto other topics.

A day or two or three later, he jumped. Sadly, on the way down he hit the side of a dumpster breaking his fall and many bones to the horror of bystanders. Hours later he died.

Late summer in my third year, my wife and I visited friends on a farm for a potluck. I helped an elderly cheerful lady bring many items from her car into the farmhouse. For some reason as we walked, we chatted about faith.

Her surprising response was straight from Pascal's Wager. Pascal said, if there is a God and you believe in God you win; but if you don't believe in God then you lose. However, if there is no God to believe in then it doesn't matter because nothing happens when you are dead. Therefore, believe in God and not matter what you win.

Here is her verbatim of her comments about her belief:

"Look. Church is my social life. I have a nice life here. If I think about my belief, I might reach the wrong conclusion and go to hell. If I am wrong in my belief, then at least I have a nice social life with my friends and have had an enjoyable time. However, if I think about it and reach the wrong conclusion, I might go to hell. Thus, I lose. So, I don't want to think about it. Thus, I win either way. I have my friends, a nice social life in church, and I don't want to think about it."

She hurriedly walked away towards her women friends in the dining room and kitchen.

While the women were in their 'rightful place' getting dinner ready, the men were sitting on the porch. One of the old men, sitting in a rocking chair, disdainfully said, "Well, we had a young pastor like you. He told us how to treat our women folk and n...s. We told him, 'We don't like that.' He kept telling us how to treat them. We kept telling him to stop. This went on for a couple of weeks. Then one day we cut off his pay. He was gone in two weeks. The bishop wasn't happy with us. But now we have a minister that we like."

I realized then I was not interested in making people happy by telling them what they wanted to hear. But, if I didn't tell them what they wanted to hear, then I wouldn't last long in a congregation. They would eventually kick me out or quietly leave like slowly deflating balloons.

Some months later, after some seminar finished, two seminary professors, several students, and I went to a local German pub. Everyone relaxed and became jovial because the event went well. When theology people get together it is natural to talk about theology.

Without hesitation, I mentioned a dream. The bedroom closet door opened. Jesus, dressed in a white robe with a long beard, walked out. While intently looking at me, he glided to the foot of the bed. Then floated right next to me. Looking down he grinned, shaking his head, and went "tsk tsk tsk." He walked back into the closet and closed the door.

One of the professors blurted out, "You saw Jesus! You saw Jesus! You saw Jesus!"

I thought, "Maybe. Or maybe it was my subconscious struggling with faith issues and making light of the struggles. Or maybe Jesus was indicating damnation awaits the doubters." Psychologists and religious people certainly have their opinions.

The M Div. (Master of Divinity) program was four years. The first two years were classes, followed by one year working in the church and then one year of class. It was a revealing experience:

No one was interested in exploring their beliefs. And the congregations expected the minister to support their view."

When in trauma, they wanted their hands held. So, they expected ministers to get them through the trauma. But then they would go back to the behaviors that caused the problem in the first place. There was no interest in changing their behaviors.

Fundamentalist leaning ministers and members were vocal about keeping purity in the teachings. They chased out those who believed anything else. They were determined to gain political power locally, in the state, the nation, and the world.

I realized that people also wanted their minister to entertain them and tell them what they wanted to hear. That people wanted a literal to semi-literal biblical interpretation and none of that fancy seminary godless interpretation. Don't mention several ways to understand the Bible as literature.

The TV, radio, papers, magazines, and culture were overwhelmingly Fundamentalist. They wanted to dominate the county, state, US, and the world. The liberal clergy and congregations were like church mice quietly going about doing their thing and helping people in the here and now.

I mentioned my feelings and observations to professors and the seminary president many times. Saying, they needed to take on the growing juggernaut of Fundamentalism. Otherwise, the churches, synods, and seminaries would drastically decline. Their reaction was to yawn, or giggle, dismissively shrug me off, and check their watches. Decades later many main-line Christian churches and seminaries declined by fifty percent while the fundamentalists gained national power.

So, I checked out alternative ministerial possibilities: Becoming a UCC (United Church of Christ) minister since a professor said they believed anything. Similarly, I checked out UU (Unitarian Universalists), the Methodists, Mormons, Mennonite, Baha'is, and several other denominations. But each had dogmatic issues on which there seemed to be little basis.

I even checked out getting a degree in counseling or clinical psychology. But then it was obvious that people went to counseling to get over some trouble and go back to the same behavior patterns that got them into their troubles in the first place. They really didn't want to change. They just wanted their troubles to go away. However, interestingly, prisoners were a bit more honest. At least they eventually told me that a judge, prison officer, or parole officer forced them to go to counseling. For them the counseling was all a game to get out earlier. They asked, "What do you want to hear?"

I replied, "The truth."

The supervisor of internship and the elderly pastor said that I had completed enough of the internship to qualify for the M.Div. (Master of Divinity degree). I reluctantly said, "No." Deep inside me, I felt my heart crumbling, my body sinking, and tears almost came. On the one hand, I would have made an excellent pastor. Yet, I wasn't going to spend a life of lying to people, my family, nor myself.

So, to avoid the pressure of having to conform for all eternity to any denominational view, I dropped my quest to become a minister.

I felt that the entire world knew the truth and that I was incompetent and defective. Not a soul listened to nor was willing to engage in meaningful discussion nor work with me on my belief questions. Not a soul. The overwhelming impression from others was that there was something deeply wrong with me. Everyone else had God's grace and by some magic knew the answers. They were the Chosen Ones. But the silence of their disengagement, their shunning, and their condescending attitude that they knew the answers was disheartening to me.

I was again the seven-year-old leaving the unknown priest. Running down the hall, seeing doors, doors, and more doors. Out onto the dark street under the uncaring streetlight with the indifferent breeze gently flowing. There was no home to go to. No one understood. The few that took a casual interest in me were more concerned about converting me to their view. A Catholic priest felt it was a waste of time to minister to one not of his flock, unless conversion was possible. Fundamentalists saw an opportunity to convert a lost sheep to their view. Some people saw an opportunity to make some money by counseling me. It felt as though they were more concerned about proving that their world view was right than being concerned about me.

But the puzzle was, how do all these people really know that they are right? I don't know if I am right about anything. Even the result of an experiment doesn't match reality accurately. Even solid logic doesn't match reality accurately. My view was, "Show the evidence to change my mind to what the data – or at least what seems to be data – and the logic says. Then, I will accept that view until better data, experiment, or logic says something different. Then I will change my mind again. Again, and again, and again as more data, information, and logic indicates."

So, how do all these ministerial students, professors, ministers, counselors and normal people all know at the core of themselves that they are right? Right about whatever happens to be their beliefs. How do they do that?

The despair was overwhelming.

To stop the never-ending pain, suicide was extremely attractive. It was warm, inviting, and a solution to the pain. Just like the fellow seminarian who jumped down eight stories. Yet, the pain of suicide exceeded the pain and torment of being the only person in the world filled with religious doubts. Plus, I had a family to support. How to support the family and find answers to simple religious questions?

A force deep within me relentlessly pushed to find out why people and institutions believe what they believe.

Thus, I resolved to explore for the rest of my life why people believed religious and non-religious beliefs. Therefore, I continued working on a MATh degree at the seminary instead of the M.Div.,[12] degree, while simultaneously working on an MS in engineering and an MBA at a local university. I graduated with the three degrees within six months of each other.[13]

Quietly, quieter than a church mouse, I resolved to pursue why people believe religious and secular beliefs while raising a family and pursuing a livelihood in engineering and business.

Eleven Suicides

Perhaps because of my personal experience with suicide, I was sensitive and accepting of suicidal people. I didn't react with horror, disapproval or a need to save them for the afterlife.

From time to time, people would quietly talk in private. Occasionally, some would slowly reveal a deep abiding hopelessness. A hopelessness that was in the depths of their being. Their minds, emotions, and their very essence

---

12   MATh (Master of Arts in Theology) and MDiv (Master of Divinity), MS (Master of Science) engineering, MBA (Master of Business Administration)

13   In case you are wondering how I financially did all that, I used the GI Bill and a half of a full-time job. Between the job, class and studies that was 60-100 hours per week. That is another story of supportive wife.

were in solitary deep black sinkholes. Their friends, relatives, and co-workers were unmerciful and thoughtless to them. Day after day, week after week, month after month, for years, and some for decades, their significant others emotionally beat on them. When they tried climbing out of their sink holes, their friends, relatives, and co-workers shoved them back down into the hole. The significant others placed signs at the top of the sink hole facing down to them. It was visible only to those in the hole. It said, "Do not come out. Do not disturb us." There was no way out. They were fully and completely alone.

These people I understood to their core. Suicide was my friend since being seven years old. It was a companion that was reliable and always available. It was someone that could supply relief. It was a touch point that pointed out there was a problem. I could ignore the problem or figure out a way to handle it and resolve it. It was one of my "idiot lights of life." When the light came on, that showed it was time to handle something. So, as the feeling of despair would come over me like a lead apron that dentists use on patients when doing x-rays, I spent time feeling, intuiting, and thinking through whatever issue was at hand. It was at least a weekly occurrence since the unknown priest chased me down the hall when I was seven years old.

So, people felt comfortable with me to chat. I was open to them and enjoyed just being with people and listening to them. Everyone had their stories. Those that had sad stories, I understood. The others with happy stories were just fun people to be around; but, at their core they were an enigma to me.

In retrospect, I realized that I knew eleven people that killed themselves. But at that time, my skills of professionally understanding suicidal people were non-existent. Of those eleven I knew; I had listened to nine people who killed themselves. They died by various means. Five shot themselves. Four of those died quickly and one floundered around with part of his face blown off and then died; one of them died as suicide by cop. Two hung themselves. Two drank themselves to death. One jumped. He lived for several hours in torment. One jumped in front of car.

Their communities uniformly reacted with shock:

How could they have done that?

We loved them so much!

They were so selfish to kill themselves.

They were so weak.

If only they had said something to us. We would have helped.

Jesus could have saved them.

Our prayers go out to them.

Yet, it just seemed that before they died, no one, not one soul cared for them. People just wanted those nine to not bother them. They seemed to say to them, "Be good. Be nice. Do your job. Get out of the way. Don't talk. Don't bother us."

The communities buried the nine alive. The communities didn't care. They did not have the time, nor the skills, nor the money, nor the interest to effectively do something. Everyone had their busy lives and interests and recreation and television. They could have listened but chose not to.

In retrospect, I too lacked the skills to hear and do something. But I didn't realize what they were saying. These were people that just quietly leaked their souls to me. Just like pipes quietly leaking water and then the pipe bursts. Is that why most people say that suicide is an impulse? Those nine people pondered suicide for years. It was not an impulse.

In their own very private ways, they were exhausted. With suicide, they solved their problem and gave themselves rest that passes all understanding. A rest that not one human would or could give them. Their life situation and despair were so deep that there was no way out. If the nine would have begun to change, then their relatives, friends, and co-workers would have to change. That would have been uncomfortable. Instead, they pushed the nine back into a bottomless lonely personal sinkhole of despair.

Most of them were hurting for decades. They were damaged goods. They were the silent walking wounded. Their lives were on frozen ground, slowly morphing into a sinkhole. There was no way out. They lacked the skills and strength to make the changes to have fulfilling lives. Perhaps they went to churches hoping for a miracle. None occurred.

Society did not provide them with the skills. It was too expensive. The idea was that the rugged self-made individual would toughen them up. The signs on the churches saying that trials and tribulations are God's ways of toughening people. The nine did not know how to reach out. Yet, it just seemed that the nine were in an impossible situation for which there was no way out. So, suicide was a healthy choice.

Yet, the church condemned suicide and was more welded to their doctrines than answers to troubling questions: Would a loving God condemn the nine to hell? Would a loving God want them to live lives of quiet desperation in an abyss of lonely hopelessness? That in the next life God would make them whole, but not in this life. If they had believed certain doctrines of a faith, would they still be alive? But believe which doctrines of which faith? "God so loved the world that he gave His only begotten son so that people would have eternal life." God seemed more interested in their sins in this life so they could have a happy afterlife. Why didn't God help them in this life? Why leave them suffering for decades? Why leave them in an abyss that also does not help their family, friends, and co-workers have fulfilling lives?

That all made no sense. Is God more interested in faith to doctrines than in helping people in the here and now to have fulfilling lives? I don't know. Ministers and religious people get angry with such discussion. So, it is easy to quietly retreat and not upset their happy, calm, and idyllic world.

The Book Donation

Perhaps it is easy to understand their happy, calm, idyllic world with what happened to my library book donation thirty-six years after graduating from seminary. My book donation to a local library clearly showed why people had little interest in understanding their religious and scientific world views.

Where I used to live, my home had a stately library. It had four windows letting in pleasant sunlight. The shelves went from floor to a ten-foot ceiling. For more than forty years, thousands of books went into the library and reluctantly pushed out some less valued ones. They were part of my treasure and where a segment of my heart and mind lived.

Just walking through the 2,000-book library, I could carry on a 'Great Conversation' with authors dead and alive. At times it felt like the Harry Potter scenes of talking pictures hanging on walls. There were times I had conversations with Thomas Paine, Benjamin Franklin, Carl von Clausewitz, Will Durant, Adam Smith, Karl Marx, St Augustine, Peter Drucker, Bart Ehrman and hundreds of others. I treasured their thoughts, their advice, their efforts to write clearly, and thus I valued the books.

But I was moving to a place that had no bookshelves and was 40% the size of our home of thirty-three years. The cost of moving the books at $.60 a pound and building shelves was at least $2,000.

It was obvious that the best place to donate most of the books was to fellow book lovers at the local library. I imagined them enjoying and thinking because of my precious donation. The books could continue living.

After deciding which five hundred treasures to keep, I began taking books to the library: 500 in one load. 500 the next day. Then the next day, I came with 500 more.

The guy who received the books said, "Hey, those books that you have been bringing, we didn't want them. So, I threw them into the dumpster over there." He pointed across the wet parking lot. The lids were left open letting in the drizzling rain.

"People only buy fiction, easy religious books, and cookbooks. Nobody wants business, science, math, history, military strategy, nor theology. If those books in the van are like the ones you brought before, then you can throw them into the dumpster yourself." He was upset. It had rained for two days and he had gotten wet.

He discarded my friends and my helpmates into a dumpster just like dead bodies discarded along roadsides and trails in Vietnam. He trashed all the thought the authors put into their writings. My friends were gone. They were dead and buried. Their treasures would not go to some other unknown inquisitive minds.

I became disheartened; instead of helping others, those books helped no one. I thought about dumpster diving to resurrect the treasures and pass them on to some other appreciative souls. But that meant drying out a thousand books that would then look like wrinkled toilet paper. Sadness descended like a dentist's lead vest that protects patients from X-rays.

No one cared about thoughtful well-crafted books. All they wanted were novels and cookbooks. Their lack of interest in thoughtful well-crafted religious and science books showed they had little interest in understanding their religious and scientific world view.

Discarding those treasurers that had so much work, thought, and feeling made me feel that few if anyone would be interested in my decades of pondering and thinking about why people believe what they believe. They just want to go on with their lives and enjoy themselves. Nothing wrong with that. They were like the little old lady who didn't want to think about her world view. She epitomized what my library book donation was about. My mania to understand religion was like Captain Ahab's mania to capture Moby Dick. Something only a few souls cared about.

Captain Ahab and Moby Dick

For forty years after seminary, while working for a living, I explored various Christian sects, Judaism, Islam, Buddhism, and Hinduism. Each faith had statements that were beautiful and wonderful for humanity. But other statements that made no sense. Answers by lay people and clergy were frustrating and elusive. They gave the standard safe answers that wouldn't get them in trouble with their hierarchy or congregation. They were not interested in understanding the issues with their views. At times their elusive answers buried their quiet anger. Sometimes laypeople and clergy would become like angry lions. That their views were right, and all others were wrong; or at best tolerated; or everyone is right. Those views were like barnacles steadfastly cemented to ships and rocks. They were impervious to change.

Figure 6.2 Similar to Captain Ahab pursuit of Moby Dick the whale, I pursued faith issues for the rest of my life.

So, I demurred, and like a gentle wind, moved away from the lions, hesitating to pursue them with troubling questions.

Yet, I wondered, "Am I alone? Are there others who question the basics of their religion such as Christianity, Judaism, Islam, Buddhism, and Hinduism? In these religions, were there laypeople, seminarians, students for the various ministries, and clergy that had questions and doubts about their faith? Do they have doubts today? Did they have doubts hundreds of years ago? Perhaps even thousands of years ago? Perhaps, just perhaps, I am not alone and was not alone in my questioning and doubts?

Yet, the questions pestered me so much, that I felt like Captain Ahab's passion in the book Moby Dick.[14] The Captain's insane drive was to get the whale, Moby Dick shown below. It drove his life. These faith questions drove my life while I earned a secular living and raised a family.

At times I felt like the traveler to the left in Camille Flammarion's engraving.[15] There an explorer like me is poking his head through the edge of the universe discovering another world. Like Captain Ahab, it was impossible to let go of the faith issues and do something else. So, I explored fourteen characteristics of Christianity, Judaism, Islam, Buddhism, and Hinduism.

Figure 6.3 Similar to the traveler above, I was about to poke into new realities.

14 (Taber 1902)

15 (Raven 2015) The engraving depicts a man peering through the Earth's atmosphere looking at the inner workings of the universe. It is a modification of Camille Flammarion's engraving by an unknown artist. It is referred to as the Flammarion engraving because its first documented appearance is in page 163 of Camille Flammarion's L'atmosphère: météorologie populaire (Paris, 1888), a work on meteorology for a general audience.

Part II – 14 Themes of 5 Religions

I reasoned that if billions of people for more than four thousand years had their religious beliefs, they must have truth. So, I explored the five major religion: Christianity, Judaism, Islam, Buddhism, and Hinduism, while raising a family, working a secular job, and being in the Army Reserves.

So, I read their scriptures, listened to their clergy and their devotees. Granted, most of the effort was on Christianity. Nevertheless, it became clear that the scriptures had a place for authority. That rituals were sources of comfort. That various scholars and clergy gave their reasons for the various beliefs. That their traditions carried immense respect and following.

People turned in innocence and trust to one of the religions and their clergy. In the depths of their despair, worries, insecurities, hopes, fears, and joys they sought solace, comfort, and meaning. The various religions supplied intellectual and emotional answers.

Most people accepted the answers without understanding. They were unwilling to pursue the basis for the answers because it would take too much time and effort, and they had lives to live, families to raise, jobs to do, and have some fun.

But there were doubters. They too didn't understand. But they were quiet. At first it seemed that they were respectful of others and didn't want to rock the boat. But they lacked the confidence to explore the various issues with their religion. They also lacked the tools to analyze the issues with the religion. They had doubts and questions, but they just quietly buried the discomfort. They didn't want others to shun them, to look foolish, or they were tired of doubting and questioning. Just like the old lady previously mentioned while I was in seminary.

Part II has religious concerns of laypeople and their clergies' responses. Here are clergy and lay-peoples' stories. The format is on the next page:

14 Themes of 5 Religions

Pain, Suffering, and Evil	Sex
Sin	God's Character
Forgiveness	Experiencing God
Faith	Afterlife
Hope	Scriptures
Joy	Authority
Love	Meaning of life

What follows, is a summary of each theme in each of the five religions, followed by a discussion of issues with each theme. Thus, the pattern is:

One theme – One Chapter
Christianity
Judaism
Islam
Buddhism
Hinduism
Discussion

One theme – One Chapter
Christianity
Judaism
Islam
Buddhism
Hinduism
Discussion

ETC.

Chapter 7

Pain, Suffering, and Evil

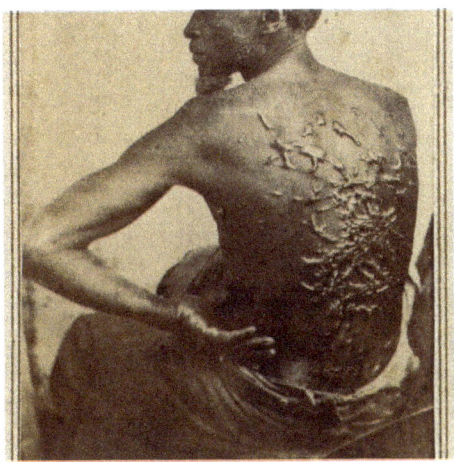

Figure 7.1 Individual pain, suffering and evil.

Figure 7.2 Corporate pain, suffering, and evil

Religions struggle with "Why does a loving, good, and just God, G-d, Allah, Buddha, or a Hindu God permit pain, suffering, and evil? If an all loving power genuinely loves people, then why does it allow so many people to suffer hour after hour, day after day, week after week, month after month, year after year, decade after decade?"

Christianity and Pain, Suffering & Evil

Christianity defines God as good and as the creator of good. Good did not create evil. Conservatives say that the devil and fallen man created evil and suffering. That humans by their very nature are now evil. That when Jesus returns all will be well for those who believe. But right now, Satan leads a war against humanity and particularly conservative Christians. So, it is the Christian duty to be a loyal soldier and fight against evil in all its' forms.

On the other hand, liberals say that individuals and groups must pray and work together to reduce pain, suffering, and evil. Most liberals do not believe in original sin from Adam and Eve and that Satan is not waging a war.

However, both conservatives and liberal Christians believe that God created free will so that people could choose between good and evil. Though often not said, there is the implication that the cumulative effect of individual and group choices between good and evil is at the heart of all suffering. The choices could come from lifestyle, ignorance, foolishness, passion, ideology, demagogues, etc. The result is pain, suffering, or evil.

Yet, Pope John Paul said for people to experience "the joy of suffering and becoming more like the Savior that suffered for our sins:"

A source of joy is found in the overcoming of the sense of the uselessness of suffering, a feeling that is sometimes very strongly rooted in human suffering. This feeling not only consumes the person interiorly but seems to make him a burden to others. The person feels condemned to receive help and assistance from others and at the same time seems useless to himself. The discovery of the salvific meaning of suffering in union with Christ transforms this depressing feeling. Faith in sharing in the suffering of Christ brings with it the interior certainty that the suffering person "completes what is lacking in Christ's afflictions"; the certainty that in the spiritual dimension of the work of redemption he is serving, like Christ, the salvation of his brothers and sisters. Therefore, he is carrying out an irreplaceable service. [16]

Thus, the reason there is suffering is "...participation in the mystery of the cross of Christ." [17]

One common theme which many Christians will say is, "God doesn't give us more than we can handle." Some say that is a misunderstanding of 1 Corinthians 10:13. That "...God will not place us in a situation where a

---

16 Christopher Kaczor, Catholic Answers Magazine, Volume 18 Number 1, http://www.catholic.com/magazine/articles/a-pope%E2%80%99s-answer-to-the-problem-of-pain

17 (Longenecker 2017)

temptation to do wrong is irresistible but will always give us a "way of escape." Essentially, it's a verse that puts the responsibility for our own sinful choices on ourselves…." [18] That is, pain, suffering, and evil are not God's doing; rather, they are mankind's fallen nature and free will.

Judaism and Pain, Suffering & Evil

Judaism does not believe that there is Original Sin where humans are born evil. Instead there are two drives. One to do good and one to do evil. The goal of Judaism is to control the impulses to do good. Sin is missing the mark from doing good. Thus, correct the error and work to make the world a better place.[19]

Life has a purpose and all that G-d does is good. Thus, even pain, suffering, and evil are good. That doesn't mean that one just accepts that. Instead work to make the world a better place. Thus, put one's faith in G-d and realize that G-d sees all, and all will work out for the best.[20]

Judaism has struggled with persecutions since the Dark Ages in Europe and Russia. Leaders struggled with the meaning of the Holocaust. "How could an omnipotent, benevolent G-d allow such calamities? Where was G-d in Auschwitz?"[21] The responses are varied:

> The whole of history unfolds under G-d's guidance. Meaning that the Nazis were his instruments. Jews abandoned the Torah, assimilated with non-Jews and Zionism (viewed by some as a lack of trust in religion and in G-d). The more the increase in evil, the sterner the

---

18 (Corey 2017)

19 Extracted from an excellent article, "Good, Evil and Freewill in Judaism." (Rabbi 2006)

20 From "Faith Lectures: Judaism, Justice and Tragedy – Confronting the problem of evil." (Sacks, Faith Lectures: Judaism, Justice and Tragedy – Confronting the problem of evil 2000)

21 (Watson 2014) Page 372

chastisement and then the closer to redemption. Thus, Nazis were instruments of the divine plan of salvation.

Suffering purifies and deepens the personality.

G-d was absent during genocides.

G-d was absent from the death camps because G-d was dead.

G-d had to be redefined – he was no longer omnipotent nor benevolent, or even a "he."

Focusing on Jewish suffering distanced Jews from the suffering of others and gradually shut Jews inside their own pain. [22]

Islam and Pain, Suffering & Evil

Islamic responses to why people suffer are:

To test humans. Those who pass the test will be in paradise. Those who fail the test will experience the consequences.

Allah has made laws. Suffering occurs when people break these laws. However, Allah does not let people suffer from every negligence.

Allah allows some people to suffer to test other people's charity and faith.

Believers face suffering with prayers, repentance and charitable deeds. The non-believers face suffering with doubts and confusions. They blame Allah or make arguments against Him.[23]

Buddhism and Pain, Suffering & Evil

Buddhism tends to view pain as the result of desire. Skip the desire and then one escapes pain. If one has inescapable physical or mental pain, then

---

[22] (Watson 2014) See pages 372-380 for details as to determine which rabbis and sects made which statements.

[23] (Siddiqi n.d.)

change the response to the pain. For example, there was a tragic accident in a swimming pool. The pain drove questions about the "truth of the human condition." [24] Eventually the person found peace and understanding:

Did I want to live, and take responsibility for my life, or did I want to give up and die? I felt that if I had chosen death, I really could have died.

I decided to live, and my life has felt qualitatively different ever since….

…In that second there was a knowledge that my reactions and fears caused much of my pain and distress. That I could be utterly free. I saw that "the present moment is always bearable."

…ever since (I) transform my moment-by-moment reactions (to) cultivate a positive mental state, even when my body is causing me trouble.

…personal suffering (creates) empathy with others who are suffering. I feel in touch with all beings that suffer, and I care deeply about them. We no longer feel so separate. [25]

Hinduism and Pain, Suffering & Evil

Karma is the natural forces of good and bad and is the sum of past actions that dictates reincarnation or eternal bliss. There are five principles:

Every motivated action attracts Karma. If there is no motivation, there is no Karma.

Every motivated action has a good or bad consequence.

Consequences arise in this life, the next life, or at some time in the future.

Karmic effects are cumulative.

---

[24] First published in 'Dharma Life', Winter 2000 (Vidyamala 2007) For the full response see https://www.wildmind.org/applied/pain/being-here

[25] First published in 'Dharma Life', Winter 2000 (Vidyamala 2007) For the full response see https://www.wildmind.org/applied/pain/being-here

Humans experience rebirth, also known as reincarnation. [26]

Karma explains evil and suffering as the result of earlier life or lives. As one improves behavior then the next life will be better. So, pain, suffering, and evil in this life are not relevant. What is important is to learn the lessons so that the next life is better. When a person is mindful, pure, has learned the needed lessons, then that person is free of this world.

Discussion
Why is there pain, suffering, and evil?

The clergy of the five religions do not like the question. If God is love, why does God allow pain, brutality, unfulfillment, hell on earth, genocide, disease, starvation, wars, third degree burns, loneliness, meaninglessness, bereavement, cheating, stealing, evil, deeply rooted evil, the Seven Deadly Sins (pride, greed, lust, envy, gluttony, wrath, and sloth), ,etc., etc., etc.? Why?

Here is a poignant example. A healthy child is born. A few weeks later because of medical malpractice, the child becomes incapacitated. For the next forty years and more, the child is unable to communicate or feed itself, lives in a wheelchair, needs care twenty-four hours a day to get out of bed, to go to bed, to change soiled clothing, etc. Where is God's love? Where is God's love for the child? Where is God's love for parents who deeply love the child and personally spent forty year taking care of the child's needs? Their lives revolved around the child. Where is God's love?

Obviously, there are millions of more examples.

These pains, sufferings, and evils continue day after day, week after week, month after month, year after year, decade after decade, century after century, millennia after millennia. Not only that, if people don't believe the right doctrines and religion, various religions say the disbelievers, unregenerate minds, hard hearted people, etc. will experience torment for eternity in hell. What

---
26 "Evil and Theodicy in Hinduism" (Willett 2015)

kind of a loving God is this?

It seems that when events are pleasant, it is God's will. When God allows suffering then some people say, "God works in mysterious ways." Or, "It is God's plan." "All will be better in heaven." Or, they mention something like Pope John Paul saying, "It is the joy of suffering and becoming more like the Savior that suffered for our sins." [27]

How tortured was my unknown priest? The poor guy suffering with celibacy and loneliness. Was that God's plan for someone that had a calling to serve God and then be tortured with desires? This is God's plan? My unknown priest's lonely suffering might have helped him to know, like the Pope, "the joy of suffering and becoming more like the Savior that suffered for our sins." Or more likely, he was suffering from natural desires in an unhealthy institutional situation.

Or, someone says, "I am suffering from spousal abuse, rape, assault, genocide, diabetes, theft, burns, or something else. So, now I know the joy of suffering and am becoming more like the Savior that suffered for our sins." That theology and thinking seems cruel and sick.

Yet, many people experience a personal God that looks after trivial things like finding a parking space, winning a sports game, or passing a test. The result of work or coincidence, they attribute to God being active in their lives. It becomes proof of God's divine love and the correctness of their faith.

Still, people believe that God, G-d, Allah, Buddha, or a Hindu God demands humans love the deity. If people don't, the deity condemns the unloving to eternal torture in hell or reincarnation until they learn. Where is the deity's love in that? On the other hand, there are religions that believe that those that absolutely love will go to heaven or Nirvana; and, those that don't absolutely love will upon death just cease to exist.[28] Some religious sects now

---

27 See previous quote and details of it on page

28 Jehovah's Witnesses

change the concept of hell. There is no hell; rather, one goes through purification and then enters heaven. There is mysticism about the process and there is no proof for any of these concepts.

These issues and interpretations negate the meaning of a loving God. Jean Meslier, a priest in 1732 France, wrote that God created humans who were:

"…pure, innocent, and good; but his nature became corrupted in consequence of sin. If man could sin, when just leaving the hands of God, his nature was then not perfect! Why did God permit him to sin, and his nature to become corrupt? Why did God allow him to be seduced, knowing well that he would be too weak to resist the tempter? Why did God create a Satan, a malicious spirit, a tempter? Why did not God, who was so desirous of doing good to mankind, why did He not annihilate, once for all, so many evil genii whose nature rendered them enemies of our happiness? Or rather, why did God create evil spirits, whose victories and terrible actions influences the human race? He must have foreseen what would happen? Finally, in all the religions of the world, why has the evil principle such a marked advantage over good principle or over Divinity?" [29]

Couldn't God have designed a better world?

If leaders ran organizations with these characteristics, people would condemn the leaders, saying they were tyrannical, inhumane, and inept. Yet, that is exactly the kind of organization or world that the Christian, Jewish, Muslim, Buddhist, and Hindu clergy say their deity made.

Isn't God all powerful and all knowing? If so, why create humans with free will that can cause pain, suffering, and evil? Why not create humans with free will that does not include pain, suffering, and evil? So that the only choices are healthy choices. In heaven or Nirvana isn't there an absence of pain, suffering, and evil? Isn't there only joy and good? Why since creation would

---

29 (Meslier 2013) LXXIV.—Absurdity Of The Theological Fables Upon Original Sin And Upon Satan.

God punish tens of billions of people? For eternity? For millennia? Or for believing the 'wrong' doctrines according to some sects of the five religions? What kind of God is that? A loving God?

Christians typically say that Jesus died on the cross for the salvation of mankind. That Jesus, by his death, absolved mankind of sins and if people accept him as Lord and Savior, then they will have eternal bliss in heaven. However, since Jesus took part in the creation of the universe, why didn't he do a better job to create a heaven on earth that the action of two people couldn't corrupt for eternity? Or if one doesn't believe in the literal Genesis story of creation, create a world without sin? Either Jesus didn't want to, or Jesus made a design flaw. Or at least, when he was on earth 2,000 years ago, why didn't he recreate a heaven on earth instead of promising heaven after death?

Jesus knew while creating the universe that he would have to suffer to make things right – right not in this earthly life – but rather right in heaven if people confess their sins and believe in him as Lord and Savior. He knowingly wanted to cast billions of people into eternal hell. With a flick of an eyelash he could have eradicated Satan and made the world right. Instead, thousands of years after the creation, he died on the cross so that a few people could have a better next life. What kind of a guy is Jesus? Is he an incompetent designer that has not admitted to his design mistake? So, he decided that he must suffer to make up for his mistake?

Yet, many clergy continue to answer that God gives people freedom to choose. The consequence can be pain, suffering, and evil. Would a parent let their child suffer with pain? Not the trivial kind of pain where the child learns not to touch a hot stove, hit the finger with a hammer, fall and bruise a knee, etc. Instead who would let a child do something that causes a lifelong debilitating problem? Something like jumping off a cliff into water and breaking a neck, taking drugs and frying the brain, getting diseases, etc. Granted, the little painful events hopefully result in learning. Why wouldn't God do likewise? Why create a world with pain, suffering, and evil?

Free Will Causes Pain, Suffering, and Evil?

The standard clergy response of the five religions as to why there is pain, suffering, and evil in the world is because people have free will and do what displeases God. If they did what God, G-d, Allah, Buddha, or the Hindu Gods want, then there would not be pain, suffering, and evil. But people by their nature are sinful and unclean so they exercise their free will causing pain, suffering, and evil. Do what God wants and then everything will be better now or in the next life.

So, people suffer because they have made poor choices. Thus, people fall and break bones because of improper action and thoughts. They don't have healthy lifestyles and get diseases. They go to war and cause destruction. If they believed in Jesus, G-d, Allah, Buddha, or a Hindu God and followed the teachings, then they might not experience pain, suffering, and evil. At least if not in this life, then in the next life. One might quibble on the preciseness of these points; yet, that is the essence of free will.

Some say God gives free will because He wants people of their own free will to love Him. He doesn't want to force people to love him. Those that love God will have eternal bliss and happiness in the next life. But....do not do what God wants, then God punishes people for 'wrongly' exercising their free will. Where is the free will in that? It is like telling a child, "Do what you want. But if you do, I will punish you for eternity."

But there is a way out. Christians, Muslims, and Jews confess sin and do penance, then God forgives those sins and one is again on the path to heaven. At least until the next set of sins occurs. In some religious sects there is such concern about absolving sins that for dying people a cleric does final absolution. Or, there is the concept of Karma. Do enough charitable deeds that outweigh the bad deeds, then one goes to a higher plain and eventually to Nirvana. Yet, there is no proof of any of this. It is a leap of faith. Might be true. Might not be true. Any proof?

If a person has no free will in heaven or karmic bliss is that a different person?

Free will is a fundamental part of the five religions. The five religions believe that without free will a person is just a zombie, an animal, or a robot. So, when a person of the five religions ascends to heaven or karmic bliss, does that person have free will? The clergy's response is, "Yes! The person is radically transformed to a purified soul who would not want to nor allow oneself to fall out of heaven or karmic bliss."

Would that radically transformed purified soul be recognizable? Most clergy would say, "Yes!"

If so, then why didn't God, G-d, Allah, Karmic force, or a Hindu God create purified souls that wouldn't fall out of heaven or karmic bliss? Why create pain, suffering, and evil for billions of people that will last for billions of years in hell or other plains of existence? Or perhaps as Buddhist clergy will say, "It is an illusion."

Seems like the deities want pure souls with free wills. Thus, the deities create people with free spirits and discard the impure ones just like gardeners and farmers get rid of weeds. The deities purposefully create eternal pain, suffering, and evil to get a few pure souls.

Then what about Satan and other angels that fell out of heaven? In Buddhism and Hinduism are there former evil deities in karmic bliss? Were they at one time pure? Would they be recognizable in their pure state?

Was it the snake or humans that first sinned?

What were Satan and the other fallen angels doing prior to the Fall? When were they created? Just after the creation of the universe? Apparently, they too had free will and fell from the eternal heaven. This implies that there were other creatures with free will existing prior to the creation of the universe. Didn't the all-knowing God know that they too would exercise free will and fall out of heaven? That the humans God created would also exercise free will and fall out of the Garden of Eden? That both those created before the creation of the universe and humans would cause sin? That really, it was the snake and not humans that caused sin to enter the world.

Seems like there is no guarantee of a permanent spot in heaven or karmic bliss.

Evil as Omission and Commission

In World War II, Adolf Eichmann went along with the system to murder twelve million people in German concentration Camps. In New York City, Kitty Genovese, on March 13, 1964 screamed for half an hour as an attacker murdered her. Thirty people who saw or heard her did nothing.[30]

These are examples of evil as an omission and commission:[31]

Evil as omission when societies do not supply health care, excellent education, standard of living, and takes advantage of people. Do not protect the elderly and enfeebled from those who steal their homes, savings and a decent life.

Evil as omission when children lack the basic education skills of reading, writing, arithmetic and thinking.

Evil as omission when ideologies and theocracies rule while people do nothing. That they don't even question the ideologues and theocrats.

Is it evil as omission when people do not engage in the politics of their society and let special interests and demagogues run the society?

Evil by omission when silent about systems that create poverty, ill health, economic depredation of one group by another group.

Evil by commission when they preach against science, LGBTQ, global

---

30 (The Learning Network 2012)

31 (Arendt, The Life of the Mind 1977) Page 4. The concept of evil as commission and omission is from Hannah Arendt and expanded here.

warming and preach that those who support those views are evil.

Evil by commission when preaching the prosperity gospel while ignoring poverty, pain, suffering, and evil.

Evil by omission when people living in totalitarian regimes now and throughout history do not fight against evil. The evil that tortures, destroys families, steals property and, sends people to jails, gulags, and isolation cells.

Evil by omission when the five religions do not effectively speak out against the drugs, violence, corruption and greed in Central America, South America, Africa, Asia, Europe and North America.

Evil by omission in WWI, when the British, French, German, American, Middle East Christians, Jews, Muslims, Buddhists and Hindus did not speak out against the war and the aftermath of hate and continued fighting after the Armistice. **Was that the real evil of WWI?** That created so many problems that still plague the world today?

Evil by omission in WWII Germany when the Catholic, Lutheran, and other clergy, and their flocks did not reflect upon nor act upon what was happening. Was that the real evil of WWII?

Evil by omission when the clergy of the five religions do not effectively engage in society but comfortably expound in their pulpits about a passage from one of their scriptures. Because they don't want to upset the congregation and thus lose membership and funding, or are they too intellectually, morally or physically lazy. That they just preach happiness and prosperity.

Evil by omission when the price the price of omission is less to pay than the price to counter evil.

Evil by omission when the almighty, all merciful God, G-d, Allah, Buddha or Karma stand by and watch the cosmic show while pain, suffering, and evil occur day after day, week after week, year after year, decade after decade, millennia after millennia. Where is the Almighty's love in letting pain, suffering, and evil happen?

Evil as omission when abortions happen, and groups turn away and do nothing; and, evil as omission, when abortions don't happen, and unwanted people are born into the world to be unloved, unwanted, and eventually fill up children's homes.

Isn't all the above the same evil of omission as Adolf Eichmann's just going along?

The clergy of the five religions answer that in the next life God or Karma will reward the followers. How do they know that? Even if that is true, doesn't that say that if God or the clergy will not intervene, then why should ordinary people get involved when there will be torture, loss of job, monetary loss, etc?

Evil caused by the absence of thought

"…absence of thought is not stupidity; it can be found in highly intelligent people, and a wicked heart is not its cause…wickedness may be caused by absence of thought" [32]

People do things that many consider stupid. "Why did so-and-so ever do such a thing? What was he thinking?" Quite common comments. They are not stupid. Rather they have not thought out what they were doing.

Yet, there are totalitarian regimes and theocracies of the five religions that focus on mind control. That is, making sure that the people think in a certain way. Those regimes and theocracies jail, ostracize, or shun those that do not think the right way. The result is group thinking where participants think only in a certain way. Innovative ideas are not allowed unless those ideas support the regime or the clergy.

Hannah Arendt said about Adolf Eichmann, "…the only notable characteristic one could detect in his past behavior as well as in his behavior during the trial and throughout the pre-trial police examination was…not stupidity

---

32   (Arendt, The Life of the Mind 1977) Pg 13

but thoughtlessness.... Eichmann differed from the rest of us only in that he clearly..."[33] did not think nor reflect upon his actions. Thus, some evil is the omission of thought, of reflection upon one's actions, of conversation with others about actions. Yet, Eichmann was part of a structure that had thought, reflection, and conversation with others about actions.

If thinking – that is full uncensored thinking with facts – is so important, then societies must demand the rigorous teaching of science and the scientific process in schools.[34] That thinking consists of logic, facts, refining the logic, and refining with more facts. That there is no final great understanding nor truth. Rather, that the search for what makes a happy, healthy, wealthy, and wise society is a never-ending work of logic, facts, and modification of ideas.

Does Pain, suffering, and evil Bring People Closer to God, G-d, Allah, Buddha, or a Hindu God?

Pope John Paul stated, "...suffering is carrying out an irreplaceable service... to provide others a chance to be charitable and for all to get closer to Christ." How does one prove it? The Catholic Church says God came to earth, soldiers beat him for a night, and then He suffered for six hours on the cross from 9 AM in the morning till 4 PM in the afternoon. Is that an answer? What happened to the other two men hanging on crosses with Jesus? How long did they hang there? Crucified criminals hung on crosses for days and weeks. Birds would eat their eyes and body while they still lived. It was excruciatingly painful. Why was Jesus' crucifixion more significant when there was less time, pain, and suffering than most if not all the other crucifixions?

If pain, suffering, and evil bring people closer to the divine, then why not let people experience pain, suffering, and evil? Why not rejoice when seeing people in pain, suffering, and committing evil? After all, they should be experiencing the divine, according to the Pope.

---

33 (Arendt, The Life of the Mind 1977) pg 4

34 (Arendt, The Life of the Mind 1977) Pg 13

God, G-d, Allah, or Hindu Gods are unwilling to end the misery except in the next life and then only for those that subscribe to the 'correct' doctrines. Some of the Christian and Muslim clergy think pain, suffering, and evil bring people closer to God or are tests. But since God knows all and knows what the results will be, why do the testing and cause such misery? What parents would allow their children to have major suffering and to be around evil? The Christian, Muslim, and Jewish God does.

At least Judaism wrestles with pain, suffering, and evil. The answers vary with extended conversations. There is an attempt by some clergy to say, 'Let's make the world a better place. At some point in the future, the Messiah will come.'

Muslim clergy say to accept pain and suffering as a test so that one can have eternity in bliss. Don't question. Don't doubt. That is for unbelievers. But why did Allah create pain and suffering so that Allah could choose who would go to paradise? Didn't Allah, the all-knowing, the all wise God, know who would pass the test? So, why create a test for which Allah already knew the answer? Why create undeserved suffering? Their basic answer is, "Just make a leap of faith. Believe the Qur'an and trust the almighty merciful Allah will take care of you and damn the infidelity of non-belief." That absolves Allah of any responsibility by making laws that Allah knows humans will fail to observe.

Buddhists' view pain as coming from desire. Drop the desire and then pain, suffering, and evil are meaningless. Thus, Buddhists seem to be in this world and not of it. The non-attachment is a useful tool to see and understand what is truly happening and to understand the world. There is a valid point that attachment to things, events, people, and ideas causes pain, suffering, and evil when those things are lost, stolen, destroyed, or get hurt. On the other hand, a life of non-attachment seems empty. It is a life waiting for bliss in the next life. Thus, non-attachment becomes attachment to the next life. It is an escape from this life to the next life.

Hinduism states that for every motivated action there is a Karmic result. That good motivated actions cancel out bad motivated actions. Yet, there is no proof of this for the afterlife. None. The idea that one's life of joy, sadness, pain, or evil is based on some past life has no proof. Rather, it is a way of population control so that everyone is striving to be good and better so that in the next life one has it better. This is a vicious assault on humanity and forces people to accept abject poverty, suffering, and a caste system.

Does God love only humans?

DNA is fundamental to the structure of all living creatures. Why do many people think that humans are so special that the creator of the infinite universe is extremely concerned only about humans? Isn't the creator also concerned about animals, plants, and bacteria?

For millennia, humans thought the earth was the center of the universe. Then they thought that the sun was the center of the universe. Then they thought that the Milky Way, the galaxy where we live, was the center of the universe. In 1924, Edwin Hubble proved that the Milky Way is one of billions and billions of galaxies. That the universe will eventually die and fade away. Others now theorize that perhaps there are other parallel universes that come into, and then go out, of existence. The point is, humans are not special creatures. Humans are just one of many life forms. Life forms that are changing and, like all species, evolving and eventually disappear.

So, does God love animals, plants, and bacteria? Animals suffer when one animal kills another, starves, has disease, are in zoo cages, or imprisoned for factory food. Yet, God does nothing for those creatures. Is there a heaven for those creatures? Will pets be in heaven? No one knows. Most people will think this is silly. Why?

Is God's love present in daily activities?

Many people believe God's love is present in daily activities of humans. They see it when they suddenly avoid an accident, meet someone special, get a good grade on an exam, find a parking spot, etc. Does God, G-d, Allah, Buddha, and Hindu Gods love animals, plants, and bacteria? How does one prove those instances? Is it wishful or magical thinking? Can one run a test of God's love? Does even trying to or thinking of running a test of God's love mean that the person is automatically unfaithful, untrusting, and shouldn't enter a relationship with God? Instead one should just love and trust God?

Why Did Jesus Only Heal Those Near Him?

Two thousand years ago, Jesus walked among and healed many people. Yet, he healed individuals. He didn't heal masses and masses of people. He had the power to feed five thousand people. That seemed important. Why didn't he heal and feed all the people around the earth? Why not heal the entire world and never again have suffering? Why was he just wandering around a few villages, teaching and healing?

Many Christians say, "Jesus is around today! He healed my broken arm. The bone was protruding out. I prayed about it. Then He healed my arm. There was no need to go to a doctor. See, that is proof that Jesus heals today!" If Jesus is healing people, then why aren't Christians in hospitals and hospital chaplains healing millions of people and emptying out the hospitals? Why do the clergy permit lingering diseases?

Or, why doesn't the visible spirit of Jesus waft through hospitals, healing? The response is that Jesus heals those that want healing. So, if the apparition of Jesus floats into a hospital room, a person sees Jesus, then the person can ask, "Lord, please heal me." That happened several times in the New Testament. Why not now? Why today is Jesus absent so much in pain, suffering, and evil? Apparently, people in hospitals don't trust the healing power of Jesus.

Some will say, that he wanted people to believe in Him, and healing people would not have helped that cause. Most are just silent.

Why did God Utterly Destroy?

In the Christian and Jewish scriptures, God commands killing, annihilating, slaughter, ethnic cleansing, and killing one's own children. For example, God commanded to "utterly destroy all that they have and spare them not; but slay both man and woman, infant and suckling, ox and sheep, camel, and ass."[35] Or in the Great Flood, wipe out every land creature on earth. There is little questioning why the loving God or G-d would allow such devastation to themselves and others. Except that he was angry. Is that an example for humans to follow?

Muslims say that Allah will destroy the enemy and those that do not worship him.

Buddhist ignore it all. Though some protest war.

Hindus have a god called Shiva that is the destroyer. It is one of Hinduism's three main gods. The other two are Brahma, the creator, and Vishnu, the preserver. Why do Brahma and Vishnu permit Shiva, the destroyer, to create misery?

Clergy answers are an attempt to defend God

Christian, Muslim, and Jewish clergy want an all knowing, loving God. They refuse to speak about suffering and evil except to help people get by, die, and then go to heaven or hell. Clergy refuse to see that God, G-d, and Allah created pain, suffering, and evil. Instead, their explanation is that their deity did not; rather, humans created pain, suffering, and evil by exercising free will.

Yet, the clergy refuse to understand that their God could have created humans with free will with only healthy choices. An almighty creator could create a world where there is free will and there was no pain, suffering and evil. After all, isn't that what God created with heaven? Instead they refuse

---

35   Samuel 15:3

to criticize their deity.

Which Faith to Believe?

So, which of the five religions to believe? Which sect of the five or fifty thousand sects of the five religions to believe? If one chooses wrong or was born to the wrong sect, then that person goes to hell? Are all the other four religions and thousands of sects condemned to hell? But there are some denominations and sects that are more tolerant and say that there are many different beliefs and God is loving. But that gives the impression that the differences don't matter, and God loves everyone. If God loves everyone, then it doesn't matter which sect one belongs to. If so, the different interpretations of various doctrines about the real body and blood of Jesus Christ, the divinity of Jesus, the resurrection of the body, the life everlasting, judging the living and the dead are irrelevant. However, these are issues that have divided Christians for millennia, and divide it from the other religions.

These never-ending differences feel more like a casino. One's eternal life is more dependent upon where one happens to be born, what family one is born into, what culture one is born into, rather than what faith one has. The casino analogy also fits to those that shop for a church or a religion. With some 4,300 different Christian denominations and sects in the world[36], it is pure luck to find the one true Christian denomination or sect, let alone the one true religion.

The variations do not make a coherent view of God or a "Loving God." So, how does one determine which religion, denomination, sect, and belief matches reality? How does one figure it out? Run a test? Run a test of, "God's love?" What would constitute a test of God's love? Pray and then God

---

36   The precise number of religions in the world is not known, but available estimates show the number to be about 4,300, according to Adherents.com. Only two religions can claim more than one billion adherents each. Christianity has approximately 2 billion and Islam 1.3 to 1.5 billion believers. https://www.reference.com/world-view/total-number-religions-world-ff89ae17c6068514

whispers the answer? If so, there are a lot of different answers; which means going to any denomination and sect is neither right nor wrong. Just choose one that fits the needs or desires. Perhaps choose the church with a nice basketball court, choir, band, and other programs that feel good.

It would be nice that "God is Love." However, a God or Karma that allows suffering doesn't seem like love. The "God is Love" people respond with, 'If everyone followed my version of God, then the world would be better, and God's love would be shown to the world."

How does one choose a faith? Just make a leap of faith to a religion??

There is no proof for any of this.

Conclusions

Religion fails to answer a fundamental issue of life: Why pain, suffering, and evil?

Neither clergy of the five religions, nor their scriptures, traditions, reasoning, and institutions supply a satisfactory answer while preaching a loving creator and blissful eternity for the true believers. Especially when there is no proof of a loving creator and blissful eternity. One insightful commentator was brave enough to say, "That human nature is evil is said to be the only empirically verifiable claim of Christianity." [37]

Based upon my understanding of world history and science, a force of some kind created the world. It is up to individuals, groups, societies, and nations to make the best of it. Or they let those that create evil by either commission or omission rule the world.

---

37 (Funk 2007) Perspectives on Science and Christian Faith, pg 207 Ken Funk also references," Genesis 3, 6:5, 8:21; 2 Chronicles 6:36; Psalms 51:5, 143:2; Ecclesiastes 7:20, 9:3; Isaiah 53:6; Jeremiah 17:9; Matthew 12:34; John 3:19; Romans 3:23, 5:12; Galatians 5:17; Ephesians 2:3."

Pain, suffering, and evil are THE Idiot Lights of Life

In a car there are warning lights. Some of the lights are either on or off. When they are on, that means that there is a problem that needs quick attention. When the oil light comes on, pull over and stop. Don't drive. Don't keep going. Stop. Now! If one doesn't stop, then the engine burns up and fails. Any idiot knows that when the oil light comes on, stop driving. Stop what you are doing. Get oil into the engine. Fix the problem. That is why the name of that type of light is an, "Idiot light."

So, expand that concept to pain, suffering, and evil. Thus, pain, suffering, and evil are, "The idiot lights of life."

When one feels pain, that is a warning. Stop. Figure out what is happening. Decide what to do to get rid of the pain, suffering or evil.

There are little pains that seem trivial. A hammer hits a finger. An instantaneous signal goes to the brain saying, "Hey you up there. Stop." If one didn't feel that pain, one would keep hammering away and eventually lose a finger. So, as annoying as that pain is, it goes away quickly. If one doesn't pay attention and keeps on hammering on the finger, the finger will be permanently damaged.

Groups can experience pain. For example, people don't get along with each other. The finances are not strong enough to support the group. The group senses that something is wrong. Sometimes the sense is subtle. Not all members feel it. Some do and some don't. That sense is an indicator to act. The problem for many is that they might not know what action to take, or they don't want to rock the boat. They also might not have the skills, the energy, or the connection to improve the organization.

States and societies can experience pain. The most obvious is war. If people did not experience pain in war, they might like it too much and destroy themselves and their nation. It is the sense of pain that keeps many groups from war. It is also the sense of pain that causes people to give up and not fight.

Sadly, few clergy of the five faiths speak out about war. Some sects and clergy are viscerally against war in any form. Others use the "'Just War' Theory" to justify some military actions. Most just seem to go along with what their country desires.

Perhaps the clergy of the five faiths can campaign for dialogue among and between the different faiths to avoid war. That dialogue might look like the warlord in the drawing. Instead of using weapons that kill, maim, and destroy, they would carry pencils and dialogue. They would advocate turning weapons into plowshares, pencils, and dialogue. One such group, is ArtLords:[38]

Figure 7.3 Warlords, instead of weapons
use pencils and dialogue."

ArtLords

are Afghan artists and volunteers

using art and culture

for social transformation and behavioral change.

Yet, a strong military is needed to hold back and defeat powers that seek to

---

38 (ArtLords n.d.) https://www.artlords.com https://www.facebook.com/ArtlordsofAfghanistan/

undermine nations seeking to create happy, healthy, wealthy and wise societies.

On the other hand, the less obvious and much more pervasive forces causing pain, suffering, and evil are corruption, lying, and stealing. It is a quiet pain that hurts individuals, families, groups, states, and societies. People are aware yet they become desensitized. The "Idiot Light of Life" doesn't shine too brightly for them.

Some pain, suffering, and evil are just the result of ignorance of how to cope with destructive natural events such as disease, tsunamis, pestilence, meteors, earthquakes, etc.

Thus, pain is a gift that prevents individuals, families, groups, cities, states, and societies from destroying themselves. Pain alerts the various levels of problems that they can choose to address. If they don't address it, then many as individuals and groups will suffer and some will die. If they are not aware, then unhealthy living conditions will be coming.

Thus pain, suffering, and evil are the idiot lights of life

When a person, family, group, society, or a nation experiences pain, suffering or evil, then change something. Choose to change, adapt, fight, or ignore. There is no need to bring God or theology into pain, suffering, and evil.

However, related to pain, suffering, and evil, is sin and Karma.

Chapter 8

Sin and Karma

Figure 8.1 The five religions have strong beliefs on individual sin or karma and some beliefs on societal sin. Healthy people and corporations create a better world.

Three of the five major religions define sin as an action against God's will. Judaism expanded the idea from an individual committing sin to the nation of Israel committing sin. Some sects of Christianity expanded that concept to include all nations. Buddhism and Hinduism focus on the cumulative effects of Karma.

So, let's look at the various views of sin and Karma.

Christianity and Sin

Typically, when Christians think of sin, they think of the first Chapter in Genesis that tells the story of the Adam and Eve as the first humans who live in the Garden of Eden. God tells them that they can eat of anything in the Garden; but they must not eat from the tree of Knowledge of Good and Evil.

There are multiple interpretations to the story. Some sects believe there was an actual Adam and Eve who ate real fruit of an actual tree. Because of their actions, sin entered the world, dooming mankind to damnation. Thus, since that moment 6,000 years ago, God condemns all mankind that are non-believers in Jesus to hell. That means that God has, is, and will condemn billions and billions of people to hell for not believing in Jesus. However, some sects believe that God does not condemn humans who have not heard the Gospel of Christ to hell. Such believers refuse to learn anything that challenges the literal concept of the Bible, because that will cause loss of faith and a falling away from God, which is a grievous sin.

On the other hand, Liberal churches view the first chapter of Genesis as a story of faith in a God and not about sin entering the world. Instead it is a story of faith that God created the world which has problems for the faithful to address. It is not a literal story.

In conservative churches, there is ambivalence about interpreting the Old Testament views of sin. Clearly, they believe in obeying the Ten Commandments. Yet, depending on the denomination, they follow some but not all the other Old Testament commandments. The sects believe that they are 'rightly dividing the word of God.' For instance, they do not go along with stoning people for some listed sins, nor avoiding eating pork and various sea foods, nor cutting off body parts that cause people to sin. For instance, Jesus stated:

> [27] "You have heard that it was said, 'You shall not commit adultery.' [28] But I tell you that anyone who looks at a woman lustfully has already committed adultery with her in his heart. [29] If your right eye causes you to stumble, gouge it out and throw it away. It is better for you to lose one part of your body than for your whole body to be thrown into hell. [30] And if your right hand causes you to stumble, cut it off and throw it away. It is better for you to lose one part of your body than for your whole body to go into hell. (Matt 5:27-30)

A literal interpretation means that anyone (male or female) looking lustfully at someone has committed adultery. Therefore, gouge out the eye and throw it away. Similarly, if one commits adultery, cut off the hand and throw it away. Though not stated, for a male to look lustfully also means penile arousal. Therefore, if one is literal, then the male should cut off his penis and throw it away. Similarly, a female should cut off her organs that cause her to sin. Specifically, that would be the clitoris and other parts of her anatomy. Thus, for both the males and females, adultery would be committed by seeing, by sexual arousal, and then by the hands and actions. Therefore, both sexes should cut out their eyes, cut off their hands, and cut off their sexual organs. Yet, not one Christian sect advocates such action.

Liberal sects have metaphorical, metaphysical, allegorical or historical interpretations to the various Old and New Testament commands and injunctions. In the sexual instance above, Jesus said to cut off anything that entices sinful behavior because the end time was near. The time is short, and the end is near. Therefore, save oneself from missing out on being in heaven by dismembering yourself. Unfortunately, Jesus didn't return in the lifetimes of the early Christians who then adjusted their views. What those Christians felt about a delay in Jesus' return to be sometime in the future is not known. It must have bothered them. But not so much that they gave up their faith nor cut off offending parts of their body. Other liberals lean more towards a loving God and self-mutilation is not what God intended.

To explain sin, both the conservative and the liberal sects believe that God gave people free-will. Therefore, they exercise their free will. Some do good and some people do evil. That is their choice. If they followed God's will and commandments, then there would be less sin and evil in the world. But mankind is by nature evil and thus continues to sin. Thus, to paraphrase Martin Luther, 'Mankind is like a drunk riding a horse. Trying to stay on the horse (be sinless), yet, continually falls to one side or the other side of the horse (committing sins).'

Many conservative churches say that God punishes nations for national sins. So, if the US doesn't do God's will, then God will punish the US. The idea is rooted in the Book of Jerimiah. God punished Israel for transgressions. Some churches believe the hurricanes, tornadoes, and acts of God are punishments for not doing God's will. Similarly, they interpret world political events as indicators of God's favor or displeasure.

On the other hand, liberal churches do not see divine providence nor God's will acting in natural nor political events. Nevertheless, in the United States during the Vietnam War and Freedom Marches for racial equality, many liberal churches campaigned for their view of Biblical justice. In the later 1800's and early 1900's some liberal churches campaigned for the right of women to vote. There is some sense that a nation was at fault for not endorsing racial equality, equality for women, and acting on other social issues.

Conservative Christians believe that by teaching the true Christian faith in schools and applying it in business and politics God's grace will descend upon the United States. They believe the US is suffering because of failure to follow God's commands and return to its' Biblical foundations. Therefore, they are politically active and anxious for the Second Coming of Jesus.

The Catholic clergy at one time was concerned about sexual sins; but in the past decades, except for abortion and abstinence, they have been quieter and quieter. Liberals discuss those issues; but tend to gently guide their followers to a healthy lifestyle, if that is possible.

The New Testament and several fundamentalist sects believe that the unpardonable sins are disowning Jesus before men or denying the Holy Spirit:

> [30] "Whoever is not with me is against me, and whoever does not gather with me scatters. [31] And so I tell you, every kind of sin and slander can be forgiven, but blasphemy against the Spirit will not be forgiven. [32] Anyone who speaks a word against the Son of Man will be forgiven, but anyone who speaks against the Holy Spirit will not be forgiven, either in this age or in the age to come." (Matt 12:30-32 NIV)

> [28] "Truly I tell you, people can be forgiven all their sins and every slander they utter, [29] but whoever blasphemes against the Holy Spirit will never be forgiven; they are guilty of an eternal sin." (Mark 3:28-29 NIV)

> [8] "I tell you, whoever publicly acknowledges me before others, the Son of Man will also acknowledge before the angels of God. [9] But whoever disowns me before others will be disowned before the angels of God. [10] And everyone who speaks a word against the Son of Man will be forgiven, but anyone who blasphemes against the Holy Spirit will not be forgiven." (Luke 12:8-10 NIV)

Decades ago, this was the basis for blasphemy laws that considered heresy, profanity, and sacrilege illegal in secular courts. Thus, a secular court conviction of blasphemy could result in fines, jail, or death. Most of these laws have disappeared or magistrates do not enforce them.

The Catholic Church considers blasphemy against the Holy Spirit as:

1. Despair (believing that one's evil is beyond God's forgiveness);

2. Presumption (hope of salvation without keeping the Commandments, or expectation of pardon for sin without repentance)

3. Envying the goodness of another (sadness or repining at another's

growth in virtue and perfection);

4. Obstinacy in sin (willfully persisting in sin, after enough instructions and admonition);

5. Final impenitence (to die without either confession or contrition for our sins);

6. Disputing the known truth (to argue against known points of faith, and this includes misrepresenting parts or all the Christian faith). [39]

✝☪︎☾❋🕉

However, many Christians ask, "Why do terrible things happen to good people?" The response is, 'God created humans with free will.' So, humans can exercise freewill to do or not to do sin at the individual or the corporate level. God is not the cause of personal nor corporate pain, suffering, and evil.[40]

✝☪︎☾❋🕉

Thus, Christianity views sin as being very personal and somewhat corporate.

Judaism and Sin

G-d's love gave the law to his people who could then live happy and healthy lives. The Law without G-d's love misses the whole point of the Law and of G-d's love. That is, G-d as a loving parent gave laws for people to live healthy lives. G-d did not give the Laws as a burden or a means to cause pain, suffering, and evil.

Thus, some Jews will consider the Holocaust as a punishment against Jews for not rigorously following G-d's laws. That is, if they had done what G-d wanted, then the Holocaust would not have happened. G-d punished them

---

39 (Wikipedia 2018) Eternal Sin

40 This was addressed in the previous section, about Pain, Suffering and Evil.

out of his love for them. Other Jewish sects do not agree. More detail is in the earlier section on, "Pain, suffering, and evil."

Conservative Jews follow the 600 plus laws in the Torah (The first five books in the Christian Old Testament).

Islam and Sin

Allah lovingly gave laws through Mohammed to people. Thus, the various laws are meant as a way for a holy and pure life. However, people are incapable of adhering to those laws; and so, they sin. Allah punishes people and nations for their sins just as a loving father punishes his child. It is to correct the sinful behavior and it is not meant as retribution.

Thus, a loving father, Allah, has given laws for all aspects of life:

1. A person
2. Families, groups, societies, business activities, and nations
3. Animals, plants, land, atmosphere, and water
4. An offense against Allah's creation is an offense against Allah.[41]

These laws are in the Qur'an, the Hadith (teachings of Mohammad), and clarifications by various clergy. A focus of Islam is to achieve everlasting life in paradise.

Muslims split into Sunni and Shia following the death of Muhammad in AD 632. Some consider that the split is a sin against Allah. Nevertheless, Muslims have not been able to resolve the split and thus remain in sin.

Buddhism and Karma

Buddhism is concerned with accumulating good and bad deeds. As one lives

---

41 (Ali 2006) Ali, M. Amir, Ph.D. "Forgiveness." Institute of Islamic Information and Education. February 24, 2006. http://www.iiie.net/forgiveness/ (accessed February 19, 2018). For more detail, use this succinct source from the Institute of Islamic Information and Education. The quote here is specifically from (Ali 2006)

with intention, then the sum of the virtuous deeds is greater than the sum of the bad or evil deeds. When the sum of the good outweighs the sum of the bad, then one has good Karma in the next life. That is, one's next life will be better than this life. When the sum of the bad deeds outweighs the sum of the virtuous deeds, then one's next life will not be as nice as this life.

A deed by itself has little value. What is important is the sum of the good and the bad deeds. The aim is to have virtuous deeds outweigh the bad deeds.

Hinduism and Karma

In Hinduism, there is no concept of sin. However, there is the concept of what one does affects one's Karma. For everything that a person does, there is a price to pay. There is no god that says, "Your sins are forgiven." Instead, when one does an act that feels 'wrong,' then there is a wrong. Although the other person who has suffered from the action might forgive, Karma demands compensating action. The scriptures and various gurus or teachers guide devotees how to live a good life. But the good life is not like the Western view which focuses on wealth. Instead, the good life focuses on following the scriptures, the teachers, and being aware of Karma.

What one does in this life affects what the next life will be like. Those that are now suffering are suffering because what they did in their past life or lives. Those that are living in opulence deserve opulence because in an earlier life they were virtuous. Those that are living in misery deserve to live in misery because of what they did in their earlier life or lives.

Discussion

The five religions view sin or Karma as actions that can negatively affect one's next life. In Christianity, Islam, and Judaism, God defines what a sin or wrong action is. In Buddhism and Hinduism there is the karmic law.

Yet there is no proof there are sins against God, G-d, Allah, or that Karma exists. Ask the clergy, "Where do these ideas come from? Are the ideas of the other religions true?" The clergy will respond that the other religions are wrong and don't listen to them. How do those clergy know the other religions view of sin or Karma is wrong and their view is right? How do they know that their definition of sin is against God, G-d, Allah's will, or Karma? They don't. It is a leap of faith.

Nevertheless, closely tied to sin, or doing that which causes pain, suffering or evil, is forgiveness.

Chapter 9

Forgiveness

Figure 9.1 Individual and corporate forgiveness
are fundamental in the five religions

The Abrahamic religions believe that God, G-d, and Allah forgives sins. Buddhism and Hinduism do not have such a concept; instead, they have Karma which means doing more good actions than bad actions.

Christianity and Forgiveness

If one believes in Jesus as God, then God forgives sins. Most sects would also include the ritual of communion where the laity make confession of sins. Then a cleric gives the believer wine or grape juice and bread or a wafer. Depending upon the sect, those are the real or symbolic blood and body of Jesus.

In some sects the laity will confess each sin; though that is not as prominent as it once was. Christianity has divided whether to have wine or grape juice, bread or wafer; and, whether these are the real blood and body of Jesus, the spirit of Jesus or, a representation of Jesus.

Some Christian sects believe in Original Sin. That was when Adam and Eve ate fruit from the Tree of Knowledge of good and evil:

> [16] And the Lord God commanded the man, "You are free to eat from any tree in the garden; [17] but you must not eat from the tree of the knowledge of good and evil, for when you eat from it you will certainly die." (Gen 2: 16-17, NIV).

From that one action, 'sin entered into the world and all humanity is now fallen and corrupted.'

The Old Testament lists something like 613 laws. Not following them is a sin.

> There are dietary laws, lying, purification of women, curing illness, modesty in dress, sexual laws, do not hold a grudge, take care of the stranger in the land, kill adulterers, only take a wife that is a virgin, work six days a week, stone those that curse, offerings, take care of the poor, no idols, tithing. (Leviticus).
>
> The Ten Commandments. (Deuteronomy 7-21)
>
> Love God with all your heart, soul and might. (Deuteronomy 6:5)
>
> Follow the commands so that you may possess the land. (Deuteronomy 8:1)
>
> Live by every word that proceeds from the Lord. (Deuteronomy 8:3)
>
> What to wear, how to plant, stone non-virgins before marriage, rapist to marry the virgin, (Deuteronomy 22). Man wounded in private parts or a bastard shall not enter the congregation (Deuteronomy 22:1-2). Rules for divorce. Two men fight and the woman grabs one

by the genitals, then cut off the woman's hand and her eye. (Deuteronomy 25:11-12)

Most Christians believe that Jesus fulfilled those laws and therefore He did away with most of the laws. The New Testament simplified the process by fulfilling the law with Jesus' atoning death.

> He (Jesus) is the atoning sacrifice for our sins, and not only for ours but also for the sins of the whole world. (1 John 2:2 NIV)

> For this reason, Christ is the mediator of a new covenant, that those who are called may receive the promised eternal inheritance—now that he has died as a ransom to set them free from the sins committed under the first covenant. (Hebrews 9:15 NIV)

> This is my blood of the covenant, which is poured out for many for the forgiveness of sins. (Matt. 26:28 NIV)

That is why Christians do not follow all the Old Testament rules for defining sin nor the rituals for forgiveness of those sins. However, in general Christians hold to the Old Testament Ten Commandments and some conservative sects hold to various sins defined in the Old Testament. Liberal sects in general loosely hold to the Ten Commandments and little if any of the other laws and rituals for forgiveness of sins. Yet, many Christians abide by some of those laws.

In any case, many Christians simply believe that Jesus' death, and their accepting Him, absolves them of their sins.

Judaism and Forgiveness

In Judaism forgiveness is recognition of one's sins as sins, remorse, desisting from sin, restitution where possible, and confession.[42]

There will be punishment for not living by G-d's commandments. But the

---

42 (Blumenthal n.d.)

punishment is like the loving parent that corrects a child for the child's benefit. The punishment can be for an individual, group or a nation. There does not appear to be a strong concept of the next life, especially when coupled with the notion of sin.

There are two ways to forgive:

> 1. Ignore the instinct for revenge. Instead, behave as if nothing happened. That will weaken or end negative feelings towards the perpetrator person, group, or nation. Eventually the negative feelings will disappear.

> 2. Change the feeling. Everything happens by divine providence for the benefit of individuals, groups, and nations. So, there is no reason to get angry. No one can harm another if G-d didn't decree harm beforehand. Once G-d decrees that harm will happen, anyone can carry out the decree. So, when something painful happens, instead of getting angry ask: "Why do I, or my group, or nation deserve this? Is it a test? Is it to strengthen? Is it a punishment? Is it an opportunity to do something unexpected? [43]

One does not decide what happens; one decides what do with what happens.

Humans are responsible for their actions. Recognize the action. Regret it. Decide never to do it again. Confess to the mistreated person. Ask for forgiveness. If done with sincerity, G-d will forgive.

However, G-d does not forgive wrongdoing until people first forgive. If people do not forgive and correct the damage, then G-d will not forgive. Only after correcting the damage and the one who suffered forgives does G-d forgive the violation of His command. Then there is a great relief. Additionally, the trauma of having to ask for forgiveness makes people think twice before hurting others again.

---

43   A succinct article well worth reading in more detail. "The Art of Forgiveness." (Shemtov 2018)

Resisting temptation to commit the same sin again shows that repentance was sincere and G-d has forgiven.

For many people, the most difficult person to forgive is oneself. Guilt feelings are an opportunity for growth. However, if guilt is demoralizing and depressing, then quickly seek help.

Joy is one of the most important values of Judaism. The only way to overcome life's challenges is through joy. From joy comes agility to handle all of life's challenges. The worst enemy a Jew has is misplaced sadness.

Spiritual failing is from enthusiasm for what is wrong and indifference to what is right.

Spiritual strength comes by filling one's mind with the Torah. Then there will be no room for guilt and negative thoughts that destroys those that harbor them.

Islam and Forgiveness[44]

The Qur'an and the historical accounts of Mohammad are the basis for forgiveness. The Qur'an uses three terms for forgiveness:
1. Pardon.
2. To turn away sin.
3. To cover, to forgive and to remit.

Forgiveness means closing an account of offense against Allah or any of His creation. Allah knows everything a person thinks but does not express in words or deeds. So, forgiveness must be sincere.

Requirements to receive forgiveness from Allah:
1. Recognizing the offense and admitting it to Allah.
2. Commitment not to repeat the offense.
3. Doing what is necessary to rectify the offense (within reason) and ask

---

44   Ali, M. Amir, Ph.D. "Forgiveness." Institute of Islamic Information and Education. February 24, 2006. http://www.iiie.net/forgiveness/ (accessed February 19, 2018). For more detail, use this succinct source from the Institute of Islamic Information and Education. The quote here is specifically from (Ali 2006)

pardon of the offended party.
4. Ask Allah for forgiveness.

By sincerely meeting the above conditions, Allah will forgive and help the sinner to not repeat the sin.

Sometimes sins are committed against non-humans. Examples are torturing animals, killing them without justification (food is a justification), defoliation and burning of trees, poisoning bodies of water, polluting air, destroying land and so on. However, it is acceptable to use land and animals to help humans.

There are many phrases and words to ask for forgiveness to use daily. For example:

> I ask forgiveness from Allah.

> Glory be to You, Allah, and with You Praise (thanks) and I bear witness that there is no deity but You, I ask Your forgiveness and I return to You (in obedience).

Forgiveness is selfishness. So, to receive forgiveness, forgive others.

Forgiveness is important:
1. For the afterlife
2. To bring happiness
3. To improve relations by bringing good reputation and respect.

Forgiveness means not taking revenge nor harming the offender. Forgiveness includes not asking that God punish the offender in this life nor in the afterlife.

However, when situations are not clear, and the parties sincerely disagree, they should get arbitration and conflict resolution. Allah teaches:

> "If two groups of believers fall to fighting, make peace between them; but then, if one of the two [groups] goes on acting wrongfully towards the other, fight against the one that acts wrongfully until it reverts to God's command; and if they revert, make peace between

them with justice, and deal equitably [with them]: for verily, God loves those who act equitably!" The Qur'an 49:9

If there is repentance, there will be a bond between the two parties. But it is not necessary for the offender to repent for there to be forgiveness. Reconciliation is desirable but not essential to forgiveness. If the victim feels that the offender has serious character flaws and it is not in his best interest to reconcile, then there is no need for reconciliation. Reconciliation means forgiving and forgetting as if the event never happened. But this might not be practical. Just learn from experiences and avoid such situations. Sometimes it is best to stop normal relationships with some people but not totally dissociate from Muslim brethren.

Buddhism and Forgiveness[45]

Forgiveness is a transactional concept that does not exist in Buddhism. Rather, a central concept in Buddhism is Karma. It means, the actions one does accumulate throughout one's life. If the total Karma is negative, then the next life will be worse. If the total Karma is positive, then the next life will be better.

Another central Buddhist concept is non-attachment. To stop reactive patterns to events and desires, cease attachment to the outcomes.

If one has hurt someone, be aware that one has hurt another. Figure out a way to stop hurting the other. It might include talking with the person. Going to a mediator. Spending time, money, effort to rectify the situation. However, the intent is not to make oneself or the other person feel better. Instead, the intent is to rectify the situation, so it does not happen again. In some cases, it might be necessary to go to court. If those actions do not work, then break the relationship. Cease attachment to the relationship and move on.

The injured person can easily become a victim and nurses the victimization

---

45 (McLeod 2017) Ken McCleod has an excellent website, tricycle.org. For thoughtful clear explanations in more depth it is worth a subscription.

for the rest of one's life. Thus, the victim stays attached to the perpetrator and to the injury. Just let it go and move on. One might need help to overcome such attachments and change the behavior and thought patterns.

If attachment stays, then both the perpetrator and the victim are in cycles of attachment that can last for generations. It is essential for both the perpetrator and the victim to let go no matter how justified either feels.

Notice the patterns in one's life. If they are helpful to others or one's self, then continue them. If they are hurtful, cease, stop and desist from those patterns.

Hinduism and Forgiveness[46]

> "If a dog bites a man, he does not bite the dog back.
> Therefore, if a wicked man injures a virtuous one,
> the virtuous one does not seek revenge."[47]

Actions that hurt others affects one's Karma and thus the next life.

In Hinduism, actions can be beneficial, hurtful or neutral to oneself, others, groups, societies, as well as plants, animals, and the earth. The actions that are beneficial add to good Karma. The actions that are hurtful add to bad Karma. The neutral actions neither add nor subtract from one's Karma. So, when one does something that is hurtful, do what is necessary to undo one's bad Karma.

When a person or group receives hurtful actions, they also create Karma. If they act with anger, vengefulness or dislike, then they add to their own Karma. Thus, when a person or group receives hurtful actions, they will improve their Karma by doing beneficial actions to the other person or group. This includes forgiving the person or group. One example of this is after World War II. The US created the Marshall Plan that helped former enemies Germany and Italy quickly recover from the devastation. That is in sharp

---

46 (Hindupedia n.d.)

47 Nītidvishashtikā of Sundara Pandya vs 68 from (Hindupedia n.d.)

contrast to after World War I when the victors demanded reparations for war damages. The hate and anger by the enemies festered to become World War II in Europe.

However, one cannot forgive an action that one has not done. Only the victim can forgive. If that victim does not forgive, then the victim adds to their bad Karma. However, there are circumstances when the perpetrator helps the injured and gets good Karma and the victim does not forgive and gets bad Karma. That is how Karma works.

There are some people that should receive punishment in this life. The punishers should not be acting with vengeance; but rather, they should be acting with a sense of justice.

It is difficult to forgive everyone for every hurtful action by others, groups, societies or nations done against themselves, their group, society or nation. Doing so can mean that the hurtful person, group, society or nation will keep on doing the hurtful actions. Such hurtful behavior benefits no one. Not taking action creates bad Karma for the perpetrators and the victims. Thus, in this life, when hurtful actions occur to others or to oneself, reduce the bad Karma and increase the good Karma by effective beneficial actions. Sometimes, these actions can be punishments or re-education.

Discussion

The five religions view forgiveness as healthy for oneself and for society. That forgiveness is a noble act and individuals, families, societies and nations should practice every day. While each of the religions and their sects may disagree on methods for forgiveness, they all encourage it. The focus tends to be on individuals forgiving others, themselves and seeking God's forgiveness or to improve their Karma. There is some mention of families, organizations, societies and nations forgiving each other. Forgiveness seems simple: Just forgive and forget. As a friend of mine said, "To quote that great philosopher, Willie Nelson – "Forgiving you was easy, but forgetting seems to take the longest time." "(OK you the reader and I the writer needed a little levity – sorry!)[48]

Yet, forgiveness is more complicated than that. Here are some topics to consider:

Blasphemy – The Unpardonable sin – and Basic Trust

Why be afraid about the next life? If God or Karma is just, then there is nothing to fear about God not forgiving sins or working out Karma. Don't worry about being good enough and repentant enough. Just do what your religion says and leave the rest up to God or Karma.[49] If you don't, you don't trust God or Karma. That is distrust, which is real blasphemy, because you don't really trust in God or Karma.

Or, doing good solely to have a better next life and not loving God, G-d, Allah, Karma, or the pantheon of Hindu gods is blasphemy. Because one does not love the deity; rather, one wants what the deity provides.

That is the true meaning of blasphemy – not trusting God or karmic action – not loving God nor Karmic action – or wanting something from God, G-d, Allah, Karma, or Hindu gods without love.

However, Christians view The Unpardonable Sin as speaking against or blaspheming against the Holy Spirit or not acknowledging Jesus before people (Matt 12:31). Typically, people think of cursing. Consequently, it was a crime to curse in public. Today conservative Christians around the world believe it is blasphemy not to publicly acknowledge Jesus. Therefore, they insist on acknowledging God or Jesus before governmental activities; acknowledging God on money, public buildings, and vehicles; acknowledging Jesus before and after sporting events; and, preaching about Jesus in public squares. To not do so is The Unpardonable Sin. Thus, they

---

48 Quotation inserted from Jim Nelson, the editor. (Nelson 2019)

49 (C. Hitchens n.d.) A variation on the statement from Christopher Hitchens. He made the essence of the statement which is elaborated here.

have the same view as Muslims, Conservative Jews, and probably also Hindus. They all want their religious views in the public arena. In their view, to not do so is also discrimination against them.

✝☆☪☸ॐ

But what happens if one recants the blasphemy or turns from not acknowledging Jesus to acknowledging Jesus before people? Will God forgive them then? For example, St Paul before converting to Jesus was persecuting Christians. Clearly that was blasphemy. Yet, Paul converted during the Damascus Road Experience. Then preached in Israel, Turkey, Greece, and Italy. Finally, Paul significantly influenced the New Testament and Christian theology. He is one of the pillars of Christianity. Thus, one would think that God forgave his blasphemy. Yet the Biblical quote (Matt 12:31) does not agree.

✝☆☪☸ॐ

Is doubt an unforgivable sin? After all to doubt is close to denying God, G-d, Allah, Buddha, Hindu Gods, Jesus, the Holy Spirit, Moses, Muhammad, along with the various traditions, writings, as well as priests, pastors, rabbis, and mullahs of the five religions. Would God accept doubters into heaven or would one's good Karma outweigh doubt? After all, could a doubter infect others in heaven and then cause others to fall out of heaven or create bad Karma in others?

Many Christians believe that Judas betrayed Christ. Yet, the New Testament clearly states that Jesus had to die on the cross. Therefore, Judas helped Jesus to die on the cross. Jesus was supposed to die on the cross. Is Judas guilty of an unpardonable sin? Wouldn't Jesus and Judas be in heaven together celebrating that they fulfilled the prophesies? Did Jesus absolve the Roman soldiers that crucified Him? Or did Jesus condemn those soldiers to an eternity of Hell?

Are there other unforgivable sins?

Guilt

Many religious people are concerned about forgiveness from God or creating bad Karma. On the one hand they are worried about guilty feelings over sins or Karma and having a nice afterlife. There are people that feel guilty in normal everyday actions. There are some that cannot stand to make a minor mistake. Something overpowers them with worry about error, a wrongdoing, etc. St Paul and Martin Luther worried about their errors and sins. Eventually, they viewed salvation as being by the grace of God and not about worrying about every perceived sin.

On the other hand, there are people that feel no guilt at all. They can hate, rape, pillage, kill, commit genocide, and enslave people without the slightest remorse.

Why did a loving God, G-d, Allah, or Karmic action of the five religions create people that are overly concerned about every possible sin or bad Karma and others that give no thought to any action they do? Why the guilt and the non-guilt?

The typical response is that humans have free will to love or to hate, rape, pillage, kill, and commit genocide. That neither God, G-d, Allah, Karma nor a Hindu god created the latter. So therefore, the gods and Karma are innocent. As a result, the gods created free will which individual humans use for their benefit to please the gods or Karma for a better life or for a worse afterlife. For the believer, this all makes perfect sense particularly if they know they will have a better afterlife. For those that are not believers in the five religions, the gods condemn them to eternal punishment. As a result, guilt consumes some people and some literally tremble with fear about the next life.

Temptation and forgiveness

The Bible is silent about why God tempted Adam and Eve with the Tree of Knowledge of Good and Evil. However, there are many theories about the passage. Most say that God gave Adam and Eve freewill, which is essential to human nature. To not have free will is to be like an animal, plant, or bacteria. Therefore, Adam and Eve made a choice that hurt billions of people. If so, that is worse than any tyrant, dictator, or other evil person that ever existed. Where is God's effective forgiveness for Adam and Eve and the billions who came later? If they use their free by not doing God's will, God will punish them forever. So, what happens in heaven? Do souls have free will there? If so, can they fall out of heaven like Satan did? Thus, in heaven there is temptation just like on earth. On the other hand, if there is no sin in heaven, there must not be free will in heaven. Then why did God create free will? What is the benefit of free will?

Is the Adam and Eve passage a statement that gaining knowledge leads to falling away from God? Is that why fundamentalists of all the five religions prefer to know only what is in their scriptures and minimize liberal learning? That learning other thoughts leads to moving away from their view of God and doing what they feel is good and not evil?

The literalist statement, "You are free to eat from any tree in the garden, except from the tree of knowledge" implies that every tree in the garden had edible food. So, picture innocent people allowed to eat from any tree. They eat from this tree and that tree. Then there is that one prohibited tree. God set a trap and caught Adam and Eve. In legal terms, it is "entrapment." What kind of God entraps? God admonishes them and does not ask them to repent. Instead, God gets angry, kicks them out of the Garden of Eden, and then punishes billions of their descendants. What kind of God does not forgive them and the billions of their descendants? This does not seem like a model for humans to forgive others. Instead it is a model to punish others.

But why tempt them? Why create creatures that are holy and innocent and then tempt them to partake of the Tree of Knowledge of Good and Evil? What parent tells a child not to do something and then tempts the child? What kind of parent is that? What kind of God is that? Doesn't God know that if the people eat of the fruit of the tree that billions of people will suffer because of the sins of one or two people? What kind of God would setup a situation like that? What kind of parent would setup a prohibition with the great likelihood that the child will experiment and then the parent viciously punishes the child and all the child's descendants? This is a loving God? Where is the forgiveness? Is this a model example of good parenting?

God created plants, animals, bugs, amoebas, germs, and snakes. Genesis says that God saw that they were good. Genesis says nothing about the talking snake being good or bad. So, since God created all and it was good, the snake must have been good at first. Was the snake tempted and then became evil? If so, why punish Adam and Eve along with billions of descendants? Why didn't God cast the snake out of the Garden of Eden before tempting Adam and Eve?

Instead, God punishes Adam and Even along with the rest of humanity. And, God punishes the snake by forcing it and its' descendants to crawl on its' belly. How was the snake getting around before? The snake as a tempter gets off lightly while Adam and Eve and their descendants get severely punished. Unless, they seek God's forgiveness. Then all is OK. So, can snakes ask and get forgiveness from God? Why did God punish Adam and Eve instead of discussing the matter with them, slapping their wrists with a mild punishment, and then telling them not to do that again? Instead, God gets angry and punishes Adam and Eve along with the rest of humanity – and the snake. For what? What was the growth for Adam and Eve?

If the snake tempted Adam and Eve, can snakes today tempt humans or commit sins? Can other animals, bugs, and amoeba tempt humans or commit sins? If they can commit sins, does God forgive them? After all Mark 15:15 says, "Go into all the world and preach the gospel to all creation." That means to preach to animals, fish, bugs, amoebas, germs, bacteria, and space aliens. Are any Christians doing that? Are those creatures also tempted and is there forgiveness for them? If there is, do they go to heaven or have a better afterlife? Buddhists and Hindus think that all creatures have an afterlife. Fundamentalist Christians imply that, but they don't say so.

Trapped in Karmic action

Since people are frail and not able to be perfect, then most humans will never be able to undo the bad Karma of all their lives. If so, that means trapping people in a perpetual cycle of reincarnation and never reaching Nirvana. It is totally hopeless for the mass of mere mortals. Furthermore, will the end of the world in a few billion years trap most people in non-nirvana, causing them to suffer for all eternity? Or do they go to other plains of existence and reincarnate there and continue the everlasting reincarnation cycles? What kind of an entity creates such a nightmare? How do the clergy know that is true? Where is the proof that karmic action is real? Ask clergy that believe in Karma to prove it is true. See what they say and how they react.

Karma also implies that Karma is not just for Buddhists and Hindus. It is a principle that applies to all people no matter what their religion or if they are non-religious. It must pertain to all eternity for anyone that ever lived. So, when did Karma start in history? At the instant of creation? Earlier? Later? Did it start with Cro-Magnon humans? Paleolithic humans? Devonian humans? Does Karma apply to non-humans? If people reincarnate as pigs, dogs, cows, birds, amoeba, can those creatures reincarnate as people? Can those creatures create bad Karma? Can the clergy prove any of this? Ask them.

Trapped in sin or Karma

The theme of sin and guilt is central to Christianity, Islam, and Judaism. Karmic action is central to Buddhism and Hinduism. The Old Testament has 613 laws[50] about all aspects of life (God, family, love, war, sex, clothing, etc.). If one is serious about following the laws, then to violate those laws creates

---

50   (Judiasm 101 n.d.)

a sense of failure and guilt. Christians take communion and then a cleric reminds the penitents that Christ died for their sins. Jews perform rituals to create a sense of relief from a guilty conscience. Muslims believe that, with sincere repentance, Allah forgives their sins just as Muslims forgive the sins of others.

However, many Christians believe that Jesus' death did away with the 613 Jewish laws in the Old Testament and the specific rituals for forgiveness. Why didn't an omniscient all-knowing being get the forgiveness process right the first time and make it simple the first time?

The followers of the five religions mean well

Yet, God, G-d, Allah, Karma, and Hindu gods set up a process of temptation or entrapment, created sin, and then punished people with eternal damnation. So, is God, G-d Allah, gods or Karma incompetent for creating such problems? But the clergy will blame the people. That is like a failing corporation where the leadership blames the people and is not willing to admit that they failed the people because of poor systems, lack of resources, lack of leadership, etc. Perhaps Christians unknowingly believe that God did not get the process right the first time and sent Jesus to correct God's error or poor judgment in setting up the process?

So, for Christians, Muslims and Jews, priests, pastors, or rabbis that administer some form of sacrament for the forgiveness of sins claim that it is mystical, wonderful action from a merciful God. For Buddhists and Hindus there is karmic action. What that means is that an omniscient God creates temptation. Then on a regular basis people must go to the clergy to get forgiveness or to improve Karma. The process is: Sin. Go to a cleric. Get forgiven. Sin some more. Go to cleric. It is an unending process. For those that take the process seriously, it can become a mental illness. For those that don't take the process seriously, they shrug and go through the ritual without understanding. They do feel better; so apparently something happens. For others it is meaningless and for some they quietly mock the process.

The followers of the five religions mean well and basically try to follow their religion. What they might do is go to the various Christian, Jewish, Muslim, Buddhist, and Hindu clergy and ask, "What is the proof that forgiveness of sins or karmic actions is true?" Keep asking. Don't just accept what they say from the scriptures, traditions, rituals or rationale. What is the proof?

Unforgiven sins

What happens if one dies between communions where God forgives the sinner of all sins or one dies without having forgiven others? That concern prompted the Catholic Church to institute Last Rites to wipe out all the person's sins before death so that at the Final Judgment the soul would as pure as possible. Most Protestant religions don't agree. They believe that believing in Jesus as Lord is enough. That God's grace mysteriously accepts believers into heaven.

In Judaism forgiveness is recognition of one's sins as sins, remorse, desisting from sin, restitution where possible, and confession.[51] What happens when one dies and has not completed these steps? Apparently, G-d does not forgive those sins? Or maybe through mercy the divine does forgive those sins of the gaps between earthly forgiveness. What does God do with the unforgiven sins of Jews?

In Buddhism and Hinduism, Karma is the adding up all the good and all the bad one does. If all the bad outweighs all the good that one does, then the next life will be worse than this life. If the bad and good are about the same, then the next life will be the same. If the good outweighs the bad, then the next life will be better. Perhaps the next life will be much better if the good in this life significantly outweighs the bad. However, the Buddhist and Hindu clergy claim that this is not transactional forgiveness as in Christianity, Judaism, or Islam.

---

51 (Blumenthal n.d.)

These are vastly different views. Are all of them correct? Are none of them correct? How do their clerics and billions of people know which view is correct? Is it because of their own sacred texts, institutions, traditions, human reasoning and personal experience which they claim invalidate the other faith's sacred texts, institutions, traditions, human reasoning and personal experience?

Corporate

Judaism has more focus upon group, society, and national sins and for-giveness than Christianity, Islam, Buddhism, and Hinduism. Yet, all the five religions focus more upon the individual than upon the corporate sin and forgiveness.

What would the world be like if Christian, Jewish, Muslim, Buddhist, and Hindu clergy focused more upon groups, societies, and nations not to be:

- Greedy,
- Self-centered,
- Hateful,
- Lying,
- Lying,
- Cheating,
- Stealing,
- And not tolerate those that do?

Politically, that would be unsustainable. Powerful political and economic forces would rebel against such intrusions into their affairs or domains. The devotees would be confused, feel powerless, and begin to distrust their political and business leaders. Anyway, most clergy will happily stay out of such issues and focus upon easier individual sins and individual forgiveness from God, G-d, Allah, or Karma.

Did God's mind change?

The Christian Bible and the Jewish Torah says,

> This is what the LORD Almighty says: ... attack the Amalekites and destroy everything that belongs to them. Do not spare them; put to death men and women, children and infants, cattle and sheep, camels and donkeys. (1 Samuel 15:2-3)

> [34] And we captured all his cities at that time and devoted to destruction every city, men, women, and children. We left no survivors. (Deuteronomy 2:34) [6] We completely destroyed them, as we had done with Sihon king of Heshbon, destroying every city—men, women and children. (Deuteronomy 3:6)

> [16] But in the cities of these peoples that the Lord your God is giving you for an inheritance, you shall save alive nothing that breathes, [17] but you shall devote them to complete destruction, the Hittites and the Amorites, the Canaanites and the Perizzites, the Hivites and the Jebusites, as the Lord your God has commanded, [18] that they may not teach you to do according to all their abominable practices that they have done for their gods, and so you sin against the Lord your God. (Deuteronomy 20:16–18)

The typical interpretation is that "God's ways are not our ways. He is fair and just. So, he must have some reason for ordering the genocide." Then there are statements that justify the slaughter because those tribes opposed the Jews entering Palestine. How does one know that? Is that a human interpretation or was there some revelation from God that makes that statement match reality of three thousand years ago? Or, why, since God gave the land to the Israeli's, didn't God just breathe upon the locals to give up the land and cheerfully welcome the Israelis? Why the slaughter?

Why didn't the Israelis do the same in 1948 or today?

Contrast those commands to Jesus' preaching:

> ...[30] and you shall love the Lord your God with all your heart and with all your soul and with all your mind and with all your strength.'
> [31] The second is this: 'Love your neighbor as yourself.' No other commandment is greater than these.(Mark 30-31)

That is an enormous difference. The Israelis invaded a land. The invaded people resist. God tells the Israelis to wipe out the opposition. So, a millennium later God says," Love your neighbor." Did the modern-day Israelis disobey those commandments listed above by not early on destroying Palestinians? Did God change his mind from destruction to love?

Jesus gave an example of a neighbor with The Parable of the Good Samaritan.

> [25] On one occasion an expert in the law stood up to test Jesus. "Teacher," he asked, "what must I do to inherit eternal life?"
>
> [26] "What is written in the Law?" he replied. "How do you read it?"
>
> [27] He answered, "'Love the Lord your God with all your heart and with all your soul and with all your strength and with all your mind'; and, 'Love your neighbor as yourself.'"
>
> [28] "You have answered correctly," Jesus replied. "Do this and you will live."
>
> [29] But he wanted to justify himself, so he asked Jesus, "And who is my neighbor?"
>
> [30] In reply Jesus said: "A man was going down from Jerusalem to Jericho, when he was attacked by robbers. They stripped him of his clothes, beat him and went away, leaving him half dead. [31] A priest happened to be going down the same road, and when he saw the man, he passed by on the other side. [32] So too, a Levite, when he came to the place and saw him, passed by on the other side. 33 But a Samaritan, as he traveled, came where the man was; and when he

saw him, he took pity on him. 34 He went to him and bandaged his wounds, pouring on oil and wine. Then he put the man on his own donkey, brought him to an inn and took care of him. 35 The next day he took out two denarii and gave them to the innkeeper. 'Look after him,' he said, 'and when I return, I will reimburse you for any extra expense you may have.'

36 "Which of these three do you think was a neighbor to the man who fell into the hands of robbers?"

37 The expert in the law replied, "The one who had mercy on him."

Jesus told him, "Go and do likewise." (Luke 10:25-37 (NIV))

That is about an individual to an individual. The Samaritans were despised people. Yet Jesus said, 'Help them in their need.'

Does that mean nations are to liberate people in oppressed regimes? Jesus said nothing about converting others. He just said to take care of your neighbor. So, why aren't Christians concerned about liberating people from the oppression of tyranny, poverty, sickness, etc. without regard to saving them for a better afterlife? Did the Christian God change its' mind and focus upon saving people for the afterlife? What is the implication for Christianity, the U.S. and other countries to help people in their need to help themselves?

Such change of mind does not appear in Judaism, Islam, Buddhism, nor Hinduism.

Deeply held religious and secular beliefs

In the various religions, if a person has deeply held religious beliefs, does that person have the right in a company to not do certain tasks? For instance, a person's religion considers homosexuality a sin. The person works as a counselor, or a pharmacist, or a teacher, or a manufacturing company, or any other place. Does that person have the right not to interact with the homosexual person or the person's parents because of deeply held religious beliefs? How does forgiveness fit with deeply held religious beliefs? Does one's faith mean that one does not work with a person of certain sins? Does a coworker have the right to choose not to work with a homosexual, fornicator, murderer, embezzler, etc.? Where does forgiveness or karmic action occur? Does one shun those people? Does one shun people who don't have the same economic or ideological views? Or is of a different social class? Jesus didn't shun people. He ate, chatted, and even made water into wine for them. It is not clear what the founders of the other religions did.

Does a faith forgive when it helps create a secular society that respects all religions and points of view? Or, does the faith remain true to core beliefs and rehabilitate society to conform to its' beliefs and actions? How to forgive those that do not look for nor attempt to change behaviors that sects/religions consider abominable? Love the sinner and hate the sin? Do not tolerate certain sins and don't do any action that supports or encourages such sin?

Why do deeply held religious beliefs trump deeply held secular beliefs? If so, which religious belief trumps the other religious beliefs? Christians say that the Judea-Christian set of beliefs trump the Muslim, Buddhist and Hindu beliefs. The other religions say their beliefs trump the other ones. Why are deeply held secular beliefs less tolerated then deeply held religious beliefs? Hindus might say, 'All the religions are like rivers that in time flow together. So, all the religions will become Hindu.'[52]

What does respect of God, G-d, Allah, Buddha, a Hindu god, or secular belief mean? Allow those of different beliefs to exercise their faith while limiting the life of those that don't have that belief?

Grace

Depending on the five religions, most focus is on either karmic actions or on personal sin and God's graciousness in forgiving individuals. There is some

---

52 I don't remember nor could find where that quote or semi-quote came from.

mention about family to family forgiveness of sin, organizations forgiving organizations, and nations forgiving nations.

The five religions say to forgive all those that hurt oneself, family, group, society, and nation. For example, someone assaults another. Does the assaulted person just forgive the one who assaulted and end of story? Therefore, there is no need for any form of punishment by society? Just use whatever the holy scriptures say for those that committed the crimes. Thus, if a Muslim commits some action against Muslim law, or Christian against Christian law, Jew against Jewish law, etc. then just apply the laws of those religions. What if, the perpetrator and the victim(s) have no religion or are of another faith? Just get them to be nice to each other and work out a healthy lifestyle for both? If someone bilks people out of their money, property, or causes loss, then what? Just forgive?

What do societies today that apply their religious beliefs look like? What do countries look like that apply Judea-Christian law and ethics? What do countries look like that apply Jewish law? What do countries look like that apply Muslim law? What do countries look like that apply Buddhist or Hindu law with Karmic action look like? Those that fervently adhere to their faith would probably say that the countries that truly adhered to their system of beliefs would be happier, healthier, wealthier, and wiser. That the reason the countries aren't better is because humans use their free will and do not adhere to their religion. Yet, what is the proof of that.? What are the examples of countries or groups that adhere to their faith? Perhaps they could be models for the rest of the world to emulate.

Why are clergy so tepid to speak out about implementing Grace?

Forgive God, G-d, Allah, Buddha, and the Hindu Gods?

Jesus walked around healing individuals and instructing them to have fulfilling lives. Yet, he rarely healed more than one person at a time. Certainly, he did not heal entire nations. Why not? With all the power of the universe, why not heal the animosity of one nation against another, of a tribe against another tribe, of a person against another person? With the flick of the wrist, Jesus could have healed the world. Yet, he only healed individuals in a tiny part of the world.

It just seems that Jesus was in error or powerless to heal. Why not make the Roman Empire a loving strong empire that empowered its' people towards fulfillment? With a flick of the wrist Jesus could have done that. With a flick of the wrist, Jesus could have avoided the tragedies of WWI, WWII, the Cold War, and so many other wars. Yet, he didn't.

The CEO of an organization is responsible for everything that happens and doesn't happen in the organization. No excuses. The CEO is responsible for the failures and non-standard performance of the entire organization. When there are systematic failures across the organization, then it is the responsibility of the CEO to correct the issues. In that sense, God, G-d, Allah, Karmic action, or a Hindu god is the CEO of the world/universe. So, why hasn't one of them effectively corrected these issues? What are they waiting for?

Can religious people forgive God for not correcting these issues now?

Imagine today if a CEO, after a major product failure that kills people, says, "My people have free will to do what they believe is right. I take no responsibility." That would be unconscionable for a CEO; yet, God, G-d, Allah, Karma, and Hindu gods seem to be saying that.

Thus, it is irresponsible for the clergy to say that because of human freewill there is sin and evil in the world. Furthermore, it is irresponsible for the clergy to say that God's ways are not our ways and He is a just God that loves people. For a CEO, let alone an all-powerful entity, to have the power to correct glaring issues and problems in the organization is a dereliction of duty.

Apparently, God can't figure out how to help people or doesn't want to. Yet, God appears to help people find parking spaces, miraculously heal a compound fracture, whispers to some to run for president, whispers to others to kill their child as a sacrifice, etc. Apparently, the deities do a lot of whispering that only individuals hear. There is no corroboration.

So, forgive God, G-d, Allah, Buddha, Karma, and the pantheon of Hindu gods for the mess they have made. On the other hand, it is about time that God, G-d, Allah, Karmic action, and Hindu gods take responsibility for what they have created and clean it up without excuses and delays. They have the power to do in less time than it takes an electron to circle once around an atomic nucleus.

Forgive God, G-d, Allah, Karma and Hindu gods:

> For creating a world where there is evil, suffering and pain. For not being clear about what healthy actions are. For creating free will. That those that do not do what 'God wants' or create healthy Karma will suffer in the next life.

> For not clearly and forcefully educating people to create happy, healthy, wealthy, and wise people, families, groups, societies, and nations.

> For staying hidden and not being clear. Would a competent leader run an organization like God or Karma lets the world run?

> For creating conflicting religions and points of view.

> For punishing people that do not voluntarily love the deity or power. Yet the devotees and clergy call their view of the deity a loving deity.

> For creating a world in which people will create harm and then suffer, perhaps for all eternity. They will suffer for not seeking God's mercy or for not improving their Karma.

> For punishing the Amalekites and others with annihilation for not voluntarily giving up their land to the Israelites.

> For encouraging Jephthah to kill his daughter as a sacrifice. Today

people would say that a person who hears God's voice saying, "Kill your child" would be insane.

For not writing in Qur'an that the Palestinians should voluntarily and happily move out of their lands to allow the modern Israelis to move in. Why punish them for not understanding? Can the Israelis and Christians forgive the Palestinians for resisting?

For creating Adam and Eve, the snake, and Satan, who sin and then God punishes most of humanity for not properly repenting nor loving God.

For the poor leadership of the Pope, priests/pastors, Imams, rabbis, Buddhists clergy, and Hindu clergy for being unable to forgive each other, and getting their people, societies, and nations to forgive each other.

For creating natural events that hurt, maim or kill people. Why would a loving God or that which created Karma allow such events?

Additional Concerns for the five religions

How to create forgiveness between individuals, families, groups, companies, organizations, local communities, states and nations?

How to prevent egocentrics and sycophants from running groups, companies, states and nations? To allow them to run such organizations an absence of forgiveness and faith?

Does forgiveness enable unhealthy behavior? Or is forgiveness after rehabilitation of the perpetrator.

What is meaningful forgiveness of actions committed decades or centuries ago? For example, current Japanese people asking China and the Koreas for forgiveness for actions done by their ancestors.

How can Sunnis and Shias forgive each other and reconcile?

Release jailed people only when they have forgiven those that they hurt? How to test sincerity?

Forgive Hitler, Stalin, Mao, ISIS, Genghis Kahn, Saladin the Magnificent or Richard the Lion Heart, Pol Pot, El Chapo, etc.? Could people forgive them in heaven or some other place or karmic plain?

The Bible tells of people wearing sack cloth, spreading ashes on themselves and doing various forms of penance to win God's forgiveness. Did or do other religions? Would literalists do the same today? If not, does that mean that they don't really believe in the literal interpretation of the Bible?

Can people and organizations forgive the five religions for not strongly encouraging actions to avert global climate change? A change that will kill billions of people. When will the clerics of the five religions take climate change as seriously as they take the fundamentals of their religion?

Can there be forgiveness without punishment or compensation?

What is the relationship between forgiveness and gratefulness? Perhaps some hurtful action results in benefit to another.

Is Genesis THE model of God or G-d's forgiveness? Do Christians and Jews take the model in Genesis and the Old Testament as a model for forgiveness?

Is sin or harm just a human condition? If not, then do animals, plants, bacteria, etc. sin? If so, is there forgiveness for and among them?

✝ ✡ ☪ ☸ ☯

Societal forgiveness includes freedom, education, health, wealth, and happiness. Yet, few clergy of the five religions say much. They focus instead upon the individual. Some clergy focus upon slavery, abortion, anti-science education, anti-LGBTQ, religious public education, and forcefully practice their faith in the public square. They partner with business and politicians to gain support. The businesses and politicians support the clergy because no funds are involved. It is a win for all sides. Meanwhile liberal clergy of all religions stay quiet, say little, and don't 'rock the boat.' They hope to retire in comfort.

Thus, neither the conservative nor liberal Christian, Jewish, Muslim, Buddhist, nor Hindu clergy effectively preach and teach forgiveness.

Why arguments between the five religions?

Thus, the five religions are strongly concerned about good and bad actions. The five religions differ as to various mechanisms for reward, absolution of their sins; yet, they all say that it works out. Christians rely on Jesus to absolve their sins. Muslims rely on the mercy of Allah to absolve their sins. Jews rely on their rituals. Buddhists and Hindus believe that Karma takes care of it all.

In a sense they are all saying the same thing. That there is a God or force that eventually rights the wrongs that have occurred, if not in this life, then in the next life. Yet, most people in the five religions view the other religions with disdain, caution, fear, and superstition. Also, the five religions believe that what one does in this life, including forgiveness, affects what happens in the afterlife. In that narrow sense, the five religions are similar.

✝ ✡ ☪ ☸ ॐ

So, what are the Christian, Jewish, Muslim, Buddhist, and Hindu understandings of faith in God?

Chapter 10

Faith

Figure 10.1 Faith is trust or confidence that one can do something like keep away from the rocks

So, let's look at the essence of what the five religions have faith in.

Christianity and Faith

While there are different strands for Christian, faith the essential Christian faith is:

- Jesus is the only son of God.
- Jesus died for the sins of mankind.
- Jesus rose from the dead.
- Jesus will judge who goes to heaven and who goes to hell.

There are several early statements of Christian faith. Among the first is the Nicene Creed, which is the very essence of Christianity, written in 325 AD.[53] Those that don't subscribe to it are non-Christian:

We believe in one God the Father Almighty, Maker of heaven and

---
53 (Council of Nicea 325 AD)

earth, and of all things visible and invisible.

And in one Lord Jesus Christ, the only-begotten Son of God, begotten of the Father before all worlds, God of God, Light of Light, Very God of Very God, begotten, not made, being of one substance with the Father by whom all things were made;

who for us men, and for our salvation, came down from heaven, and was incarnate by the Holy Spirit of the Virgin Mary, and was made man, and was crucified also for us under Pontius Pilate.

He suffered and was buried, and the third day he rose again according to the Scriptures, and ascended into heaven, and sitteth on the right hand of the Father.

And he shall come again with glory to judge both the quick and the dead, whose kingdom shall have no end.

And we believe in the Holy Spirit, the Lord and Giver of Life, who proceedeth from the Father and the Son, who with the Father and the Son together is worshipped and glorified, who spoke by the prophets.

And we believe one holy catholic and apostolic Church.

We acknowledge one baptism for the remission of sins.

And we look for the resurrection of the dead, and the life of the world to come.

Here are two examples of confessions or articles of faith by various Christian religions.

The Lutheran Church's statement of faith is typical of most mainline Christian churches:[54]

Article I: of God.

1. Our Churches, ... teach that the decree of the Council of Nicaea

---
54 (Andreae, Jacob; Chemnitz, Martin 1530)

concerning the Unity of the Divine Essence and concerning the Three Persons, is true and to be believed without any doubting;

2. that is to say, there is one Divine Essence which is called and which is God: eternal, without body, without parts, of infinite power, wisdom, and goodness, the Maker and Preserver of all things, visible and invisible; and

3. yet there are three Persons, of the same essence and power, who also are co-eternal, the Father, the Son, and the Holy Ghost. And the term "person"

4. they use as the Fathers have used it, to signify, not a part or quality in another, but that which subsists of itself.

5. They condemn all heresies which have sprung up against this article,

Article II: Of Original Sin.

1. Also, they teach that since the fall of Adam all men begotten in the natural way are born with sin, that is, without the fear of God, without trust in God, and with

2. Concupiscence (strong sexual desire; lust); and that this disease, or vice of origin, is truly sin, even now condemning and bringing eternal death upon those not born again through Baptism and the Holy Ghost.

3. They condemn (all) who deny that original depravity is sin, and who, to obscure the glory of Christ's merit and benefits, argue that man can be justified before God by his own strength and reason.

Article III: Of the Son of God.

1. Also they teach that the Word, that is, the Son of God, did

assume the human nature in

2. the womb of the blessed Virgin Mary, so that there are two natures, the divine and the human, inseparably enjoined in one Person, one Christ, true God and true man, who was born of the Virgin Mary, truly suffered, was crucified, dead, and

3. buried, that He might reconcile the Father unto us, and be a sacrifice, not only for original guilt, but also for all actual sins of men.

4. He also descended into hell, and truly rose again the third day; afterward He ascended into heaven that He might sit on the right hand of the Father, and forever reign and have dominion over all creatures, and sanctify

5. them that believe in Him, by sending the Holy Ghost into their hearts, to rule, comfort, and quicken them, and to defend them against the devil and the power of sin.

6. The same Christ shall openly come again to judge the quick and the dead, etc., according to the Apostles' Creed.

The Confession continues for 28 articles: Justification, The Ministry, New Obedience, The Church, What the Church Is, Baptism, The Lord's Supper, Confession, Repentance, The Use of the Sacraments, Ecclesiastical Order, Ecclesiastical Usages, Civil Affairs, Christ's Return to Judgment, Free Will, The Cause of Sin, Good Works, The Worship of the Saints, Abuses Corrected, Both Kinds in the Sacrament, The Marriage of Priests, The Mass, Confession, Distinction of Foods, Monastic Vows,

Article 28: Of Ecclesiastical Power.

"…is a power or commandment of God, to preach the Gospel, to remit and retain sins, and to administer Sacraments…. Whosoever sins ye remit, they are remitted unto them; and whosoever sins ye retain, they are retained.... Go preach the Gospel to every creature."

Note the last part of Article 28. The pastor has power to absolve or not absolve sins (remit and retain). They are to *preach to every creature*. Preach to cows, horses, birds, bees, etc. like Francis of Assisi?

The Church of England's The Westminster Confession of 1646 says:[55]

> I. The grace of faith, whereby the elect are enabled to believe to the saving of their souls, is the work of the Spirit of Christ in their hearts; and is ordinarily wrought by the ministry of the Word: by which alo, and by the administration of the sacraments, and prayer, it is increased and strengthened.
>
> II. By this faith, a Christian believeth to be true whatsoever is revealed in the Word, for the authority of god himself speaking therein; and acteth differently, upon that which each particular passage thereof containeth; yielding obedience to the commands, trembling at the threatenings, and embracing the promises of God for this life, and that which is to come. But the principle acts of saving faith are, accepting, receiving, and resting upon Christ alone for justification, sanctification, and eternal life, by virtue of the covenant of grace.
>
> III. This faith is different in degrees, weak or strong; may be often and many ways assailed and weakened but gets the victory; growing up in many to the attainment of a full assurance through Christ, who is both the author and finisher of our faith.

Conservative churches emphasize believing in Jesus Christ as one's Lord and Savior. Do that and one has eternal life. They emphatically and strongly believe that the Bible is literal and inerrantly true. That, the Holy Spirit wrote every word in the Bible by guiding the hands and fingers that held the writing instruments of those who then transcribed what they Holy Spirit said. Their faith rests upon that assumption. Furthermore, they emphasize a personal

---

55 (Church of England 1646)

relationship daily with Jesus and the Holy Spirit. Just like the picture of Jesus knocking at the door, Jesus is inviting himself into one's life. Accept Him in and then one has eternal life. People who reject the invitation will be in hell for eternity.

On the other hand, liberals view the Bible as texts written by many authors over a period of a thousand years. The authors lived in a culture with a world view that is reflected in the texts. The scriptures are expressions of faith in God that works in mysterious ways beyond the understanding of mere mortals.

Yet, the liberals come to the similar conclusions as the fundamentalists about the key tenets of faith as shown in the two creeds above.

The difference is the emotional and intellectual intensity. The conservatives are significantly much more emotional and intense in their faith than the liberals are. As a result, conservatives are more emotionally active in politics and evangelizing communities, states, and nations than liberals.

This gives the appearance that Conservative Christianity is vigorous, growing and more forceful than liberal Christianity which appears to be receding and dying.

Faith and prayer go together. When praying, pray quietly, and simply pray:

> [5] "And when you pray, do not be like the hypocrites, for they love to pray standing in the synagogues and on the street corners to be seen by others. Truly I tell you, they have received their reward in full. [6] But when you pray, go into your room, close the door and pray to your Father, who is unseen. Then your Father, who sees what is done in secret, will reward you. (Matt 6:5-6)

> [7] And when you pray, do not keep on babbling like pagans, for they think they will be heard because of their many words. [8] Do not be

like them, for your Father knows what you need before you ask him. (Matt 6:7-8)

⁹ This, then, is how you should pray:

> 'Our Father in heaven,
> hallowed be your name,
> ¹⁰ your kingdom come,
> your will be done, on earth as it is in heaven.
> ¹¹ Give us today our daily bread.
> ¹² And forgive us our debts,
> as we also have forgiven our debtors.
> ¹³ And lead us not into temptation
> but deliver us from the evil one.

¹⁴ For if you forgive other people when they sin against you, your heavenly Father will also forgive you. 15 But if you do not forgive others their sins, your Father will not forgive your sins. (Matthew 6:9-14)

However, many Christian sects vigorously push for public prayer so that God's presence will manifest itself upon the nations. On the one hand they say it is for the benefit of the people. If the people would have prayer in all parts of their lives, (school, work, politics, home) then society would be better. They say that societal troubles are from a lack of a relationship with Jesus. Thus, society will be better with prayer throughout each day and publicly in politics, school, business and athletic events.

Christians have a mixed view about science. On the one hand happily accepting the benefits of science in industry, medicine and many conveniences. Then on the other hand, some view science that conflicts with their religious beliefs as troublesome, or a point of discussion, or false/fake science. A typical example is the age of the earth as being 6,000 years old compared to science saying that it is 4.5 billion years old.

Judaism and Faith

Judaism is a tight knit group that think and discuss every point of the relationship between the G-d, mankind, and the land of Israel.[56] Orthodox Jews will be more literal and stricter in their interpretation of their scriptures and traditions than the liberal Jews. While Judaism does not have a formal mandatory belief system, there are 13 principles of faith that most Jews adhere to in varying degrees:

1. G-d exists.
2. G-d is one and unique.
3. G-d is incorporeal.
4. G-d is eternal.
5. Prayer is to G-d alone and to no other.
6. The words of the prophets are true.
7. Moses' prophecies are true, and Moses was the greatest of the prophets.
8. The Written Torah (first 5 books of the Bible) and Oral Torah (teachings now contained in the Talmud and other writings) were given to Moses.
9. There will be no other Torah.
10. G-d knows the thoughts and deeds of men.
11. G-d will reward the good and punish the wicked.
12. The Messiah will come.
13. G-d will resurrect the dead.

Orthodox Judaism follows the 613 commandments given by G-d in the Torah as well as laws instituted by the rabbis and long-standing customs; while liberal Judaism debates most of the laws and does not as strictly adhere to them.

Judaism views science as part of the natural order. Though there are some that frown on that view. Judaism has made substantial contributions to

---

56 (T. R. Rich, What Do Jews Believe? 2011)

science. E.g. Albert Einstein.

Islam and Faith

Islam means 'submission to God and is a 'way of life'. [57]

To be a Muslim:

> There is one God, and Mohammed is his prophet.
>
> Pray 2-5 times per day (Sun rise, early afternoon, late afternoon, sunset and, night).
>
> Give to the needy.
>
> Fast during Ramadan (one month).
>
> Make a pilgrimage to Mecca, for those that are capable.

When one has sinned, just ask Allah for forgiveness. Allah is the final judge. No human is. The sinner should make efforts to end the sinful act and never do it again. However, Allah can punish sins in this life with minor to severe punishments which include death. If the sin was against a person, group, society or country, then the sinner is within reason to undo as much as possible the damage and ask the other person, group, society, or country for forgiveness.

Muslims also have faith that Allah sees the intentions of individuals, groups, societies, and nations. That there is divine destiny in all events. That there are many prophets: Adam, Abraham, Noah, Isaac, Jesus, Moses, with Muhammad being the last prophet. These prophets will go to heaven. Finally, Muslims believe in a day of judgment.

Muslim clergy forbid scholars to research, critique, and have debates about the authenticity of the Qur'an. [58]

---

57 (Bhat 2015)

58 (McCandless 2012)

Muslims tend to view science as an explanation of God's world, and some have concern about science illiteracy.

Buddhism and Faith

Faith in Buddhism means being willing to start on the Eightfold Path. Faith prepares one for the journey and sustains the devotee. It is concentrating energy on the ideal that one has not yet reached. Faith supplies an attitude of serenity and joy when doubt and fear occur. It prepares the mind for meditation. Faith is the willingness to be patient and to trust until evidence fills the doubts and concerns with results. One starts with faith and eventually one knows.[59][60]

Faith becomes knowing by understanding the teachings of the Buddha, with guidance from a skilled teacher and being part of a Buddhist community. While there are differences among the various Buddhist communities, schools, and traditions, in general most substantially have the same views to faith.

Buddhists tend to accept science as part of the natural order.

Hinduism and Faith

Hinduism has a wide range of beliefs. One clear writer, Jayaram V, says a Creator God is not central to many Hindu schools of thought. The way he presents the general concept of faith is like the other religions. He says that true faith does not depend upon proof nor reason; rather, faith is a belief in something to be true.[61] Reason uses the mind while faith uses the heart and knows. Hindu traditions have truths and eternal laws which lead to liberation. So have faith and dedication in the gods, who will strengthen one's faith.

---

[59] (Bloom 2018)

[60] It is tempting to state that this paragraph also applies to the other four major religions.

[61] (V, What is Faith? Faith in Hinduism n.d.)

Faith arises from trust, devotion, loyalty, commitment, dedication and assurance. It may arise from observations, facts, inference, intuition, assurance, experience, common sense or a simple belief. Faith is difficult to sustain because the world is an appearance, and people have delusions and are ignorant. [62]

By worshiping with faith, the faithful eventually break the cycle of births and deaths.

For a deeper understanding of the Hindu faith consult Jayaram V's writings. They are excellent, succinct, and clear. Here is a brief summary of Hindu faith:

Nature has three modes and 23 realities. The modes create patterns of behavior and attitude in beings. They influence thinking and actions. A person's essential nature is determined by them. The three modes are:

1. Gentle and pleasant. All actions are directed to God without expectations. By working to achieve liberation and experiencing the supreme bliss of self-realization, the true nature of mortal existence and the need to become free from it.

2. Ambitious and competitive. One expects God to fulfill selfish or conditional desires.

3. Harsh or cruel. Having envy, contempt, or tries to control him or manipulate God. Therefore, faith is foolish, vain, and delusional.

The 25 realities are:
1. Nature,
2. The great principle – Dharma, *
3. Discriminating, reasoning, and causative intelligence.
4. Eternal soul,

---

62 (V, What is Faith? Faith in Hinduism n.d.)

5. The brain,
6. The five sense organs (ears, eyes, nose, tongue, skin), [63]
7. The five organs of action (feet, hands, rectum, genitals, mouth), [64]
8. The five subtle elements (hearing, sight, smell, taste and touch),[65]
9. The five gross elements (earth, water, air, fire and ether).[66] [67]

*Dharma is the foundational force that guides, orders and regulates worlds and beings. Everything animate or inanimate being in the universe has its own Dharma.[68]

Hindus tend to accept science as part of the natural order.

Discussion

The five religions state that faith is belief without proof nor reason. That with faith one begins and eventually partially understand one's religion. Therefore, have faith and walk the path of one of the five religions. But which one? Just choose one and walk its' path in faith?

The five religions differ in their beliefs. Yet, there is a commonality. They believe that a force is present and active in the lives of devotees, organizations, states, and the world. However, the five faiths differ on how, who, what, and why that force is. Some say that no one has disproven the existence of one or multiple deities. Theists state that the mere existence of the universe(s) implies a deity.

Never-the-less, most religious people claim that the deity cares for humans and is interested in what is eaten, sexual relations, sickness, health, wealth,

---

63 (Pratyahara (Con't) – The Sense Organs n.d.)
64 (Pratyahara (Con't) – The Sense Organs n.d.)
65 (Wikipedia 2016)
66 (V, The 24 Tattvas of Creation in Samkhya Darshana n.d.)
67 (Pratyahara (Con't) – The Sense Organs n.d.)
68 (V, The Abiding Principles of Hindu Dharma n.d.)

thoughts, wars, etc.[69] Various people claim proofs in their daily lives by noting how God answered prayer to heal a person, get a job, avoid being shot, get a good grade in school, find a parking spot, meet someone, punishes for evil actions, etc. These events are proof enough that their faith is true and what the clergy say is true. Therefore, unanswered prayers mean that the all-knowing all-wise God knows better. So, they just trust. Just have faith. Thus, faith trumps any proof, facts or reason to the contrary.

For many people of the five religions, when they have doubts, have a need to confess a misdeed, want to know more of their religion and traditions, they go to a clergy of their faith. This is like when one is sick one goes to a healer who might be a medical doctor, an herbalist, dentist, eye doctor, surgeon, chiropractor, reiki healer, etc.

The difference is that for the most part, there is a rigorous science for these healers. There is checking, confirming, and rechecking the procedures, medications, etc. When professionals cannot replicate the results, they call the process into questions. Then they make improvements and prosecute if there is fraud or negligence. Good intentions are not enough.

However, if one of those certified healers, like a medical doctor, tries to heal people based upon personal revelations that are untested, their certifying organization would probably punish them, and someone would sue them in court for damages. Good intentions are just not enough to heal. 'Just imagine a doctor or pharmaceutical company responding to a lawsuit by replying, "but we prayed good and hard for success! What more do you want?"' [70]

Yet, in religion, the clergy make statements that lack proof, facts, or reason. There are no lawsuits against clergy for false proofs, facts, or reason. There are no lawsuits for not showing proof of eternal life, sins against a deity, ab-

---

69 (C. Hitchens 2007) Pages xviii-xix. It is not clear if the entire quote is from Dr Victor Stenger or is a mixture of Dr Stenger's quote and Christopher Hitchens thoughts.

70 (C. Hitchens 2007) Page 279 From a section by Daniel C. Dennett

solving the sins against a deity, a deity being active in the world, a deity being present during calamities, the prayers of thanksgiving for people who escaped death or injury while many others survived, etc. No court in the world would handle such cases. No politician will touch such issues.[71] During a calamity like a tornado or hurricane, some clergy claim that a deity is punishing evil people. Apparently, all the people that suffered were evil. Or an airplane crashes and half the people die. The other half walk away. Many who escaped tragedies thank a deity for sparing them. Apparently, the others were wicked and needed judgment. Were there no faithful devotees there? Why aren't there lawsuits against the clergy who say a deity saved the ones that walked away? After all, there were faithful among those that died. But the response is, "God works in mysterious ways."

As a result, the clergy of the five religions make statements for which there is little to no proof, facts nor reason, and make a living doing so.

Thus, the clergy of the five religions and their institutions make a leap of faith.

To put it another way, here is a paraphrase of the conversation earlier told between Charles Templeton and Billy Graham.[72]

> I said to the Christian, Jewish, Muslim, Buddhist, and Hindu clergy, "But, it's simply not possible any longer to believe, for instance, the scriptural accounts of creation, deities, sin, dogmas, pain, suffering,

---

71 (C. Hitchens 2007) Page 280 From a section by Daniel C. Dennett. "If you would even consider filing a malpractice suit against a doctor who made a mistake in treating you, or suing a pharmaceutical company that didn't conduct all the proper control tests before selling you a drug that harmed you, you must acknowledge your tacit appreciation of the high standards of rational inquiry to which the medical world holds itself, and yet you continue to indulge in a practice for which there is no known rational justification at all, and take yourself to be actually making a contribution. (Try to imagine your outrage if a pharmaceutical company responded to your suit by blithely replying, "But we prayed good and hard for the success of the drug! What more do you want?") "

72 (C. Hitchens 2007) This is my paraphrasing Dennett's document that in Hitchens's book pages 282-283.

and evil. A deity a few thousand years ago did not create the world in a few days; it has evolved over millions of years. It's not a matter of speculation; it's demonstrable fact. There is no demonstration of an afterlife. There is no proof that pain, suffering, and evil are tests for the afterlife, or tests of faith, or punishments for not following commandments. There is no proof that angels like Gabriel or spirits inspired or dictated word for word the scriptures of any of the five religions."

All the clergy said together, "We don't' accept that; and there are reputable scholars who don't."

"Who are these scholars?" I said. "Men in Christian and Jewish colleges and seminaries, as well as Muslim madrasas, Buddhist and Hindu schools?"

"Most of them, yes," the clergy said. "But that's not the point. We believe everything in the scriptures. We've discovered something: when we proclaim the scriptures as the Word of our deity, our preaching has power. When we stand on the platform and say, 'God, or G-d, or Allah, or Buddha, or a Hindu god says,' or 'the scripture says,' there are results. Wiser men than you and we have been arguing questions like this for centuries. We don't have the time or the intellect to examine all sides of each theological dispute, so we've decided to stop questioning and accept our faith's scripture as authority."

"But clergy," I protested, "you can't do that. You don't dare stop thinking about the most important question in life. Do it and you begin to die. It is intellectual suicide."

We don't know about anybody else," the clergy said, "But we've decided that's the path for us."

Of the thousand people I have listened to, I have yet to meet one person that isn't troubled by the basis of their faith. Yet all of them found comfort in one of their five religions. My guess is that their sense of comfort is the basic standard of measurement. Would most of them follow one of the five religions, or any faith, if there was no comfort? Is that why many devout people distrusts or shy away from science?

Miracles

Jesus and healers of the various religions didn't use medicine nor farming to feed the people. They just did miracles. There are a few sects that adhere to faith healing. For example, a clergy person heals people on stage. Why doesn't the healer just heal everyone in the audience instead of just a few people? Why don't the clergy wander the halls of all hospitals healing people? Instead a few make a stage production while others shroud their healings in mystery and away from science. "Shush. Don't say anything." Why?

The response tends to be, "It doesn't work that way." There is no intention to massively heal people. Instead, the other response is that a person must want their deity to heal them and have faith. That implies that those in or out of hospitals suffering with some physical or mental ailments do not want healing. That they want to suffer and refuse a deity's cure.

Have faith healers duplicated the feeding of the multitudes? Why don't they go to where the starving people are and feed them? This does not count potlucks where people bring extra food to feed others. So, where today are the miracles of healing and feeding the hungry?

The church has tremendous emphasis upon personal sins; yet, has effectively no emphasis upon miracles to heal and to feed the world. Instead, secular type institutions do that. Some of the five religions claim that their deity is working through science to heal and feed.

An Experiment

If you are sense of the five religions try this experiment.

Get the parallel version of the Christian Gospels of Matthew, Mark, Luke and John, and a red-letter Bible (Jesus statements are in red letters). Read the red-letter statements. Find them in the parallel version. Understand what Jesus is saying. Compare the statements as they appear in the other Gospels. Forget any church doctrine. Just put yourself in a follower of Jesus who does not know any modern views two thousand years later. What conclusion do you draw? Then read the Pauline material. Compare the two. What is the difference between the Jesus quotations and the Pauline letters? Note the similarities and differences.

Read the Qur'an, Teachings of the Compassionate Buddha and the Bhagavad Gita. Highlight the statements that are valuable for all time in one color. Use a distinct color to highlight the statements that are in cultural contexts of the writers' times. What are the similar messages among all five religions? What conclusions do you make?

Then consider: Why didn't the various inspired scriptures of the five religions give the same instructions on how to be happy, healthy, wealthy, and wise for individuals, groups, societies, and nations for all time? Why is one of the five religions right and the other four wrong? Why the diverse ways to interpret the divine will of God, G-d, Allah, Buddha, or Hindu gods? Why weren't they saying the same thing? The same thing for all the ages? Why weren't those truths revealed quickly around the world at the same time. Why use selected individuals separated by hundreds and thousands of years?

Leap of faith?

Some people have a need for assurance that all is well with the universe and that there is a way to have a good life, or at least a good afterlife. Others are willing to accept that there is no assurance; and that they have faith and trust in a divine force that created what people now experience. Perhaps the root issue is that many people fear death, do not know how to fully live, seek ways to influence the world around them, and have varying degrees of guilt or worry.

Unfortunately, at the very basis of their faith is a the "leap of faith." A leap for which there is no proof. Just a sense of what seems right. If you want to be a Christian, then take "a leap of faith" and be a Christian. If you want to be a Muslim, take a leap of faith. If you want to be a Jew, take a leap of faith. If you want to be a Buddhist, take a leap of faith. If you want to be a Hindu, take a leap of faith. After that leap of faith, take another "leap of faith" for a literalist or a liberal interpretation of the faith's scriptures. Then another leap of faith for the faith's traditions, revelations, clergy, human reasoning, ethics, politics, and individual experiences.

But the response will be, 'But science also is a leap of faith. How does one know that science is right? That human reasoning and testing can match what is in the universe that God created and is a match for the divine? God is beyond what human reasoning and science can understand. Therefore, my faith is in Christianity, Judaism, Islam, Buddhism, or Hinduism is true.'

Science is not quite a leap of faith. Properly done, science is testing and changing one's theory and understanding as needed. While difficult to impossible to do, good scientists struggle to avoid bias. Confusions happen with differing interpretations of facts, conflicts of egos, and personalities that won't let go of their pet theories. Ideally, scientists are above that; yet, scientist are humans. Nevertheless, science has made a lot of progress that benefits mankind. Compared to religions that are several thousand years old with outdated world views, science is the best way to understand the world. Perhaps someone will develop something better. So, in this sense, science is and is not a leap of faith.

So, how do the five religions base their truth upon the scriptures and authority? Can they prove that their view is reality? That it is true and more exact than the other religions? Or, is accepting their scriptures and authority just a matter of faith? Is it a leap of faith? "Try it. You will like it"?

The clergy and devotees of the five religions are willing to believe that their faith is based upon scriptures, traditions, clergy, institutions, human reasoning, experiences, and revelations. That their faith is merely a way for humans to express that which is beyond the human experience. That overtime, faith will change as humans get a better understanding. That God working beyond human understanding and in mysterious ways uses fallible, corrupt, and ignorant people for ultimate purposes. That God, G-d, Allah, Buddha, and Hindu gods even use evil people for divine purposes. So, clergy and devotees make alliances with powerful political forces to control masses of people.

How about testing every dogma in the five religions? For example, test life everlasting, Karma, revelations, in-errancy of the scriptures, eternal punishment, punishment after death, sin, devil, angels, spiritual guidance, etc. Why would it be a sacrilege to run such tests even assuming it would be possible? Just because the five religions state something is true does not mean one should not question it. Why hide behind the mystery that humans cannot explain the divine and the actions of the divine? That one shouldn't be so brazen, overconfident, arrogant, bold, audacious, forward, familiar, impertinent, insolent, impudent, cocky, cheeky, rude, impolite, uncivil, bumptious, foolhardy, and hubristic to question the deities, the clergy, the traditions, institutions, and human reasoning of the five religions? Why not question the authority of the five religions?

How and on what basis do the clergy of the five religions know that their religion is true?

Is God, G-d, Allah, Karma, or Hindu gods strong enough to answer the questions in terms that normal average humans can understand? Aren't humans strong enough to accept reality for what it is? Are humans afraid to know reality for what it is? Or, are the clergy of the five religions afraid that they do not have the answers? Or, that political, business, and religious leaders fear that people seeing reality for what it is, will create chaos?

Is a leap of faith to Christianity, Judaism, Islam, Buddhism, or Hinduism enough to base one's life, family, group, society, and nation's happiness, health, wealth and wisdom on?

In some ways yes. The five religions have valuable insights into hope, joy, and love as explained in the next three chapters

Chapter 11

Hope

Figure 11.1 Hope is an expectation or desire like this is the last hill.

The painting shows thirteen-year-old Mary Goble Pay pulling a handcart loaded with food and belongings across snowy plains, hills, and mountains. Feel her hope and faith, blended with fortitude, conviction, determination through biting cold, physical fatigue and loneliness. What she endured was trail of hope; then climbing a hill and then there was another hill.

Her family with six children left Brighton, Sussex, England May 19, 1856 and arrived at Salt Lake City, Utah on December 11, 1856. Just as they arrived her mother died. On the journey two sisters died. Mary never spoke of the crude amputation of all her toes. She went on to have 13 children.

Each of the five religions have such people of such great faith and determination. Each of the five religions provide comfort, solace, and hope.

For many people, faith and hope are the same. They have faith that they will have an afterlife and they have hope for a blissful afterlife. While faith and hope are similar, they are not the same.

Faith is the complete trust and confidence in someone or something.

Hope is a feeling of expectation and desire for an event to happen.[73]

A simple example. Faith is knowing that one can walk from one's home to a friend's home. That one has the skill, strength, and knowledge to be able make the walk. Most people don't even think about it. One just walks there. On the other hand, hope is that one can walk, perhaps with crutches, to the friend's home; yet, there is a concern that maybe the friend's home is too far and thus is impossible to walk.

Faith in the afterlife is having complete trust and confidence that there is an afterlife, and perhaps even having complete trust and confidence that it will be better than the current life. On the other hand, hope is note sure that there is an afterlife or that it will be better than this life. There is a sense of some doubt. A sense that this life might be all there is. A sense that there is no proof. For many there is a conflict between having a nice afterlife and a doubt that there is an afterlife let alone assurance that it will be happy.

Thus, most Christians, Jews, Muslims, Buddhists, and Hindus proclaim faith in an afterlife and their religion's teachings, while quietly having hope for next life and the faith's teaching just like Mary Gobles Pay pulling the handcart up the last hill. So, let's look at hope in the five religions.

Christianity and Hope

Based upon scriptures, clergy, institutions, and traditions, most Christians have faith that Jesus Christ rose from the dead, paid for the sins of humanity, and therefore have assurance of a happy afterlife. That is the foundation of Christianity. They have hope. It is a hope that also sustains and keeps their faith going. By weekly restoring hope, they renew their faith. With renewed faith they strengthen their hope. So, faith and hope strengthen each other. So, without that hope, most people would have little interest in keeping the

---

73 (Admin 2015) Difference between faith and hope

Christian faith. Thus, faith supports hope and hope supports faith. [74]

For conservative Christians, the future is secure knowing that there will be a resurrection and a heaven. For many, there is a fear that they will not pass the judgment and be eternally in damnation. So, they are afraid. Yet, they get solace from the scriptures, clergy, institutions, and traditions that proclaim they have blessed assurance that their future is secure. This frees them to love and work while on this earth. Otherwise, conservative Christians believe that liberals and non-believers are greedy living in the here and now, concerned with self-preservation, self-enhancement,[75] and live Darwinian lives of survival, unable to have loving relationships with families and others.

On the other hand, liberal Christians quietly accept that through faith in the scriptures, clergy, institutions, and traditions, people can have hope. A hope that allows people to love and to work. That people will be concerned for and help their family, their organizations, society, and the world. Church and Bible study renews their hope and strengthens their faith. Their hope is that "Faith comes by hearing and hearing by the word of God" (Romans 10:17). That, "He who did not spare his own Son but gave him up for us all, how will he not also with him graciously give us all things?" (Romans 8:32)

Thus, for both conservative and liberal Christians, hope comes from the promises of God rooted in the work of Christ as explained in the scriptures, and by clergy, institutions, and traditions.

Judaism and Hope

Judaism is a religion of the future. A religion of hope. 'To be a Jew is to ask and answer, "Has the Messiah come? Not yet." [76]

Jews have hope in the future. That nothing is inevitable, and that people

---

74   (Moultman n.d.) Introduction, section 2.

75   (Piper 2008)

76   (Sacks, Future Tense – How The Jews Invented Hope 2008) Future Tense – How The Jews Invented Hope

decide the type of society to make. Thus, "Judaism is a set of laws and narratives to create a people, families, communities, and a nation that can defeat despair." It is no accident that Jews built a nation based upon hope. A nation whose national anthem titled, "The Hope," [77] says:

> As long as within our hearts
> The Jewish soul sings,
> As long as forward to the East
> To Zion, looks the eye –
> Our hope is not yet lost,
> It is two thousand years old,
> To be a free people in our land.

Thus, many Jews believe that it is no accident that Judaism has been opposed by every empire seeking to deny people the freedom to be equal-but-different. It is no accident that Israel is still today the only free society in the Middle East. Israel has hope in its' people and for the future of mankind.

Islam and Hope

Virtuous deeds and hope go together. Without virtuous deeds, hope is just dreaming. Therefore, do virtuous deeds, study the Qur'an, and hope that Allah will forgive sins, accept the virtuous deeds, and draw believers closer. The opposite of hope is despair, which is not believing in Allah's mercy. Therefore, despair is a sin.

To have hope one must dwell on Allah's promises of great rewards, generosity, and kindness. Strengthen one's hope by reciting from memory and really knowing the multitudinous names and attributes of Allah. Strengthen hope and purify doubt through devotion and obedience to Allah. [78]

---

77 (MJL Staff n.d.) Hatikvah, the National Anthem of Israel.
78 (Having Hope in Allah The Almighty - I 2015)

Buddhism and Hope

When one has hope then there is a deficiency, a lack, that can at worst consume one's being and, at best, creates a void in one's life. There is uncertainty if one hopes.[79] It could be a thing, a love, an afterlife. It could be something trivial or monumental. Having hope creates suffering in varying degrees because the thing, the love, the next life, etc. owns the person. Thus, not having and hoping for the thing, the love, the next life, creates doubt, unease, suffering, etc. Through non-attachment and skilled practice, one can have the thing, the love, and the next life.[80]

Hinduism and Hope

Maturing of the soul takes many lifetimes. Thus, a Hindu has hope and belief that because of Karma and reincarnation there are many opportunities for growing and maturing. That, eventually, one will achieve bliss and happiness in Nirvana. This hope brings inner peace and self-assurance.[81]

Discussion

In the five religions:

> Christians have hope that through Jesus Christ one's sins are forgiven and that they will have a happy afterlife. They have hope that the teachings of their sect are true.

> Muslims have hope that their deeds and faith in Allah will result in the afterlife in eternal bliss.

> Jews have hope that the Messiah will come and make the world right.

> Buddhists believe that skilled use of non-attachment creates joy and

---

79 (Rasheta 2016)

80 (Robin 2013)

81 (Himilayan Academy, Saiva Siddhanta Theological Seminary at Kauai's Hindu Monastery n.d.)

peace.

Hindus believe that through Karma, reincarnation, and maturing, souls reach peace and bliss.

Thus, all five religions have similar, though varying, ways of expressing hope for the afterlife. Some Christians, Muslims, and Jews have hope that God, G-d, or Allah is involved in their daily activities.

For many their hope is a blessed assurance. They feel and believe that a person's lack of hope shows up in a lack of joy. A lack of hope is a sin. A lack of joy is a sign of the lack of hope and faith.

For many in the five religions, doubt or to question is a lack of hope which becomes a lack of faith. That is, doubt and hope is blasphemy, a sin, or negative Karma. Thus, a worse next life. So, don't think if there is a Christian, Jewish or Muslim heaven/Paradise or if Karma and reincarnation are true. Just cling to the hope and belief. That way if true, then one wins. If not true, one has not lost.

How do Christians, Jews, Muslims, Buddhists, and Hindus know that their hope is not a wish? Devotees of the five religions hope their faith is true. The don't know that it is. So, they make a leap of faith and cling to it fearing that their faith might be in error. Through hope they convince themselves that their faith is true.

What is the consequence of having faith and hope? It would appear to be joy.

Chapter 12

Joy

Figure 12.1 Joy is a deep sense that life is satisfying and meaningful.

Joy is a deep, long-lasting sense that life is satisfying and meaningful. It can be a life filled with a sum of many small happy events such as time with friends, enjoying the sunrise or sunset, etc. Or it is knowing that even through suffering one has made life better for others. They may not have been happy; but they had joy by making the life of others better. Joy can be outward smiling and laughing, or it can be an inward quietness. It can be frolicking with friends, or it can be deep solitude in meditation.

So, how does Christianity, Judaism, Islam, Buddhism, and Hinduism view joy?

Christianity and Joy

Christians tend to view God as a merciful father figure that has great concern for his followers. That He sent his son to die for the sins of humanity. Therefore, true Christians free of sins will feel the joy of the Spirit of God that non-believers cannot have. Conservatives and a few liberals believe that if one is not feeling joy, then one must look at one's beliefs and practices. Then understand what to change and then make the changes. Joy in one's life is a sure sign of one's belief and trust in Christ. If there is no joy, then there is no true belief, which some believe is a sin.

Therefore, submit to Jesus, pray unceasingly, trust that God answers all prayer, give up false beliefs, be thankful for everything that happens, trust that God will prevail, and that Jesus is always present, even when it appears He is not. Know that Jesus is enough for all one's needs. Sing songs of praise. Be grateful for the forgiveness of sins, and that Jesus will welcome believers into eternal bliss. Doing so, hearts will fill with joy.

On the one hand, Conservatives seem more effervescent, bubbling, and showing their joy. Their theme song would be, "There is joy, joy, joy down in my heart, down in my heart, down in my heart." On the other hand, Liberals seem more muted in their joy. It is a quiet muted contentment.

Conservatives vigorously add: Tolerating sex outside of marriage, pornography, abortion, homosexuality, and feminism kills joy. When there is a lack of joy there is a great chance that one of these sins against God is occurring. Therefore, don't allow such sins in one's life nor in society.[82]

Judaism and Joy

The meaning of life is to live in a community and to have joy. "Joy connects us to others and to G-d. Joy is the ability to celebrate life as such, knowing that whatever tomorrow may bring, we are here today, under G-d's heaven, in the universe He made, to which He has invited us as His guests." With such joy, enemies can never defeat Jews.[83] So, no

---

82 (Murray n.d.) "8 Sources of Joy vs. 6 Thieves of It" plus a multitude of other sources and personal observations.

83 (Sacks, The Pursuit of Joy n.d.)

matter what, serve G-d joyfully and smile.

Islam and Joy

The goal of Islam is to reach Paradise. When one is not happy, then one is has not submitted to the will of Allah. It is a sign to correct something. Therefore, find what needs improving in one's submission to Allah by learning from an Islamic teacher or scholar to improve one's world outlook, emotional, sexual, physical, mental, family, social, financial, political, and spiritual health. Since beliefs shape expectations, it is imperative to have healthy beliefs that are from Allah. For most people, it is difficult to impossible to form healthy beliefs. So, an Islamic teacher or scholar can help mold those healthy beliefs.

To experience joy, submit to Allah in everything. Self-centeredness, fear, negativity, and a lack of trust in Allah kills joy. It is a Muslim's duty to be joyful. Therefore, Islam creates healthy individuals and societies in the present time with the knowledge of Paradise to come. [84]

Buddhism and Joy

Attachment to anything creates desire which hinders joy. Desiring things, activities, wealth, power, sex, peace, and joy create longing and disturbance. Instead, train the mind through meditation to live in peace.[85] Be grateful for a minimal number of things necessary for life. Be grateful for all that is around and has happened. Be grateful for friends, relatives, history, the future, bugs, plants, animals, and everything. When one is profoundly grateful and meditates, then joy naturally happens. Do not seek joy. For joy is like a river. When one tries to capture a river, it is no longer a river. It might become a lake, or it just flows through one's fingers. Just be grateful and joy will follow.[86]

---

84 (Spiritual Excellence 2013) plus, a multitude of other sources and personal observations.

85 (Buddha n.d.)

86 (Quotations on: Joy, Happiness n.d.) Thich Nhat Hanh, Dalai Lama and Ven. Tenzin Dongak.

A lack of joy and contentment shows attachment to something. Whatever that attachment is, it is controlling one's life. Let go of the attachment and joy will happen. The purpose of life is to be joyful. Joy will come by knowing the Four Noble Truths and following the Eight-fold Path:

The Four Noble Truths

Life is suffering.
Suffering arises from craving.
Eliminate cravings
The Eightfold Path eliminates craving and suffering.

The Eight-Fold Path is:

Right view/understanding
Right intention/thought
Right speech
Right action
Right livelihood
Right effort
Right mindfulness
Right concentration

Hinduism and Joy

Attachment clouds the mind and the senses. The purpose of spiritual activity is to turn the mind and the senses away from the world, from the cycle of births and deaths, attachment and suffering. Therefore, cultivate detachment and liberation.[87] Then, without seeking joy, joy will come.

Discussion

The five religions value joy. Christianity, Islam, and Judaism imply that an absence of joy results from improperly applying the principles of their faith.

87 (V, Ananda, the State of Bliss or Happiness n.d.)

That there is some sort of sin in their life or lives. Buddhism and Hinduism do not advocate seeking out joy in the same way the Abrahamic religions do. Yet, they too use joy as a measure of a person or a society not properly applying the principles of their faith.

Thus, the five religions say that, when there is an absence of joy in a person, a family, a group, a society, or a nation, then something is missing. The five religions say that joy is lacking because of not applying or improperly applying the principles of their faith. If people properly applied the principles of their faith, then individuals, families, groups, societies, and nations would have joy.

Thus, the five religions say, "Apply the principles of our faith and you will have joy. Don't apply the principles of our faith and there will not be joy." They say the same idea and yet they create such different approaches to life.

✝ ✡ ☪ ☸ ॐ

Can there be joy without the five religions? Can those who do not believe the views of the five religions have joy? Can those of other religions or no faith have joy? Here are some other views:

The conclusions of a 75-year study is that good relationships keep people happier and healthier than those without good relationships: [88]

1.) Social connections are healthy. Loneliness kills. The socially connected are happier and live longer. The brain sizes of those that are lonely decrease, live shorter lives, and are not healthier.

2.) It is not the number of friends that creates joy. It is the quality of the relationships. Living in conflict is not healthy. It is worse than divorce. By age 50, those that were satisfied were the healthiest in their eighties. Those that were not satisfied were unhealthy.

---

88 (Waldinge 2016) A summary of the Harvard 75-year longitudinal study of 724 men of Harvard and additionally included poor boys in the Boston area and now studying more than 2,000 of their children. The Harvard men were sophomores in college in 1938.

3.) Being in a secure relationship protects brains. Those that cannot depend on relationships had physical brain decline and memory loss.

Most people want a quick fix. Relationships are messy and complicated. It takes a lot of work over decades. The 75-year study shows that leaning into relationships creates a healthier life. Family feuds take a terrible toll on those that hold the anger. Mark Twain said, 'There isn't time for bickering, heart burns, callings to account, etc.. The good life is built with good relationships." [89]

The possibilities are endless. Replace screen time with face to face people time.

✝☪☪☸ॐ

As screen time increases day by day, week by week, month by month, year by year, and decade by decade, face to face time decreases. Slowly, like a drying river, joy slips away. Life becomes a desert of two-dimensional, vicarious experiences and 'avatar friends. It is no longer a full life. Rather, it slowly becomes an empty, lonely life. The simple skills of face to face time wither away and for the following generations might never exist. Imagine generations of societies that are unable to communicate face to face. What kind of world will that be?

✝☪☪☸ॐ

Paraphrasing Benjamin Franklin, "The aim in life is to be happy, healthy, wealthy, and wise." What else is there to have in life? Is life worth living without joy and happiness? Yet, it is difficult to live without some amount of wealth and wisdom. With wealth one can have the necessities of life, wisdom, and health. For without basic wealth, it is exceedingly difficult to have a joyful and happy life. That is one of the reasons many people strive for wealth but not the skills to be happy, healthy, wealthy, and wise.

So, some people say, "Believe one of the five religions and you will have

---

[89] (Waldinger 2016)

happiness and joy. If not in this life, then in the next life." So, people accept that statement. They hope to be happy, if not in this life, then in the next life, which might or might not happen. For many, their proof of a next life is how they feel in this life.

✝✡☪☸🕉

To create joy in life, create the wealth that allows happiness and joy. Realize, that happiness and joy come from meaningful work, love, and relationships with others. Realize when one is unhappy. Accept it. Determine why. Decide to improve or change. If not able to improve or change, then get help and accept it. Happiness is a deeply personal individual experience. What makes one person happy and content can make another person miserable. To compare one's happiness, health, wealth, and wisdom to others creates misery.

✝✡☪☸🕉

To have joy, spread joy, love, forgiveness, share your gifts with the world, and most of all center your life around love.

Chapter 13

Love

Figure 13.1 Love is the most important activity of life.

As different as the major religions appear to be, they have similar views about love. They all believe that love is the most important activity of life. That love makes the heart sing and fills life with joy. They seem to imply that when there is despondency and depression, love is absent. In all the religions, when there is an absence of love, there is an absence of God, G-d, Allah, or positive Karma.

So, let's look at the various faiths' views of love.

Christianity and Love

Christianity seems a bit torn by love. On the one hand the Old Testament tends to view love as a set of commands. If one does not follow those commands, then one does not love God and God punishes in return. Some Christian sects view the punishment like a loving parent correcting a child. That is, the punishment is for the child's benefit. This can happen to an individual, a family, a group, a society, a nation, or even the entire planet. Usually, they refer to the commandments in the Old Testament.[90]

> God chose the Israelites as His special people because He loved them (Deuteronomy 4:37, 10:15, Isaiah 43:1-4).
>
> Hear, O Israel: The LORD our God, the LORD is one. Love the LORD your God with all your heart and with all your soul and with all your strength. (NIV, Deuteronomy 6:4-5)
>
> Show love by serving God and obeying His commands (Deuteronomy 10:12-13, Joshua 22:5).
>
> Do not seek revenge or bear a grudge against one of your people but love your neighbor as yourself. I am the LORD. (NIV, Leviticus 19:18)[91]

However, the New Testament emphasizes love is the greatest commandment; though, the wrath of God is still present. So, there is a tension as to whether salvation is by works (lovingly following the commandments). Or salvation is by grace (God is love, love God, and then joy, good works, and salvation naturally follow.

---

[90] Parts of this section incorporate the excellently stated views of Cliff Leitch. However, while including his views, my views are also mixed in. I think Clifff Leitch might agree with my statements. Not sure. Never-the-less, "Copyright © by Cliff Leitch, The Christian Bible Reference Site, www.ChristianBibleReference.org." (Leitch, What Does the Bible Say About Love? 2010)

[91] Related Verses: Genesis 24:67, 29:18-20, Deuteronomy 7:9, 1 Samuel 18:20, 2 Samuel 13:1, Psalms 31:23, Daniel 9:4

Here are some essential quotes from the New Testament about living a humble loving life:

> God is love, and all who live in love live in God, and God lives in them. (NLT, 1 John 4:16)

> Hear, O Israel, the Lord our God, the Lord is one. Love the Lord your God with all your heart and with all your soul and with all your mind and with all your strength. (NIV, Mark 12:28-30)

> Love your neighbor as yourself. (NRSV, Mark 12:31)

> All people are neighbors. (Luke 10:25-37)

> If I do not have love, I gain nothing. (NRSV, 1 Corinthians 13:3)

> ...love your enemies! If you love only those who love you, what good is that? (NLT, Matthew 5:43-48)

> Love is patient; love is kind; love is not envious or boastful or arrogant or rude. It does not insist on its own way; it is not irritable or resentful; it does not rejoice in wrongdoing but rejoices in the truth. It bears all things, believes all things, hopes all things, endures all things. Love never ends. But as for prophecies, they will come to an end; as for tongues, they will cease; as for knowledge, it will come to an end... And now faith, hope, and love abide, of these three the greatest of these is love. (NRSV, 1 Corinthians 13:4-8, 13)

Jesus expanded the scope and importance of love, saying love of God and love of fellowman are the most important of all the commandments. The apostle Paul said Christian love was the greatest and most essential of all the spiritual gifts. Throughout the New Testament, people are commanded to live in peace with all God's people (e.g., Romans 12:17-18) and commit to love and caring for others (e.g., 1 John 3:17-18). Thus, many Christian sects (for example Mennonites) believe love is quiet action in everyday life.

In the first two hundred years of Christianity, Christians were known by their love. Sixty percent of the Roman Empire were slaves, property to be bought and sold. Their masters used them for any purpose and punished them even with death. So, when Christianity preached and lived love, the slaves were attracted to a God that loved them. Tertullian, around 200 A.D. in Carthage, Africa, now Tunisia, said, 'Romans say, see how Christians love one another… how they are ready even to die for one another.'

So, there is a strong tension between various Christian sects in how to express love in oneself, one's family, groups, society, nation, the world, and with other religions.

Judaism and Love

Judaism's view of love is simple and straight forward. The two greatest commandments are:

> Thou shalt love thy neighbor as thyself. (Leviticus 19:18)[92]

> Thou shalt love the Lord thy God with all thine heart, and with all thy soul, and with all thy might. (Deuteronomy 6:5)

Love for one's spouse:

> Enjoy life with your wife, whom you love, all the days of this meaningless life that God has given you under the sun—all your meaningless days. For this is your lot in life and in your toilsome labor under the sun. (Eccl 9:9). In other words, enjoy love for what it is worth, but do not expect it to provide you with more satisfaction or fulfillment than it can. Otherwise, you will inevitably find yourself disappointed.[93]

Love means selflessly loving G-d, spouse, neighbors, gentiles, all creation

---

[92] The full quote is, "Thou shalt not avenge, nor bear any grudge against the children of thy people, but thou shalt love thy neighbor as thyself. "And a near duplicate, "The stranger that dwelleth with you shall be unto you as one born among you, and thou shalt love him as thyself; for ye were strangers in the land of Egypt." (Leviticus 19:34)

[93] (R. J. Maroof 2010)

such as the earth, animals, and plants. For some sects it means when terrible things happen, then G-d is correcting the person, the group or Judaism with love. For some sects, the Holocaust happened because G-d was correcting Jews for not following the commandments. However, other Jewish sects vigorously debate that point. Jewish laws apply to Jews, gentiles, animals, and the earth.[94]

Islam and Love

In Islam there is only belief if one loves; if one does not love, then one cannot believe. Only with belief and love can one enter paradise.[95] However, one must love Allah more than one loves anyone or anything.[96]

Because Allah loves, he creates mates for all people; therefore, it is good to marry and to love each other.[97] They are to fulfill each other's emotional, financial, physical, and sexual needs. If they have desires for others, then they are to hurry home so that their spouse can satisfy them.

Because of love, believers are of one body; thus, when one part of the body aches, the whole body feels it. Therefore, out of love for Allah and to enter Paradise:

Communicate love in words and actions.

Spend wealth for the poor and never feel hatred nor ill will towards anyone.

Believe in God, the Last Day, angels, Scripture, and the prophets.

Give away some wealth to relatives, orphans, the needy, travelers, and beggars, thus liberating those in debt and bondage.

Pray and pay the prescribed alms.

---

94 © Copyright 5756-5771 (1995-2011) (T. R. Rich 1995-201)) The summary text was modied.

95 Quran, 10:62

96 Quran 2:165

97 Quran 30:21

Be steadfast in misfortune, adversity, and danger.

Keep your promises.[98]

Buddhism and Love

In Buddhism, "Love is without attachment."

Love refers to the wish that everyone be free of suffering.

For many people, the everyday experience of love includes pain and suffering.

Worldly love is possessive and binds people with fixation and attachment. Love frees from fixation and attachment.

Love cannot exist in isolation. Love is connection with family, friends, coworkers, society, the world, and the earth. But to develop love, diminish fixations and attachments particularly those limited to family and friends.

Love and compassion include those perceived as unlikable, unlovable, untrustworthy, and enemies.

Recognize karmic connections with people that exist over many lifetimes.

When there are friends and enemies, there will be attachment to some and hatred towards others. The more protective of friends, then the more hatred towards enemies.

To avoid suffering practice loving kindness without attachment.[99]

---

98 Qur'an 2:177

99 Quotes from a speech by His Holiness Kayalwang Karmapa (Karmapa 2016)

Hinduism and Love

Hindus believe that, "God is love."[100] It is an all-encompassing love for people, animals, plants, and the earth. Love and pleasure are important purposes of life to include the magic of erotica preserved in the ancient doctrines for thousands of years. Such love creates a harmonious and happy family between the spouses and their children.[101]

Love extends beyond the family to all living creatures. Selflessly love all creatures with compassion. Be patient, contented, loyal, and free from hatred.[102] However, first is God's love and loving God.

Those that do well in life is because of actions in their in past lives. They serve as models for those in the lower castes. Because of past transgressions, the lower castes suffer in their current life. However, with right love to others, good works and attitudes, the lower castes can do better in their next life. That is why Hinduism firmly embeds the caste system in the social hierarchy.

Discussion

All five religions say to love yourself, your neighbor, life, and the world. They say, "God is love."

The Trouble with Love

Yet, people have trouble with love. If it is so basic a part of humans and agreed upon by religions, why are billions of people struggling with love? Christians would say because of free will to sin. Judaism would say that it is not following the covenants and the laws. Islam would say that it is a lack of faith in Allah. Buddhism says there is too much attachment to loving a person or thing; of not letting the person or thing be what it is. Hinduism says it is not loving all creatures and not letting God's love be foremost in life.

---

100 (Wikipedia 2017)

101 (Shakya n.d.)

102 From a Hindu scripture the Bhagavad-Gita (Gita, Xii. B, 14) per (Shakya n.d.)

Thus, the five religions say that individuals have trouble with love because they do not do what the sacred texts, institution, traditions, reason, law, and clergy say. However, the failure of billions of people to fully love is a failure of the religious leadership, the fundamentals of the five religions, or both. When an organization fails, it fails because of the leadership not the people.

The Absence of Love

The five religions imply that whenever one person causes discomfort, pain or suffering to another person, there is the absence of love. This would include lies, fibs, making fun, gossiping, stealing, giving unfair advantage to some, prejudice, demeaning comments or actions, etc. In a broader sense the absence of love includes denying the opportunity for happiness, health, wealth, and wisdom.

Is there an absence of love when there is anger in politics? When one religious side is determined to have its' view to be the law of the land? Yet, how can the various sects of the religions claim love and know God's will while the political laws they want are different than the laws the other sects want? Why is it that, if they all believe in God or at least some form of God, there is so much dissension, hostility and anger? Where is the love in this?

Two forces are at work. One is deeply personal and the other political.

With the deeply personal, it seems as if people love for what they can get out of the love. One loves another with the purpose of getting money, sex, power, and personal satisfaction. If so, then the love is not about loving another; rather, love is about satisfying oneself and one's needs. With the deeply political love, it seems as if people want their views imposed upon others to satisfy a lust for power and getting the world to conform to their views. Yet, how do they know they are right?

Love God, G-d, Allah, Buddha, or Hindu God for a Reward?

It seems that in the five religions loving God is to ensure that the next life is either in paradise or at least better than this life. One rarely loves God just to love God. That is not love. It is manipulative love.

Would billions of people love God if there was no reward?

Doesn't an all knowing, all powerful God or Karmic action know what lurks in the hearts of people that profess a love that is just wanting a better afterlife? That really, the people don't care about God; but rather, the people care about what God or Karma has to offer? Why not love God, Karma, and others with no expectation of any reward? What would that be like? Why not love the deities even if there is no afterlife nor a better next life?

If people love God, G-d, Allah, or Karma only for the afterlife, then they are ignorant as to what love is. They do not know how to love oneself, family, social groups, work, society, nations, and the physical things close and far away. This is a fault of their leadership – the clergy. Yet, the clergy will vociferously deny this. However, their results are clear in local, regional and world politics of never-ending confrontations and wars. The clergy cause confrontations by commission and omission of their actions.

There is something deeper going on that has nothing to do with God, nor God's love, nor the love of people for one another. At the root of the religious politics is the desire for power. Power by the clergy and many of the adherents. Power is intoxicating and supplies a lot of satisfaction. Yet, as previously said, the five religions in principle have similar views of love. There are some differences. Yet, those differences are not so great that they should tear their religions and political systems apart.

Love in the five religions means creating societies with laws that help people to love one another. The laws, the politics, the economic, and political structures would encourage people to pursue happiness, health, wealth, and wisdom. Rather it appears that sects in the five religions either try to pass laws that they believe please their God, or they quietly distance themselves from engagement in politics. Some sects quietly do work without expectation of reward or power. Yet, it seems that none of the five religions encourage the political will to create societies where people can be happy, healthy, wealthy, and wise in this life.

The fault lies in the inability, ignorance, or unwillingness of the clergy in the five religions to teach and practice what love is. Instead the clergy, political, and business leaders work for their selfish aims. It is clever and smart politics. The clergy see an opportunity to further enhance their views in society by supporting politicians and business leaders; who then use the clergy to implement laws with little if any cost. Thus, the clergy of the five religions, the politicians and the business leaders corrupt each other. In this vicious cycle it is the absence of love which hurts the masses.

Giving love in the expectation of a reward is manipulation. It is not love.

The absence of love is sin or bad Karma.

So, what is love and sex?

Chapter 14

Sex

Figure 14.1 Sexual desire is one of the most basic, misunderstood, and manipulated drives of life.

In general, the five religions consider sex as proper and healthy within marriage and prohibit it outside of marriage. There are varying degrees of tolerance about premarital and extramarital sex. However, there are some sects of the five religions that consider sex an evil.

Christianity and Sex

Most Christian sects tend to view sex as a natural and normal function only in marriage. Premarital sex and adultery are either prohibited or frowned upon. Officially, the Catholic Church and some denominations view sex as only for creating children. Sex used for any other purpose is sinful.

The Catholic Church and Conservative sects view sex as only in marriage and between one man and one woman. That to have, or to even think of, sex outside of marriage is a sin against God's holy order, and abstinence is the best action. If one cannot abstain, then get married. The only sexual education in schools is abstinence; because, even the mentioning of birth control, sexual diseases, abortion, sexual anatomy, and sexual practices encourages promiscuity, sin, and out of wedlock pregnancies. Society is to avoid every kind of pornography, masturbation, movie, literature, pictures, talk, provocative dress, and thought that even hints of sex outside of marriage or to have lustful desire other than for a spouse. The Catholic Church and some fundamentalists sects teach that sex is only for making babies and sex for pleasure is a sin.

Some sects of Christianity view all sexual activity as sinful. Their ideal is not to have sexual desires; if one cannot be celibate, then get married. Also, few if any denominations, are literal about Jesus' admonition to cut off body parts that cause one to sexually sin (Matthew 5:29-30 and 18:8-9). No Christian has advocated making it a lawful punishment to remove body parts for sexual crimes.

Liberal churches emphasize the spiritual and relational aspects of sex and strongly suggest avoiding premarital sex. In the schools they tend to advocate teaching healthy sexual practices. Yet, they are not as verbal nor as strongly against the practices as Conservatives are. They also tend to be more accepting of homosexuality, abortion, and contraception.

Judaism and Sex[103]

Judaism is positive about sex and considers it a divine gift and a holy obligation — both for the purposes of procreation and for pleasure and intimacy. A husband must be intimate with his wife and must sexually satisfy her. But Judaism discourages celibacy, even for those devoted to the spiritual life. Judaism is broadly permissive when it comes to sex in marriage. The same is not true for sexual activity outside of a committed relationship.

Orthodox Jews forbid premarital sex. Many ultra-Orthodox communities are

[103] Extracted from "Judaism and Sex: Questions and Answers" (MJL Staff 2018)

stringent about separating males and females in large part to reduce the likelihood of romantic encounters between the unmarried. Liberal Jews reserve sex for marriage. Reform rabbis dropped references to marriage as the only context for sexual activity; yet, they continue to urge fidelity and exclusivity in sexual relations. They consider extramarital affairs — whether conducted in secret or with a spouse's consent — as sinful and forbidden.

Both the Reform and Conservative movements have affirmed that their attitude toward sexual ethics applies equally to heterosexual and homosexual relationships.

Traditionally, there are prohibitions against male masturbation. Some sects consider spilling seed needlessly is the same as murder. The Talmud considers male masturbation as adultery with one's hand. Some authorities prohibit female masturbation based on lustful thoughts; while other rabbis see no problem with women masturbating.

The liberal sects have a more accepting approach. Some sects consider it is unreasonable to expect complete abstention from all sexual pleasure until one's wedding night. In part to avoid such choices, some Orthodox communities encourage young people to marry by their early 20s, if not earlier.

Traditional Jewish law opposes pornography. They avoid looking at a woman's finger or her clothes to avoid sinful thoughts and actions and ban pornography.[104] Some rabbis view pornography as a grave threat to the morality of people and to family stability

Many rabbis are permissive about sexual activity between husband and wife such as using pornography, fellatio, sex toys, and manuals. Other rabbis are against some or all such activities.

The current prevailing view is that a man may do with his wife as he wishes, provided that he has her consent. Few rabbis are concerned about spilled semen. Some rabbis forbid staring at a woman's genitals. Other rabbis allow a

---

104 "Tzitzit, the Fringes on the Prayer Shawl" (MJL Staff 2018) & (MJL Staff 2018)

man to kiss any limb of his wife's body that he wishes.

Islam and Sex

In Islam sex and marriage are in complete harmony with human nature. The Qur'an and the Prophet state:[105]

- The literal legal term for marriage is sexual intercourse.
- Sexual urge is God's command.
- Marriage shows God's power and blessings
- Marriage is an act of virtue:
- Even in poverty people should get married.
- It is in no way associated with evil, guilt or sin
- It helps reach spiritual perfection. It protects Muslims from sin and worship.
- It is not just a platonic relationship between husband and wife
- Monasticism and celibacy are unacceptable
- Sex is not just for procreation
- To meet Allah in purity, then he should meet Him with a wife.
- In Paradise nothing is more desirable than sex.
- When attracted to a woman, hurry to the wife.

Islam does not suppress sexual urges. Instead it promotes sexual fulfillment in a responsible, nurturing, and lawful way.

Fulfill sexual desires, without harming nor destroying oneself and not at the expense of the rights of others.

Thus, in Islamic societies there is no sexual suppression and no need for a sexual revolution.

However, some sects equate women to Satan[106]:

---

105 Extracts from, "Chapter Two: The Islamic Sexual Morality (1) Its Foundation", (Rizvi 2018)

106 Extracts from, "Chapter Two: The Islamic Sexual Morality (1) Its Foundation", (Rizvi 2018)

The Prophet said, "When the woman comes towards you, it is Satan who is approaching you. When one of you sees a woman and he feels attracted to her, he should hurry to his wife. With her, it would be the same as with the other one."

Thus, some sects believe that:

Sexually active women are a distraction and thus a danger to the social order.

There should be no emotional investment in women; that is, a man should have no love for his wife.

Devote love, emotional investment and attention to Allah alone in the form of knowledge-seeking, meditation, and prayer.

Use women to provide the Muslim nation with offspring and quenching the tensions of the sexual instinct.

Buddhism and Sex[107]

The happiest situation is when sexual activity is an expression of love within a committed relationship. A healthy sex life can lovingly bind two people together for many years. It is often a barometer for the emotional well-being of the partners. It can be a motivation to let go of unnecessary negativity and be the reward for letting go. A mutually satisfying sex life is sharing, trust, acceptance, and understanding.

Being with someone who loves what the other loves is a basis for an enduring relationship. Sharing creates the deepest bonds.

Intercourse with people who are committed to another partner, or who are

---
[107] The unknown author of the blog states in the About section or introduction to the blog, "… it seems to me that the most helpful thing I can offer others is a clear description of the ethical teachings of the Buddha. There are scores of highly qualified meditation teachers, and many, many books about the various techniques. But there is very little written about the behavioral trainings the Buddha encouraged, and hardly anything directed at 21st century, "first-world" readers. So – here it is." (https://buddhasadvice.wordpress.com/about-this-blog-and-me/) (Unknown 2018)

vulnerable in some way, is a betrayal of trust and harms those involved. Even flirting harms. The most common way is leading someone on. The pretender gives an insincere commitment, or none, and takes advantage of hopes and desires.

Sex is an impersonal force. It is a force that just flows through us and uses the most wonderful and inspiring emotions for its own ends, which are totally concerned with the continuance of species. The idea that it is just a private and wonderful thing between people is merely a part of our general illusion.

Key to seeing this great illusion is knowing when sexual desire distorts feelings. Sex can be a mindfulness exercise. It is an invitation to closely see actions and motivations as they happen. Before being in a situation think seriously about what would happen weeks and months later. Will everyone be happy, and no one hurt? If a desire to confess an attraction to an inappropriate person arises, just wait and breathe until the urge passes.

Appreciate the wholesomeness in current sexual and non-sexual relationships. Broaden the idea of sensual energy to include all the energies exchanged with others. Non-sexual relationships can be close and have significant, wholesome elements in them. Notice how speech, thought, and simply being present with someone is a means of exchanging energy. These are all non-sexual ways to interact with others that can express and build intimacy, trust, and love.

Hinduism and Sex[108]

Sexual union beautifully draws husband and wife together for procreation. Hinduism does not legislate sexual matters. Though it offers guidance.

Sexual intercourse is a natural reproductive function, a part of the instinctive nature, and its pleasures draw man and woman together to conceive a child. Intimacy expresses love and nurture. It is love which endows sexual intercourse with its higher qualities, transforming it from an animal function to

---

108 "Dancing with Siva, Hinduism's Contemporary Catechism" pages 89-90, (Subramuniyaswami 2003)

human fulfillment, subject to community laws and customs. The scriptures state, "May all the divine powers together with the waters join our two hearts in one!"

Wisdom restricts sexual intercourse to marriage. Marriages that are between a virgin man and a virgin woman are the truest and strongest, seldom ending in separation or divorce. This is because their psychic nerve currents, grow together and they form one body and one mind. Conversely, if the man or woman has had intercourse before the marriage, the emotional-psychic closeness of the marriage will suffer, and this in proportion to the extent of promiscuity.

Each partner should grow to understand the other's needs and take care to neither deny intercourse nor make excessive demands and keep a healthy, unrepressed attitude. Instruct boys and girls to value and protect their chastity as a sacred treasure, and to save the special gift of intimacy for their spouse. Teach them the importance of loyalty in marriage and to avoid even the thought of adultery.

Discussion

Very broadly, the five religions advocate to varying degrees that sex is for marriage and they differ in the details. Some sects say that there must be punishment for lust, while other sects want punishment only for sexual assault. Some sects say that sex is only for marriage, while some sects are more open. Some sects say that the soul enters the sperm, some say that life begins at conception, while others say life begins at birth. Some sects say LGBTQ, prostitution, free sex, and pornography are against nature, while other sects say that is normal.

Lust and Punishment

The Christian Bible has strong words about sex. A rarely implemented punishment for illicit sex in Christianity, Judaism and Islam is:

> If a man commits adultery with another man's wife—with the wife of his neighbor—both the adulterer and the adulteress must be put to death. (Lev 20:10)

Yet, neither Judaism nor Western cultures kill nor torture adulterers. However, Jesus said:

> Do not think that I have come to abolish the Law or the Prophets; I have not come to abolish them but to fulfill them. I tell you the truth, until heaven and earth disappear, not the smallest letter, not the least stroke of a pen, will by any means disappear from the Law until everything is accomplished. (NIV, Matthew 5:17–18)

That statement is clear that the law still pertains until heaven and earth disappear. Thus, all the laws in the Old Testament hold for Christians today. Yet, there is an argument that Jesus did away with all the ceremonial actions and focused on the heart and the mind. That leaves a muddle for the average person particularly about sexual urges.

One very thoughtful response is:

> Jesus did not abolish the moral and ethical laws that had been in effect from the time of Moses. He affirmed and expanded upon those principles, but He said obedience must be from the heart (attitudes and intentions) rather than just technical observance of the letter of the law (Matthew 5:21-44). [109]

This agrees with St Paul:

> [16] Do you not know that he who unites himself with a prostitute is one with her in body? For it is said, "The two will become one flesh."

---

[109] This is one of the best most thoughtful commentaries on the topic of Jesus fulfilling the law and doing away with parts of the law. If you want more detail, see http://www.christianbiblereference.org/Copyright.htm (Leitch, What Does the Bible Say About the Old Testament Law? 1996-2014) "Copyright © by Cliff Leitch, The Christian Bible Reference Site, www.ChristianBibleReference.org. Used by permission."

¹⁷ But he who unites himself with the Lord is one with him in spirit. ¹⁸ Flee from sexual immorality. All other sins a man commits are outside his body, but he who sins sexually sins against his own body. ¹⁹ Do you not know that your body is a temple of the Holy Spirit, who is in you, whom you have received from God? You are not your own; ²⁰ you were bought at a price. Therefore, honor God with your body. (1 Cor 6:16-20)

⁹ But if they cannot control themselves, they should marry, for it is better to marry than to burn with passion. (1 Cor 7:9)

So, sexual desire outside of marriage is a sin. If one lusts, then get married. Therefore, Catholic priests and nuns that lust should get married. Also, how does Paul know that the body is a temple of the Holy Spirit? Paul states:

⁴ The wife does not have authority over her own body, but the husband does and likewise also the husband does not have authority over his own body, but the wife does. ⁵ Stop depriving one another, except by agreement for a time that you may devote yourselves to prayer, and come together again lest Satan tempt you because of your lack of self-control. (1 Cor 7:4-5)

Thus, Jesus did not get rid of the Old Testament laws nor change them. He was noticeably clear about cutting off body parts that cause one to sin.:

²⁷ You have heard that it was said, 'Do not commit adultery. ²⁸ But I tell you that anyone who looks at a woman lustfully has already committed adultery with her in his heart. ²⁹ If your right eye causes you to sin, gouge it out and throw it away. It is better for you to lose one part of your body than for your whole body to be thrown into hell. ³⁰ And if your right hand causes you to sin, cut it off and throw it away. It is better for you to lose one part of your body than for your whole body to go into hell. ³¹ It has been said, 'Anyone who divorces his wife must give her a certificate of divorce. ³² But I tell you that anyone

who divorces his wife, except for marital unfaithfulness, causes her to become an adulteress, and anyone who marries the divorced woman commits adultery." (Mat 5:27-32 NIV)

And if your hand or your foot causes you to sin, cut it off and throw it away. It is better for you to enter life crippled or lame than with two hands or two feet to be thrown into the eternal fire. [9] And if your eye causes you to sin, tear it out and throw it away. It is better for you to enter life with one eye than with two eyes to be thrown into the hell of fire. (Mat 18:8–9).

Not one fundamentalist Christian minister nor Catholic priest convicted of sexual crimes or who has had lustful thoughts has cutoff their penis and scrotum, gouged out their eyes nor cut off their hands. Perhaps if they genuinely believed what Jesus said they would cut off their offending parts. Not one of the them advocate legal punishment against rapists, voyeurs and any form of sex crime should be gouging out perpetrators' eyes, cutting off their offending sex organs and hands. Perhaps if they honestly believed what Jesus said they would cut off those parts. Not one of them advocate for their followers or themselves to legally or illegally cutoff the body parts of adolescents, adults, priests, and nuns that have lustful thoughts outside of marriage, take part in pornography, commit sexual crimes, etc. Not one.

Yet, both conservative and liberal churches are silent on these specific passages. Though many follow Jesus' directive and advocate against divorce and adultery.

Some Islamic sects while quoting Qur'anic texts encourage and demand stoning those that violate sexual laws. Similarly, Jesus did not tell a crowd of men that were about to stone an adulteress not to stone her. Instead, he said, "Let he who is without sin, cast the first stone." That is not a strong argument against stoning. It is an argument that only the sexually sinless should stone her. Is Jesus advocating that churches and society should use stoning?

Perhaps the Pope who gleefully said, "I never ever had a lustful thought," [110] should stone those in adultery.

Oddly, Jewish rabbis seem to be silent about killing men and women for adultery (Leviticus 20:10).

Sexual Urges and Marriage

However, many Christian clergy do carefully address sexual urges. Fundamentalists say wait till marriage and keep sex only in the marriage. Liberal clergy vary tremendously in their guidance. Most say that sexual urges are to be in marriage; yet, they tend to be more lenient than their fundamentalist counterparts.

The omnipotent Christian God clearly knew that Adam and Eve would give into temptation after eating the fruit and then have sexual lusts. The Christian God knew that millennia later Jesus would say that if one gives into the temptation of lust, that they should gouge out their eyes, cut off their hands and cut off their genitalia. Why?

Why did the deities of the five religions create sexual curiosity in children, lust in adolescents and adults, and then claim it is all a sin or bad Karma? What kind of a deity does that and then the answer is to get married? Instead, why didn't the deities of the five religions create humans with a desire for marriage and then only in marriage would the partners have lust for each other? It seems as if the deities created a system designed for most people to fail, and that God, G-d, Allah, or Karmic action will punish people in this life, in the next life, and possibly both in this life and the next life.

However, many devotees have said, "Well, I can resist the temptation. So, others should and can do also. Therefore, they should also wait to have sex

---

110 I read the statement or something similar in a biography of perhaps Pope John XXIII or another Pope some sixty years ago. It made a deep impression. That is an impression of why God would bless people with sexual desire and then call it lust and sinful if one exercised that desire. Then I wondered why would a Pope consider it wonderful that he never had a sexual desire.

till they are married!" Though they seem to be angry when saying so.

The soul enters the body at …

A few priests and fundamentalist ministers have quietly said to me, "The sperm contains a human soul. So, by having sex for pleasure means that one is killing thousands of souls which is against God's will."

Naively, I asked about the rhythm method where a woman determines when she is ready to have a baby by taking her temperature. "So, then it is ok to have sex only near those few days when the female is ready to have a baby and murder the unused sperms? But to have sex when a woman is ready to make a baby is murdering all the sperm? Seems as if over a lifetime, that the average male murders more sperm and their souls than Hitler, Stalin, etc. ever murdered."

"Anyway, where do the souls go? Immediately to heaven? Hell? Get recycled? Get reincarnated?"

"How and when does the soul enter the sperm? Or is there one soul lurking in the scrotum ready to jump into the sperm that will successfully implant into the female's egg? Are souls flitting around searching for likable parents? Then at the moment of conception entering the female egg?"

"Is that why having sex for enjoyment only is considered sinful because it is murder?"

"How do you know any of this?"

By that time the various priests or fundamentalist ministers were irate and stormed off. Catholic priests would mumble, "Just accept Catholic Doctrine and you won't have these issues." Fundamentalists would pronounce, "Just accept Jesus and you won't have these issues."

That is a tough sell, telling males that their sperm holds millions of souls.

Therefore, only use sperm to make babies. Otherwise males would be committing genocide on a larger scale than Hitler, Stalin, and others. Thus today, the idea that the soul is in the sperm has fallen out of favor. Neither the sperm nor the egg now has a soul. So, since there are no souls in the sperm, there is no sin in having sex just for pleasure.

Now, the dominant conservative concept is that the soul mysteriously enters the egg at the precise moment that the sperm enters the egg. That is not provable and is an assumption and easier to sell to men and women. This way, sex does not kill millions of souls.

The mysteriousness of the soul entering the egg at the precise moment the sperm enters the egg is fascinating. When a couple is having sex, is there a soul lingering around the egg ready to join the lucky sperm? Perhaps there are several souls lingering around in case there will be twins, triplets, etc. How do the souls know when to show up? Or are they always hovering around women's eggs? If the women don't give birth to all those eggs, is that a sin? Apparently not, since there are no souls in the eggs. What happens to all those souls hanging around to be born, yet never get a chance to be born? Do they go to heaven, hell, purgatory or cease to exist? Do they move on to other women?

Many Christians believe that at the moment of conception, whether inside a woman or in a test tube, God created a complete human. Therefore, it is murder to have an abortion. They also believe that all humans have souls. Therefore, the soul mysteriously appears at the moment of conception. Did God create the soul at that moment or were souls hanging around waiting to be born? Either way, at that moment of conception, the baby or fetus is sinful. Its' nature is sinful at that very moment. It has not done anything. Yet, it is sinful. What kind of a God makes such a creation? However, there is no proof for any of this logic nor proof for any of the answers.

But if a human soul becomes a human at the moment of conception then doesn't that mean that there is no sin if there is no conception and no abortion. Therefore, it is OK to have premarital or extra marital sex?

Homosexuality, Prostitution, Free Sex, Pornography

The five religions in general are against homosexuality, prostitution, free sex, and pornography. It violates their sense of religion or nature's order. However, sizable portions of their devotees quietly indulge themselves. Some feel it is a natural inclination. Some because they have sexual drives and no other outlets or just don't have the skills or believe they are attractive enough. Some because they are too lazy or afraid to try the traditional views of the five religions.

The five religions in general condemn these practices yet few offer helpful guidance except to stop and to get married to one of the opposite sex. In general, in all five faiths, sexual taboos are implicit and strong. Though many followers being mortal humans go their own ways.

Sex in the Afterlife

The five religions view sex as a powerful force and place a lot of attention on it. All basically advocate sexual activity within marriage. So, do couples have sex in the afterlife? If married multiple times, do they have sex with multiple partners? Is there free love in the afterlife? Why when most of humanity loves sex, wouldn't there be sex activity in the afterlife?

Some Christian sects believe that there are neither male and female in heaven (Galatians 3:28) and thus there is no sex in heaven. However, some sects say that is a fundamental misunderstanding of God's order; thus, there are male and female in heaven and there is sex in heaven.

Islam is particularly clear that, "In Paradise nothing is more desirable than sex." Perhaps that is why so many jihadists are willing to quickly go to Paradise instead of living to old age.

Judaism, Buddhism, and Hinduism appear to be quiet about sex in the afterlife.

The Sexual Ideal of the Five Religions

The Christian, Jewish, Islamic, Buddhist, and Hindu ideal for sexual activity and desire is in a loving marriage. And yet, sexual pain, suffering, and evil is prevalent in the world.

So, what is the character of God, G-d, Allah, Buddha, or Hindu gods to create such a system of sexual pain, suffering, and evil, and then blame humans for their problems? What is the character of such a deity or deities?

Chapter 15

God's Character

Figure 15.1 God's character is enigmatic and debated for millennia

The Abrahamic religions (Christianity, Islam and Judaism) have similar yet different concepts of God. Buddhism does not portray God as an entity. Hinduism has gods and a vast set of lesser deities.

In general, the Abrahamic religions believe that the one God is omnipotent, all-powerful, all-knowing, all-good / benevolent, judgmental, and all present. That means that God knows the past, present, and future. God can do anything including suspend the so-called laws of nature. Thus, God can intervene in human affairs to stop the earth from rotating, raise the dead at will, create revelations to one or a few people that no one else experiences, etc. The three religions will not agree on all their points; but in general, their concept of God in a very general sense is similar. Obviously, they differ about the Trinity.

In Buddhism and Hinduism, there are forces that one works with. Use the forces wisely and there are benefits. Use the forces unwisely, then there are hurtful consequences. In Buddhism the forces are impersonal; while

Hinduism personalizes the various forces as deities.

Christianity and God's Character

The Old and the New Testaments describe God's character.

The Old Testament states God is jealous:

> You shall not worship other gods or serve them; for I, the LORD your God, am a jealous God, visiting the iniquity of the fathers on the children, on the third and the fourth generations of those who hate Me, Exodus 20:5

> --for you shall not worship any other god, for the LORD, whose name is Jealous, is a jealous God—Exodus 34:14

> For the LORD your God is a consuming fire, a jealous God. Deuteronomy 4:24

> So, watch yourselves, that you do not forget the covenant of the LORD your God which He made with you, and make for yourselves a graven image in the form of anything against which the LORD your God has commanded you. "For the LORD your God is a consuming fire, a jealous God. Deuteronomy 4:23-24

> They made Him jealous with strange gods; With abominations they provoked Him to anger. Deuteronomy 32:16

> You shall not worship them or serve them; for I, the LORD your God, am a jealous God, visiting the iniquity of the fathers on the children, and on the third and the fourth generations of those who hate Me, Deuteronomy 5:9

> ...for the LORD your God in the midst of you is a jealous God; otherwise the anger of the LORD your God will be kindled against you, and He will wipe you off the face of the earth. Deuteronomy 6:15

> Then Joshua said to the people, "You will not be able to serve the LORD, for He is a holy God He is a jealous God; He will not forgive your transgression or your sins." Joshua 24:19

> How long, O LORD? Will You be angry forever? Will Your jealousy burn like fire? Psalm 79:5

> For they provoked Him with their high places And aroused His jealousy with their graven images. Psalm 78:58

God is compassionate, merciful and slow to anger:

> And he passed in front of Moses, proclaiming, "The LORD, the LORD, the compassionate and gracious God, slow to anger, abounding in love and faithfulness. (Exodus 34:6 NIV)

> The Lord is your God, for he is gracious and compassionate, slow to anger and abounding in love, and he relents from sending calamity. (Joel 2:13 NIV)

> ...you are a gracious and compassionate God, slow to anger and abounding in love, a God who relents from sending calamity. (Jonah 4:2 NIV)

There are more characteristics[111]:

> All-wise, All Knowing – (Isaiah 40:28)
> Sovereign – (Isaiah 46:9)
> Holy – (Psalm 78:41)
> Jealous – For I am a jealous God (Exodus 20:5)
> The way, the truth, and the light – (John 14:6)
> Trinity – (Not explicitly stated in the Bible.)
> Faithful – (1 Cor 1:9)
> Love – God is love (John 3:16 and 1 John 4)
> Loving – (Romans 5:8)

---

111 (Attributes of God 2018)

Eternal – (Hebrews 13:8)

Never changes – (Numbers 23:19 plus dozens more)

Perfect – (Romans 12:2)

Just – (Revelations 6:17)

Merciful – (Romans 5:8)

Truth – (John 14:6-7)

Grace – (John 1:14)

A very central doctrine of Christianity is the Lordship of Jesus. Typically, this means that Jesus is very God of very God, begotten not made, is of one substance with God, will come to judge the living and the dead. Thus, He is THE Lord and all people should worship and commune with Him daily.

"He that hath seen me hath seen the Father." (John 14:9)

"All things have been committed to me by my Father. No one knows the Son except the Father, and no one knows the Father except the Son and those to whom the Son chooses to reveal him." (Matt 11:27)

"And Jesus came and said to them, "All authority in heaven and on earth has been given to me. Go therefore and disciple all nations baptizing them in the name of the Father and the Son and the Holy Spirit, teaching them to observe everything I have commanded you." (Matt 28:19)[112]

"For although they knew God, they neither glorified him as God nor gave thanks to him, but their thinking became futile and their foolish hearts were darkened." (Rom 1:21)

"[1] In the beginning was the Word, and the Word was with God, and

---

[112] There is some disagreement among scholars that Matt 28:19 was modified at a later date to reflect the Trinitarian concept. There exist no documents to directly prove such a hypothesis. Also, there is no proof that the Emperor Constantine modified the phrase from "…baptizing them in my name…" to "baptizing them in the name of he Father and the Son and the Holy Spirit…" to become a Trinitarian formula. The reader is invited to search the internet for further discussions of this verse.

the Word was God. ² He was with God in the beginning. ³ Through him all things were made; without him nothing was made that has been made. ⁴ In him was life, and that life was the light of all mankind. ⁵ The light shines in the darkness, and the darkness has not overcome it. …¹⁴ The Word became flesh and made his dwelling among us. We have seen his glory, the glory of the one and only Son, who came from the Father, full of grace and truth.

¹⁶ Out of his fullness we have all received grace in place of grace already given. ¹⁷ For the law was given through Moses; grace and truth came through Jesus Christ. ¹⁸ No one has ever seen God, but the one and only Son, who is himself God and is in closest relationship with the Father, has made him known…²⁴

"²⁷ Then he said to Thomas, "Put your finger here; see my hands. Reach out your hand and put it into my side. Stop doubting and believe. ²⁸ Thomas said to him, "My Lord and my God!" (John 20:27-28)

Christianity has a strong concept of Messiah from Judaism. Christians passionately believe that Jesus is the Messiah because he fulfilled prophecies in the Old Testament with verification in the New Testament. Jesus as the Messiah will return to usher in the Messianic Age, known as the Second Coming. Then all Jews will gather in Israel, the Temple will be rebuilt in Jerusalem, and there will be world peace. However, Judaism completely disagrees with using the Old Testament in such a manner. The arguments and logic of Jesus as Messiah, the related events, and Judaism's disagreement are beyond the scope of this book.[113]

God loved humans so much that he created them with freewill to experience and create love, life, happiness, pain, suffering, and evil. People are free to choose what they want. That is, they are free within the bounds of their

---

113 There are multiple on-line and hard copy analyses supporting and some contra to Jesus as the Messiah.

society. Their society is free to create what the society wants. Though in most cases people choose corruption, greed and self-centeredness. God gives them that choice out of love for humanity. Thus, it is because of the choices they have made that condemns them to hell. If they choose to love and honor God, then God will love and honor them by giving them eternal life.

Judaism and God's Character[114]

The characteristics of God from the Jewish Scriptures (the Old Testament) are listed above and are not repeated here.

In general, Judaism views the existence of G-d as a prerequisite for the existence of the universe. The existence of the universe is proof of the existence of G-d.

There is only one G-d, which is indivisible, described by attributes that are nor male nor female. Showing G-d in physical form is idolatry and forbidden and references of G-d as a body are a figure of speech.

G-d is everywhere and sees all that people do. Is the G-d of all nations, not just the Jews.

G-d can do anything and has reasons for allowing good and evil to occur.

G-d knows all things, past, present and future including all thoughts.

Everyone is a child of G-d.

Judaism believes that the Messiah will come, gather all Jews in Israel, rebuild the Temple in Jerusalem, and create world peace. However, the Messiah is not Jesus. The arguments and logic of the related events, and Christianity's disagreement are beyond the scope of this book.[115]

---

114 (T. R. Rich, The Nature of G-d 2011)

115 There are multiple on-line and hard copy analyses supporting and some contra to Jesus as the Messiah.

Islam and God's Character

Islamic view of God's character is similar to the Christian and Jewish views. Islam has over a hundred descriptions for Allah. A few are:[116]

- The creator of all
- The King – Dominion and no imperfection
- The Holy – pure from any imperfection
- The Source of Peace
- The Mighty - The Strong, The Defeater
- The Compassionate – has mercy to believers and blasphemers
- The Compeller – nothing happens without his will
- The Subduer – overcomes anything
- The All-knowing – nothing is absent from His knowledge
- The Judge
- The Gracious – kind to His slaves
- The Grateful – gives a lot of reward for a little obedience
- The Responsive – answers if asked and rescues if called upon
- The Loving – loves and is merciful to believing slaves that love Him
- The Creator of Death – makes the living dead
- The Governor – owns and manages things
- The Source of Goodness – is kind, supportive, protective, and is merciful
- The Avenger – prevails over enemies and punishes them for their sins
- The Pardoner – forgives broadly
- The Gatherer – gathers the creatures on the Day of Judgment
- The Everlasting – non-existence is impossible for Him
- The Patient – does not quickly punish the sinners.

---

116 (jannah.org 2018) Abstracted from Islam 101.

Buddhism and God's Character

Buddhism rejects the notion of a Supreme God. Buddha is not a god; rather, Buddha is a supremely enlightened human teacher who has come to his last birth in the Buddhist cycle of existence.

Buddhism is a mental discipline of escape from the worldly ills. Buddha is more interested in personal salvation, to improve mankind in this world and in the worlds to come than about a deity's existence or character.

Liberating mankind means shedding delusions. One of the delusions is the existence of God. A person that is deluded by the existence of a deity is not able to follow the Buddhist path. So, a correct understanding of all the ramifications of the God-idea is essential for progressing along the Buddhist path to total liberation. [117]

Hinduism and God's Character

Hindus have a broad range of beliefs about God's character. For some, formless reality is God; others accept God as personal Lord and Creator. Some Hindus believe that God is female, while others believe that God is male, and still other believe that God has no gender because that is an aspect of physical bodies. However, in general, Hindus believe that God is transcendent, in all things, is the creator and the creation. God is not remote but is within all as the essence of everything.[118]

Hinduism has a large pantheon of divinities. For example, one of the most popular is the elephant-faced Lord Ganesh, who brings luck, power, and protection; thus, it is common to see his statue in stores, in front of buildings, and entrances to temples. Although Ganesh places obstacles to enhance the devotees learning and growth.[119]

---

117 (Gunasekara 1997)

118 (Hindupedia 2009)

119 (Newlyn 2017)

There are gods for a variety of activities and powers. A few examples are gods of yoga, learning, art, music, wealth and culture, health, and harvest.

Discussion

Interestingly, the above descriptions of four of the five religions view of God, G-d, Allah, and Hindu gods are remarkably similar except for the Christian Trinitarian view. With such similarities one would think that four of the five religions would figure out a way to come together. Yet, they don't.

Just and loving?

In the Biblical narrative, God created a beautiful, nice, and pleasant world. Then Adam and Eve ate a forbidden fruit. They gained knowledge of good and evil. Knowledge that God and Satan had. God kicked them out of the Garden of Eden, forcing them and billions of their descendants to misery, pain, disease, war, famine, poverty, slavery, etc. Just for the actions of two people?

Many Christian believers say God was just to kick Adam and Eve out of the Garden because they disobeyed God's command not to eat of the fruit. If they hadn't eaten of the fruit, then they would have remained in the Garden and billions of people would not have suffered for thousands of years and be sent to hell.

Is this a model of a forgiving, just, and loving God? Is this a model for parenting and governing groups, societies, and nations? It is hard to believe so.

On the other hand, liberals avoid the issue by saying that the story is not history; rather, it is just a story of God's creation and man's propensity to sin. Meanwhile love God and make the world better.

True believer and suffering

In another Biblical story, God tests Abraham by commanding him to kill his son Isaac as a sacrifice. Was that for Abraham or Isaac's sins? When Abraham lifts the knife high in the air ready to thrust it into his son, an angel suddenly informs Abraham to stop. Abraham passed the test. So, God blesses Abraham with generations of descendants.

Today, if someone heard an angel say, "Sacrifice your child," that person would not be honored as faithful by sacrificing the child. The medical community and societies would label the person insane. However, that story is not much different than the people who kill in the name of Christianity, Islam, Judaism, Buddhism, or Hinduism.

A Pope was suffering before dying, and said his suffering made him closer to God and Christ. Is the Pope saying that God's character is such that to get closer to God, one must suffer as Christ suffered? If so, people should have been happy that the Pope was suffering. They should be dancing in the streets to know that God was purifying the Pope and that he was on the way to being with Christ. People should also be happy that God is purifying everyone that suffers during life, just before dying, and after death. After all, that is God lovingly correcting his devotees.

So, Jews and Muslims have a similar view of suffering.

Apparently then suffering from diseases, abuse, poverty, war, famine, and many other types of suffering brings people closer to God, G-d, or Allah. If so, then people should rejoice in the suffering of others. They could happily point to them saying, "That person is becoming closer to God, G-d, or Allah. Yeah for that person." So, the Palestinians suffer because they are not pleasing God by simply giving up their land to the Israelis. The people of Aleppo suffer because they are not giving up their land to Assad.

God or G-d is a jealous God (Exodus 20:5 and 34:14). So, God is jealous yesterday, today, and tomorrow. Thus, He both allows and makes people suffer through disease, abuse, poverty, war, famine, etc. Therefore, whenever there is pain, suffering, or evil, consider what was done to make God or G-d jealous.

Why would God, G-d, or Allah of the infinite universe be jealous of the actions of tiny humans? That feels more like a tyrannical dictator that watches over every little action of its' subjects and then severely punishing the slightest little offense. This is like a loving parent, allowing a child to suffer the consequences of actions. However, what loving parent would allow a child to suffer brutal consequences and consequences that can last a lifetime or even eternal damnation?

God uses suffering like a tyrant or a loving deity?

Many people follow their deity's will and suffer. While many others did follow God's will and prospered. So, which is it? Follow and still suffer or follow and prosper? Could be both. There is no guarantee. Seems like God, G-d, Allah, Karma, or Hindu Gods are fickle. But many people believe that their deity or Karma works in mysterious ways. They trust and fear that the deity or Karma will be nice to them. That is like a tyrant being arbitrarily nice and wicked. The reward will be in the next life. So be nice now for a better future in the afterlife.

Was the devastation of WWI, WWII, the Cold War, genocides in Rwanda, Sudan, Cambodia, Laos, etc. a result of God's jealousy, absence, uncaring, punishment, etc.? Was the fall of Constantinople by the Muslim army on May 29, 1453 because God punished Christians or was Allah blessing Muslims for their true faith? Or perhaps both? Or was it just a more powerful army defeating a weaker city?

Or, does God, G-d, Allah, Karma, and Hindu gods use suffering as a loving parent chastises a child, or a boss disciplines an employee? The five religions would say that their deity is a loving parent and not a tyrant. Yet, their deity does nothing to effectively stop pain, suffering, and evil in this world. Instead the deity will fully act for humans in the afterlife – if the humans are good enough, or pass the test, or, or, or.

Basic Trust

Why did God give humans freewill? To tempt people? To allow humans to torture, maim, kill, steal, etc.? To reward those that don't displease God with a wonderful afterlife? What is the character of God, G-d, Allah, the creator of Karmic action, and/or Hindu gods to allow such suffering?

Yet, Christians, Muslims, Jews, Buddhists, and Hindus believe variations of just trusting their deity. One does not know if one will have a blissful afterlife as compared to eternal suffering. That is pure trust in a deity's Judgment. Live a life as best as one can and then perhaps the next life will be eternally wondrous or horrible. That ambivalence seems like the characteristics of a fickle tyrant.

So, just believe and trust the doctrines of the five religions and all will be well – perhaps.

Proof?

How does one know or prove that statements made by the five religions between 1,400 to 5,000 years ago about God's character are true? Just accept statements in the various scriptures, or traditions, or by clergy, or by reasoning? If so, that is a leap of faith. Even if one says that the variations in the five religions are simply different understandings of some power greater than what humans can understand it is still a leap of faith.

Are there experiments to prove some of the deities' characteristics? Or, does one just trust and accept whatever the five religions say about their deity or deities?

When seeing what people create with their effort and lives, one understands their character. Thus, look at the world as the handiwork of God, G-d, Allah, or Karmic action, or a Hindu god. So, these deities created blessings, happiness, joy, pain, suffering, evil, and eternal torture. The deity wants the world that way because the world is that way. This is the same as builders

CHAPTER 15 - GOD'S CHARACTER

creating faulty structures. The builders are responsible for what they created. They might blame those that use the structures to absolve themselves. But ultimately, the designer is at fault. Thus, it is the character of God, G-d, Allah, and that which created Karmic action that is responsible for pain, suffering, and evil in both this world and the afterlife.

Even when discussing these issues, the typical two responses are:

> Have a personal encounter with the divine. Then you will know in your heart. Just accept the divine into your life.

> The original sacred texts are literal and inerrant. Therefore, the doctrines are true.

Yet, what is the proof? How does one know those statements are reality? One doesn't. It is a leap of faith.

For instance, how to prove the doctrine of the Trinity? If one makes a leap of faith that the Bible is literal and inerrant, then there is a convoluted proof of the Trinity. But why, if it is so important to the Christian faith, is the proof convoluted? For believers, the process is obvious. But for the non-believers, the proof is reading conclusions into the Bible that really aren't there. Why didn't God make the Trinity so clear that there is no question? No question from the time of the cave man till now all around the world? No question by all the five religions? Why reveal that basic character so late in human existence? For conservatives it would be the last 2,000 years of a 6,000-year-old universe. For liberals that would be 2,000 years of 200,000 years of human existence or of 4,500,000 years of the earth's existence.

One response is that the scriptures of the five religions are not for the non-believers. The scriptures are for the believers. That is circular reasoning. Also, the scriptures of the five religions are not to convince the non-believers; instead the scriptures are for the believers.

How does one prove that Christian, Jewish, Muslim, Buddhist, and Hindu statements about God and the universe are true? Especially when Muslims and other sects are prohibited from questioning.

How does one prove that the statements in the Jewish Testament about God's character are true?

How does one prove that the statements in the teachings of the universe by the compassionate Buddha are true?

How does one prove that the statements in the Hindu literature about the many Gods and spirits are true?

If the five religions' statements about the supernatural character are all true, then what kind of supernatural character is there? Perhaps combine all the various attributes of the five religions together. If all but one of the religions are in error, then how does one decide which is true? Run experiments? Study all the religions? Make a leap of faith like Billy Graham and then charge on with life? Walk away from all religion because an all-knowing deity would have been clearer about revealing what is true? Or, pray daily and commune with what appears to be a deity. Then claim proof when the desired result happens? But when the prayers are not answered, claim that the deity has a greater purpose in mind? Or, just feel the presence of the divine and know in one's heart that a faith or sect is true?

Freewill

What is the character of God, G-d, Allah, the creator of Karmic action, and the Hindu gods that create a world that allows free will and then clobbers people for inappropriately or ignorantly exercising free will? Then forgives them if they are contrite enough and love one of the deities back enough? Finally, gives them eternal blissful in life only if they love the deity enough or have great Karma. Those that don't love the deity enough go to hell to suffer for eternity. Though some religions state that there are multiple incarnations until one has reached a state that God or a force finds acceptable. Some sects believe that God created an afterlife for those that love him, and for those that don't there is nothing - one just ceases to exist.

The five religions have similar and differing views of God's character. Do they also have similar and differing views of experiencing God?

Chapter 16

Experiencing God

Figure 16.1 People experience their God in nature, meditation, groups, and many other ways.

Devotees of the Five Religions experience God, G-d, Allah, Karma and Hindu gods in similar yet separate ways.

Christianity and Experiencing God

A popular song reflects a common Christian experience:

1. I come to the garden alone,
While the dew is still on the roses,
And the voice I hear falling on my ear
The Son of God discloses.

Refrain:
And He walks with me, and He talks with me,
And He tells me I am His own;
And the joy we share as we tarry there,
None other has ever known.

2. He speaks, and the sound of His voice

> Is so sweet the birds hush their singing,
> And the melody that He gave to me
> Within my heart is ringing.
>
> 3. I'd stay in the garden with Him,
> Though the night around me be falling,
> But He bids me go; through the voice of woe
> His voice to me is calling.[120]

The hymn gives a warm reassuring feeling of a personal God that personally cares and feels for people. A God that one can call on without concern about criticism. A God that will counsel and recommend. A God that responds just by asking. Hymn books of many denominations convey that sense of warmth and reassurance.

This painting conveys what millions of Christians sense. [121]

Figure 16.2 "Jesus at your heart's door."

Jesus is constantly gently knocking at one's door. All one must do is open the door and invite him in. Jesus will not force himself into one's heart. Just open the door – the door to your heart – and you will have eternal life. It is that simple. Don't open the door, then the loving Jesus condemns the person to hell for all eternity. Several hundred people, both conservative and liberal, explain their encounter with Jesus as:

- He appeared to me.
- I just know it was Him.

---

120 (Miles 1913) "In the Garden" Also, in https://creativecommons.org/licenses/by-sa/3.0/

121 (Geissler 1802-1872) I stand at your door and knock

- When in prayer, I know He is there.
- The Bible says so.
- There are so many books that give testimony.
- In Holy Communion, I feel the presence of Jesus.
- I had a near death experience and met Jesus in the light.
- I knew it was Jesus when He saved me on xyz date and time.
- I came forward at altar call and Jesus saved me.
- I just know that He is my personal Lord and Savior!
- Look at the books that have been written!
- Don't be logical. Just believe and you will see. You can't understand. Just accept.
- Who are you to doubt two thousand years of Church testimony?
- Don't pay attention to the scholars. They just make things up.
- Why do you even care? Just let people believe what they want. It makes them happy.
- You are of the devil. Get out of here.
- I don't want to think about it. I might be wrong and go to hell. This way I win even if I am wrong.

Judaism and Experiencing G-d

Many describe experiencing G-d as:

> The presence of G-d? Yes, I remember... I was on a hike, walking in nature." She stretched her arms out, her voice tone changed, there was softness in her eyes, as she continued. "It felt like: I love the whole world so much, that I want to hug all of it in my arms. Everything is good. Everything is so peaceful, so quiet. What could ever be wrong? I was crying and laughing at the same time." [122]

There are times when a spiritual experience can dawn on us as a surprise, a complete gift. Such moments can envelop us with a sense of

---

122 (Nachman, Rabbi 2014)

blissful euphoria even during our most mundane chores or activities.

G-d is an immanent—an immediate and felt presence. G-d is in every encounter, in each experience, and in every aspect of the world.

The Creator is here right now and wishes to give you everything that you need for your spiritual growth. People feel: [123]

- Safe
- Protected
- Harmonious
- Loved
- Fantastic
- Happy
- Able to do anything

So, relax and think about the Creator being right here, right now. "What am I supposed to see when I think about G-d?" The answer is "nothing." On one hand, it is impossible to see the Creator, and on the other hand, everything that exists is a manifestation of the Creator. Just focus on the Creator's presence here and now. [124]

Martin Buber describes two kinds of relationships with the divine as the "I-It and the "I-Thou": [125]

The I-It relationship is… detachment from others … in which one uses another as an object.

In the I-Thou relationship, each person fully and equally turns toward the other with openness and ethical engagement…characterized by dialogue and by (being totally present with concern) for the other person.

G-d is the "Eternal Thou." G-d is the only Thou which can never become an

---

123 (Svirsky n.d.)

124 (Svirsky n.d.)

125 (Beit-Halachmi n.d.)

It. ... in a genuine relationship with G-d, G-d is not a means towards an end.

One meets G-d through other human beings and natural events. "Meet the world with the fullness of your being and you shall meet G-d …."

Islam and Experiencing Allah

For a Muslim:

> Love of God causes one to enjoy life more fully and to know that God is the only non-changing reality and Truth. To love Allah, one must have faith. It is a decision to worship that which is unseen and un-seeable in this life.
>
> Developing love for God begins with worship, prayer, and meditation. Then one with reverence becomes a seeker of God's Greatness.
>
> Love of God brings out the best and benefits others. Out of love for God, the Muslim will do everything, from waking moment to sleep, courageously battling lower desires to please her/his lord and sacrificing what she/he is in possession of for the sake of the Beloved. [126]

Buddhism and Experiencing ...

Buddhists tend to say that:

> Profound absorption in meditation can bring about a deepening and widening, a brightening and intensifying of consciousness, accompanied by a transporting feeling of rapture and bliss.
>
> After rising from deep meditative absorption, view the impermanency, liability to suffering, and absence of an abiding ego or eternal substance to achieve liberating insight. By developing that skill, there will not be uncontrolled emotions and thoughts, nor interpretations not called for by facts.

---

126 (Green 2015)

Experiences are evidence for the existence of a personal God or an impersonal godhead.

The spiritual is ... directed ... towards a state utterly transcending this world. (There is no) absolute separation between the beyond and the here and now (so) aim at the highest realization in this present existence (to make) this world a better place to live in.

The law of cause and effect accepts survival, not of an eternal soul, but of a mental process subject to renewed becoming. By one's efforts, there is no suffering and there is the eradication of greed, hatred, and delusion.[127]

Hinduism and Experiencing Gods

Because Hinduism is so broad, it is a bit difficult to describe how a billion adherents experience God. In general, Hindus accept almost all paths to experiencing God or Gods. Each person is free to find a way that suits them. It could be devotion, meditation, yoga, service, withdrawal, etc.[128]

The key is devotional worship. While education is helpful, it is not necessary to experience God or Gods. What is important is to believe in God, see God in the eyes of others, spend time in devotion, meditation,[129] and be ready to receive. Yet, it is helpful to be with likeminded people, gurus, and listen to lectures. Uneducated people experience God; so, education is not necessary even though that helps. However, for most people it is best to have a skilled teacher that guides the follower to spiritual liberation.[130]

---

127 (Thera 2013)

128 (Hindupedia 2009)

129 (Himilayan Academy, Saiva Siddhanta Theological Seminary at Kauai's Hindu Monastery n.d.)

130 (Himilayan Academy, Saiva Siddhanta Theological Seminary at Kauai's Hindu Monastery n.d.)

Discussion

The above statements sound like the same experience. Since the experience seems the same, then perhaps the experience is the same. If people of different religions have the same experience with the divine, then perhaps they are all experiencing the same divinity. That God, G-d, Allah, Karmic action, and the Hindu gods are different terms by frail humans separated by thousands of years, differing cultures, world views, and language structures to describe the same deity.

If so, then it might be possible for the many different religions to become tolerant of each other. Perhaps the many different religions can work together to create a happy, healthy, wealthy and wise world that benefits all of humankind.

Perhaps it not that difficult. Just be willing to be tolerant; and then, be tolerant. But, how does one be tolerant when the various religions insist that their world view dominate the political power of their nation and the world? That their experience of their deity trumps all other experiences and thus is the right one?

The answer lies in the desires of the conservative and liberal clergy of the many religions. If they push for, practice, teach, and live tolerant lives then eventually their followers will do likewise. But, if they preach that their view is the only right view, then there will continue to be divisiveness and the world will not be a better place. The world is facing issues that need unified, healthy actions. Instead, the clergy of the world are creating divisions based upon their interpretations of experiencing their deity, personal lust for power, and fear their sect will ostracize them.

Nevertheless, believers in their religions have what they call experiences that confirm their beliefs. The intellectual arguments or discussions do not convince people to believe. Though the arguments or discussions can convince people not to believe. The believers will read or hear this or that argument in support of their faith and will nod and continue believing. If they do not understand the argument or have some doubts about the argument, they will quietly push it aside. Or, they will say something like, "Many brilliant minds have wrestled with these questions for thousands of years. Who am I do to doubt their arguments and lose my faith? So, I will just accept what they say about God."

Thus, it is the experience of God that creates believers. For example, people are in a religious setting. The music is playing. A cleric gives an inspiring message and the audience feels inspired. There is artwork or no artwork in the setting. The group has a shared experience they name spiritual. Some people talk with their religious entity and they receive responses. Some pray for a healing for themselvhes or a loved one who, perhaps, gets better. Some feel the presence of past relatives, fond memories, and many traditions going back decades and millennia. All this convinces people to accept one of the five major religions.

Then there are non-religious settings when people become convinced that a deity was active in their life. Some ask their parking angel to find a parking place in a huge crowded parking lot. A car suddenly pulls out creating a space. They are convinced of divine intervention. When experiencing pain, suffering, and evil, like wars, they see their deity active and stay convinced in their faith. Some call that experience the absence of the divine or the divine's way of punishing while believing that humans don't understand.

✝ ✡ ☪ ☸ ॐ

Non-believers state that most of what people experience as God's presence is a pleasant feeling, or a coincidence, or the work of someone else like a doctor in healing.

Nevertheless, people are having an experience what they might call as Jesus, the Holy Spirit, G-d, Allah, Buddha, a Hindu god, or a spirit, or a force. Is it one of those or something else? How does one prove that the encounter is more than some psychological experience?

Clearly, there is an experience of something. Perhaps it is like the earlier European explorers mapping the world. The early maps were crude and the best representations that technology and understandings could provide.[131] Perhaps more tools, skills, financing and unbiased interest to research what people are experiencing will add clarity. For the believers of the five religions, experiencing God is core to their religion. It could be that God, in some form as represented by each religion, quietly knocking at the devotee's door. Could be. How does one know that the experience of God is hormonal, or dreaming, or something else?

Responses by the faithful typically are:

- Who are you to doubt two thousand years of Church testimony?
- Who are you to doubt over a thousand years of Muslim testimony and history?
- Who are you to doubt six thousand years of Jewish testimony and history?
- Who are you to doubt thousands of years of Buddhist testimony and history?
- Who are you to doubt thousands of years of Hindu testimony and history?
- Perhaps the five religions should willingly and enthusiastically fund research of, "The Experience of God" to better understand:
- What six billion people are experiencing.
- What drives part of their politics, world view, economics and

---

131 (Vesconte 1321) Pietro Vesconte's world map of 1321 is crude; yet, there is a sense of becoming accurate..

ideology.
- How to enhance world health.

So, the people of the five religions have similar and different experiences God, G-d, Allah, Karma, and Hindu gods. So, are their descriptions of the afterlife similar and yet different?

Chapter 17

Afterlife

Figure 17.1 The five religions have similar and different views of the afterlife.

A driving force in the five religions is the afterlife. Many devotees look forward with joy, some with fear, and some with doubt, to their afterlife experience. They hope for a pleasant afterlife. Yet many people fear eternal punishment or a worse next life. The purpose of funerals in the five religions is to reinforce belief in the five religions and to provide comfort.

Christianity and Afterlife

Many committed Christians have said, 'If the resurrection never happened, my faith is in vain. My whole reason for existence is the resurrection. It causes me to rise enthusiastically in the morning and labor all day.'[132] For them the resurrection is the core of one's belief, world view, and identity. Without the resurrection, life is meaningless.

The scriptural basis for everlasting life is:

> For God so loved the world that he gave his one and only Son, that whoever believes in him shall not perish but have eternal

---
[132] Quoted with slight variations from many lay Christians, pastors, priests, seminary professors, and two seminary presidents'

life. (John 3:16 NIV)

Whoever believes in the Son has eternal life, but whoever rejects the Son will not see life, for God's wrath remains on them. (John 3:36)

But whoever drinks the water I give them will never thirst. Indeed, the water I give them will become in them a spring of water welling up to eternal life. (John 4:14 NIV)

Very truly I tell you, whoever hears my word and believes him who sent me has eternal life and will not be judged but has crossed over from death to life. (John 5:24 NIV)

I give them eternal life, and they shall never perish; no one will snatch them out of my hand. (John 10:28 NIV)

Now this is eternal life: that they know you, the only true God, and Jesus Christ, whom you have sent. (John 17:3 NIV)

The world and its desires pass away, but whoever does the will of God lives forever. (1 John 2:17)

I write these things to you who believe in the name of the Son of God so that you may know that you have eternal life. (1 John 5:13 NIV)

For the wages of sin is death, but the gift of God is eternal life in Christ Jesus our Lord. (Romans 6:23 NIV)

But for that very reason I was shown mercy so that in me, the worst of sinners, Christ Jesus might display his immense patience as an example for those who would believe in him and receive eternal life. (1 Timothy 1:16)

Whoever sows to please their flesh, from the flesh will reap destruction; whoever sows to please the Spirit, from the Spirit will reap eternal life. (Galatians 6:8 NIV)

So that, just as sin reigned in death, so also grace might reign through righteousness to bring eternal life through Jesus Christ our Lord. (Romans 5:21 NIV)

[18] A certain ruler asked him, "Good teacher, what must I do to inherit eternal life?" [29] Jesus said, "no one who has left home or wife or brothers or sisters or parents or children for the sake of the kingdom of God [30] will fail to receive many times as much in this age, and in the age to come eternal life." (Luke 18:18 & 29 NIV)

People want assurance that doing the right things will grant them eternal life. Yet, the assurances are words written almost two thousand years ago. Today preachers quote the words to provide their followers with the assurance that whatever miserable or happy lives they have today, that there will be a happy afterlife. Some clergy will qualify the statement that the believer must believe the right dogmas, then they too will have a happy afterlife. Some clergy demand that they must absolve all sins just prior to the believer's death; otherwise, the person will go to hell or purgatory.

There are lay people, professors, and clergy who claim afterlife experiences. Some claim that they communicated with a loved one. Some say that they met Jesus or the Virgin Mary. Some say that a loved one died and within a few moments, they experienced the presence of the dead person. Then they felt the dead person leave.

One professor conducted double blind experiments with mediums who communicated with dead relatives of their subject. He used this as proof that there is an afterlife. Furthermore, he said that it might be possible to do further experiments to find souls that have passed on to find out how to cure illnesses. Though not said, it might even be possible to get the hosts of angels and afterlife people to help mortals here now to end war, suffering, and evil.[133]

The purpose of a Christian funeral is to provide comfort for the bereaved, reinforce belief in the afterlife, persuade unbelievers to believe, and to honor those that have died.

Judaism and Afterlife

Judaism is ambiguous about an afterlife.[134] A few groups believe that there is a resurrection of the body that unites with the imperishable soul. Reformed Jews tend to believe in the immortality of the soul; while the Orthodox Jews tend to believe that in the resurrection the body will unite with the soul.[135]

The Jewish Bible says little about the afterlife. Daniel 12:2 implies that after the resurrection there will be a day of judgment. Those judged favorably will live forever and those judged as wicked will suffer eternally. G-d will destroy those souls who G-d judges neither favorably nor unfavorably. Thus, those souls will not experience an afterlife. Isaiah 25-26 also implies a resurrection.

Various authorities in the past millennia have written that the resurrection will occur during the messianic age, others say at the end of the age, and others just say the soul will continue. They tend to say these events will happen with the creation of the full state of Israel and the rebuilding of the Temple. That is why some want to create now the full State of Israel, which is the current State of Israel and the Palestinian Territory. It includes rebuilding now the Temple on the Temple Mount and making Jerusalem the capital of the full State of Israel.

Some sages discussed doing virtuous actions just to do virtuous actions or

---

133 (Schwartz 2002) I don't remember the page number. It was perhaps the last chapter.

134 (MJL Staff n.d.)

135 (MJL Staff n.d.)

for the result. If believers felt they were not capable of doing enough virtuous actions then they might give up and ask, "Why do virtuous actions if there is no reward?"

Therefore, a highly respected Medieval scholar, Maimonides wrote, "Therefore, in order that the multitude stay faithful and do the commandments, it was permitted to tell them that they might hope for a reward and to warn them against transgressions out of fear of punishment." In time, they might awaken to truth and serve God out of love. The hope is that people will eventually become virtuous out of love for others, their community, and the world, without regard for a reward.[136]

The funeral is to honor the dead and comfort the bereaved. There is no viewing of the body prior to burial. Burial allows the body to decompose naturally and takes place as soon as possible after death.

Islam and Afterlife

Islam believes that there should be harmony between the love of this world and the love of God. If there is any conflict between the two, then love of God takes precedence. Keeping this balance ensures that the believer will have a blessed afterlife. Not keeping the balance means eternal chastisement.[137] Thus, this earthly life is a test. Those that pass the test go to heaven. Those who fail go to hell. On the last day, there will be both reward and penalty for the deeds done.[138] The reward will be ten times for virtuous deeds and the penalty

---

136 (Arkush, Immortality: Belief in a Bodiless Existence - Everlasting life was not always guaranteed to the Jewish soul. n.d.)

137 Extracts from, "Chapter Two: The Islamic Sexual Morality (1) Its Foundation", (Rizvi 2018)

138 (Shakir, M.H. 2004 9th U.S. Edition) Surah 99, page 628, "6 On that day men shall come forth in sundry bodies that they may be shown their works. 7. So, he has done an atom's weight of good shall see it. 8. And he who done an atom's weight of evil shall see it. "

onetime for evil deeds.[139] For unbelievers, there is eternal hell.[140]

The funeral is to honor the dead, comfort the bereaved, and remind the faithful of Allah's mercy. Within two days of death, four men carry the body to the graveyard. A procession of relatives and friends follow. There is no open casket. The buried body faces Mecca.

Buddhism and Afterlife

Buddhism does not believe in the soul as a permanent entity of a personality that exists on earth. The entity of the person dissolves into nirvana (eternal bliss) or reincarnates. To stop the eternal cycle of reincarnation, avoid desire, and identity.

Buddhism believes that the sum of one's virtuous deeds and bad determines the next life. If the virtuous deeds outweigh the bad deeds, then there will be a better life. If the bad outweighs the virtuous deeds, then a worse next life and one relearns life lessons.

Buddhists and Hindus views of Karma are remarkably similar.

The funeral has prayer, meditation, and chanting. Cremation releases the soul from the physical form.

Hinduism and Afterlife

Death is a natural set of cycles of birth and rebirth because souls are immortal and imperishable. With each new life the soul can learn needed lessons. What

---

139 (Shakir, M.H. 2004 9th U.S. Edition) Surah 6 # 160, page 134 "Whoever brings a good deed, he shall have ten like it, and whoever brings an evil deed, he shall be recompensed only with the like of it, and they shall not be dealt with unjustly.

140 (Shakir, M.H. 2004 9th U.S. Edition) Shurah 17 #10, page 261 "…those who do not believe in the hereafter, We have prepared for them a painful chastisement."

one does in this life decides what will happen in the next life. The sum of the activities in this life determines whether the next life is suffering, better, or bliss.[141] The Karmic effect depends upon the sincerity, intent, and righteousness of the action as well as the chosen means.[142] One reaches a better afterlife through discipline, guidance from a guru, and the grace of God.[143]

Here are some examples, to create good Karma:

- Don't hurt anyone.
- Do unto others only what you want done to yourself.
- Do those actions that bring happiness to oneself and does good to others.
- Do not speak harshly.
- Wish only good for others.
- Do not hesitate to take up weapons to protect oneself or others.[144]

While Karma certainly is the major factor in deciding what happens after death, there are several other factors. For instance, what one thinks at the instant of death can significantly affect the next life. So, thinking of family, one will be born again into that family. Thinking of money, one might become a banker, a financier, money changer, merchant, a poor person, etc. When one thinks of God at the instant of death then one goes to a much higher place.

Also, what one is doing at the instant of death has a considerable influence. Soldiers killed in battle will be with other soldiers. Those that are doing charitable deeds will be better off. Those that die during a religious activity will go to a higher world.

---

141 (V, Death and Afterlife in Hinduism n.d.)

142 (Khandavalli n.d.)

143 (V, Death and Afterlife in Hinduism n.d.)

144 (Khandavalli n.d.)

Liberating oneself from desire moves one to bliss.

When children properly perform the rituals, then the departed will quickly move on to the next world. However, if they do not, then the soul waits. Then of course God might choose to move a soul to eternal bliss, perhaps because of a particular action.

There are troubled souls who have not moved on. They search for humans with unclean hearts and habits. However, good souls are in the vicinity of religious activities.

Cremation releases the soul to the proper place for further learning. A sacred river like the Ganges, which purifies sins, receives the ashes. Because death pollutes the family and visitors, they stay away from others until the family and visitors perform purification rituals.[145]

To reach a better afterlife, one needs discipline, guidance from a guru, and the grace of God.[146]

Discussion

Certainty of an afterlife.

The five religions have a belief in some form of an afterlife. It is based upon scriptures, traditions, institution, clergy, reasoning, and perceived experiences. Five or six billion people now living and billions who have died, all claim there is an afterlife. They differ on the details; but they claim there is one. Thus, one might conclude that, because there have been and there are billions of people believing there is an afterlife, there must be an afterlife.

However, just because billions of people believe something doesn't make it true. That just means that billions of people believe in something. In this case, they believe in some form of afterlife.

---

145 (V, Death and Afterlife in Hinduism n.d.)

146 (V, Death and Afterlife in Hinduism n.d.)

How do so many people know that the afterlife of some sort is reality? How do they know that, when their body dies, they do not completely cease to exist? Some say that there will be a bodily resurrection. Others say that their deity resurrects only the soul. Some followers say that it is and will be possible to recognize the departed loved one; others say that is not possible. Others say that the resurrection of the soul occurs around the time of death. Others say that when their body dies, they completely cease to exist. For all these statements there are no reliable proof one way or another.

Some people claim to have died and have come back to life. They describe what it is like on 'the other side.' While they might be describing immediate life after death, they might also be describing the decaying brain functions that have not died but are not registering on instruments. The typical definition of death is flatline of brain waves. While that is the standard, there is some thought that the brain continues to function for a while as it continues to die. Therefore, it is possible for people to experience sensations after the brain flatlines. Then the person is brought back to life and people feel they have experienced life after death; when in reality they have experienced sensations past the point of a flat lined brain and before the brain and body has fully died.

Believers rely on the Christian, Muslim, Jewish, Buddhist, and Hindu scriptures, traditions, reasoning and experiences that are one to five thousand years old in cultures, world views, language structures and science that are vastly different than now to prove that there is life after death. However, those are not proofs. Nevertheless, the five religions take their views as solid, unmovable rocks, true for all eternity. Their devotees view those that have strong solid faith with great honor.

Yet, there is no verifiable proof. But that is why people also call religion, "Faith."

If there is free will in heaven,
can souls fall out of heaven or karmic bliss?

In heaven, will souls have free will and thus fall out of heaven? If not, then why here on earth? What force, reason, or need did a deity have to create beings to worship and love it? Then if the beings don't love it, God, G-d, Allah, or Karmic action condemns them to suffer or to recycle until they learn. Does this also mean, that Christians, Muslims and Jews that fall out of heaven have another chance to go back to heaven? If so, this seems like Karma. Does it ever end? Does that cycle of going to and falling out of heaven last eternally, with some souls progressing for a while and then falling back to some sort of hell? What happens when the universe as humans now think it will be, ceases to exist? Does the cycle of souls going to heaven and some falling back stop, or does it continue in a different form?

This description feels like Karma. If so, the five religions are describing the same process of Karma.

✝︎✡︎☪︎☸︎ॐ

Conservative Christians consider Satan to be a fallen angel. Which implies there is temptation in heaven like on earth. Thus, there appears to be free will in heaven as on earth. Thus, souls did and, perhaps, continue to fall out of heaven. People today that go to heaven might not stay there. If so, people trying to live pure holy lives on earth might again suffer temptation in heaven, as on earth, and then fall out of heaven. Therefore, there is no guarantee of eternal bliss in heaven.

Similarly, in Nirvana or Karmic bliss. If there is free will in Nirvana or Karmic bliss, then souls or entities can fall back to a lower plain.

Or perhaps there is no free will in heaven or Nirvana. If so, then why have free will on earth that God, G-d, or Allah condemns people to eternal damnation? Or for believers in Karmic action that they continue eternally on a path towards or away from enlightenment?

In the future, does God or Allah destroy Satan and all evil? If so, why not now instead of condemning billions to eternal damnation? In the future will all souls or entities reach Nirvana or karmic bliss?

If Christian, Jewish, and Muslim souls can fall out of heaven or paradise, where will they go? Back to earth? Where will they go ten billion years after the earth, the sun and the solar system no longer exist?

Can Satan and other fallen angels repent and return to heaven? If so, can the souls of dead humans repent and then go to heaven? That would mean one can sin, sin, sin, go to hell, repent, and then go to heaven. Therefore, righteous Christians, Jews, and Muslims could happily meet Hitler, Pol Pot, Stalin, Roman Emperors, etc. in heaven. They would all rejoice since all will be forgiven.

But, since they all have free will in heaven, they could fall out of heaven to start the process all over again. Then it appears that the Abrahamic religions are close to reincarnation like the Buddhists and Hindus.

People reincarnated as animals, bugs, microbes, etc. experience Karma. That means they experience life based upon past lives. So, to progress to a higher state, they must learn. Which implies that animals, bugs, microbes, etc. have free will. Maybe some Buddhists and Hindus come back as some form of Christian, Jew, or Muslim…. After which they might come back as a Buddhist or Hindu or something else….

Does this also mean, that Christians, Muslims, and Jews that fall out of heaven have another chance to go back to heaven? If so, this seems like Karma. Does it ever end? Does that cycle of going to and falling out of heaven last eternally, with some souls progressing for a while and then falling back to some sort of hell? What happens when the universe as humans now think it will be, ceases to exist? Does the cycle of souls going to heaven and some falling back stop, or does it continue in a different form?

These descriptions feel like Karma. If so, the five religions are describing a similar afterlife

Karmic action for societies?

Karma is the sum of one's actions and highly determines if the next life is painful, suffering, filled with evil, or that is happier, or even blissful in Nirvana. If one sums up all people's lives and then looks at societies, then are the people in those societies the result of past lives? Therefore, one might conclude that a society that increases good Karma increases the happiness and wellbeing of society. A society that increases bad Karma decreases the happiness and wellbeing of society.

If so, people should not be interested in alleviating poverty, pain, suffering, evil, etc. here in this lifetime. Instead, all people should be concerned about creating societies focusing upon creating good karma. When most everyone has good karma, then the next experiences on this world will be better. Within sixty years entire societies should improve.

But, for thousands of years many societies wallow in pain, suffering, and evil, so it appears that people are not making much progress towards improvements. Thus, the religious, political, and business leaders are failing their societies.

Fear

Quite a few people physically shake with fear at the thought of being dead.[147] They dread it. Fear it. That is normal. But, they also fear abandoning their faith because then they might go to hell. They don't want to suffer in the next life. So, they won't think that the dogma of their Christian, Muslim, Jewish, Buddhist, or Hindu cleric might be wrong. They hope it is right and refuse to consider any other alternative. They greedily grasp at their faith for the reward they hope to get. Their clergy consider this great faith.

While the fear of death is normal, it is a lack of trust in God, G-d, Allah, or the Karmic process. If one trusted their deity to be fair, loving and considerate, then whatever decision deity would make would be fair, loving, and

---

[147] Based upon my conversations with over a hundred people about being dying and being dead.

considerate. To be afraid about the decision is normal; yet, it means that the person with the fear shows a lack of trust in their deity. If one was not good enough, then one was not. If one sinned, then one sinned. The five religions have various rituals, prayers and actions for the forgiveness of sins or to improve one's Karma. But then the cycle of sinning or creating bad Karma continues. The fear lingers, and the devotee is stuck wondering if the next world will be nice or not.

Another way of considering this is that people want a quid pro quo. If they live a holy life, confessing sins, believing certain doctrines, going to services regularly, praying unceasingly, and other actions, then they will have a happy eternal life or better reincarnated next life. Yet, there is no guarantee. How do they really know? They might go to a better afterlife; perhaps not. Perhaps all their virtuous deeds, prayers, wishes, and hopes will make no difference in reaching a happy afterlife. There is no proof that working one's way to a happier afterlife happens.

Usually when discussing such questions, people have said, "Well, then I may as well do what I really want and screw around a lot. Then in the latter part of my life, I will repent and get my reward in heaven. I will just concern myself with me, me, me. To heck with everyone else. Life is all about me in the here and now. God or the entity will take care of the rest. There is no surety of an afterlife (or improving Karma). So, why be virtuous? If my spouse does not treat me well or my child doesn't do what I say or people around me don't do what I want, then I will throw them out."

Seems hard hearted. But that is a reason some religious people advocate teaching that, upon death, there is a judgment which determines the next experience. The basic feeling is that, if people don't fear the judgment, then they won't be good. That they will have selfish animal like behavior, which will hurt themselves, their family, friends, society, nation, and perhaps even the world.

So, the five religions use scriptures, traditions, reasoning, and perceived experiences as proofs that there is eternal life. Eventually devotees just 'submit' and go along. They get assurance that there is eternal life, or their Karma is improving. They have hope. They make a leap of faith.

What drives the devotee is the comfort that all is and will be well. No matter what happens now, God, G-d, Allah, Karmic action, or Hindu gods will eventually make everything right. Yet, they have some unease about the interpretations by the clergy. So, they choose not to think about it and just believe to be comfortable.

Proving life after death

Some religious people cite experiences of others about moments after death. Usually, a medical person determines a person is clinically dead. Then miraculously the person comes back to life. The person can describe what happened. Believers take the description as evidence of an afterlife. Disbelievers or doubters attribute the event to the brain not being fully dead and it was able to recall part of the experience which the person attributes to an afterlife.

More solid research in this area can confirm or disprove such events. For instance, get one hundred death explorers to voluntarily die for thirty seconds and then medical teams bring the departed back to life. Then repeat the process by lengthening the death times and bringing the dead person back to life. Each time medical people check the brain and vital signs and then get detailed reports of explorers' experiences. Of course, there is concern the explorers won't come back. Certainly, there are other and better ways of conducting such experiments.

A complete or incomplete soul?

If the soul lives on, then does the memory and personality of the person live too? Will the wonderful and the not so wonderful to horrible memories also live on with the soul after death? If not, then how is that a complete soul? Purification ends bad memories and sins from the soul. But horrible people are condemned to hell remembering only their 'sins' for all eternity. Or perhaps all memories of past life or lives vanish.

Or perhaps only the personality lives on? If one is a happy person, then will one be happy through all eternity? Or can the personality change in heaven to be sad, happy, blissful? Those that believe in Karma seem to think that the personality can change.

What happens to people born mentally unstable, suffering debilitating injuries, etc.? Is their soul made whole to be pure, or do the infirmities continue in eternity? Does ending an infirmity change the essence of the person? If so, what is the essence of a person? If not, then where is love of the deity?

Perhaps this is the meaning of going to heaven or reincarnation to a higher plane - that the soul is reborn and has no memory of the past. Just like few people today claim to have any memory of what happened before they were born into this world.

Happy to die?

Yet, people go to mediums and talk with deceased family members. They recognize each other. If true, then the personality must continue, at least for some souls. If not, then how can the soul continue? Some say that the soul continues just as the seed of the butterfly creates a caterpillar which morphs into a butterfly. Thus, there might not be memory. But then how do the mediums 'chat' with dead souls?

Many people have terminal illnesses. If they genuinely believed their faith, wouldn't they happily, yet with some fear, look forward to being dead? Wouldn't they refuse medical care and let the dying process take over? Perhaps some would want palliative care to reduce the pain. Otherwise, they are just hanging on to every enfeebled day, which means they don't believe what their religion has professed.[148] If they really believed their faith, then they would be willing to die. In fact, no matter what their religion is, they would be deliriously happy to be dead.

☨✡☾✦ॐ

If criminals believe that there is an afterlife, then they might kill others because that dead person is living in an afterlife and is not dead. Their victim might be in a better place.

If there is a better place, then why not suicide? How do the clergy know that suicide is a ticket to hell? What is the proof?

On the other hand, Muslims say that a person that dies in battle goes straight to heaven and has seventy virgins.[149] Seems to encourage never ending war. Why have peace, when one has a lousy life now, when one dies in war, one goes directly to heaven and has seventy virgins with eternal sex? Doesn't that mean the God, G-d, Allah, or Karmic action favors war and warriors and that humans should engage in more wars? Therefore, kill, kill, kill, and destroy. The reward will certainly be in the afterlife.

☨✡☾✦ॐ

In a very general sense, the five religions have some sort of belief in an afterlife whether it be one time or multiple times. Yet, there is no scientific proof. That is why belief in an afterlife or Karma is a leap of faith.

So, what are their scriptures and why are they valid for faith?

---

[148] Elaborated on from a suggestion by Gary E. Schwartz, PhD in "The Afterlife Experiment," pg 248, (Schwartz 2002)

[149] Elaborated on from a suggestion by Gary E. Schwartz, PhD in "The Afterlife Experiment," pg 246, (Schwartz 2002)

Chapter 18

Scriptures

Figure 18.1 Scriptures are crucial to all five religions.

Scriptural authority is strong in the five religions. Devotees use their scriptures for guidance, inspiration, comfort, and assurance. It is a lighthouse for their lives. Without the scriptures millions and billions of people would feel lost.

Christianity and Scripture

The Christian Scripture consist of the Old Testament and the New Testament. The Protestant Old Testament consists of 39 books which correspond to the Jewish 24 books. There are some differences of order, text, and dividing some of the books; otherwise they are the same. The Catholic Church's Old Testament has 46 books. The Eastern Orthodox and the Oriental Orthodox Churches have up to 51 books

The Old Testament was based upon an oral tradition and written between 1,250 BCE and 165 BCE. Some believe that God dictated the first five books around 4,000 BCE to Moses who then authored the books word for word as dictated to him.

The New Testament consists of the Gospels and letters. The Gospels tell the story of Jesus and his teachings. The letters tell some of the work of the apostles, Paul, and the issues within the early church. Various authors wrote the Gospels between 65 and 110 CE. The Letters, written mostly by Paul and others between 48 and 110 CE. Under the influence of Emperor Constantine, the writings became part of the Church official document in the early third to fourth centuries. It was an effort to merge the church's teachings from many various other documents in various parts of the Mediterranean world.

How to interpret the Christian Scripture is an extremely basic and fundamental difference between conservatives and liberals. The difference is so great that it deeply polarizes US politics and society. That polarization has spread throughout the entire Christian world.

At the root of the difference is why and how the various authors wrote what is now known as the Bible. The Conservative Biblical interpretation is every word is literal in the original language of Hebrew and Greek. Therefore, read the Bible just as one reads a newspaper. "It says what it says." The Liberal interpretation is that the Bible is a set of documents written over several thousand years; therefore, to interpret the text, it is necessary to consider the history, language and the context of each text.

One of the leading conservative seminaries in the US said in their primary theological texts:

    1. The inspiration and authority of the Scriptures are assumed. [150]

---

150 (Chafer 1947 Eleventh Edition 1973) page 7 Volume 1

2. The meaning of the truths of Scripture is best expressed in original languages.... A perfect induction is formed when all the teachings of the Scripture, according to their precise meaning, are made the basis of a doctrinal statement.[151]

3. He not only opened the scriptures to them but that He opened their understanding that they might understand the Scriptures (Luke 24:27-32,45) ....it is the spiritual Christian who discerns all things (1 Cor 2:15).[152]

4. Thus, there is introduced into the pursuit of the science of Systematic Theology a pedagogical law which is foreign to other laws of research, namely, that divine illumination, by which alone the revelation maybe comprehended, is made to depend on a state of heart which is not only yielded to God, but is ever ready to be conformed to the Word He has spoken.[153]

5. ...the Bible is incomprehensible to the unregenerate man and the unspiritual Christian, the doctrines are, to a large degree, sealed to them; and as Systematic Theology has largely to do with doctrine, that vast science is closed to multitudes who are not lacking in education and culture, but who are lacking in that inward personal adjustment to God, which alone insures a spiritual understanding.[154]

6. Too often the seminary has taken the attitude that the study of the English Bible for its spiritual content has no place in a theological curriculum...[155]

7. Rationalism has ever been seeking admission into the Christian

---

151 (Chafer 1947 Eleventh Edition 1973) page 8 Volume 1
152 (Chafer 1947 Eleventh Edition 1973) page 9 Volume 1
153 (Chafer 1947 Eleventh Edition 1973) page 9 Volume 1
154 (Chafer 1947 Eleventh Edition 1973) page 9 Volume 1
155 (Chafer 1947 Eleventh Edition 1973) page vii Volume 1

church...It is a short step ...from the ignorance of doctrine to the rejection and ridicule of it, and it can be safely stated that there is no rejection of sound doctrine which is not based on ignorance.[156]

8. Those who have not gained a working knowledge of the original languages can hardly be expected to realize what a wealth of disclosure that ability imparts.... It is exceedingly easy to twist or mold the Word of God to make it conform to one's preconceived notions. To do this is no less than "handling the word of God deceitfully" (2 Cor. 4:2) and is worthy of judgment from Him whose Word is thus perverted.[157]

9. ...the Bible presents no theory regarding its own inspiration...The question is not what men-even great scholars-think a workable theory is as to the manner in which the Bible was written; it is what the Bible declares concerning itself.[158]

10. (Inspiration) is so embedded in the Oracles of God, no saint or apostle could do otherwise than to believe the word God as spoken.[159]

11. If the Bible contains errors as seen by God, the case would be serious; if it contains errors as seen by men, the difficulty may be wholly accounted for in the sphere of human misunderstandings.[160]

12. ...all facts concerning the doctrine are doubtless capable of being harmonized and comprehended where sufficient understanding exists.[161]

---

156 (Chafer 1947 Eleventh Edition 1973) page viii Volume 1
157 (Chafer 1947 Eleventh Edition 1973) page 118 Volume 1
158 (Chafer 1947 Eleventh Edition 1973) page 63 Volume 1
159 (Chafer 1947 Eleventh Edition 1973) page 64 Volume 1
160 (Chafer 1947 Eleventh Edition 1973) page 66 Volume 1
161 (Chafer 1947 Eleventh Edition 1973) page 67 Volume 1

13. The Scriptures give abundant teaching as to the fact of inspiration but do not offer explanation of this phenomenon. The how of every miracle is wanting, and inspiration is a miracle. Concerning this and all miracles, man is called upon to believe and not to elucidate.[162]

14. As to how He transmitted that Word to them and secured inerrant oracles at their hand, the Scriptures are silent.[163]

15. Those who are disposed to disagree with these conclusions must reckon with Christ, the apostles, and the prophets upon whom, after all, we must depend for any knowledge of any truth whatsoever. If their testimony is broken regarding the trustworthiness of the Scriptures, it is broken regarding all else.[164]

On the other hand, the basis of liberal Christian faith takes a fair amount of effort to understand it. For the mainline churches the Bible is a set of books by various authors and purposes written two to three thousand years ago, over a one-thousand-year period by people with a different world view, a different culture, and a different language structure. Also, the various authors wrote the Biblical texts decades or more after the events from oral traditions. Furthermore, liberal scholars state that several of the books are consolidations of older texts that were also based upon oral histories.

Furthermore, liberals state that the Holy Spirit did not dictate the various writings. Each writing had a purpose. For instance, Job explains great faith when suffering trauma; however, it is not a literal historical event. That is, God and the Devil did not discuss the person named Job; nor did the events described in the book happen to Job. The Book of Jeremiah laments about

---

162 (Chafer 1947 Eleventh Edition 1973) page 82 Volume 1
163 (Chafer 1947 Eleventh Edition 1973) page 88 Volume 1
164 (Chafer 1947 Eleventh Edition 1973) page 88 Volume 1

the fate of Israel and people's faith, the same as religious political commentators describe events today to show God's current active participation in human affairs. Thus, the prophet Jeremiah said that God was active in the events of Israel because Israel was faithlessness to the commands of God. In the New Testament, documents like Paul's letter to the Ephesians simply described what the local church should do in Paul's opinion about several issues. The authors of the four Gospels (Matthew, Mark, Luke and John) wrote about parts of Jesus' life and teachings decades after Jesus' death. Those unknown authors had their points of view and agendas in writing the texts.

Liberals read each book of the Bible in its' historical context and style of writing. Parts of the texts are allegorical, some are historical, some theological, and a few are liturgical. There are contradictions and errors within the Bible and with science and history. The clearest example is the Creation Story in Genesis 1. The vast scientific consensus is that the earth is billions of years old while the literal reading of the Genesis story is six thousand years old. So, Liberals read Genesis as a story describing that there is faith in a creator that over billions of years formed and created the universe, animals, and people through natural processes. Conservatives read Genesis as a literal story with God creating the universe in six days. God created humans as one currently sees them. That is, there was no evolution. There is sin, suffering and evil in the world because two people Adam and Eve did not obey one command of God.

Furthermore, Liberals believe that the ancient people orally transmitted the stories and had a world view with hell below, earth where one lives, heaven above, and the entire universe revolved around the earth. God was active in the wind, rain, and wars, and was concerned about one's personal and corporate sins. However, that world view is vastly different from the modern world view, where the earth is a tiny speck, spinning around an insignificant sun, in a medium size galaxy, which is one among trillions of other galaxies. Nevertheless, many Liberals pray for divine guidance and hope that God is active in their lives.

Additionally, liberals believe that the Aramaic language of the New Testament was more metaphorical when compared to today's descriptive language. When Jesus taught, he spoke in Aramaic. The writers of the Gospels thirty to sixty years later wrote them in Greek. Also, many Biblical scholars believe the writers did not even live in Palestine. So, the writers had a different language and cultural perspective. Take for instance the Lord's Prayer. Here is the version in standard English translation, a version from Hebrew, and a version translated from Aramaic. Note the differences. Remember, that this prayer has morphed from Aramaic to Hebrew to Greek to English over more than two thousand years, from a different culture, world view, and grammatical structures.

In the standard English:

> [9] Our Father in heaven,
> hallowed be your name,
> [10] your kingdom come,
> your will be done,
> [11] Give us today our daily bread.
> [12] And forgive us our debts,
> as we also have forgiven our debtors.
> [13] And lead us not into temptation,
> but deliver us from the evil one
> On earth as it is in heaven.[165]

From Hebrew to English:

> Our Parent which art in heaven,
> be gracious to us, O Lord, our God;
> hallowed be thy name
> and let the remembrance of thee be glorified in heaven above

---

165 (Gregorie n.d.)

> and in the earth here below
> Let thy kingdom reign over us now and forever.
>
> The holy men of old said,
> Remit and forgive unto all men whatsoever they have done against me.
> And lead us not into temptation but deliver us from the evil thing.
> For thine is the kingdom, and thou shalt reign in glory
> forever and for evermore.[166]

From Aramaic to English:

> Oh Thou, from whom the breath of life comes,
> who fills all realms of sound, light and vibration.
> May Your light be experienced in my utmost holiest.
> Your Heavenly Domain approaches.
> Let Your will come true – in the universe just as on earth.
> Give us wisdom for our daily need,
> detach the fetters of faults that bind us,
> like we let go the guilt of others.
> Let us not be lost in superficial things,
> but let us be freed from that what keeps us from our true purpose.
> From You comes the all-working will,
> the lively strength to act,
> the song that beautifies all and renews itself from age to age.
> Sealed in trust, faith and truth.
> I confirm with my entire being.[167]

There is a sense that the three say the same yet, there is a sense that there is a fundamental difference. Also, the literature disagrees with various Aramaic translations.

Just above, there was a brief description that Mark appears mostly word for

---

166 (Gregorie n.d.)

167 (Gregorie n.d.)

word in both Matthew and Luke. Conservatives and Liberals disagree as to why. Conservatives state that there is no problem. The Holy Spirit dictated the three Gospels; therefore, there would be word for word agreement in sections of the three Gospels. In fact, that is proof that the

> Holy Spirit dictated every word of the Gospels.

However, many liberal seminaries interpret the facts differently. Matthew included Mark and a source labeled Q (the first letter of the German word Quelle which means source). Luke used Mark and Q. This is the "Two-source Hypothesis." Shown in the adjacent chart.[168] Note that the colors n Matthew and Luke correspond to the amount of material used from the various sources. The purple shows the percentage of material in Matthew and Luke that are common to Mark. The blue shows the material in Matthew and Luke that are common to the unknown source Q. The remaining two colors show independent material appearing solely in Matthew and Luke and Mark. There are three and four source theories.[169] The basic process is still the same n the theories.

The 'side-by-side' version of the Gospels show more detail. Their layout shows the verses in columns labeled Matthew, Mark, Luke and John. One reads a verse in the Matthew column and then goes left to right to make verse by verse comparisons. After a while the basic patterns will become obvious to the reader. Though it does take some careful reading and patience.

Figure 18.2 Two source hypothesis of the three Gospels

---

168 (Wikipedia n.d.) Two Source Hypothesis

169 (Wikipedia n.d.) Synoptic Gospels – Wikipedia. Shows more charts

To make the effort stand out, use colored pens. One color for what is the same in two Gospels. Another color for what is the same in three Gospels and a distinct color for what is the same in four Gospels. For what appears only in one Gospel, don't use any color. This will sharpen the clarity of the various source theory. As the process unfolds, flip the pages and just notice the colors. The process will reveal there are common verses.

This chart shows more detail.[170] It shows the percentages of each of the sources in the various gospels. For instance, 76% of Mark appears in Luke and Matthew. 41% of Luke comes from Mark while 45% of Matthew comes from Mark. The triple tradition means the material is common in Mark, Luke and Matthew. The double tradition is the material common only in Luke and Matthew. That is the Q source mentioned earlier. Note that 35% of Luke is unique to Luke and that 20% of Matthew is unique to Matthew.[171]

The process gives an understanding of the formations of the Gospels. The authors found information they agreed with and wrote it into the various texts. This is the same process as biographers today write histories of famous people. They consult documents and then author the story. The result is that there are slightly different versions of the same event. For example, compare only a few verses from the story of the Centurion of Capernaum. The first quote is from Matthew (the first column in the "Side by Side") and the second quote is from Luke (the third column in the "Side by Side"). They show a common source. Notice the word for word similarities. In this case the two quotes are not identical but do tell the same story:

- "Lord, I am not worthy to have you come under my roof: but only say the word, and my 8-servant will be healed. For I am a man under authority, with soldiers under me; and I say to one 'Go,' and he goes, and to another, 'Come,' and he comes, and to my slave, 'Do this,' and he does it." When Jesus hear him, he

---

170 (Wikipedia n.d.) Two Source Hypothesis

171 (Wikipedia n.d.) Two Source Hypothesis

marveled, and said to those who followed him, "Truly, I say to you, not even in Israel have I found such faith." (Matt 8:8-10 RSV)

- "Lord, do not trouble yourself, for I am not worthy to have you come under my roof; therefore, I did not presume to come to you. But say the word, and let my servant be healed. For I am a man set under authority, with soldiers under me; and I say to one, 'Go,' and he goes; and to another, 'Come,' and he come; and to my slave, 'Do this,' and he does it." When Jesus heard this, he marveled at him, and turned and said to the multitude that followed him, "I tell you, not even in Israel have I found such faith." (Luke 7:6-9 RSV)

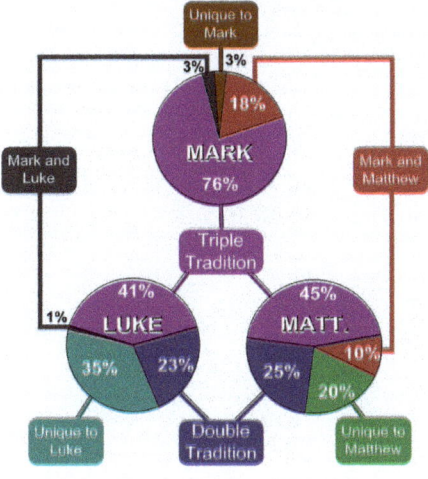

Figure 18.3 Percentage relationship between three Gospels

However, conservative scholars might agree with the entire process above. They argue that the Holy Spirit guided the hands and fingers of individual authors to write every word in the original Greek New Testament and the Hebrew Old Testament. That is why there is so much commonality in Matthew, Mark and Luke. Furthermore, wherever there is a conflict or problem, that merely shows a lack of human understanding.

A further example of conservative versus liberal interpretation can be understanding the book of Job. The conservative interpretation of Job is a literal one. Job is a faithful servant of God.

The Devil has a real conversation with God. The Devil says to God that Job is faithful because God has rewarded Job. So, they agree to visit various calamities upon Job to test Job's faith. Job gets boils, loses property, family dies, and still Job is faithful. Job's friends mock him. Nevertheless, Job is faithful though he has many doubts of faith. Eventually, God blesses Job and once again all is well with Job.

The literal interpretation is that Job is an exact description of what happened several thousand years ago. Job is a real person along with his family and friends. Job in fact did physically suffer. Job did suffer trials of faith; but he remained steadfast no matter how much doubt. That, no matter how much pain and suffering one has, be faithful and strong in the faith. Though one lacks understanding as to why there is pain and suffering in the world, just remain faithful. God will supply reward, if not in this life, then in the next.

The liberal interpretation is different. Job is not a literal book. Rather, it is a story for people to remain faithful. It is an example of great faith. In that sense, it is no different than children's stories encouraging children to believe in oneself and persevere. For instance, the "Little Engine That Could" is a story about a little train engine that had a heavy load to pull up a hill. It pulled and pulled a heavy load that was important to get to the other side of the hill. The Little Engine said to itself, "I think I can. I think I can. I think I can." The little train gets to the other side and delivers the load. Everyone is happy. The tale has inspired many children to persevere.

It is in that light, that liberals interpret Job. Maintain faith and all will be well. Don't concern oneself that the Devil and God are having a real conversation. That is not what the story is about. That, while one might not understand why there is pain and suffering, one should remain in the faith, and that God loves the faithful.

Judaism and Scripture

The Jewish scriptures consists of rabbinic literature and the Tanaka (which is what Christians and most of the world would consider to be the Old Testament[172]). Both were first oral and then written from about 4,000 BCE to about 430 BCE. There is some thought that authors wrote the oral traditions between 1,200 BCE and 165 BCE[173] in Biblical Hebrew and with some texts in Biblical Aramaic (mostly Daniel an Ezra).

The rabbinic literature consists of the Midrash and the Mishnah. The Midrash is commentary on the Tanaka. The Mishnah has topics and is more in depth that Midrash.

Torah is the first five books of the Hebrew Bible: Genesis, Exodus, Leviticus, Numbers, and Deuteronomy. According to Jewish tradition, God handed down the Torah directly to Moses, who wrote it word for word. It is the Written Word.

However, the Holy Spirit did not inspire the scriptures by dictating every word, jot and title, as Christian Fundamentalists state. Instead, the Jewish Scriptures have authority because of the community not because of inspiration.[174]

On the other hand, the Talmud is the Oral Word of God – handed down at the same time and repeated by generations. Eventually, various rabbis and their students wrote the Talmud in Jerusalem and Babylon.

The Talmud has passages from the Torah and discusses what the passages mean. The discussion could be between rabbis who lived generations apart. The Talmud gives insight and explains the Torah, considering the Rabbis' discussion. [175]

Islam and Scripture

Qur'an is the word of God revealed by the archangel Gabriel to the final

---

172 The Old Testament is what Judaism names as the Tanaka. It consists of the Torah (Five Books of Moses), Nevi'im ("Prophets") and Ketuvim ("Writings"). The first letters of each TNK become TaNaKh.

173 (Drane 2011)

174 (Marc Zvi Brettler 2012) Page 56

175 (Exstein 2015)

Prophet Muhammad by archangel Gabriel beginning on December 22, 609 CE and concluding in 632, the year of his death. Companions of Muhammad wrote the revelations. Shortly after Muhammad's death scribes joined the revelations into a standard version. There are some slightly different versions with minor variations.[176]

Only the Qur'an written in the Arabic language is the word of God. A translation of the Qur'an is not Qur'an because God revealed it only in Arabic. A translation is the word of the translator not the word of God. Hadith has reports of Prophet Muhammad's sayings, deeds, approvals and explanations of the Qur'an. It is the second source of Islamic knowledge and legal system.[177]

The Qur'an has 114 chapters[178] of varying length and each has a name and a number in consecutive order. Translators use either Roman or Arabic numerals for numbering the chapters. Verse numbers are in Arabic numerals and numbered within the chapter in consecutive order.[179]

There are many Hadith collections and each primary collection goes by the collector's name. There are secondary collections of Hadith, coming from primary collections and arranged according to the topic; such collections go by the name given by the collector. It is much easier for untrained people to use secondary Hadith collections than the primary collections.[180]

Buddhism and Scripture

The three Abrahamic religions (Christianity, Judaism and Islam) have well-defined scriptures. Buddhism instead has histories of the words and teachings of Buddha. The three major texts are: Pali Canon[181], Mahayana Canon, and the

176 (Wikipedia n.d.) Quran

177 (Ali 2006)

178 Chapters are called Suras.

179 (Ali 2006)

180 (Ali 2006)

181 (Dhammika n.d.)

Tibetan Book of the Dead. These Canons are very voluminous. The English translation of the Pali Canon is forty volumes.[182] However, it is best to learn from masters instead of following only authorized and non-authorize texts or books. Consequently, different sects of Buddhism follow scriptures to varying degrees.[183] For instance, Zen Buddhism emphasizes transcending intellect, logic, and language to experience the meaning of life through meditation.[184]

For example, Buddha states, "… if you are in doubt, uncertainty is born…. Don't go by reports, by legends, by traditions, by scripture, by logical conjecture, by inference, by analogies, by agreement through pondering views, by probability, or by the thought; instead contemplation is the teacher." For example, when one knows that one is unskillful and wise teachers criticize, then abandon those actions[185] and learn to become more skillful.

Typically, Western cultures have trouble understanding Buddhism. In some cases, teachers present it as a science, or a psychology, or psychotherapy to make the understanding easier. Instead, it is best to find a skilled teacher and be on a retreat to understand and practice Buddhism.[186]

Hinduism and Scripture

Hinduism is 4,000 years old and includes many different sects and views among the one billion or so adherents. The Vedas, Upanishads, Puranas and the Epics are some of the sacred scriptures depending upon the sect[187]:

The primary texts are the Vedas which have hymns, incantations, and rituals from ancient India. They were orally composed about 1500 BCE and written between 600 to 300 BCE.

---

182 (Dhammika n.d.)

183 (Moran, Mark CEO 2018?)

184 (Moran, Mark CEO 2018?)

185 (Payne n.d.) ibid, pg 20

186 An excellent description by Ken McCleod (McLeod 2017)

187 (Hare 2010)

The Upanishads explain how the soul unites with the ultimate Truth and Karma. Authors wrote them between 800 and 400 BCE.

The Puranas have the history of the Universe from creation to destruction, genealogies of the kings, heroes, demigods, cosmology, and geography. They appeared a bit after the Vedas.

The Mahabharata and Ramayana are the national epics of India. To get a good understanding of Hinduism, read the Bhagavad Gita which is a subset of the first Mahabharata.[188] It is a philosophical dialog between the god Krishna and the warrior Arjuna as they ride into battle and written between 540 BCE to 100 CE.

There are many other texts of varying importance to Hindus.

Discussion

For Christians the method of interpretation causes a great divide between conservatives and liberals. Conservatives trust a literal reading of the Bible and God's promises as revealed in the Bible. Liberals trust God and use the Bible as a guide.

Literal versus non-literal Biblical Interpretation

The Conservative interpretation of the Bible means reading the Bible like one reads the newspaper. Every word, sentence, paragraph, and book says what it says in plain meaning. For example, the book of Job is true word for word. Thus, God and Satan had a real conversation about Job. They make a wager. Yes, they make a bet as to who wins Job's soul. God bets that Job will be faithful and true. Satan bets that when the going gets tough, Job will give up faith and God. Job gets disease, loses property, and his family dies. In the end, Job stays faithful. So, God wins the bet. That means God get Job's soul and Satan doesn't.

---

188 (Prabhupada 2001) This edition in Sanskrit with an English translation and commentary. It is well worth the read to better understand Hinduism.

For the Conservative to interpret the book of Job non-literally means the promises of the Bible might not be true. Therefore, faith as Jesus as God and the guarantee of the afterlife might not be real. The firm promise of a happy afterlife would not be firm. That shakes Conservatives to their core. So, they cling to literal in-errancy for security. A security for which there is no proof.

For liberals, faith is a nebulous leap of faith. The Bible has truth, though not in literal form. One just trusts in God. As a president of a seminary once said, "The Bible is inspired because it inspires us!" [189]

Yet, the basic conclusion for Conservatives and most Liberals is the same: Jesus is Lord and Savior who will come to judge the living and the dead. But the different Biblical interpretations needlessly tear apart the Christian Church. Furthermore, it creates further divisions and conflicts by various denominations which create many sects such as Mennonites, Lutherans, Catholics, Methodists, Moravians, Baptists, Gospel Churches, Unity, Science of Mind, etc. etc. All claiming to have the correct interpretation of the Faith. Instead of living in love for one another, they divide into groups that are suspicious of one another. They fight each other for political control of societies by making deals with politicians. In the process they forget Jesus' commands about what it means to love sinners.

Five Religions passing values from generation to generation

The historical documents and traditions of the five religions are more than one-thousand four-hundred years old. They supply guidance for the present and glimpses of what the next life will be like. The reader can believe the account or not. What matters in those events are the values that the stories relate to the world today. People like some of the stories because they like the values in the stories. Or, they like the story because their person or tribe did something noble or won a battle. National histories are stories about noble

---

[189] A seminary president said that to me between 1977 to 1978.

values, about freedom, overcoming hardship, and creating a nation. Most of the stories pay little attention to brutality of slavery, genocide, theft, etc. Nevertheless, the sagas are an inspiration. Undoubtedly, there are errors in the details; but it is conveying the values that matters most. A leap of faith in the accuracy is irrelevant. What is relevant for the Five Faiths is passing values from generation to generation.

Jesus spoke Aramaic – Mohammed spoke Arabic

Jesus spoke Aramaic. There were Aramaic documents from which the writers gathered materials for what is now the New Testament and the Old Testament translated into Greek. Yet, very few scholars, let alone Christian clergy, bother to master Aramaic, let alone Hebrew and Greek. There is a fundamental difference in understanding the thought process of Aramaic. The example shown earlier of the Lord's Prayer in English and a translation from Aramaic shows a difference in understanding. If those writings are so important, one would think that all Christian scholars and clergy would master Aramaic, Hebrew and Greek as well as the several ways to interpret the Scriptures. Because of time constraint and laziness, they don't. Instead, they take a view and run with it for the rest of their lives. The result is that there is conflict between the various Christian sects.

Mohammed spoke Arabic. The angel Gabriel dictated the Qur'an to Mohammed. His scribes wrote what Mohammed said. The Muslim view is that any translation of the Qur'an is a translation according to the translation. Therefore, the translation is not the word of Allah; rather, it is the word of the translator. Therefore, only read and study the Qur'an in Arabic.

Sin like a drunk riding a horse

Few Christian conservatives who believe in the literal interpretation of the Bible willingly would take Jesus' command to cut off body parts that cause one to sin, nor to stone sinners. They avoid such drastic measures. Instead they ask forgiveness of sins and then take communion to have forgiveness of sins. Then sin again and ask for forgiveness. They repeat the ceremonies for the rest of their lives. For those that are truly trying to follow Jesus' commands, that pattern can drive a tremendous guilt complex. Those that casually accept the Biblical interpretation and follow that pattern don't give much thought to any of it. They sin, ask for forgiveness and feel all is well.

It appears that for this quote of Jesus, the liberals just shrug their shoulders and go on with their lives. Some will follow the command; some will make attempts, and others will just ignore it.

Similarly, Jews, Muslims, Buddhists, and Hindus take their scriptures very seriously and struggle to keep the commands.

Therefore, the literalists and the liberals of the Five Religions have the same result. Sin like a drunk riding a horse. Sit upright asking for forgiveness. Then slide to the other side of the horse. They keep repeating the process for the rest of their lives but can't fully follow their beliefs.[190] They do their best and trust in the forgiveness of God, G-d, Allah, Karmic action, or Hindu gods.

Healing the sick

The scriptures of the five religions show God, G-d, Allah, and Hindu gods as active in people's lives. However, Buddhism is more of a mental attitude towards this life.

Based upon the Bible, Christian literalists and liberals have similar views about healing the sick. For instance, Jesus sent the disciples out to heal the sick. Today only a few clergy heal the sick. They pray for the sick and then encourage their flocks to work with medical doctors and pray. Very few expect ministers to heal the sick. Instead, ministers pray, which comforts people, perhaps changes mental attitudes to the positive, which in turn helps healing.

However, some clergy make public demonstrations of healings. Others claim

---

190 Comes from Martin Luther.

they heal the sick. But then refuse to empty out hospitals with their prayers of healing. Their claim is that the hospitals do not allow them to go into hospitals to heal the sick. So, they heal people in secret. To find such healers, people find people that know people who know where to find faith healers.

There are varying sketchy reports that similar healings occur in Islam, Judaism, Buddhism, and Hinduism. However, this line of investigation shows that only fringes of those religions practice faith healing. So, there is no definitive conclusion about healing.

However, considering that Judaism and Islam view G-d and Allah as active in the world, helping and punishing people then G-d and Allah should be actively and massively healing and feeding people. That rabbis and imams would pray to heal and feed their devotees. That there would lots of healed, well fed, and wealthy people. Instead, the history of both shows illness, hunger, and poverty. Why is that? Why are their deities active in their lives but not healing, feeding, and creating wealth for their devotees? Is it because their devotees are being punished for wrong action, beliefs, or something else?

Lack of human understanding

Conservative Christians deeply believe that the errors in the Bible are a lack of human understanding. Just have faith and God will eventually make all clear. Just accept the Bible as inerrant and true. On the other hand, liberals accept fallible people wrote the Bible in their cultural context in a different language and with a radically different world view from today. They believe that a literal Biblical interpretation makes a mockery of the Biblical message and Jesus.

Take the Creation Story. Conservatives believe that God made the world and all the creatures in it in six days, and God rested on the seventh. Using that as a starting point and the genealogy in the Bible, Bishop Ussher calculated that the world and the universe was created in the evening of

October 23, 4004 BCE.[191] On the other hand, liberals believe that science states that the universe is approximately 14 billion years old and the world is 4.6 billion years old. That evolutionary processes occurred over millions of years, creating the diverse living creatures that today inhabit the world.

This is an enormous difference. Some conservatives propose that the since the Bible is infallible, they must find the scientific facts that back up the literal interpretation of the Bible. They say that human understanding lacks information and it is not Biblical error. Some conservatives go so far as to say science that contradicts the Bible is a lie. That problems in the world happen because the world does not accept the Bible as literally true. That Darwinism proposes evolution of creatures and humans is a root cause misunderstanding, causes a degenerate society, and leads people away from salvation and to everlasting hell. Therefore, no elementary school, no high school, nor university of any type should teach evolution. Nor should any government advocate it. Though for political reasons, the anti-science literal Biblical view should be at a minimum taught alongside of evolution.

Liberals start with physical evidence, propose theories that create cohesion, and as researchers find more evidence, they painstakingly revise the theories. It is a torturous process. Some theories have so much evidence in supporting the theory that it becomes bedrock for understanding all of science. If detailed evidence and work appears that supports alternatives, then eventually changes in understanding will happen.

Conservative emotions run high on this issue; while liberals tire of the issue. There appears to be no way to bridge the gap of literalism versus science. The arguments go into vast details, with neither side persuading the other.

The difference seems rooted in the Conservative deep need to have assurance of a blessed afterlife. Anything that casts doubt on that assurance creates

---

191 (Linder 2004) See, "Bishop James Ussher Sets the Date for Creation" by Doug Linder (2004) for a very interesting explanation and use of Bishop Ussher's twenty-year work.

distress and therefore they attack it. On the other hand, liberals accept that one just trusts that God will be just in making decisions about one's afterlife. One might go to heaven or could go to hell or just cease to exist.

Similarly, with the Jewish, Muslim, Buddhist, and Hindu scriptures. Anywhere there is trouble understanding the various scriptures, traditions, rationale, and clergy, there are typical responses. For instance, 'Just trust.' 'Just believe.' 'You show lack of faith.' 'Eventually you will understand.' 'There are many mysteries.' "Some form of evil has a hold of you.' 'Just follow the traditions of thousands of years and all will be well.' 'The clergy are trained more than you; so follow their guidance.' 'Who do you think you are?' Etc.

Fundamentally Christianity, Judaism, Islam, Buddhism, and Hinduism have a basic trust in the judgement of God, G-d, Allah, Karma, any of the Hindu gods. In that sense, anyone questioning or doubting the five religions commits blasphemy. Conservative Christians particularly commit blasphemy by insisting on the literal word of God instead of trusting the creative force that created this universe. There is more trust in their interpretations than in science. It is a fundamental and perhaps unbridgeable division between conservatives and science.

The end times

Popular in Jesus' time were end time movements (apocalyptic movements). Jesus' taught that the end times were near. He emphasized that the time was near. That the world would end shortly and therefore people should prepare. After His death he returned for a brief time. Followers were concerned that the end times did not happen. They struggled with the issue. Some left the faith while others continued with the faith believing that there were unknown reasons.

For the following two millennia, based upon the Biblical interpretation, there have been preachers saying the end times are near. They gave dates. People waited in expectation. Sometimes people sold their possessions and gathered in an appointed place to see the show. Nothing happened. Life went on.

Today, there are clergy that insist that the end times are imminent and make predictions. Currently, without proof of their views, they highly influence US internal and foreign politics.

Similarly, Judaism and Islam have apocalyptic threads based upon their scriptures. There are sects, along with Christian sects, that believe that the Armageddon is near. A large segment of Christianity and Judaism push for the formation of Greater Israel to usher in their view of the Messiah coming. Islam views it as a day of judgement. All three look forward to the vast conflict with joy and glee. So much so that it influences their world view and national political actions. Yet, outside of their scriptures, there is no proof that such events will happen.

Why not one clear concise scripture?

Why isn't there uniformity in the scriptures of the five religions? Why not address the social issues of the time to end greed, corruption, murder, sloth, the seven deadly sins, tolerance of those that are different, slavery, equality for all members of society, create health care system, create education systems, create just economic systems, equality of the sexes, equal rights for all people, the way to end war, etc.?

✝☪☮☸🕉

If the Holy Spirit dictated each letter and word of the Bible, then why isn't there one uniform New Testament? That is, why were there four Gospels and the Letters by various authors? Why not have one uniform and truly clear explanation of what was important to God? Why explain God's intentions in parables and sayings that need interpretations that clergy, let alone normal people, differ in their interpretations? Seems like Jesus did not even consider creating a happy, healthy, wealthy, and wise world. If he did not, then why should Christianity today say that those issues are important? Instead, the emphasis is on the next life. Just get through this life.

If the Bible is not completely verifiable, then Christianity is a leap of faith. One just trusts in God.

However, many devotees do claim that they find truth, meaning, and solace in Christian principles and the Bible. Therefore, they claim their experience makes Christianity true and confirms the scriptures.

☦ ✡ ☪ ☸ ॐ

Judaism has same basic issues as Christians do with scriptural interpretation of the Torah, Talmud, Midrash, and Mishna, as well as the traditions, reasoning, and experiences. How does one know that the scriptures, rituals, traditions and rabbinical statements are true? How does one verify them? They too start with the assumption that these are the word of G-d and have been handed down for millennia. Who are humans to challenge such assumptions?

If the Torah, Talmud, Midrash, and Mishna are not verifiable then Judaism is a leap of faith. One just trusts in G-d.

However, many devotees do claim that they find truth, meaning and solace in Jewish principles. Therefore, they claim their experience makes Judaism true and confirms the scriptures.

☦ ✡ ☪ ☸ ॐ

There are similar issues with the Muslim scriptures. Because the Archangel Gabriel dictated the texts to Mohammad, who then related it to scribes who wrote down word for word what Mohammad said. Thus, the Qur'an is sacred. There is great uniformity in the texts from the earliest times. For Muslims that is proof for the authenticity of the texts.

Yet, how do Muslims know that Gabriel dictated the texts and that neither Mohammad nor the scribes made no errors? Why was the Qur'an written with the longer texts first and the shorter texts last? Why are there conflicting statements in the Qur'an? Why didn't Gabriel dictate that Allah is a Trinity like the Christian God? That means the Christian concept of God is not true. Or it means that Gabriel made a mistake in dictating to Mohammed. Or that Mohammed made a mistake in dictating to the scribes. Or there was an error in transmission in the early years.

Just because Muslim clergy, institutions, traditions and scriptures make statements doesn't mean those statements are true. It just means that people made statements without proof. They had thoughts that many people agreed with in ancient times. To blindly accept those statements in the Qur'an and the Hadiths, traditions, dogmas, rituals, clerical and institutional statements is anti-science.

Is Allah the same as a generic name for God or G-d of the universe? Aren't the three, God, G-d and Allah really the same essence? How does one prove they are or are not the same essence?

If the Qur'an is not verifiable, then Islam is a leap of faith. One just trusts in a concept of Allah and the inspiration of the Qur'an and Hadiths.

However, many devotees do claim that they find truth, meaning and solace in Muslim principles. Therefore, they claim their experience makes Islam true and confirms the scriptures.

✝ ✡ ☪ ☸ ॐ

Buddhism has a complex set of sacred documents. How does the lay person know that they are true and what the trained leader says of them is true? For instance, a person has many lives. That Karma decides what will happen in the next life. That attachment causes suffering. Therefore, do not attach to anything. *How does one know those statements are true?*

If Buddhist scriptures, such as the Pali Canon, Mahayana Canon, and the Tibetan Book of the Dead, are not verifiable, then Buddhism is a leap of faith. One just trusts in Karma and the Eight-Fold Path. However, many devotees do claim that they find truth, meaning and solace in Buddhist principles. Therefore, they claim their experience makes Buddhism true and confirms the scriptures.

☨✡☪☸🕉

Hinduism being the oldest of the five religions has the most complex set of sacred scriptures. The same issues exist with those scriptures as with the other four religions. How do believers and non-believer know that those scriptures are true? How do they know that Krishna and Arjuna are really riding in a chariot on their way to battle? That they have an extended dialogue about many interesting topics. The topics and the philosophy are interesting and does make sense. So, if one just views it as a philosophical story, that is one thing. But if one views it as a real god and Arjuna talking, then how do the believer and non-believer know that was reality?

To blindly accept Hindu traditions, dogmas, rituals, scriptural interpretations, clerical and institutional statements is anti-science and a leap of faith.

However, many devotees do claim that they find truth, meaning and solace in Hinduism. Thus Hinduism is true.

Conclusion

The five religions interpret their sacred scriptures in diverse ways. Some sects interpret their holy documents as literal. Others interpret their scriptures metaphorically, or even metaphysically. Some sects believe that there are truths in the texts of other religions. Some sects believe that only their view of the sacred texts is correct. So, where is the truth in the stories?

With such differences between the five religions in interpretations of their scriptures, Christianity, Judaism, Islam, Buddhism, and Hinduism each appear to be a leap of faith. *How does one know those statements are true?*

So then, what is authority in the five religions?

Chapter 19

Authority

Figure 19.1 (left to right) Christian, Jewish, Muslim, Buddhist, Hindu authorities

In the five religions, authority comes in varying degrees from sacred texts, clerics, institutions, traditions, human reasoning, and personal experience.[192] Some of the religions or, sects of their religions, will place more emphasis on one aspect of authority than on the other aspects of authority. Most religions tend to hold that their sacred texts are the most important. For instance, they hold that their sacred text and personal experience are extremely important while minimizing their institutions, traditions, and human reasoning. Some religions might place the institution as primary and allow the institution to determine the beliefs based upon the institution's understanding of the sacred text.

Thus, section will examine the role of texts, institutions, traditions, human reasoning, and personal experience in forming authority in each of the five religions.

Christianity and Authority

The Christian Church consists of Catholicism, Protestantism, Orthodox, and Eastern Orthodox. Estimates range from 30,000 to 50,000 very minor

---

192 (Numrich 2018) Excellent framework to understand religious authority and ethics.

subsets[193] for a total of 2.3 billion followers.[194] The differences range from very minor to very major. For instance, a belief group might have five different major groups each with the same principle beliefs but differ upon a specific interpretation of scripture. Others will argue that is irrelevant, that there are not in practice that many subsets. The differences flow from interpretation of the sacred texts, their institutional structures, their different reasoning about faith, the different subjective experiences, and different personalities, cultures, languages and history.

The Catholic Church claims about half of the Christian believers with Protestantism claiming the other half. Protestantism splits into conservative and liberal branches.

The Catholic Church places primacy on the Pope and the Papal Institution to determine faith, dogma, ethics, actions, etc. The Papacy interprets the sacred text of the Holy Bible, which includes added books to the Protestant Bible. The Catholic hierarchy expects that Catholics around the world will believe and follow Papal announcements and dogma. However, the hierarchy expects that each Catholic will individually examine their faith and where it differs from the teachings to pray and seek reconciliation.

Protestantism has a wide range of authority. In general, there is a deep split between conservative Protestants who place a literal interpretation of the Bible and personal relationship with Jesus as the authority. Conservatives consider the entire Bible to be THE Word of God and rigorously adhere to every statement in it. "If the Bible says it, it must be true." Every single word and sentence. Devotees must accept a literal Biblical understanding of salvation and actions in this life. The institutions set dogmatic beliefs and correct Biblical interpretation that all must adhere to. When human reasoning does

---

193 Some argue with the numbers claiming some denominations are not Christians, that some blocks of Christians are really united together and shouldn't be counted as divided, etc.

194 (Wikipedia 2018)

not agree with a literal interpretation of the Bible, a personal relationship with Jesus, or the institution, that means that there is a lack of understanding or faulty reasoning. Thus, one must find the error in the reasoning and not with the cleric, Biblical interpretation, or personal relationship with Jesus.

The liberal churches have a fluid view of authority. Human reasoning and science interpret the Bible, institutions, traditions and personal experience. The Bible is sacred and is a document written by humans over a one-thousand-year period more than two thousand years ago. They had linguistic, cultural, and scientific comprehension different from today. So, understandings from two to four thousand years ago need reinterpretation for today's culture. God is active in the world through the actions of people. Liberal institutions tend to have statements of belief formed by the clergy and parishioners; though that varies with in degrees with the various denominations. Where there is disagreement, there is conversation. Personal experience tends to be – personal – that is quiet in prayer and meditation. There is a hope that followers will experience the divine.

✝☪☮☸🕉

In either the conservative or the liberal interpretation, there is a fundamental problem of pain, suffering, and evil. How does a loving God allow pain, suffering and evil? The conservative approach implies that God is testing people with pain, suffering, and evil to see if they will remain true to their faith. That pain, suffering, and evil are a result of humans exercising their free will by not following God's commandments and loving God with their whole heart, mind and soul.

Liberals on the other hand tend to say that pain, suffering, and evil are the result of free will and natural causes. If one has pain, suffering or there is evil, then it is necessary to find the causes and take corrective actions.

Most Christian sects view adhering to tradition as important. For example:[195]

> "…the Church has no authority whatsoever to overturn what God has definitely taught. No one—not even a pope—can change the truths of Scripture, Sacred Tradition, or the doctrines definitely put forth for our belief by the Magisterium."

> "Tradition means giving a vote to the most obscure of all classes, our ancestors. It is the democracy of the dead."[196] Their voices and their example still matter. To those who erroneously seek truth in opinion polls: Don't forget to poll the "dead," who are still very much alive and a part of the Church! They get a vote, too. The Church cannot simply concern herself with the needs, views, and demands of her current earthly members. She regards all of her members, past, present, and future.

> The Church cannot simply reinvent herself to conform to current demands or preferences. She is in service of her Lord, Savior, Groom, and Head. She exists to proclaim His teachings and to hand on the sacred deposit of faith, which He died and rose to give to His Apostles. She is to reflect Him who is truth incarnate, not the changing mores of the world.[197]

Though today, there appear to be a willingness to change or even abandon traditions. For example, having women ministers.

✝ ✡ ☪ ☸ ㉟

For the overwhelming majority of Christians' personal experience determines their fundamental belief and trust. The traditions, reasons, institutions, and clergy strengthen their beliefs; but it is the experiences that make them

---

195 (Pope 2017)

196 Pope's quotation from Chesterton.

197 (Pope 2017)

believers. Paraphrasing an author:

Pray and hope that God will to tell you what to believe, to do something, to commit oneself to a career, to marry someone, etc.[198] Pray or meditate sincerely and with conviction. Ask God to reveal His intention. Then if one is sincere and God considers it is appropriate, God will answer. This is not something that is rational. Instead you must experience it. Just trust God. Every day, first thing in the morning, pray and meditate. Let God guide the day's activities. Then the days will be wonderful, knowing that God is guiding and protecting in all activities and experiences. Try it, you will like it.

Judaism and Authority

Judaism has no dogma, no formal set of beliefs that one must hold to be a Jew. In Judaism, actions are far more important than beliefs, although there is certainly a place for belief within Judaism.[199]

Judaism is a comprehensive way of life, an integral part of one's existence, and improves one's spiritual life and relationship with the Divine. Thus, it has rules and practices that affect every aspect of life[200]: what to do when waking up in the morning, what to eat and not eat, what to wear and not wear, how to dress, how to conduct business, who one can marry, how to observe holidays and the Sabbath, and how to treat G-d, how to treat neighbors and animals.

The basis is from the Torah, laws instituted by rabbis and from tradition. The rabbis interpret the texts for the congregations. Universities and seminaries educate rabbis and lay people.

As in all the religions, there is the liberal and the conservative forces. The difference appears to be in how much in detail one follows the Jewish way of life. Those that follow the details as much as possible are conservative and those

---

198 (Pope 2017)

199 (T. R. Rich, Beliefs 2011)

200 (T. R. Rich, Halakhah: Jewish Law 2011)

that are more open and don't are liberal. While it might seem strange, there are secular or atheistic Jews. They consider themselves Jewish and follow little to none of the way of life. Rather, they identify with Jewish traditions without all the practices.

Judaism has a rich and varied history. The written history is roughly four-thousand-years old. It is the basis for Christianity. Islam refers to it with varying degrees of respect, disrespect and emotion.

✝✡☪☸☥

In general Judaism places authority upon the Torah, other documents and the rabbis. Rabbis have authority to interpret the texts. They have the skills to interpret the true meaning of the Divine text. In antiquity, it was rare for either religious or civic text to be normative. It was the rabbinic interpretive approach to biblical texts, developed over millennia, that elevated the authority of texts above that of custom.[201]

✝✡☪☸☥

Pain, suffering, and evil happen by not adhering to the Jewish laws and customs.

Islam and Authority

The Qur'an, the teachings of Mohammad (Hadiths), and the clergy form the central basis for authority in Islam. It forms the basis for the totality of an Islamic society. Islam is more than a personal religion; it is a total way of life.

The Qur'an is a book of spiritual guidance and a source of laws regulating daily life. "Islam," means "submission to the will of God." [202]

"It is not for any believer, man or woman, when God and His Messenger

---

201 (Satlow n.d.)

202 Extracts from, "Chapter Two: The Islamic Sexual Morality (1) Its Foundation", (Rizvi 2018)

have decreed a matter, to have the choice in the affair. Whosoever disobeys God and His Messenger has gone astray into manifest error." (Sura 33:36)

Muslims believe that the archangel Gabriel revealed the Qur'an to Muhammad from 610 to 632 CE. Scribes of Muhammad accurately wrote the divine revelations. Thus, the Qur'an is the word of God. Hadiths are the collections of Muhammad's teachings and sayings. There are various collections of sayings which are named after the collector.[203] The Hadith contains reports of Prophet Muhammad's sayings, deeds and, approvals, and is the second source of Islamic knowledge and legal system.[204] There are secondary collections of Hadith, meaning they are culled from primary collections and arranged according to the topic; such collections go by the name given by the collector. It is much easier for untrained people to use secondary Hadith collections than the primary collections.

The Qur'an is the word of God revealed in the Arabic language. Translations are not the Qur'an, because a translation may have the message of the Qur'an, but it is the word of the translator, not the word of God.

✝✡☪☸🕉

Islam is a total system for personal, business, social and political actions. Therefore, individual parts of Islam do not work well in isolation. For example,

If the Islamic welfare system is in place, then the Islamic legal system works.

If the Islamic moral system is in place, then the Islamic family and social system works.

If the Islamic political and legal systems are in place, then the Islamic economics work.

Countries that do not have all the Islamic systems in place are a mess.

---

203 (Cavendish, Marshall 2011) pages 59-61

204 (Ali 2006)

Therefore, countries should adopt the total Islamic system.[205]

Thus, have a strong say in all aspects of personal, political, economic, education and religious aspects of life. As a result, Muslim clergy train, educate and dictate to societies how to be Muslim.

✝☆☪☸︎㊌

Western scholars accept that Islam states that the angel Gabriel transmitted the Qur'an to Muhammad between 610 and 632 CE. However, Western historians point out that there was no definitive, written version of the Qur'an until the ninth century. Thus, there is no definitive link between the Prophet and the Qur'an. However, Islamic scholars maintain that the Qur'an was accurately orally transmitted from 632 CE until the ninth century.[206] Furthermore, that scribes with Muhammad accurately and divinely transcribed what the archangel Gabriel revealed to Muhammad. Islamic scholars consider such Western statements and scholarship as being hostile to and ignorant of Islam.

Islamic scholars believe it is a sacrilege to do scholarly research on the Qur'an and the Hadiths, as scholars have done in Western societies on the Bible.

✝☆☪☸︎㊌

There are two main divisions in Islam: Sunni and Shia. It started shortly after the death of Muhammad with arguments about who is the rightful prophet. That division has lasted for a millennium and is extremely divisive in the Muslim world.

✝☆☪☸︎㊌

Humans cannot understand Allah's actions, particularly about pain, suffering and evil.[207]. Muslims and hopefully all humans agree that

---

205 (Ali 2006)

206 (Cavendish, Marshall 2011) page 60

207 (Al-Munajjid 1998)

Allah is fair, just, wise and knowing. That means whatever Allah does is legitimate, although humans might not understand why. It is not for any of his creatures to question Allah's actions, but Allah will question humans about their actions. (Sura 2: 23)

Thus pain, suffering and evil, are due to human sins (Sura 42:30): In times of crisis, humans get closer to Allah and start to repent, while in times of ease and comfort humans commit sin after sin. Thus, there is pain, suffering, and evil. Allah gave humans the power and will to choose. Therefore, humans are accountable for deeds and punishments. In this world pain, suffering, and evil are merely tests. The results will be known in the hereafter, and Allah knows best.

Buddhism and Authority

Buddhist authority relies upon one's practice and experience, Buddha's teachings, and teachers to guide followers.

Buddha did not want people to take the teachings upon faith.[208] Rather, they are to look to their daily lives to see the results and adjust. The best progress is studying the teachings of Buddha and following the guidance of skilled teachers. Coupled with sustained practice the follower sees results and makes corrections.

So, Buddhism is a melding of learning, practice and improvement. Thus, the teachings of Buddha are key to daily living. The teachers are accomplished students, who continue learning themselves, and understand what and how to improve their own and their student skills. Therefore, Buddhism is a never-ending process of improvement[209]. There is no central authority like the Pope in Catholicism, rabbis in Judaism, or Imams in Islam.

Although there are three major schools of Buddhism and many sub-sects,

---

208 (Blanchard 2012)

209 (Blanchard 2012)

Buddhist authority is practice, improvement, experience, study the Buddha teachings and listen to teachers.

✝ ✡ ☪ ☸ ॐ

Buddhists view that life is about delusions, desires, and attachments which cause pain, suffering, and evil. Therefore, follow the Four Noble Truths:

1. Life is suffering.

2. Suffering arises from craving.

3. Eliminate craving or attachment.

4. Follow the Eight-Fold Path.

And practice Buddha's Eight-Fold Path[210]:

- Right Understanding
- Right Thought
- Right Speech
- Right Livelihood
- Right Action
- Right Effort
- Right Mindfulness
- Right Concentration.

While this seems simple, it requires practice, experience, and improvement with a skilled teacher.

Hinduism and Authority[211][212]

The written Vedas "Knowledge" (1500 BCE to 500 BCE) are considered the most ancient of the Hindu scriptures and are a basis for many other later scriptural documents as described in the section, "Hinduism and Scripture."

---

210 (Peto 2011)

211 (Encyclopedia Britannica 2018)

212 (Anonymous 2016)

Therefore, while the Vedas have the most scriptural authority there are many other scriptures that are very influential. The Brahmans have spiritual supremacy from birth, though there are others that believe that the status is from scholarship and practice. They interpret the scriptures and officiate at weddings, funerals and other ceremonies.

There is no central authority in the Western sense like a Pope. Instead, there are schools of thought, Brahmans, and individual experiences with divine entities.

In general, Hindus believe that truth comes from many sources. One view is that Hinduism is truth that has many rivers flowing into it. In that sense, some Hindus believe that, "Eventually all religions will converge together. So, we are all Hindus." For instance, Hindus believe that truth comes from the Vedas, other scriptures, Brahmans, human thought such as science and philosophy. While on the one hand Hinduism seems to be quite fluid, there are very rigid thought structures. Humans, the divine, and Karma shape the world, which is flawed. There are deep bonds with family, society, and the divine beings. Thus, various divine beings influence everyday activities. The other rigidities are the caste system, role of women, personal actions, etc. However, the fluidness of Hinduism means that even these are changing, though slowly.

✝☆☪☸︎ॐ

Thus, one's Karma, natural events, and interactions with divine beings cause pain, suffering, and evil, which are a part of life.

✝☆☪☸︎ॐ

Authority in Hinduism is a 4,000-year-old search for truth, constrained by time, history, age, gender, consciousness, education, social position, social and economic conditions, geographic location, and stage of attainment. Thus, Hinduism is fluid, constrained, changing and a total way of life.

Discussion

The five religions claim authority by appealing to six areas: ancient scriptures, traditions, revelations, clerical authority, human reasoning, and personal experience. Why are the claims to those areas true? How does a devotee of one religion know that the six authority claims of the other religions are not true? That the devotee's religion is the one true religion? How does one prove that the claims of the five major religions in the six areas are true?

In the scientific sense, there is no proof that the six areas of authority of the five religions are true. Thus, it appears that to believe any of the six areas of the five religions is a "leap of faith." Unprovable. Could be true. Then again, it might not be true. Perhaps all five religions are true. Perhaps they are true in the sense that some, but not all, of what they claim is true. Perhaps the basics of all the five religions are not true. When there is so much disagreement among the followers and between the five religions, that implies there is an incomplete understanding of reality.

In the past four hundred years, science has done and continues to explain reality better than any of the five religions. However, science does not provide the solace, comfort and security that the six authority claims of the five religions offer.

Though, from my listening, reading, and seeing, it seems as if many of the devotees have a sense of not being sure. That they are unwilling or unable to express their doubts. That when a few do express doubts, the clergy and other devotees use group think and other unconscious methods to get the doubters back in line. If that doesn't work, they shun or physically or mentally abuse the doubters.

The Centrality of Jesus to Christianity.

It matters not whether one is conservative or liberal. Jesus is central to Christianity. But that centrality is based upon who Jesus is, obtaining a better afterlife, and differing impressions of what Jesus and Paul's teachings meant.

Assume that you are living back in Jesus' time and place. You know nothing about the New Testament, the birth, the life, the death, and the resurrection of Jesus, nor any of the creeds. You might or might not be Jewish. You have heard in the marketplace and from friends about this Jesus who says things that interest you. So, you decide to follow Jesus a day or perhaps even for several years as one of the anonymous people in the crowds. There is no interpretation by others. You are only hearing Jesus' words. The Apostles' Creed, the New Testament and the Christian Church did not exist. There was only Jesus' words and deeds.

What does Jesus say?

- ^{30} Love the Lord your God with all your heart and with all your soul and with all your mind and with all your strength.' ^{31} The second is this: 'Love your neighbor as yourself.' There is no commandment greater than these. (Mark 12:30-31)
- Man shall not live on bread alone, but on every word that comes from the mouth of God. (Matt 4:4)
- Do not put the Lord your God to the test. (Matt 4:7)
- Worship the Lord your God and serve him only! (Matt 4:11)
- Come, follow me," Jesus said, "and I will send you out to fish for people (Matt 4:19)

The beatitudes (Matt 5:3-11)

- ^{3} Blessed are the poor in spirit, for theirs is the kingdom of heaven.
- ^{4} Blessed are those who mourn, for they will be comforted.
- ^{5} Blessed are the meek, for they will inherit the earth.
- ^{6} Blessed are those who hunger and thirst for righteousness, for they will be filled.
- ^{7} Blessed are the merciful, for they will be shown mercy.
- ^{8} Blessed are the pure in heart, for they will see God.

- [9] Blessed are the peacemakers, for they will be called children of God.
- [10] Blessed are those who are persecuted because of righteousness, for theirs is the kingdom of heaven.
- [11] "Blessed are you when people insult you, persecute you and falsely say all kinds of evil against you because of me.
- [12] Rejoice and be glad, because great is your reward in heaven, for in the same way they persecuted the prophets who were before you.
- Proclaiming the good news of the kingdom and healing every disease and sickness among the people. (Matt 4:23)[213]
- Let your light shine before others, that they may see your good deeds and glorify your Father in heaven. (Matt 5:15)
- Watch out for the teachers of the law. They like to walk around in flowing robes and be greeted with respect in the marketplaces, [39] and have the most important seats in the synagogues and the places of honor at banquets. [40] They devour widows' houses and for a show make lengthy prayers. These men will be punished most severely. (Mark 12:38-40)
- Be careful not to practice your righteousness in front of others to be seen by them. If you do, you will have no reward from your Father in heaven. [2] "So when you give to the needy, do not announce it with trumpets, as the hypocrites do in the synagogues and on the streets, to be honored by others. Truly I tell you, they have received their reward in full. [3] But when you give to the needy, do not let your left hand know what your right hand is doing, [4] so that your giving may be in secret. Then your Father, who sees what is done in secret, will reward you. (Matt 6:1-4)

---

213 Jesus healed every illness and sickness. Why did the healing stop when he died and then rose from the dead?

- ⁵And when you pray, do not be like the hypocrites, for they love to pray standing in the synagogues and on the street corners to be seen by others. Truly I tell you, they have received their reward in full. ⁶ But when you pray, go into your room, close the door and pray to your Father, who is unseen. Then your Father, who sees what is done in secret, will reward you. (Matt 6:5-6)[214]

Jesus clearly says to keep prayer private. Perhaps this simple prayer like the Lord's Prayer.

² Father,

hallowed be your name,

your kingdom come.

³ Give us each day our daily bread.

⁴ Forgive us our sins,

for we also forgive everyone who sins against us.

And lead us not into temptation (Luke 11:2-4)

Public prayers are meant as having God present in all and to be thankful. Many people have a need to have all events blessed and believe that Christianity formed the basis of the United States. Therefore, they believe, it is imperative to inoculate people with Christian beliefs at every possible moment. So, they want public prayer to do God's bidding and to enhance a Christian society. Which is the same as the Muslim call to public prayer and drive to make Muslim societies. Similarly, with variation in Judaism and Hinduism.

Go read Matthew Chapters 4 – 20. Notice that Jesus makes many statements like the ones just quoted. Prayer is private. Healing is public. Miracles are public. There are quotes about sex, murder, taking care of the poor, reward for good behavior either now or in the afterlife, ask and you will receive, and many others. What is the impression from a literal and a liberal perspective?

---

[214] Contrast Jesus' statement with today many people push to have Christian prayer in public places like school, government meetings, dinners, sports events, etc. Many get irate when prayer isn't done.

Reading Matthew, as well as the other Gospels, this way creates an impression that emphasis is upon unconditional love, childlike obedience to the teachings of Jesus Christ, and separation from the world.[215] Neither literal nor liberal interpretation is important. Just love and do what Jesus said. Leave the rest up to God.

In the first three centuries love characterized the entire church. Roman society took note. Tertullian reported that the Romans would exclaim, "See how they love one another!"

Justin Martyr said, "We who used to value the acquisition of wealth and possessions more than anything else now bring what we have into a common fund and share it with anyone who needs it. We used to hate and destroy one another and refused to associate with people of another race or country. Now, because of Christ, we live together with such people and pray for our enemies."[216]

Do modern Conservative and Liberal Churches adhere to such statements? Or are they more concerned about a better afterlife? They seemed focused upon sex, power, wealth, and comfort in the here and now with guarantees about a blissful afterlife. Would Christians remain Christians if there was no "Blessed assurance" that there is a pleasant afterlife?

✝ ✡ ☪ ☸ ૐ

Yet, there is a powerful sense that Jesus was apocalyptic. That He preached the end times at hand. That one must be ready.

> "Truly I tell you, there are some standing here who will not taste death until they see that the kingdom of God has come with power." (Mark 9:1; cf. Matt 16:28 and Luke 9:27)

> "Truly I tell you, this generation will certainly not pass away until all

---

215 (Bercot, What was the early church like? n.d.)

216 (Bercot, Love Without Condition n.d.)

these things have happened." (Mark 13:30)

"When they persecute you in one town, flee to the next; for truly I tell you, you will not have gone through all the towns of Israel before the Son of Man comes." (Matt 10:23)

"For nation will rise against nation, and kingdom against kingdom, and there will be famines and earthquakes in various places …. For at that time there will be great suffering, such as has not been from the beginning of the world until now, no, and never will be …the sun will be darkened, and the moon will not give its light, the stars will fall from heaven and the powers of heaven will be shaken." (Matt 24, cf. Mark 13 and Luke 21)

"When the Son of Man comes in his glory, and all the angels with him, then he will sit on the throne of his glory. All the nations will be gathered before him, and he will separate people one from another as a shepherd separates the sheep from the goats, and he will put the sheep at his right hand and the goats at the left …. And these will go away into eternal punishment, but the righteous into eternal life." (Matt 25:31-33, 46)

So, John summoned two of his disciples and sent them to the Lord to ask, "Are you the one who is to come, or are we to wait for another?" When the men had come to him, they said, "John the Baptist has sent us to you to ask, 'Are you the one who is to come, or are we to wait for another?'" (Luke 7:18-20)

Jesus had just then cured many people of diseases, plagues, and evil spirits, and had given sight to many who were blind. And he answered them, "Go and tell John what you have seen and heard: the blind receive their sight, the lame walk, the lepers are cleansed, the deaf hear, the dead are raised, the poor have good news brought to them. And blessed is anyone who takes no offense at me." (Luke 7: 21-23)

> For since we believe that Jesus died and rose again, even so, through Jesus, God will bring with him those who have died. For this we declare to you by the word of the Lord, that we who are alive, who are left until the coming of the Lord, will by no means precede those who have died.[217] For the Lord himself, with a cry of command, with the archangel's call and with the sound of God's trumpet, will descend from heaven, and the dead in Christ will rise first. Then we who are alive[218], who are left, will be caught up in the clouds together with them to meet the Lord in the air; and so we will be with the Lord forever. (1Thess 4:14-17)

(Paul says, "we who are alive." He did not say, "we who will be alive" meaning some future distant time. The emphasis is on immediacy.)

Yet, the end times did not occur. For two thousand years Christians have waited for the end times. There are popular books about disappearing into the heavens, leaving the non-believers behind. There is no rationale as to why the end times did not occur when Jesus said they would. So, the present view that the end times are near is a leap of faith. It is demanding that God do what they believe the Holy Spirit dictated word for word through the authors of the New Testament. There is no proof that such dictation happened. Nor is there proof that the scriptures are true to the exclusion of the other four major religions. Thus, the fantasy about the end times is blasphemy.

The literal versus liberal understanding of scriptures.

The literalists insist that the authority of the Bible as inerrant must be adhered to. That one must live according to Jesus' commands in detail. When fallible humans can not follow the law, then they must take communion for the forgiveness of sins. The most important aspect of life is being saved for the next life in eternity. In comparison, nothing else matters. On the other hand, the

---

217 My emphasis.

218 My emphasis.

liberals emphasize the grace of God. That people love one another, trust God and leave salvation up to God.

The arguing and pondering over such issues create thirty thousand different religious sects and religions. There are plenty of books that describe the various beliefs, with attempts at justification of those beliefs. One can spend a lifetime reading them. The differences are important to the adherents; but, from Jesus' perspective, the differences don't matter. What matters is love in action. What matters is love and trust in God.

In every one of the sects and religions there are the issues of pain, suffering, jealousy and free will. What is the authority on which these various religions or sects base their beliefs?

To be a Christian, then, is to make a leap of faith whether one is conservative or liberal. A leap of faith to believe in Jesus as one's Lord and Savior, to make a leap of faith that Jesus died for the sins of the world, or that Jesus is just someone who shows a way to live a full life. Others will make attempts to meld reason and literal faith, reason and liberal faith. Some will just use reason. Others will just use faith.

My guess is that the majority of conservative and liberal Christians sense that their faith is based upon "knowing and not reason. That one must put reason aside and go deep inside."[219] Great pride is taken in meetings by making that or similar statements. Supporters nod in agreement.

Dietary

Four of the five major religions prohibit eating pork. Because of Peter's vision, God undid the prohibition to eat pork. Why does God prohibit eating pork

---

[219] This is not a stratified random sample of conservatives and liberals. It is based upon listening to more than a hundred people for several decades and noticing the predominant theme of "I just know the truth" or variations of the words. The reader might notice that it is also mentioned in some of their reputable books.

and allow Christians to eat pork? Why did God change the commandment only for Christians but not for the other four religions? By what authority did the various authors conclude and write that devotees are not to eat pork and how does one know that Peter's vision was valid to allow eating pork? Billions of people eat pork today. With proper cooking, the pork is clean, edible and nutritious which is proof that eating properly prepared pork is sanitary and healthy. It is not unclean, as the various as Muslims and Jews say. On what basis do Buddhist and Hindus decide to not kill animals? Though some hedge a bit and say it is ok to kill an animal for eating. Did a god reveal that? Why do Buddhists and Hindus believe that it is ok to kill in war?

> [6] And the hare, because it chews the cud but does not part the hoof, is unclean to you. [7] And the pig, because it parts the hoof and is cloven-footed but does not chew the cud, is unclean to you. [8] You shall not eat any of their flesh, and you shall not touch their carcasses; they are unclean to you. (Leviticus 11:6-8)

> [10] And he (Peter) became very hungry, and would have eaten: but while they made ready, he fell into a trance, [11] And saw heaven opened, and a certain vessel descending unto him, as it had been a great sheet knit at the four corners, and let down to the earth: [12] Wherein were all manner of four footed beasts of the earth, and wild beasts, and creeping things, and fowls of the air. [13] And there came a voice to him, Rise, Peter; kill, and eat. [14] But Peter said, Not so, Lord; for I have never eaten anything that is common or unclean. [15] And the voice spoke unto him again the second time, What God hath cleansed, that call not thou common. [16] This was done thrice: and the vessel was received up again into heaven. (Acts 10:10-16)

> "He [God] has forbidden you only dead animals, and blood, and the swine, and that which is slaughtered as a sacrifice for other than God." (Quran 2:173)

In Buddhism, the views on vegetarianism vary between different schools of thought. According to Theravada, the Buddha allowed his monks to eat pork, chicken and fish if the monk was aware that the animal was not killed on their behalf. The Mahayana schools generally recommend a vegetarian diet; according to some sutras, the Buddha himself insisted that his followers should not eat the flesh of any sentient being. Monks of the Mahayana traditions say that follow the Brahma Net Sutra are forbidden by their vows from eating flesh of any kind.[220]

One can never obtain meat without causing injury to living beings... therefore abstain from meat.... The man who authorizes, the man who butchers, the man who slaughters, the man who buys or sells, the man who cooks, the man who serves, and the man who eats – these are all killers. There is no greater sinner than a man who, outside of an offering to gods or ancestors, wants to make his own flesh thrive at the expense of someone else's. (Manusmriti, 5.48-5.52) But one can eat meat in a time of adversity.[221]

The five religions absolve God

The five faiths absolve their deities of creating a world where there are wars, diseases, disfigurements, abuse, theft, loneliness, etc. They all do not answer the issue of why a loving God creates free will that allows suffering that goes on for hours, days, weeks, months, years or decades? As one noted scholar said, Conservatives and Liberals try to defend God from what is indefensible. That "the Bible fails to answer our most important question – why we suffer."[222] Thus the reason for pain, suffering, and evil challenges the authority of Christian sacred texts, institutions, traditions, human reasoning

---

220 (Wikipedia 2018) Buddhist vegetarianism

221 (Wikipedia 2019) Diet in Hinduism

222 (B. D. Ehrman 2008) Title page

and personal experience(spiritual).

Pain, suffering, and evil challenge the authority of all the five religions' sacred texts, institutions, traditions, human reasoning and personal experience.

The five-faiths state that their authority is correct

Conservative Christians state that the Holy Spirit guided every stroke of the hand of the Biblical writers, and they focus on a personal relationship with Jesus Christ and the Holy Spirit. Based upon that understanding, they seek to convert the world to believing in Jesus Christ and are very involved in politics. Liberal Christians have a fluid view of authority as a historical understanding of the Bible and they have some experience of the divine. They accept the traditions of their church or sect and their vague experiences of the divine. The clergy, institutions, and some of the parishioners use human reasoning to understand their faith in an historical context to explain the truths contained in their faith in God. Based upon that understanding, as a group they do not look to convert, nor are they a coherent political force. However, both conservatives and liberals believe that pain, suffering, and evil are due to humanity's free will and humanity's fall from God.

Conservative Judaism's authority is rooted in rabbis interpreting a literal view of the scriptures and the commentaries. Liberal Judaism's authority is a fluid view of authority as an historical understanding of the scriptures, understood with reference to rabbinical interpretations. As a group they are very political and do not look to convert the world. Judaism tends to believe that pain, suffering, and evil are G-d's way of educating people, as a parent trains a child.

Both Sunni and Shia divisions of Islam accept the divine revelation of the archangel Gabriel to Muhammad, which his scribes quickly wrote down. They also accept the various collections of Muhammad's sayings and teachings. Based upon that understanding, they expect to convert the world and are a worldwide political force in the world which they expect to convert. They believe that pain, suffering, and evil are merely tests; the results of the test(s) will be known in the hereafter; and that Allah knows what is best and the purpose for human pain, suffering and evil.

Buddhism accepts the authoritative teachings of Buddha and expects that, with guidance of skilled teachers, followers will have more understanding and be better skilled in Buddhism. Though there are Buddhists who are very politically active and seek converts, they tend not to be a political force in the world and tend not to convert the world. Pain, suffering, and evil are an illusion. By understanding Karma and following the Noble Path, one will achieve liberation.

Hinduism accepts the authority of various ancient scriptures, Brahmin interpretations, personal experiences, and traditions thousands of years old. While it seeks truth and can be quite fluid in beliefs, it is also very rigid in many views. It is a political force in countries where it has a significant population. It does not appear to be seeking converts. One's Karma, natural events, and interactions with divine beings cause pain, suffering and evil.

Is the authority of the five religions correct?

How does one know that sacred texts, institutions, traditions, human reasoning and personal experience(spiritual) of the five religions are correct? Particularly how does one know that their view concerning pain, suffering, and evil are eternally true? Just because some people say it is so, doesn't make it so. It is purely a leap of faith to assume that what people wrote some one to three thousand years ago is true for all eternity. Those people who pondered, thought, and wrote had a world view and experiences far different than now. They meant well. They had insights that are worth pondering and considering today and in the future. But people do not need to be bound by past traditions and thoughts. They can, if they want to be. But that does not mean it is true, nor match reality.

Testing for validity of the five religions

The reason is that the five religions have no way of testing that the basis for their religions are true.[223] While there are appeals to individual experiences, group experiences, traditions, human logic, and archeological finds, they provide no proof that the fundamental basis of their religions are factual, true and without error. Just because people claim a revelation, have an experience, gain an insight, have inspiration, know that the truth is in them, know they are right, etc. does not mean that their faith is true. Rather, it just means that they have an experience or thought and make a leap to concluding that the experience or thought faith is true. Thus, their religions are a leap of faith.

So, some of the responses to doubt are:

- Try it. You will like it.
- You are standing against traditions that are thousands of years old.
- You are doubting the scriptures that are thousands of years old.
- Who are you to question the religions?
- Just accept and you will understand.
- God works in mysterious ways that are beyond human understanding.
- Any conflicts in the scriptures or understanding are just a limitation of humanity.
- People have free will to accept or not. So, accept and receive the rewards.
- Look at the world. It conforms to what the scriptures and traditions say. You are blind.
- You are of the devil to question the faith.

---

223 However, Buddhism does claim to test what is taught. Use the experiences with the help of a skilled guide to make improvements. However, one of the fundamental beliefs of Buddhism is the pain, suffering and evil are illusions. The other is that there is karma and multiple lives. These points are probably not testable; though it would be interesting to somehow create a series of replicable tests.

- If you just accept the faith, you wouldn't have questions nor doubts.
- Everyone has doubts. It is God's way of strengthening faith.
- Someday you will understand.
- It is disrespectful to question people's religions. They have their truths.
- Faith provides comfort. Why are you trying to undermine their comfort?
- Some adherents believe, that any conflict with science shows science is wrong.
- Some adherents believe, that any conflict with science means to do more dialogue.

Can beliefs of the five religions be proved?

Basically, it seems that some clergy forcefully claim divine revelation or insight into their scriptures. When people speak with authority, many people believe them, whether the person speaking with authority is correct or not. There is some deep-seated psychology in humans, that when one speaks with authority, whether correct or not, that many people will believe that person. Perhaps it just takes too much time and effort to ferret through the various claims that authority figures make. So, they go along.

For example, Charles Templeton interviewed Billy Graham:[224]

> I said (to Billy Graham), "But Bill, it's simply not possible any longer to believe, for instance, the biblical account of creation. The world wasn't created over a period of days a few thousand years ago; it has evolved over millions of years. It's not a matter of speculation; it's demonstrable fact."
>
> "I don't' accept that," Bill said. "And there are reputable scholars who don't."

---

[224] (C. Hitchens 2007) Pages 282-283

"Who are these scholars?" I said. "Men in conservative Christian colleges?"

"Most of them, yes," he said. "But that's not the point. I believe the Genesis account of creation because it's in the Bible. I've discovered something in my ministry: when I take the Bible literally, when I proclaim it as the Word of God, my preaching has power. When I stand on the platform and say, 'God says,' or 'the Bible says,' the Holy Spirit uses me. There are results. Wiser men than you and I have been arguing questions like this for centuries. I don't have the time or the intellect to examine all sides of each theological dispute, so I've decided, once and for all, to stop questioning and accept the Bible as God's Word."

"But Billy," I protested, "you can't do that. You don't dare stop thinking about the most important question in life. Do it and you begin to die. It is intellectual suicide."

I don't know about anybody else," he said, "But I've decided that that's the path for me."

Templeton's dialogue with Graham is most likely similar to the basic position of most if not all clergy of the five religions. They really do not know, and are unwilling to admit, that they don't know if their faith is really true. Instead, they forcefully speak about their faith as Graham did, because the preaching and writing has power, or they meekly push aside answering the questions as shown above.

So, Graham is saying, 'There are too many smart people who can't figure this out. So, I am taking the faith as true and will convince others.' In that sense, he wasn't sure if he was right or wrong. He only knew that he couldn't figure it out. He went with what felt right with him. Did Graham ever have doubts about his faith while he was convincing millions of people? Was it ethical to speak with such conviction when he just forced himself to be convinced and, perhaps over the decades, he became convinced? On the other hand, was Graham right in making a leap of faith and pretending there was no doubt? Did he know he was right because he had a feeling of power? Did he persuade millions because "he taught as one who had authority"[225]?

Testing or proving the five religions is sacrilege

Many believe that using a scientific world view to study the basis of Christianity, Judaism, Islam, Buddhism and Hinduism is a sacrilege. The standard response tends to be, 'Religion deals with the ultimate questions of humanity. Science deals with the world. The two overlap a bit; but they deal with different domains of the human experience. Some believe, it is not valid to bring science into religious understanding.' Another typical response is, "Science guys always have trouble with religion. Just accept the faith. It has been around for thousands of years. Who are science guys to question that kind of faith?" There are other similar quotes previously listed.

Yet, there are many who believe that religion and science are complementary. That they are different views of that world and both should respect each other. They presume that religion and science can coexist together and have truths for all mankind. That is possible. However, that is not the scientific process. The scientific process does not try to meld any points of view just to get them to agree. Instead, the overly simplified science process is:

- Gather facts as best as one understands the facts
- Create a theory
- Test the theory
- Modify or discard the theory as appropriate.
- Use the theory.
- Issues? Start again.

Thus, accept the theory until questions arise or develop a better theory. Then replace the earlier theory. Ideally, there is no attempt to force competing

---

225 Matthew 7:29 and Mark 1:22, describing how Jesus spoke with authority.

theories to fit the facts or the facts to fit the theory. The facts and theory are what they are. Using the scientific process, one might conclude that one of the five religions is more accurate. The scientific method is not to prove a faith is true. That is not science. Instead, that is ideology masquerading as science and at best it is pseudo-science.

The scientific examination of the five religions would examine and test each dogmatic statement, creed, and presupposition. Then if factual or plausible, so be it. If not, so be it. Drop the dogmas and put them in museums. As with good science, then take the results and create something from the five religions.

Most clergy feel a calling

Most clergy of the five religions, probably feel that they have a calling to take care of their flocks. To help and guide them in their times of need. To offer comfort and solace and a hope of a better afterlife. To rejoice with them in the happy times and cry with them in the sad times. To be defenders of the faith and guide people to a stronger faith in their deity.

However, there are clergy who want political influence. And there are politicians more than willing to use the clergy to bolster their political positions. So, they bolster each other. In the meantime, the literalists and the liberals fight each other in what they perceive as important battles of faith and truth.

The literalists believe that there should be no limits to expression of their faith. Thus, there are clergy that believe that their views should dominate the world, societies, nations, groups, families and individuals. Missionaries travel the world to convince people to accept their views. Meanwhile in secular societies, they advocate freedom to choose to whom they supply services and products. If someone is of a belief or faith that they feel is against their faith, then they have the duty not to provide those people with services or goods.

On the other hand, the liberals should in love supply services or goods to anyone no matter what their beliefs are.

Each side believes the other is imposing their religious views on the other. Because of the leaps of faith, the gap is too wide to bridge.

It would be interesting for the resurrected Jesus, Muhammad, Buddha, Moses, and Ramanuja[226] to visit and make some comments about wedding cakes, wedding licenses, refusal to serve LGBT, birth control, prayer at sports events, prayer before political meetings, blessings for war, etc. Would they take sides, or would they speak in love? Which of their scriptural verses would they quote? My guess is they would say, "Love one another. Stop the various denominations and sects quarreling about doctrine and scriptural interpretations."

They might say that the quarrelling lacks basic trust in God. It is grasping for guarantees for righteousness to have the surety of a happy next or eternal life. There is a refusal to have a loving life with those outside of one's religious sect or viewpoint.

Total view of social, political, and economic activities

Both conservatives and liberals of the five faiths have a total view of social, political and economic activities. While the conservatives are full of energy to impose their belief system on society, the liberals are tired, exhausted and unable to express their views, trying to bridge the unbridgeable gap. The literalists preach assurance, while the liberals preach uncertainty. In these times, people are searching for assurance, which the liberals are incapable of delivering. Consequently, the liberal churches are dying while the conservative churches are growing in numbers and with political influence.

Message of love in the first few centuries

The Roman Empire was based upon slavery, conquest, and power, while the basic Christian message was love. People began to feel that they were

---

226 Born c. 1017, Shriperumbudur, India—died 1137

valued, lovable, and free. This was a threat to the Roman power structure. Consequently, there were persecutions. However, by the time of the Emperor Constantine, Christianity was widespread. To control the threat to slavery and power, Constantine gathered the bishops together. It was an effort to solidify control so that the basic structure (slavery, conquest and power) of the Empire remained intact. The church would support Constantine and in turn, Constantine would support the church. Control was the key for both the clergy and the emperors. Together they would control the population. Without slaves, the economy and political life would have been in turmoil. The nature of the church changed from love to control. Eventually, the dominant theme became "You are by nature sinful and unclean." "You will have freedom in the afterlife." A phenomenal way to control a slave population. It became a means of oppression, so that the rulers could rule and keep the economy stable. The Church supplied stability and control. In turn, various states supported the church for nearly two thousand years.

Literal versus liberal scriptural interpretation

Another fundamental issue in the five religions is the literal versus liberal interpretation of the scriptures in the five religions. Many people believe that only the literal interpretation of scriptures is correct; that the traditions have authority; that the clergy must be listened to; that human reasoning, when it agrees with the faith, is correct; and, that peoples' experiences to include revelations that confirm the faith are acceptable.

Unless both sides are willing to engage in long term dialogue focused on obtaining truth, there is no hope of bridging the gap. The five religions have well over 30,000 different sects divided by differing interpretations of their scriptures, adhering to traditions, differing institutions, human reasoning, individual experiences and revelations. Each sect tends to believe they have the right interpretation. Some of the sects are more open to the idea that they have a glimpse of what is right. Unless forced by declining numbers and finances, they cling to their views and won't budge from the righteousness of their position.

For example, interpreting the Christian Bible from a literal perspective means that the Bible is completely harmonious and without error. Anything that appears to be an error shows the limitations of human understanding, copying errors, or translation errors. When science or logic conflicts with a literal understanding, then science and logic is in error, not the Bible.

For example, the Bible has various stories. In one, a talking snake entraps two innocent people for not obeying God's order and then God punishes mankind forever. In another, God tells a father to sacrifice his son. Then, when he is about to, God praises him for faith. In another, God tells people to kill all the people in the land and conquer it. Today that is genocide. The same God tells Noah to build an ark because He will wipe all living beings off the world because he is angry about human sin. So, God kills all land creatures except the ones on the ark in pairs of two. The sea creatures were apparently ok to God; so, they all lived. Apparently, the sea creatures ate all the carcasses of the land creatures that died. Then God sent his son to be a child, teach, and heal a bit. Jesus died on the cross for the sins of the world. People who don't believe in that, God condemns to hell for an eternity of suffering. Thus, God says, "Love me or I will torment you forever. Also, you have free will; so, it is your fault that you suffer for eternity." Finally, original sin and freewill cause pain, suffering and evil. What kind of God creates such a system? A loving God? A sane God?

On the other hand, interpreting the Bible from a liberal perspective treats the Bible as a collection of documents that were written over a period of several thousand years, in different languages, cultures, and scientific understandings. One must step into the very shoes of the authors, as best as one can, to understand what they were trying to say. Then one brings the basic essence of what was said into today's culture. Finally, the priest or minister explains it to a local congregation in whatever context or issue they face. This allows a huge amount of room for interpretation. The liberal interpretation tends to focus on love, and then almost anything else goes. They tend to gloss over pain, suffering, and evil, perhaps mentioning original sin and free will to do what one wants.

✝☆☾✡☸️ॐ

The same basic issue is in Judaism, with the Orthodox Jews claiming their view, while the Reformed Jews take a more nuanced and accepting view. For example, Orthodox Jews have extremely strict and detailed dietary rules. Meanwhile, Reformed Jews are more open about the rules, they still follow the intent. Both seem to believe that G-d is active in punishing people and nations that don't follow the laws. Therefore, there is pain, suffering and evil.

✝☆☾✡☸️ॐ

The same basic stance occurs in Islam with the Sunni Muslims claiming authority from one line of prophets and the Shia Muslims claiming authority from a different line. Therefore, there is pain, suffering, and evil which are tests for followers to pass to get to heaven.

✝☆☾✡☸️ॐ

The same occurs somewhat in Buddhism, with various schools of thought, though it is not as pronounced as with the Abrahamic religions. Pain, suffering, and evil is just an illusion caused by attachment.

✝☆☾✡☸️ॐ

Hinduism is more open in accepting many different views. However, deep divisions are beginning as forces inside of Hinduism challenge the basic tenets of their faith. Some of the challenges are about the caste system, human rights, the role of women in society and the home. At the root cause of the conflict is accepting the idea that one's past lives cause pain, suffering, and evil in this life. That people should do better now for a better next life.

Drop that view and the other issues will tend to go away. Yet, there is a strong conservative push to implement strict views of Hinduism in their societies.

It would be satisfying to prove that one of the authorities of the five religions have the truth. Or that, there is some sort of commonality in the five religions that everyone can agree on. Or that, the five religions are merely representations by humans of the divine, which is beyond all understanding, and therefore all religions are true from their historical context. The analogys of the five blind men touching an elephant. They try to explain what it is. One touches the trunk. Others touch a leg, a tail, the body and another the head. They all come up with an explanation of what they perceive as the truth of the elephant. Yet, while each one is correct, each misses the whole of the elephant. Thus, the five religions have their representation of the divine, which is at best only a part of the whole. Thus, fallible humans continue with the five religions, believing that they have the truth. Some believing that their faith is literally true, and the other religions are in error; while others believe that their faith is a representation of truth.

To answer these basic questions, devotees of the five religions accept their sacred texts, institutions, traditions, human reasoning and individual experiences to explain pain, suffering, and evil by making leaps of faith.

Chapter 20

A Meaningful Life

Figure 20.1 The five religions are concerned about people in this life, while some are more concerned about the afterlife. Here the Good Samaritan is concerned about a person. Does he care about the afterlife?

Religious people in the five religions say that their faith gives their lives meaning. That without their faith, life has no meaning. So, the five religions tell people what the meaning of life is. This section examines those various meanings of life.

Christianity and The Meaning of Life

According to Ecclesiastes life is meaningless:

> Enjoy life with your wife, whom you love, all the days of this meaningless life that God has given you under the sun—all your meaningless days. For this is your lot in life and in your toilsome labor under the sun. (Eccl 9:9).

According to Jesus:

> ^{37} Jesus replied: "'Love the Lord your God with all your heart and with all your soul and with all your mind.' ^{38} This is the first and greatest commandment. ^{39} And the second is like it: 'Love your neighbor as yourself.' ^{40} All the Law and the Prophets hang on these two commandments." (Matthew 22:37-40)

Therefore, the primary purpose of life is to love God with all one's heart, mind, and soul, in order to have happy everlasting life. But when one does not love and know God, then there is no real everlasting joy in one's life, and life is without meaning. That does not mean that an earthly life will be wonderful and blissful. Rather, it means that by loving God, studying the teachings of Jesus, being faithful in giving, and being at Church, the meaning of life becomes clearer. Eventually, the faithful will be with God in the afterlife.

Many Christians also believe that the real meaning of life is only for God's glory. That people are to praise and worship God while proclaiming God's greatness and doing his will. [227] That one's life is solely for God, and to do what God planned. It is up to the individual to express that plan. By trusting in God's guiding spirit, through good times and severe adversity, individuals will know the meaning of life. Eventually, the faithful will reunite with God in the afterlife.

Jesus condemns to hell for all eternity those that:

- Follow their own desires,
- Do not trust in God's guidance,
- Do not study God's word,
- Do not pray,
- Do not take part in worship.

Judaism and The Meaning of Life

According to Ecclesiastes life is meaningless:

---

227 (Slick 2012)

Enjoy life with your wife, whom you love, all the days of this meaningless life that God has given you under the sun–all your meaningless days. For this is your lot in life and in your toilsome labor under the sun. (Eccl 9:9).

Therefore, the primary purpose of life is to love G-d with all one's heart, all one's mind, and all one's soul. When the Jew responds to that call, keeping the commandment of the Torah is a blessing and a joy. It is a blessing and an encounter with the divine. That encounter is the true meaning of life. When that happens, there is no question and no doubt - just understanding that is difficult to explain. One just understands and feels the meaning of life. [228] One's life then has meaning, has a purpose and power. The force is so strong that one is willing to sacrifice one's life for it. That is why, throughout history, Jews have been willing to sacrifice their lives.[229] It is better for a Jew to die for G-d than to live without G-d.

G-d created people to serve their maker by fearing G-d, studying the Torah, and building the spiritual capital of the world in Jerusalem (which means "perfect awe"). These are steps towards the coming of the Messiah, when the world will know and worship G-d. The world will then be like the Garden of Eden. [230]

Islam and The Meaning of Life

The primary purpose of life is to worship the Creator and pass the test of life. Those that pass it will have eternal bliss.[231] Allah will help those that accept the help to enjoy the pleasure of His presence, guidance, admonitions and Paradise.[232] Those that do not pass the test of life pay the price.

---

228 (Fackenheim 1965)

229 (Weinberg n.d.)

230 (Izquierdo 2017)

231 (Malaekah 2001)

232 (What is Islam? 2010?)

Buddhism and The Meaning of Life

The primary purpose of life is to liberate oneself from suffering, [233] for oneself and for others to be happy, [234] and to achieve Nirvana. People suffer because they strive for that which does not give lasting happiness. This does not mean non-attachment from all things, people and experiences. Rather, it is recognizing that nothing is permanent. Enjoy things, people, and experiences; but do not become attached to things, people and experiences. The attachment causes suffering. The true meaning of life is helping others be free from suffering, to realize their true potential,[235] and to eventually achieve bliss. The point is not to become a Buddhist; but rather, to become a better you who is free from suffering and helping others [236].

The Four Noble Truths and the Noble Eightfold Path guide people to achieve the meaning of life.[237]

Hinduism and The Meaning of Life

The primary purpose of life is release from the cycle of births, deaths, disease, suffering, and attachment.[238] The key to Hinduism is not worshiping one of many gods; instead, it is devotion to someone or something to surpass the ego and achieve oneness with the other.[239] Thus, one develops wisdom and discretion to pursue wealth and happiness while achieving liberation.

---

233 (The Meaning of Life in Buddhism 2016)

234 (Chugh 2016)

235 (What is the Purpose of Life in Buddhism n.d.)

236 (Quotations on: Joy, Happiness n.d.)

237 For explanation of Four Noble Truths and the Eight-Fold Path, see the section Buddhism and Joy

238 (V, Ananda, the State of Bliss or Happiness n.d.)

239 (V, Introduction to Hinduism 2012)

Discussion

A better next life

The five religions say that the meaning of life is a better next life. Nothing else matters. One might suffer all one's life, or one might be joyful all one's life. That doesn't matter. Being rich or poor doesn't matter. Being in sickness or in health doesn't matter. Only a better next life matters. For Christians and Muslims there is only one chance, and that is in this life. For Jews there is the Messiah, who will eventually come. Judaism has different opinions as to what happens after a Jew dies and before the Messiah comes. For Buddhists and Hindus, it is passing through cycles of births, deaths, and suffering to eventually achieve eternal bliss.

Yet, there is no proof that the five religions are right. They offer as proofs their sacred texts, institutions, traditions, human reasoning and personal experience. They say that one cannot prove those wrong. Therefore, their view is true. No one has proven the essence of their views wrong. Especially, that there is no proof that their meaning of life is wrong. Therefore, they say their meaning of life is true. How can one prove what happens or doesn't happen in the next life? Or if there is a next life? How does one prove that the essence of the five religions is true or false?

A leap of faith

An informal survey over a forty-year period of a thousand people[240] show that religious people claim to experience God. They seem unsure of the doctrines of their faith. But they are quite clear that they experience something; which they use to accept whatever their cleric says about their faith.

For instance, "Experiencing God is like a soft gentle comforting breeze that

---

240 This is my impression of listening to people for more than forty years. So, on the one hand it is not statistically rigorous. On the other hand, it indicates that a more rigorous process might or might not validate the impressions built upon listening to perhaps a thousand people.

blows on a hot humid day." One notices it. One feels it. One is joyful for it. And then it is gone. Yet, the sense of God is still there. For others, it is more forceful. But for most that have experienced God, it is a present stillness that is mysteriously active. Once one meets that presence, then one changes forever. Thus, in their view clerical and scholarly writings and speeches are just meaningless musings unless they agree with their experience. What is real is the indescribable experience of God.

The worry and arguments about a loving God that allows pain, suffering, and evil to happen are insignificant compared to the experience of God. Some people will say that, through pain and suffering, one experiences the transcendence of the divine. But why does a loving transcendent God allow pain, suffering and evil?

Typically, people of the five religions will say, "How does one describe the love for another person? One can use many words, such as 'the heart sings.' The soul joyfully floats on a street where the beloved lives. Their religious songs are about love. Yet, all these attempts do not adequately explain love to those that have not loved," or have loved imperfectly. For those with such experiences, the intellectual explanations are irrelevant and miss the whole point.

And so, the conversation ends. Those who do not understand the experience of God feel dismissed as a dumb child incapable of understanding what others so easily understand with the effortlessness of a god. Or, they give respect to the religious descriptions and people that claim to have the religious experiences. Thus, a gap grows between those that claim the experience of God and those that don't.

But the five religions say, those that have experienced God might at times say to the unfortunates that have not experienced God, "Try it. You will like it." Or, "Just submit and you too will experience the divine. We will show you the way. It is easy." To non-believers, those are words that sound like a salesperson hawking a thing or service that is a scam. Something just doesn't seem right. One is to put away one's logic and intuition and then just experience something. Then accept the joyful, wonderful and indescribable experience. Those that have experienced God tend to say, "See, see, you just experienced God."

Some people say, "I believe, that we humans are souls having an earthly experience. That when I die, I go on to experience another existence." I just know that. That is the meaning in my life.

Make a leap of faith or not?

Is choosing a religion like choosing a car, food, house, or a spouse? One just likes it. Religious people say, "True faith depends upon neither proof nor reason, but belief in something to be true. True faith is self-existing. It is sustained by itself, either by intuition or belief, but rarely by an external proof."[241]

Clergy have devoted decades to learning their profession. The Christian priest or pastor, the Muslim mullah, the Jewish Rabbi, the Buddhist monk and the Hindu priest will suffer significant loss to give up their faith. Their families, relatives and followers will shun them. They will suffer a huge monetary impact. They will have to learn a new trade, get a new job, explain to future employers what happened. For someone in their forties or fifties, this is a near impossible task.

Emotionally for the clergy and followers it will be devastating because their faith helps them make sense of the world and guides them through struggles and uncertain moments. They fervently believe that their faith heals their mind and their body. They will claim that people cannot get through devasting periods of their lives without one of their five religions. That the five religions have formed civilization and are the basis for the modern world.

---

241 (V, What is Faith? Faith in Hinduism n.d.)

They will say to lay people that crises of faith are tests that make devotees stronger in one of the five religions. That the Christian, Muslim, Jewish, Buddhist or Hindu clergy will help the crisis pass. One will be stronger and be able to lead others in the faith and to salvation, bliss, or a better next life depending on the faith.

Losing that loving feeling

Then there are a few that 'experience God,' only to reflect on it and lose the loving feeling. Just like losing a loved one. One remembers the joy and wonder of the other person and then, with daily activities, the memories fade. Occasionally, wistfully one remembers the person or the spirit of the person like a gentle comforting breeze on a sweltering day. A memory that creates sadness that the wonderful experience is gone.

Perhaps that is why many believers in the five religions shy away from thinking about their faith. They might lose the sense of wonder. That when one is in love, one does not want to think about what the other person is really like. It is like the saying, "Love is blind." That love is blind to the foibles, irritations, misperceptions, and all the idiosyncrasies that the other person has. Instead, one is just delighted to be in the presence of "The Other." When a devotee fills with joy of the divine, the illogic of human feelings of the divine are irrelevant. Some devotees will point to the non-intuitiveness of quantum mechanics as being like their faith. "Look, scientists say that quantum mechanics is mysterious just like the grace and experience of the divine."

Clearly, religious people are experiencing something. What is it? Something deeply rooted in human biology which religious people interpret as God? Something strong enough that they will deny the beliefs of other sects and of the other four religions? They deny others because of diverse cultures, vocabulary, institutions, doctrines, and clergy rather than different experiences. Perhaps the masses of people are right that they are experiencing something they call divine, and their clergy claim it as proof of their faith. Perhaps not.

Why did God, G-d, Allah, Karma, and Hindu Gods choose to make divine revelations?

Why were there revelations to just a few individuals sporadically for five thousand years? Why not make the revelations across the earth all at one time, in the local languages? Why make the revelations that focus upon the sins and evils of people as compared to how to have healthy lives, healthy societies, how to avoid war, best way to run economies, healthy human interactions, the way to do science, politics, education, sex, etc.?

Instead, God allows misery and suffering for thousands of years (if one believes the earth is six thousand years old) or for hundreds of thousands, if not millions of years. Why? What is the purpose? What kind of God does this?

Ask Christian, Muslim, Jewish, Buddhist, and Hindu clergy what the basis of their beliefs are. Keep pressuring them to give an answer that is not 'a leap of faith.' Go ahead. While they won't be as clear as Billy Graham was, they might say something like, "I am not smart enough to answer the basic philosophic questions of faith, so I take the Christian, Jewish, Muslim, Buddhist or Hindu scriptures of my faith and will proclaim their meaning." Most likely they won't say that. In a limited survey every cleric I have interviewed has equivocated.[242]

That stand is misleading people. If the foundation of their faith is not provable, then they are misleading people. If the foundation of their faith is provable and they don't explain how it is provable, they do not understand the fundamental basics of their faith. Granted they can explain in detail what their faith is. However, they cannot and will not explain their leap of faith. They equivocate, saying, "Science has its' domain. Religion has its' domain." As though that makes their faith true. Then the clergy of the five religions

---

242 My survey is probably around two hundred clerics over a period of fifty years. It was not statistically recorded nor subsequently validated.

take that leap and pronounce to the world that they have THE truth. Though there are some that are not as adamant. In either case, they make a leap of faith. Then they claim that they have the true faith.

Readers really should push their clergy on this point of leap of faith. They should ask "How do they know that their leap of faith is true and that one must believe them instead of some other faith or philosophy?" The clergy can't. They will get angry and mumble some words like:

- Experience it. Don't be logical.
- Try it you will like
- Logic will never lead one to faith
- I have studied these issues and therefore I am right.
- Show facial displeasure with the questions
- Your sins consume you – repent then you will believe
- What is wrong with you
- The devil is playing with you.
- The devil has a hold of you.
- Go someplace else.

The clergy take pride that their faith trumps logic and facts. Some clergy attempt to meld logic, science, and their faith.

What kind of creator gives free will and then punishes?

The clergy respond to free will issues with, "You have a choice. God gives you the free will. You are choosing to believe what you want, and God allows you to believe what you want. The result is what you choose. If you choose what pleases God, then the reward is bliss. If you choose what does not please God, then the reward is less than bliss and probably Hell. So, God is not forcing you. You are doing the choosing. Why do you blame God for what you want to do? Choose my belief and you will have a meaningful life."

Religious violence

Each of the five religions have religious leaders that advocate violence in the name of their religion. What is the meaning of life for religious leaders that advocate violence against others?

What kind of meaning?

Do God, G-d, Allah, Buddha, Karma, and the Hindu gods say, "The meaning of life is to get through life to commune joyously and eternally with the divine.... But.... First believe the right set of doctrines, dogmas, be good enough, and be pure enough."?

Other people say.... "It is solely by God's grace one goes to heaven." Or, as some religions say, "You have multiple lives to improve yourself and prove yourself worthy to have eternal bliss."

What kind of God says, "The meaning of human life is to please Me in this life, so you will have a better next life"?

What is the meaning of life when the Christian, Jewish, Muslim, Buddhist, and Hindu deities or forces:

- Created or allowed evil to exist?
- Created sex drives only for marriage?
- Created sex drives only for procreation?
- Created people having trouble loving?
- Promises an afterlife without any proof?
- Allowed individual and corporate sin to exist?
- Forgives people of their sins, but does not give power to stop sinning?
- Created suffering instead of eradicating all disease, illness, and war?
- Created free will and then punishes people for inappropriately using freewill?

- Allows so many misinterpretations of experiencing something that people call a deity?
- Claim that their scriptures, traditions, clergy and thoughts are THE truth?
- Condemned most of humanity to hell but promises joy in the afterlife to their believers?
- Created the meaning of life to be getting through life to have a better life in the afterlife?
- Created the five religions to be a leap of faith which might or might not be true?
- Claim authority without proof?

How do the clergy know any of these statements and know that other religions are wrong? Wrong enough in some cases to preach violence against people of other beliefs?

Is it enough that the clergy of the five religions know that they are right according to their sacred texts, institutions, traditions, human reasoning, and personal experience? Is that enough? One cannot prove the faith portions of their beliefs through rigorous testing. Their beliefs are a leap of faith. Thus, their view of the meaning of life is a leap of faith.

Nevertheless, Christians, Muslims, Jews, Buddhists, and Hindus seem to say,

- Why do you have to prove it? Our faith just is.
- Why do you have to understand it? Just accept the faith.
- How do you know we are wrong? We just know we are right.
- How do you know our scriptures are in error? God divinely revealed them.
- Submit to the will of God. Give up your free will and you will have a better afterlife.
- Experience our faith? Try it, you will like it.
- Our experience is not a leap of faith. It is a complete and total experience. So, it is true.

- Why do you try to destroy our faith which gives us meaning and comfort?
- Life has no meaning without our faith.

Make sense of the world

Perhaps it is as two psychiatrists said[243],

> Life has no meaning. The only meaning it has is what we ourselves give it, and, sadly, we often forget we are the ones who gave it the meaning.

> Man has a deep need to worship, and if he doesn't worship the true and living God, he ends up worshipping false gods that are merely projections of himself.

Perhaps then, the five faiths are creations by humans to make sense of the world, to feel better about their lives, to just get through their lives without knowing they are responsible for what happens and doesn't happen in their lives and their societies, or to satisfy the desire of leaders to control people. Or the five religions are like totalitarianism, which controls every aspect of one's life. Perhaps the priests, pastors, rabbis, imams, Buddhist monks, Hindu priests, religious scholars of the five religions, etc. are part of an apparatus that controls people for the benefit of the rulers.

Fact and fiction

Hannah Arendt wrote in *The Origins of Totalitarianism*,[244] "The ideal subject of totalitarian rule is not the convinced Nazi or the convinced communist, but people for whom the distinction between fact and fiction (i.e. the reality of experience) and the distinction between true and false (i.e. the standards of thought) no longer exist." "That people will believe the fiction of their religion by not being able to distinguish between fact or the reality of experience

---

243 (Wiesner 2006)

244 (Arendt, The Origins of Totalitarianism 1966) Part 3, Ch. 13, § 3

and fiction. That they will not have the standards of thought to distinguish between truth and falsehood of religions."

People are good at lying

People are good at lying to themselves, as individuals, families, groups, societies, and nations. People tend to believe what they believe and believe it with great assurance. Nothing can change their minds. So, if people believe a falsehood, most people will cling to that falsehood as a fact. For some reason, people who know less about a topic are more willing to talk as if they know more about that topic than they really do.[245]

After interviewing more than one hundred clergy over a period of forty years, I noticed a pattern. They are good at repeating back their faith's beliefs. However, they do not understand and are incapable of pondering the assumptions of their faith. They do what Billy Graham did. They just accept the assumptions without realizing that those are assumptions and they go on with their lives. The clergy that are tolerant of other religions try to get along with the other religions. They realize or vaguely realize that there are areas of their lives that they do not understand and are willing to live with some level of nebulousness. However, there are other clergy, usually the fundamentalists of the five religions, that are intolerant of any other faith. They claim to KNOW what is true and that they have the truth.

People needing reassurance like the clergy that speak with authority and assuredness. There is something about people that can speak on any topic, whether religious, politics, business, personal, etc. with great confidence. They attract followers. Those that speak timidly, or give the feeling that the understanding is tentative, do not attract followers.

---

245 (Goldhill 2018), "The person who's best at lying to you is you." This is known as the Dunning-Kruger Effect.

Lying is a cooperative act

When one person lies and the other person accepts, then both are agreeing to the lie. This happens with individuals, families, groups, societies, and nations. People unwillingly and unknowingly take part in the lie. They might suspect that something doesn't seem right, yet they go along. They are taking part in the lie. They feel comfortable with what the person is saying, so they go along with the lie because they feel good about it. In principle people are against lying; yet, people take part in lying all the time. Maybe people are too lazy to stop the lying, or it makes people feel good. Or they don't want to rock the boat. In any case, many people believe their lies.[246]

Ask, "How do you know?" "Why believe what a Christian, Muslim, Jewish, Buddhist, or Hindu cleric is saying?" It will be a roller coaster ride of difficulties, and for the believer many more downs than ups because of responses mentioned earlier. Nevertheless, keep respectfully asking.

Conclusion

Part I was my personal journey about seeking meaning in religion. Part II was a consolidation of the doubts many people whispered to me. The topics were theirs with clerical responses and the discussion was a consolidation of their whisperings. So, you are not alone with doubts, shunning, and depression. Part III provides a short guide for you to create a meaningful life with or without religion. Take heart and drive on.

Thus,

- Christian liberalism is a leap of faith
- Christian fundamentalism is a leap of faith
- Christian Orthodoxy is a leap of faith
- Orthodox Judaism is a leap of faith
- Reform or liberal Judaism is a leap of faith

---

246 (Meyers 2011)

- Islam is a leap of faith
- Buddhism is a leap of faith
- Hinduism is a leap of faith
- Probably all religions are a leap of faith.

So, how to create meaning in life with or without Christianity, Judaism, Islam, Buddhism, Hinduism, or any religion?

Part III

Creating a Meaningful Life

What is a meaningful life?

How do you create a meaningful life?

You make it up! You create it![247]

---

[247] Adapted (Fritz, The Path of Least Resistance - Learning to Become the Creative Force in Your Own Life 1989)

It is that simple – and complicated. The clergy of the five religions will argue this point: "You create your own meaningful of life?" They will vociferously declare that their faith, their interpretation of their scriptures, their traditions, and their logic are what gives meaning to life. That the next life is more important than this short life.[248] Though there are some clergy who will not agree with that point.

If you have followed this writing from the beginning, it be might clear that what the clergy of the five religions say might or might not be true. Thus, the five religions are a leap of faith. So, in the absence of proof what choices are there?

You can create meaning in your life by:

- Making a leap to be a Christian, Muslim, Jew, Buddhist, or Hindu.
- Making a leap to whatever all or parts of the five religions say.
- Making a leap to one of the many thousands of other religions.
- Making a leap to some political or economic ideology.
- Making a leap to life is meaningless, pointless, depressing, or make the best of it.
- Making a leap to reality for what it is and not what it appears to be.
- Making a leap to use the scientific method.
- Making a leap to create good or evil.
- Making a leap to love, work, and contribute to a healthy society.
- Making a leap to be happy, healthy, wealthy, and wise.[249]
- Making a leap to help create a family, group, nation, and society that are happy, healthy, wealthy, and wise.

---

248 Depending on the faith, it could be eternal life or another life.

249 Adapted from Benjamin Franklin, "Early to bed and early to rise, makes a man healthy, wealthy and wise."

- Making a leap to use combinations of all the above statements in whole or in part.
- Making a leap to create something else.

The choice is up to you.

It is your free will to choose. It is your free will to create a world that you want. The same free will that is central to the five religions. The same free will that their god or theology says creates sin in this world and punishment in the afterlife. They are saying to submit to their interpretation of God, G-d, Allah, Buddha or Karma, or one or many Hindu gods, etc.

Paraphrasing those who seek converts to their faith, they say, "Accepting this faith is the most crucial decision in your life. To decide or not to decide is to decide. So, save yourself for eternal life or the next life and believe what God, G-d, Allah, Buddha or Karma, or one of the many Hindu gods offer you."

Instead, use your free will to create your meaning of life. You create the meaning of life for yourself, family, group, nation, and society. The key words are "you create." Don't just blindly accept what the clergy of the five religions say.

You can choose to have a meaningless or a meaningful life. That is a choice. It is that simple. With practice you become more skilled in creating a meaningful life with any of the above choices, or with other choices. It means making decisions, commitments, and doing. And then be willing to adjust as your created life unfolds.

Most people do not know what they want to create nor how to create it. So, to help you, what follows is one example of what a meaningful life is. You will undoubtedly disagree with parts or even all of it. You will undoubtedly have other views. Good. Cancel, add, and change what you want. Create something that is entirely different.

Here is an example outline to get you started:

> Meaning comes from love, work, and guests in our lives.

Keep it simple. Your meaning is probably something different. OK. If you don't know it, then figure it out. By the way, why "ours?" Because there are acquaintances, friends, relatives, and strangers, even people far away whom we never met. We all affect each other. So, we are guests in each other's lives.

So right now, make a simple one sentence for what your meaning of life is or will be.

Then add more detail to clarify what that means. For instance:

> Meaning in life comes from love, work, and guests in our lives,
>
> which creates a happy, healthy, wealthy, and wise life,
>
> when used with Maslow's hierarchy and
>
> coupled with basic finance, economic, and psychological principles.
>
> I will use my free will in a creative life, not a reactive life,
>
> with the guests in my life like my family, friends, groups, and society.
>
> Creating that life might not happen. Just because I want it, doesn't mean it will happen.
>
> My meaning of life happens in Our Town.

Part III is an explanation of the above. You will undoubtedly want to cancel, add, change parts of it or even the whole approach. Good. After all, it is only example, and you are obviously free to create or not what you want. It is like music. There are millions of songs and types of music. People love some types of music that others might detest. You are free to love your type or even types of music; just like you are free to create your music or meaning of life for yourself and for others

Chapter 21

Love and Work

Figure 21.1 Love gives the ultimate meaning to life.

Figure 21.2 Work is a contribution to society, family, and oneself.

For reasons I do not understand nor am able to explain, love and work gives me satisfaction, completeness, and a reason for living.

A life without love is a life not worth living. But how does one describe love? Many have tried. Those who are in love understand it. For those that are not, love is as unintelligible as a foreign language. To know love is to experience it. Strange how something so important is so difficult to describe. Love has many forms. There is love for a spouse, children, family, and friends. Then there is love of things, activities, ideas, groups, organizations, and a country

Decide what you love. For example, I love listening to people and enjoy their company. Just listening. Though at times, the urge to talk is strong and at other times the urge is to be too helpful solving 'their problems.' I enjoy family, friends and groups, and miss them; and, love to understand the structures of people's thoughts, feelings and what they do. Also, it is a delight to be with math, physics, history, theology, groups, society, and my garden. Why? No idea. Just do.

Fortunately, I have lived and worked in a country that allowed and encouraged creating that kind of life with basically enjoyable work. Otherwise, to have been born at a different time, place, race, genetics, economic, and social position, sex, etc. that might not have been possible. Also, it is a result of industriously working sixty to a hundred hours per week for many decades. Just working those hours today might not create the lifestyle you want. Times have changed. For the past fifty years if people did the work, kept their nose clean, then they probably had a good chance to create the life they wanted. However, today, I am not sure that is true for most young people. Not sure.

There are many types of work. That is doing tasks that are drudgery, difficult, tiresome, and annoying. Then there is work that is delightful and fun. They kind of work where one says, "They pay me to do this! I love it!" In between the two extremes there is all kinds of work. For those that are trying to get by and survive, one trades one's time and energy for doing work to make money. Some do the same and are slaves, with or without pay.

Your social situation, time, place, race, genetics, economic position, sex, etc. might make it easy to create the life you want. On the other hand, it might make it extremely difficult to create the life you want for yourself, family, friends and society.

In any case, you want what you want. That point is extremely important. I'll repeat it again to make the point: You want what you want. But whether you can create that is a different matter. It might be difficult, yet possible. There will be setbacks because of your stupidity, errors, or events beyond your control. It might be impossible. You won't be able to create it. Yet, you can decide that at least you will help create conditions so that others can create the life that they want to have.

So, write your one simple sentence of meaning in your life. You probably know that already. If you are not sure yet, just write it out. You can change it in a little while or even years from now. Just write it out. Perhaps there are two, or three, or more. Don't worry about that. Write them all out. Put them together or just choose one. Point is, write it. Choose.

Using that simple sentence then consider including the chapter and chapter subheadings in the rest of this writing.

In addition to love and work, I want for myself, my family, group, nation, and society to be:

Chapter 22

Happy, Healthy, Wealthy, and Wise

Figure 22 Happy, Healthy, Wealthy, and Wise

This is just a choice. You might choose something else. I have chosen, like Benjamin Franklin, to be happy, healthy, wealthy, and wise. By the way, my definition of wealth is to have enough cash flow for my wife and me to do what we want with our time and talents. I am not interested in spending money to impress others. You might be. OK. Just be aware of what and why you are trying to create. Is it to impress others like parents, family, friends, or strangers? Or, are you creating your life because that is what you deeply want? Figure out the why to that.

For many people making such choices is not possible, or they are just not doing the necessary tiring, boring, never ending work to create the results they want. They spend 99% of their time on inspiration and do 1% of the work, instead of the reverse, which is 99% of the time on the work and 1% on the inspiration.[250] They just float along like logs on a river. Whatever comes along comes along. Wherever the river goes, they go. Nothing wrong with that. They just allow life to dictate to them. They are being reactive to life, instead of being proactive with their life force.

Here are some basics to consider for a happy, healthy, wealthy, and wise life for you, your family, organization, nation, and society;

---

250 A modification of a statement Thomas Edison made. The source I don't know.

Be clear about what you want in happiness, health, wealth and wisdom.

Plan
- Needed resources
- Financial plan
- Measure
- Implement

Have a few people that support you.
- Be realistic
- Don't take it personally
- Adjust plans as needed
- Remember that experiences are more valuable than material things.

Through love and work to create happiness, health, wealth, and wisdom, there is a structure to consider.

Chapter 23

Maslow's Hierarchy

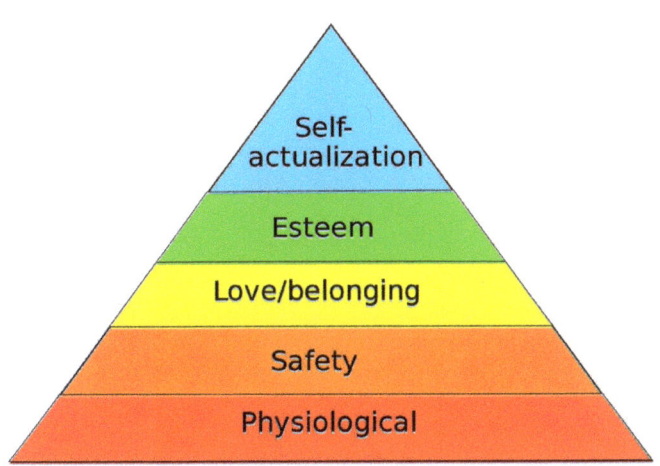

Figure 23.1 Simplistic view of how Maslow viewed human needs in life.

One approach to creating a life structure is to use Maslow's Hierarchy. It is about as good as any approach and has the basics. Use a different one if you like.

Maslow's Hierarchy outlines life in five levels. The bottom level is basic survival. Then if you can, choose to progress upwards towards a fulfilling life. People often mistake the top of the pyramid as the goal for all people. This is not so. A few might be able to achieve that fulfillment for brief periods in their life. Some might be able to experience it just momentarily. Most people aren't interested in reaching fulfillment. They just want to get by and hopefully be happy. They just want to reach some of the basics, and that is fine with them. What level do you want?

The point is, to decide what one wants in life with each of those levels. One can be at each of the levels at the same time or move around the levels at the same time. One can be concerned about survival level and belonging level at the same time. These levels are not discrete. One can be in multiple levels at the same time. However, if one is mostly concerned about survival, then concern about safety will not be as important. Then the lower levels will dominate one's activities.

So, use the hierarchy as a guide to what one wants to do for oneself, one's family, organization, nation, and society.

There will be leaders that will use the hierarchy to control people, by forcing them to focus on the lower levels. For them, having fulfilled people in their organization takes a lot of work and does not fit their ego. Their aim is to keep others down and themselves up higher. They also build societies structured to keep the masses on the lower levels of Maslow's Hierarchy.

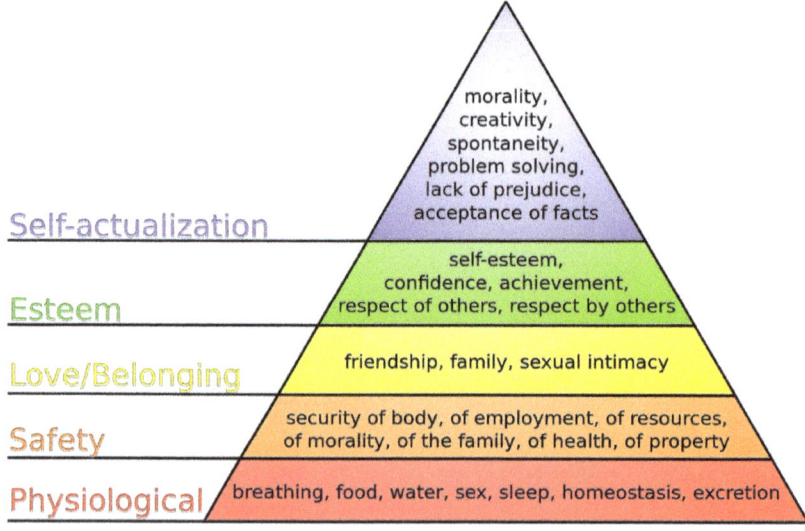

Figure 23.2 More detailed view of Maslow's hierarchy

Frequently consider how your major goals fit into the Maslow's hierarchy or whatever similar life structure you choose. For work, find an organization that supports people in their personal Maslow's hierarchy. Or if you create your own company, create it so that it is profitable and supports people in their personal Maslow's hierarchy. When that happens, life is healthy and a wonderful place. On the other hand, people interested solely in making a living might be interested in work that supplies enough income to do what they want outside of work. That too is a fit

For me, loving and working to create a happy, healthy, wealthy, and wise life by using Maslow's Hierarchy [251] (or any other such concepts) was not easy and took a long time. Similarly, your major goals might take a significant amount of dedicated effort. Granted, there are those that are born with the right set of privileges, genetics, and wealth to do so. However, most of us are not so fortunate. As Mike Tyson said, it is a decision that usually needs prolonged actions:

> Falling in love with the process of pursuing goals and the hardship that comes with it.
>
> "Do what you hate to do but do it like you love it." [252]

One must work to get the skills. At times the work will be a nuisance, uncomfortable, boring, and tiring. That is the difference between those that achieve what they want as compared to those that only dream. The dreamers fall in love with the thinking and planning and never effectively get to the doing. To paraphrase Thomas Edison, "Achieving goals is one percent inspiration and ninety-nine percent perspiration."

Most people won't do it. It is ok not to do the work and go along with what is comfortable. There is nothing right nor wrong about that. It is simply a choice. A choice that will have consequences. Understand what the consequences will be. When looking back on your life will it be,

> Gee, I wish I had created....

> Or, will it be,

---

251 (Finkelstein 2006)

252 (Oshin, The Iron Mike rule: The one thing successful people do differently 2018) Adapted from The Iron Mike rule: The one thing successful people do differently

It was a good life. Yes, there were troubles. But it was a good life.

There are some more basic items to consider.

Basic Trust

Trust is one of the most fundamental parts of life. Trust will vary, depending upon past experiences with various people and situations. There are people who will help, harm, or be indifferent to you. The key is to know what will happen if someone violates your trust.

One way is giving 100% trust and then see where it goes, but only if the penalty for violating the trust is not high or recovery is easy. Give a 100% trust and verify. Trust and verify. Just don't be naive. Recognize that there are plenty of people more than willing to take advantage of others, which includes you. So, if the penalty for violating trust is high, then be diligent about what might or might not happen. So, be aware of what is happening in the various situations you are in at home, work, shopping, etc. A feeling of trust and distrust is an indicator of something. Be aware of what it means. Be conscious – not fearing – just conscious of life and of what is going on.

Joy

Joy is a personal experience that can be different for each person, society, and nation. Joy can range from a life of outward happiness with laughter and smiles to a life of quiet contentment or contemplation.

There are probably as many ways to have a joyous life as there are people. One way to be joyous or, perhaps, even fulfilled is "being open, creative, loving, spontaneous, compassionate, concerned for others, and accepting of themselves."[253] Another said, "feel good about who you are, and see the world as a safe and positive place.

If your response is mainly negative, then you may feel unhappy with who you

---

253 (Lumen Learning n.d.) Maslow

are.... There is the ideal self and the real self. The **ideal self** is the person that you would like to be; the **real self** is the person you are.... When thoughts about the real self and ideal self are similar—in other words, when our self-concept fits reality --- that is **congruence**. [254]

When there is congruence in you, your family, your group, your society, and nation, then there will be joy in you, your family, your group, society, and nation. Perhaps there is such a nation or society. Nevertheless, at least focus upon creating a congruent you and your family. See reality for what it is. With some luck, perhaps you and your family will have a congruent group, society, and nation.

However, when the ideal self is determined by others, then the individual, society, and nation will probably develop incongruence. Thus, the greater gap between the real self and the ideal self, the greater the incongruence and not being joyous.

Joyous questions for individuals, societies and nations:

How congruent are we?

What do we exist for?

Do you want congruency as an individual, society, and nation?

Forcing people to exist incongruently at certain levels in the hierarchy creates a lack of joy in the individuals, societies, and nations. On the other hand, if people can exist congruently at the various levels of the hierarchy, then there might be joyous individuals, societies, and nations.

Consider that deep within humans there is a "...free spirit that is doing everything it can to escape from within...." Yet, individuals, societies and nations restrain their spirits by thoughts, words, and deeds. Eventually their spirits

---

254 (Lumen Learning n.d.) Carl Rogers

turn into stone. [255] Stones that weigh people, societies, and nations down. Stones that people carry their whole lives. Stones that hobble and slowly destroy people, societies, and nations. So, free your spirit and don't let it turn to stone.

There are groups that have joy by being vicious, mean, and evil. They range from petty thieves, to those that enjoy putting other people down, to creating ways to transfer wealth from others to them while causing others to have less, to ideologies and theologies that constrain people with lies and hurt others, to enjoying the maiming, slaughtering of people, to stealing land, life, and liberty from others. They enjoy creating misery for others. Some may say and believe with all sincerity it is for the benefit of others. So, just because there is joy, doesn't mean that it is healthy.

Also, genetics, accidents, family, society, and/or nations might purposefully or inadvertently push people down. Constrain them from a life of joy. There are somethings and times that it is better for people to accept what is and create a joyful life. Then there are somethings that people can choose to change in their family, society, or nation. Those changes might be rapid; or, it might take generations to create the necessary changes for people to be joyous.

Thus, for some people to be joyous is an easy decision with quick results. For others it might be a difficult decision with a lifetime of work. Then sadly for others, joyousness will not be possible.

Joy is usually an indicator of living a congruent existence as an individual, society, and nation. Deep down people know if there is joy in their life.

---

255 (Murakami 2011)

Hopefully, they will act to create healthy joy. To create joy that also creates a happy, healthy, wealthy, and wise society and nation while respecting freedoms of others to be joyous or not joyous.

As previously said, a key to joy is basic conscious trust towards life, people, and events.

Measuring

To know you are making progress in creating and achieving what you want you need standards of measurement. It will include timetables, needed resources, financial progress, task lists, charts, etc. Without the measurements and tracking against the measurements only luck will bring fulfillment and meaning.

Measurements will be daily, weekly, monthly, quarterly, and yearly. They must be quantifiable and verifiable. But too many measurements are overwhelming and meaningless. Too few measurements will result in falling behind and not making corrective actions quickly.

Figure out what your standards of measurement are and how often to measure.

Part of measuring is being aware of what is known and unknown. The Johari Window is one approach. You can use it for yourself, family, organization, nation, and society. All of which have common knowledge known to all and shown in the top left square. The other three squares can be issues. Different people, groups, organizations, societies, and nations will have different knowledge on the same topic. What is blind to one is known to others. What is unknown to one group is known to others. Depending on what one is trying to do, it is vital to understand where you and the others are in the

The Johari Window

1 Open Known to self and to others	2 Blind Not known to self but known to others
3 Hidden Known to self but not to others	4 Unknown Not known to self or others

Figure 23.3 Four quadrants of the Johari Window

Johari Window. In simple creating for oneself, then the chart is simple. In working with larger groups then this becomes quite complex and is not easy.

The other issue with using the Johari Window Model is basic trust. How much do you trust what you know, and others know? How reliable is the information?

Because of the complexity and the boringness of measuring most people won't measure. Or, they will start to measure and then drift away. Just like driving a car and not paying attention to the speedometer and then get a speeding ticket. It is easier to use feelings and intuition. For most activities this will work and produce results. Consequently, people are comfortable with using feelings and intuition in part of one's life. But to effectively create, then you need to measure and apply the Johari Window Model or something similar AND use individual and group feelings and intuition.

Feelings and intuition are important indicators in the creative process. When the feelings are intuitions are saying that something is not right. Pay attention. That might be showing that events are not going the way you want. Or, it might just be needless worry.

The point is to understand the current reality that is related to what you are creating. This takes time, money, effort, and it is often boring. For further details on the creative process I strongly recommend that you use the process developed by Robert Fritz.[256]

Here is one standard of measurement that is crucial to creative living:

Pain, suffering, and evil – "The Idiot Lights of Life"

In cars and trucks there are some lights that come on when there is a problem needing immediate attention. For instance, when the oil light comes on, that means the engine does not have enough oil. Stop the vehicle now. Don't stop in five minutes, ten minutes, or sometime later. Stop now and get oil. Otherwise, the engine will seize up and fail. Any idiot that sees that light come on knows to stop the vehicle and get oil. That is why a name for the oil light is an "Idiot light."

When feeling pain, suffering, and/or evil, STOP. It is an indicator that there is a problem. Decide what you will do about it. Your experience of pain, suffering, and evil will affect you, your family, organization, nation, and society. Their experience of pain, suffering, and evil will affect you, your family, organization, nation, and society. Pain, suffering, and evil anywhere will eventually affect many others. Decide if it is worth doing something about it or just living with it.

If people did not experience of pain, suffering, and evil from war, there would be more of it. Work to create peace and those the work to end pain, suffering, and evil. Instead of working or fighting with weapons that kill, maim, and destroy, use pencils:

Available at https://www.artlords.co

https://www.facebook.com/ArtlordsofAfghanistan/

Figure 23.4 Warlord with Pencils

---

256 (Fritz, The Path of Least Resistance - Learning to Become the Creative Force in Your Own Life 1989). Fritz also an excellent course, "Technologies for Creating." This is a powerful process and I highly recommend it.

ArtLords are Afghan artists and volunteers using art and culture for social transformation and behavioral change.

Also, to create a meaningful congruent existence, consider applying basic finance, economic and psychological principles

Chapter 24

Finance, Economics, And Psychology

Figure 24.1 Understanding household finances and basic economics helps to do pretty much what you want.

When basic finance, economic, and psychological principles are in place you can do pretty much as you want. So, determine the required income to live at the various levels of Maslow's Hierarchy or whatever life model you use. That might take a lot of thinking and adjusting through the years. There will be constantly changing economic conditions of yourself, work, family, city, state, nation, and world. That is a lot of variables that are beyond your control. Yet, that is the way it is.

Basically, keep expenses less than income. Determine how to increase the income to meet what is desired; or, determine how to live a joyful life with the current and future incomes. Read a book and take a course about household finances. There you will learn what is involved with buy and selling car. How to finance a home. Here are three good easy books to master:

Rich Dad Poor Dad by Robert T. Kiyosaki

Rich Dad's Cashflow Quadrant by Robert T. Kiyosaki

The 80/20 Principle: The Secret to Achieving More With Less by Richard Koch.

The last one fits for finances, economics, psychology, and life in general.

So, enjoy the journey. To live for the time when money is plentiful is to waste years and perhaps decades of life. Enjoy the present moments. Yet make a financial lifetime plan. A plan that you will adjust usually for reasons beyond your control.

Here are a few psychological keys:

- Don't take anything personally
- The world is not about you – very few people if any care about you
- Be aware of your emotions, what they are telling you, and what to do with them.
- 20% of what you do gives you 80% of what you want. Figure out what that 20% is and structure your life towards that.[257]
- Others are free to be who they are. There is a responsibility to others and society.
- There are manipulative people more than willing to take advantage pf you. Don't let them destroy you.
- There are many good-hearted people in the world.
- Know what you really want and figure out how to get it without harming others.
- To everything there is a season. Life changes and one's mental and physical powers change.

A key is to notice biases in oneself, family, friends, groups, societies, and nations. For example:

- Over reliance on the first idea, comment, or understanding.

---

257 (Koch 1998) An excellent book, "The 80/20 Principle: The Secret to Achieving More with Less." Strongly suggest using it.

CHAPTER 24 - FINANCE, ECONOMICS, AND PSYCHOLOGY

- Overestimating the importance of some bits of information. Not understanding more.
- Going along with the group.
- Not seeing blind spots.
- Not seeing or understanding current reality.
- Seeing patterns in random events.
- Looking for data or information that confirms your view instead of reality.
- Not accepting new evidence.
- Avoiding action by looking for more useless information
- Ignoring conflicting data
- Judging decisions solely based upon outcome instead of also understanding how the outcome happened.
- Being overconfident or under-confident.
- Believing in magic – that something will happen, therefore it will just happen.
- Not knowing the pros and cons. Not everything is all positive.
- Accepting the latest information instead of solid information.
- Not focusing on the key issues.
- Stereotyping people, ideas, places instead of knowing the reality.
- Accepting only complete or high degree of certainty.

Add, cancel, and change these psychological and bias principles as you see fit. The lists can go on indefinitely and will change as one goes through life.

Consider whether you will use your free will to have a creative or reactive stance in life.

Chapter 25

Freewill - Creative or Reactive life

Figure 25.1 Freewill is one of the most contentious issues in the five faiths and life. How much freewill do you have?

You can decide to use your free will to live a creative or reactive life.

Being reactive is when circumstances pushes you instead of you shaping the circumstances. It is you blindly reacting to the circumstances. There are a variety of ways to be reactive. Fans at a sporting event react to what the various teams do. They yell, scream and enjoy or get angry at what one or both teams do. It is a lot of fun. Nothing wrong with being reactive. Most activities tend to be reactive. Waking up, eating, working, being with friends, going to bed are usually reactive. Just realize what you are doing.

But those same activities can be creative if they support the life you want.

The creative life is – freedom. Normally people do not associate freedom with a creative life. But that is what freedom means. Freedom means forming and creating the life one wants for oneself, family, group, society, and nation.

Individuals, families, organizations, societies, and nations can be creative or reactive. It depends upon what the leadership and culture will want and tolerate. Consciously or unconsciously, with or without religion you, your family, organization, nation, and society are creating structures for people's lives. It can result in pain, suffering, and evil. Or, it can result in happiness, health, wealth, and wisdom. Or, it can result in nothing.

To be creative: [258] [259]

- Decide what you want to create.
- Figure out a plan and the needed resources
- Have standards of measurements
- Start creating.
- Adjust as activities progress
- Consider mistakes or failures as learning opportunities. Makes life a bit easier.
- Ask for help.

In the creative process there can and will be people that come into your process for a brief time and others for a long time. They are like guests in your creative process or life. They are guests in your life.

---

258 (Denning 2018)

259 (Fritz, The Path of Least Resistance - Learning to Become the Creative Force in Your Own Life 1989) This is the single best source on living a creative life that I have come across. It should be more popular.

Chapter 26

Guests in Our Lives[260]

Figure 26.1 We are all guests in other people's lives. They too are guests in our lives.

People come into and out of our lives in many ways. Some we invite in, others drift in, and a few barge in. Some people invite us in. Sometimes we barge into people's lives. Some stay for a few minutes, a few hours, a few days, and a very few for a lifetime. Some are wonderful, delightful, and fill our lives with joy. Hopefully, we can do the same for others as a guest in their lives.

Then there are those that we are delighted when they leave. Hopefully there are very few that we dislike so much that we have a party for them after they leave. Hopefully, people are not delighted with us when we leave.

Whoever they are, enjoy their presence, their history, and the precious limited time with them. For eventually we all leave. Some say goodbye. Some just slip away like a setting sun. We suddenly realize that they are gone and will never

---

260 (Pilgrim 1983) I think the term, "Guests in My Life" is taken from the book "The Peace Pilgrim: Her Life and Work in Her Own Word."

return.

We are all guests in each other's lives. Let's treat each other like guests. Let's celebrate the time with us. Even those that we don't like.[261]

Sadly, some guests, and events do cause us pain, suffering, and are evil.

Grateful

We can choose to be grateful to the millions and billions of people who have come before us. That in their ignorance, greed, selfishness, lust, and their good-naturedness and idealism they created the world we now have. Everyone has in their own way created, and are creating, the world around them. Sadly, progress for individuals, families, groups, societies, and nations has not been smooth nor pleasant. Yet, millions of normal people have quietly worked to drain swamps, create roads, grow crops, raise families, create inventions, etc. that have helped a few to millions and billions of people. We can choose daily to be grateful for these unknown people.

We can also choose to be grateful for every guest in our lives. We can be grateful for each of the people, from those that have been with us all our lives to those that pop into our lives for a few seconds and pop out. Each one has a story. Each one can be a blessing to us or to many others. We can even choose to be grateful to those that have caused us pain, suffering, and evil.

The attitude of gratitude can help people become happy, healthy, wealthy, and wise. This includes those people that we forgive. They are all part of our experience. We are all part of the long silent people going back hundreds of thousands of years that have and are creating the world we live in. Let's be grateful to them, who like us, have strengths and weaknesses. Like us, they in their own ways educated their children, who in turn will educate generations of future children.

Let us be grateful for the generations of people who came before us and

---

261 (McCoy 2019)

grateful for our children, their children, and the generations of children to come. They are humanity's future.

Identity and Society

A fundamental structure of languages is:

Singular: I, you, he/she/it

Plural: We, you, them

Notice that of the six grammatical positions that only one is "I." Yet, it is the "I," that dominants most of human feeling and thinking:

- I want this
- I want that
- I want that person
- I didn't do it
- I feel sad
- I feel happy
- I want salvation
- God loves me
- God told me to….

We look at the world through the "I" and, "Me, me, me." It is normal and natural. However, too much focus on the "I" misses the you, he/she/it, we, you and them. There is a broader world than "I" and "Me, me, me."

The world also consists of individuals, families, groups, societies, and nations. Most of us, in varying degrees, are a part of a family and a group. Most people don't consciously choose how they will fit into the range from individual to societies. It just happens because of birth, culture, education, and growing interest.

Another subtle and important aspect of "I" is identity. It is a fundamental aspect of living. What is your identity? Perhaps it is Christian, Jewish, Muslim,

Buddhist, Hindu, New Ager, atheist, or something else. It could include being white, black, brown, mulatto, red, etc. Being from a country, a state or province, a city. Being married or not married. Being a grandparent, parent or not a parent. Type of work one does. Etc.

Identifying people this way creates divisions.

There is another fundamental way. First, we are humans. Humans who have needs, wants, feelings, thoughts, and experiences. That is really our real identity. The list in the earlier paragraph is what society and nations put on official documents for people to carry around. It becomes our barcode. That is not really 'us.' What is us or you or me, is our needs, wants, feelings, thoughts, experiences, and relationships with people. That is what unites us. The official identity divides us.

The next time someone asks who you are, consider responding with something like, "I love to walk, read, talk, be with my children, enjoy my spouse, etc."

That is completely different than responding with, "I am a fundamentalist or liberal Christian, Jew, Muslim, Buddhist, Hindu, or some other religion." Or even to say that I am from the US, Mexico, Africa, South America, Asia, etc. Which statement unites? Which divides?

Instead, think of what we really are. We are humans that have needs, wants, feelings, thoughts, and experiences.

What responsibility do you have and what role do you want with your family, friends, groups, and society? Some of you will consciously or unconsciously choose to have no role. Some of you might believe that you are totally and completely self-made, with no need of others. Some of you will consciously or unconsciously choose wider roles, all the way to being involved with world societies. Those that are or will be involved with roles wider than oneself will be talking, writing, and dialoging with many people.

Having meaningful dialogue needs a willingness to step into the very shoes of other people. To be willing to abandon one's positions. If you are not willing to abandon your positions, then the discussion is positional, which means that the participants will be in a win-lose position, compromising or war, until one side or the other is exhausted and 'goes home.' The discussions and work become, instead of figuring out a healthy outcome, a matter of winners and losers. Sadly, when one deals with winner takes all mentality, then it is warfare. The so-called dialogue then becomes a matter crushing or holding off the enemy or the competition.

A healthier way is to be willing to give up a point of view when the evidence shows that there is a better view. Thus, to become happy, healthy, wealthy, and wise, means learning the skill of tolerance.[262] To learn to engage and discuss the basis of our fundamental beliefs. Which means being willing to give them up and take on new beliefs.

The struggle is to create meaningful open dialogue to create happier, healthier, wealthier, and wiser self, family, friends, societies, and nations. That takes tolerance, patience, and a willingness not to identify with any particular point of view, identity, and a willingness to change. It is a focus on what is healthiest for the community and not solely for oneself or economic class.

That also includes being willing to forgive oneself and others.

---

262 (Van Loon 1927 Revised 1940)

Forgiveness

Families, groups, societies, and nations carry the hurts, wrongs, injustices, thefts, humiliations, etc. Some take immense pleasure in going over and over the hurts, wrongs, injustices, etc. A few will spend their whole lives working to get even with others. Thus, whoever created the pain and suffering hurts them not once, but over and over. Sometimes the hurting goes on for generations.

Instead, to have a meaningful life, free oneself from real or imagined hurts. Acknowledge the hurt. If needed and possible, take legal action. Take effective action. Don't associate with those that create pain. Or, if you must associate, then figure out a way to handle the problem. Put it behind and move on. Don't let the hurt dominant your life or the life of your family, group, nation or society. Letting the hurt remain creates a double hurt. There is the first hurt. Then the second hurt is living with the memory and possibly letting it affect your life. After doing the above, it is time to move on and stop reliving the experiences.

That is forgiveness.

That is another difference between living a creative or a reactive life. The creative person, family, group, nation, and society will figure out some way not to let others hurt them. The reactive person, family, group, nation, or society will live with and remember the pain and suffering, day after day, week after week, month after month, year after year, decade after decade, for generations.

To carry the memories of past events affects the body, the mind, and the very essence of being. It is impossible to forget the trauma, whether big or small. But to remember and dwell on it hurts not once, but over and over. A hurt that goes on for a lifetime and even generations. Free yourself by forgiving.

That does not mean letting others, families, groups, nations, and societies be bullies. Decide to stand up to bullies and to evil people. Sometimes it might not be worth the time and effort. Sometimes it might be helpful to many other people. Sometimes standing up to bullies takes tremendous effort. Sometimes it just takes a bit of force to put them in their place.

In any event, forgiving means deliberately[263] freeing oneself of the past and creating a happy, healthy, wealthy, and wise life now.

Understand what forgiveness is not. Do not deny your pain or hurt nor make excuses for what happened. There is no obligation to right the wrong that has happened, to release them from legal actions, nor to get even. Do not put up with more of the same.

Instead, let go of negative feelings. Deal with it and move on. While you might not forget what happened, you can create a life that is freer of the pain, suffering, and evil.

Why Practice Forgiveness?

- Forgiveness makes us and others happier.
- Forgiveness protects mental health. With, and perhaps without, therapy, forgiveness improves depression, anxiety, and reduces suicidal tendencies.
- Forgiveness improves physical health. Forgiving reduces physical stresses such as blood pressure, heart rate, and strengthens the immune system.
- Forgiveness improves trust and commitment.
- Forgiveness in marriages creates strong and more satisfying marriages (most of the time). The couples are better able to effectively resolve conflicts. However, when a spouse mistreats a more forgiving spouse, they become less satisfied with their marriage.
- Forgiveness boosts kindness and connections towards others.
- All these benefits apply to families, groups, societies, and

---

263 (Luskin n.d.)

nations. However, that does not mean they let perpetrators get away with the actions that cause pain and suffering.[264]

Some of the precious guests in our lives are children.

Educating Children

If we choose, we can raise competent, capable, independent people that think for themselves and become happy, healthy, wealthy, and wise. However, there are many politicians, religionists and educators that want children to accept magical thinking and religious thinking instead of scientific thinking. They want children to grow into adults that become dependent upon a powerful entity. There are unscrupulous leaders that want power and money for themselves and their key backers. So, they create education systems that teach sloppy and magical thinking. When they come across data and ideas that conflict with their views, they teach their children to respond with:

- Ignoring
- Shunning
- Vigorous hostility
- Politeness and not engaging
- Seizing the opportunity to convert the person
- Praying for 'the ignorant or heathen' who oppose the religionist views.

Religionists respond that way because:

- There is a need for security
- There is a need to have a clear world view

---

264   (Kornfield n.d.)

- People are willing to accept authority figures
- There is vast ignorance about scientific thinking and process
- Political forces use the religions for political and economic gain
- There isn't time, luxury nor interest to probe the various world views.

For children to become competent, capable and independent adults they need skills to:

- Be creative, not just reactive
- Be happy, healthy, wealthy, and wise
- Apply Maslow's hierarchy or something similar
- Be appropriately trusting
- Master finance, economics, and psychological principles
- Realize that what they want might not happen
- Know what standards of measurements to have
- Be skilled in handling pain, suffering, and evil
- Practice healthy sex from puberty until senior citizen
- Practice forgiveness and gratitude
- Understand their responsibility to society
- Understand what authority is and is not
- Create their own meaning of life
- Master the mundane skills of reading, writing, mathematics, and science.

The aim is to:

- Create competent, capable, independent people that have the skills to function and contribute for themselves, their family, group, nation, and society.
- Teach expectations and values to be happy, healthy, wealthy, and wise children and adults.
- Seek out healthy inspiration to create meaningful lives for the

- here and now.
- Teach the children that this life is not a test for the next life and that there is no proof of a divine being watching every action. That there is no divine being willing to condemn billions of people in the past and future to eternal damnation, suffering, pain and thus evil. Instead teach that this life is a natural creation. They are born, live, and die. What they create is in part up to them and in part influenced by their family, friends, groups, society, and nation.
- Teach them to be skilled in handling life and its' challenges. That includes thinking, intuiting, the scientific method, and all the skills of reading, writing and mathematics to be skilled in using the power of their minds.

So, consider these thoughts. A seventy-five-year Harvard study concluded that quality relationships yield happy, meaningful lives.[265] And, it is the unimportant things that add up. The daily activities of being with others, that is love. Just being with others. These are guests in our lives whether we like them or not. Enjoy them as much you enjoy sex.

---

265 (Waldinger 2016)

Chapter 27

Sex

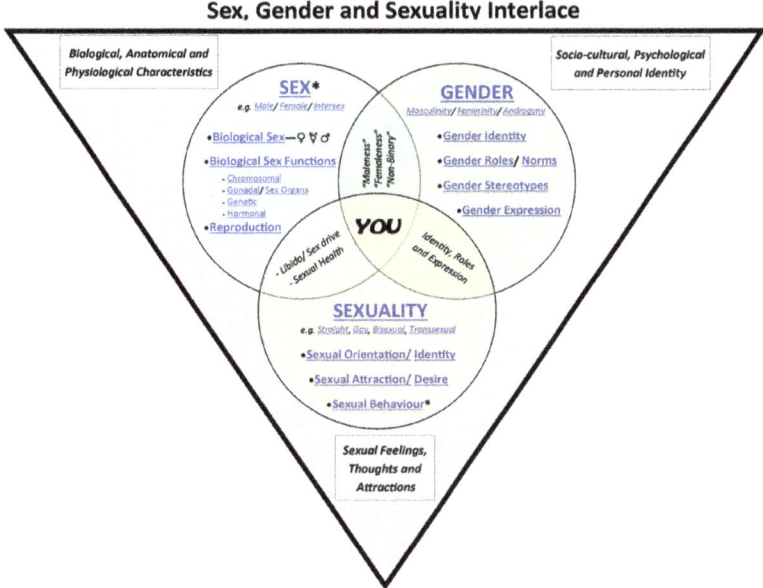

Figure 27.1 Sex can't be this complicated! Can it?

Doesn't that look complicated? For some people it is. For others sex is simple: sex is between one man and one woman only in marriage and the man determines when and how. For others it is a partnership. Then others have different ideas. So, yes, sex can be complicated and simple. A better understanding of the chart is beyond the scope of this book. See the reference material for in-depth explanations. Suffice it to say, the chart says that sex includes biology, social, psychology, feelings, thoughts, attractions. Here are a few comments to consider.

Sexual intimacy is a force that can bind couples together or pull them apart. It can be a delightful, ecstatic experience; or, it can be a physically and emotionally painful experience, and everything in between. For many people it is one of the greatest experiences in life. It connects couples with each other, with other people, and for some the universe. It adds a sense of fulfillment and meaning in life. Life without sex for many people is a meaningless life and quiet bitterness. Thus, for most people to have a meaningful life means having enjoyable creative sex.

Yet, many people have a hunger for sex and are frustrated by it. Many people suffer a deep yearning for pleasure, fulfillment, satisfaction, and connection that comes from sex. Yet societies around the world don't understand the basic male and female physiological drives. They don't understand the emotional and psychological forces of sex. Religions treat sex as a super spiritual experience or as an evil that should only be in marriage between one man and one woman. Some religions believe that the ideal life is no sex; but if one must have sex then get married. Religions seem willfully ignorant of reating a healthy atmosphere for sex for a lifetime.266 Their actions create broken relationships, abuse, heartache, loneliness, and much more. The media portrays hundreds of different healthy and unhealthy vicarious ways to have sex.

It seems that people are unskilled in fulfilling, satisfying, pleasurable sex that leads to connection to others and the world. A fulfilling sex that creates mental, physical health, and fulfillment as in Maslow's Hierarchy. This includes sex in the various stages of life as young adults, adults, and senior citizens. Individuals, families, societies can choose to educate their own and others on how to have fulfilling, satisfying, pleasurable sex which has so many benefits.

Yet today, while more people connect to the Internet, they are less and less connected to each other. People struggle with their sex desires. For some, healing from sexual abuse takes a lifetime. Sexual issues inside and outside of marriages create frustration, feelings of being unloved, undesirable,

---

266 (Beltran 2016)

unattractive, and loneliness. Loneliness can lead to heart problems, increased blood pressure, and premature death. Some men cheat to remain in a sexless marriage. Some women cheat to leave a sexless marriage.[267]

Healthy people can have sex into their nineties. A lack of sex drive is a sign of mental illness and/or poor physical health.

There are medical and social issues with sex outside of committed relationships. Sexually transmitted diseases (STDs) are powerful reasons for keeping sex only between two people. Some of the mild to serious diseases are:

- Bacterial STDs
- Vaginitis
- Chlamydia
- Gonorrhea
- Syphilis
- Pelvic Inflammatory Disease
- Viral STDs
- Herpes
- Human Papillomavirus
- Hepatitis B
- Hepatitis C
- Human Immunodeficiency Virus (HIV)
- Parasitic STDs
- Trichomoniasis
- Pubic Lice
- Fungal STDs
- Vaginal yeast[268]

---

267 (S. 2016) Page 3. & (M. McGrath, No Sex Marriage – Masturbation, Loneliness, Cheating and Shame 2016)

268 (US Government 2015) All Types of STDs and STIs, STD Symptoms, STD Pictures, STD Treatment, July 20, 2015, http://www.std-gov.org/blog/types-of-stds/

As with anything else in life, there are risks and results. For some people they engage in the risky behavior and absolutely nothing happens. Then there are others, who for the first time engage in sex and a pregnancy results, while others have lifelong diseases and others have no adverse effects.

Nevertheless, the reality is, the safe way to have sex is only between two people and no one else. The more partners there are the more the risk of STD and people problems. While using prophylactics reduces the disease risks, they are not one hundred percent effective and can have side effects. As with anything, there are risks in life. You can choose to have sex with many partners and run the risks of disease and problems with other people, or to have sex with only one other person. That is the reality.

Sex is a basic natural primal force is that can be fulfilling, pleasurable, and can be exceptionally fulfilling. Consider:

A sexually satisfying world from birth until death!

Sexual desire is a result of sexual activity.[269] Use it or you lose it.

Every day sexercise to have a happier healthier life[270] If enough people do, then civilization will be happier, healthier, wealthier and wiser.

"Sex can be fun, safe, and you deserve a healthy fulfilling sex life with partner(s) you trust."[271]

Teach science-based sex education that helps people have a happy healthy life

---

269 (M. McGrath, No Sex Marriage – Masturbation, Loneliness, Cheating and Shame 2016)

270 (M. McGrath, No Sex Marriage – Masturbation, Loneliness, Cheating and Shame 2016)

271 (Beltran 2016)

from childhood to senior citizens.[272]

So, consider sex as part of your having a fulfilling and meaningful life. As with all desires or plans, one can be reactive or creative. Reactive means that your sex life is the way it is and there is no way to change it. Creative means figuring out a way to create a fulfilling sex life. On the other hand, that might not be possible. Just because you want something – even sex – doesn't mean you can or will have it.

---

[272] (Beltran 2016) Explains a strong comprehensive sex education structure. Highly recommended. Covers all areas, but not in detail.

Chapter 28

Might not Happen

Authority and Power of Your Mind

Figure 28.1 Will what we want happen? It might..it might not.

It is not enough just to imagine, or wish, for what you want, or even plan for what you, your family, organization, nation, or world want. Crucial in creating what you want is measuring progress or lack of progress towards what you want (as previously discussed), deciding which authorities to use, AND harnessing the power of your mind. Yet realize that even doing all that, the desired events might not happen.

Might not Happen

In creating your meaningful life, you might make all the necessary plans and perfectly execute them. Yet, the results you desire might not happen. Perhaps due to lack of skill, knowledge, effort, illness, competition, financial issues, enemies, corruption, incompetence of others or oneself, war, hurricane,

volcanoes, or something else. Things go wrong. Look at the engraving of the

Titanic sinking.[273] It was well constructed, financed, and filled with hopeful passengers. Yet, due to problems with fire in the boiler room, lack of care by the Captain, or an errant iceberg, insufficient lifeboats, etc. the ship sank, and 1,496 drowned. The point is, stuff happens.

Figure 28.2 No one planned for the Titanic to sink. Stuff happens in life.

Then what?

- Abandon ship and move on to something else?
- Do nothing and sink?
- Adjust plans and carry on?

At some point, when your plans for a meaningful life don't happen, decide what to do. Your choices are like being on the Titanic. Sometimes you can make a small or even a large course correction. Then you are back on your way.

Sometimes making changes is just like rearranging the chairs on the sinking Titanic.[274] It is fruitless. It does nothing to avoid the iceberg, or in your case,

273 (Stöwer 1912)

274 (Making myths out of the Titanic (From Book, Titanic Lives, by Richard-Davenport Hines, Harper Press) 2012 (Picture taken on Titanic 1912))

achieving the results that you want. Decide if your emotions glued to your desired results are blinding you to the reality of the situation.

Figure 28.3 When a problem is about to happen, people do meaningless actions like rearranging the deck chairs on the Titanic instead of addressing the problem.

Sometimes you can push through with tremendous force and luck to achieve the desired results. Literature and movies are thrillers and inspirational with such stories. Yet, that is not the reality for most of us.

Endings

Everything ends. Everything. Daily events end. Times with friends, family, work, etc. end. The daily time with children ends when they grow-up and leave. Work ends.

Realize that while we have desires, wishes, hopes, and plans the time to have them or do them or complete them comes to an end. Time to do whatever ends. There is a time period for everything. Every event, desire, want, wish, hope, etc. has a length of time to be fulfilled. Whatever it is that you want might not be accomplished in that time.

The point is: Figure out the time period for what you want or must do.

If not, then when the time runs out, regret might set in.

If you want something like love, things, etc. figure out the time period for it. Otherwise, there is a good chance that the time runs out. Sadness and regret enter your life. Perhaps a little sadness and regret. That will always happen. What are the major desires you want in life in the time you have?

Most become aware that everything ends.

Also, this is crucial, no matter what your religious and spiritual orientation, time in this life is not eternal. Our lives do not go on forever. There is an end. There is a season for everything and everyone.

Recognize that this is your time of youth, or being an adult, or a senior person. Not someone else's. You own your time. If you don't own it, you are a slave to whomever does own it. The same is with your family, organization, state, and nation. This your time in the sun. Live it. It doesn't go on forever.

If things are not unfolding with your plan, what do you do? While deciding, continue to consult competent authorities and use the power of your mind.

Authority

In every step of the process of creating a meaningful life, consult competent authority. For finance, economics, psychology, project/time planning, etc. of everyday life, there are plenty of authorities. Those authorities are common enough to find on the Internet or the library.

However, there are many other versions of authority to consider. Some people claim, "I know my own truth!" or, "I know the Truth about …." They are adamant and have no doubt. Anyone or any evidence that contradicts their view of truth on any topic, they do not consider, and they dismiss it. There are other people that just "Go with the flow." "Everything is ok." "Everyone is entitled to their own opinion." Then there are the rest of us somewhere in between.

Also, there are a variety of other authorities, such as political leaders, business leaders, movie stars, athletes, medical doctors, alternative health practitioners, professors, religious leaders, friends, relatives, strangers, newspapers, etc. etc.

Where does that leave us normal average humans? On what authority to decide anything? How to eat healthy? How to exercise if needed at all? Get vaccines? Vote for candidate x, or y or z? Is global climate change true or a hoax? Is communism, socialism, capitalism or libertarianism bad or good? Free love or abstinence? How to determine a meaningful life?

Figure out who your competent authority figures are. Some are family, friends, co-workers, bosses, classmates, neighbors, advertisers, clerics, politicians, books, magazines, etc.

Figure out if they are supportive, against, or neutral to your efforts of creating a meaningful life. Sorting this out can, and will, be confusing.

Then constantly evaluate if those authority figures should remain as your guide, if it is time to move on to other authorities, and how they support your quest for a meaningful life. For some of you, this is easy. For others, this will be a lot of work – a lot of ongoing continual work. For most of us, there are no magic pills.

So, using Part III of this book, and applying the scientific method:

- Determine your meaningful life
- Know what your reality is
- Collect data
- Study relevant literature, laws and 'authorities'
- Run tests if needed
- Pay attention to your intuition
- Revise as more data comes in
- Go back to beginning – create and adjust
- Meanwhile, live, love, and work with guests in your life, or whatever your meaning in life is.

There is no way that the average person is going to do all that for everything in one's life. One might do that for buying a house, a car, a bicycle, getting a job, marrying someone, etc. But most of one's life people will use intuition, accept what the cleric of their five religions says, what their politician says, what their boss says, what their teacher says, what their news media says, what a pop star says, what a sports hero endorses, what the general says, what a sacred text, institution, tradition, reason, religious experience, secular experience, etc. says. It is much easier that way.

So, they just go with the flow, prejudices, and culture. To sort through all that takes time, money, patience, personal vulnerability, and a willingness to handle fuzziness, unknowns, and frustration. It is difficult emotionally, intellectually, and socially to figure out reliable authorities, such as people, data, analysis, logic, and tests.

Figure out who the reliable experts and authorities will be in your life for love, work, happiness, health, wealth, wisdom, sex, and anything else you are interested in. While doing this work, harness:

The Power of Your Mind

Napoleon Hill, after interviewing many successful people, had a realization. He noticed that successful people had developed their independent minds, were clear about what they wanted to achieve, and did the work, had a much better chance of achieving what they conceived. As a result, he said, "What the mind can conceive, the mind can achieve."[275]

The creative or non-creative life is the basic stance in one's life. To create a meaningful life, and live the creative life study these books:

- Napoleon Hill, "Think and Grow Rich."[276]
- Maxwell Maltz, "Psycho-Cybernetics."[277]

---

275 (Hill n.d.)

276 (Hill n.d.)

277 (Maltz 1989)

- Robert Fritz's works, one of which is, "The Path of Least Resistance."[278]
- Richard Koch, "The 80/20 Principle: The Secret to Achieving More with Less"[279]
- James Clear, "Atomic Habits: An Easy & Proven Way to Build Good Habits & Break Bad Ones"[280]
- Thornton Wilder, the play "Our Town"[281]

Even though you might not be able to create your life, family, organization, or nation the way you want. Nevertheless, recognize what you want. You want, what you want. And importantly, now is your time - not later - to…

---

278 (Fritz, The Path of Least Resistance - Learning to Become the Creative Force in Your Own Life 1989)

279 (Koch 1998)

280 (Clear 2018)

281 (Wilder 1938 Book 1940 Movie)

Chapter 29

Create Your Own Meaningful Life

Figure 29.1 Life is filled with choices.
Decide which choices will you make.

Thus, Part III was just an example. You make up your meaning of life. You have the freedom to make up the meaning that you want, or to accept what someone or some organization says, or to have no meaning. It is up to you. As time goes on, you will change, add, and drop various parts, or even all of it. But that is part of creating the life you want.

Purposefully or not, you are right now creating your own meaning of life. It matters not whether you have seventy years left or one day left. You are creating your meaning of life. So, consider these areas:

- Determine your theme: Perhaps it could be, love, work, and guests in our lives
- To be happy, healthy, wealthy and wise
- Maslow's Hierarchy
- Finance, economic and psychological principles
- Free will and the creative life – use a standard of measurement
- Guests in your life

- Happy and fulfilling sex
- Might not happen
- Other areas?

It will take work to achieve what others, because of their birth situation, achieve with effortlessness of gods. But if you don't do the work, then you are being reactive and just accepting what society says your meaning of life will be. The choice is up to you.

Yet, using your freewill to be creative does not mean that you will get the life you, your family, organization, nation, and society wants. It is not a panacea that automatically gives the results you want. Mistakes happen. There is competition. There are events like wars, illness, accidents, economic collapse, etc. Or one loses interest, gets bored, or becomes exhausted. Life just happens. All comes to end. Everything and everyone has an end.

Nevertheless, create your meaning in life. Then live it:

As for me, my meaning in life is to be happy, healthy wealthy, and wise through love and love and work with guests in our lives in

"Our Town"

Read and see the play, "Our Town."[282] Keep in mind the play takes place in a home and a graveyard. For the purposes of this book, it could be anywhere in the world which I call, "Our Town." Here is the key scene:

> Emily Webb died and joined the 'community of the dead' in the local cemetery. She wants to relive her twelfth birthday. She sees her parents and brother in their home doing normal activities. They do not see her.
>
> She grows frustrated with the blindness of ordinary people.

---

282 (Bauer 2016) Page 302-303. To read the play, "Our Town," Susan Bauer recommends the best edition is in Harper Perennial Modern Classics (2003). Go see the play!

Emily blurts out, "Oh mama, just look at me one minute as though you really saw me. Mama, fourteen years have gone by. I'm dead. You're a grandmother. Wally's dead, too....Don't you remember? But just for a moment now, we're all together. Mama, just for a moment we're happy. Let's look at one another."

Mama goes on cooking not knowing that Emily is there.

Emily sobs. "It goes so fast. We don't have time to look at one another. Do any human beings ever realize life while they live it? Every, every minute?"

The stage manager says, "No. ...Everybody knows in their bones that something is eternal, and that something has to do with human beings."

So, Create Your Own Meaningful Life In Our Town The World.

Figure 29.2 The world is like the play "Our Town"

**My meaningful life is to
be happy, healthy, wealthy, and wise
through work, love, and guests in our lives.**

**Your meaningful life may be quite different
and might or might not include religion.**

Bibliography

Andreae, Jacob; Chemnitz, Martin. "Chief Articles of Faith." The Book of Concord. 1530
   http://bookofconcord.org/augsburgconfession.php (accessed March 14, 2018).
Admin. "Difference Between Faith and Hope." Ipedia. December 15, 2015
   http://pediaa.com/difference-between-faith-and-hope/ (accessed March 19, 2018).
AIG. "What Is the Meaning of Life?" Answers in Genesis. n.d.
   https://answersingenesis.org/what-is-the-meaning-of-life/ (accessed March 27, 2018).
Ali, M. Amir, Ph.D. "Forgiveness." Institute of Islamic Information and Education. February 24, 2006.
   http://www.iiie.net/forgiveness/ (accessed February 19, 2018).
All Types of STDs and STIs, STD Symptoms, STD Pictures, STD Treatment. n.d.
Al-Munajjid, Sheikh Muhammed Salih. "Explaining human suffering and why Allaah does not prevent it ." Islam Question & Answer. November 11, 1998.
   https://islamqa.info/en/answers/2850/explaining-human-suffering-and-why-allaah-does-not-prevent-it (accessed October 22, 2018).
Altucher, James. "The Six Things The Most Productive People Do Every Day." The Medium. May 28, 2018.
   https://medium.com/the-mission/the-six-things-the-most-productive-people-do-every-day-fba2fe17ed45 (accessed May 281, 2018).
Alumkal, Antony. Paranoid Science - The Christian Right's War on Reality. New York: New York University Press, 2017.
Anonymous. "religous authority: Hinduism." ReligionFacts.com. November 19, 2016.
   http://www.religionfacts.com/hinduism/authority (accessed March 13, 2018).
Arendt, Hannah. The Life of the Mind. San Diego New Yor London: A Harvest Book a division of Harcourt Brace & Company, 1977.
—. The Origins of Totalitarianism. New York: Harcourt, Inc, 1966.
Arkush, Allan. "Immortality: Belief in a Bodiless Existence - Everlasting life was not always guaranteed to the Jewish soul." My Jewish Learning. n.d.
   https://www.myjewishlearning.com/article/immortality-belief-in-a-bodiless-existence/ (accessed August 3, 2018).
—. "Immortality: Belief in a Bodiless Existence." My Jewish Learning. n.d.
   https://www.myjewishlearning.com/article/immortality-belief-in-a-bodiless-existence/ (accessed March 2, 2018).
Armstrong, Karen. The Battle For God. New York: Alfred A. Knopf, 2000.
Arsenal| HistoryNet. "CH-47C Chinook Helicopter." historynet.com. n.d.
   https://www.google.com/search?q=Vietnam+Chinook+helicopter+pictures&newwindow=1&client=firefox-b-1-d&tbm=isch&source=iu&ictx=1&fir=ndcwZaPVJBMrdM%253A%252CU6BfELmRJGmQS-M%252C_&vet=1&usg=AI4_-kQNJIj6shgIpyLwj-58BAF4qCnmuQ&sa=X-&ved=2ahUKEwja5Pm-6JjiAhUE658K (accessed May 15, 2019).

ArtLords. "Warlord with Pencils." ArtLords. n.d. https://www.artlords.co (accessed August 2, 2019).

"Attributes of God." All About. 2018. https://www.allaboutgod.com/attributes-of-god.htm (accessed October 5, 2018).

Bauer, Susan Wise. The Well-Educated Mind - A Guide to the Classical Educaton You Never Had. New York: W.W. Norton & Company, Inc, 2016.

Beit-Halachmi, Rabbi Rachel Sabath. "The Experience and Nearness of God." My Jewish Learning. n.d. https://www.myjewishlearning.com/article/the-experience-and-nearness-of-god/ (accessed March 1, 2018).

Beltran, Victoria. "Sex Education…With Pleasure ." TEDxUSFSP. January 6, 2016. https://www.youtube.com/watch?v=R-gwxS-7h9o (accessed December 5, 2018).

Bercot, David. "Love Without Condition." History of the Early Church. n.d. http://www.earlychurch.com/unconditional-love.php (accessed November 14, 2016).

—. "What was the early church like?" History of the Early Church. n.d. http://earlychurch.com/index-old.html (accessed November 14, 2016).

Berger, Jonah. Invisible Influence - The Hidden Forces That Shape Behavior. New York: Simon & Shuster, 2016 June.

Berman, Robby, and Samantha Lee. "When You Can't Afford to Make a Mistake, This'll Keep You Sharp (20 cognitive biases in a chart that could keep you from making a bad decision)." Big Think. April 19, 2016. https://bigthink.com/robby-berman/a-chart-of-brain-busting-cognitive-biases-hang-it-on-your-wall (accessed September 23, 2018).

Bhat, Tehreem. "Do Muslims believe that there is no way but Islam to experience God?" Quroa. March 18, 2015. https://www.quora.com/Do-Muslims-believe-that-there-is-no-way-but-Islam-to-experience-God (accessed March 1, 2018).

Bhikkhu, Thanissaro. "All About Change." A Theravada Library . 2004 .https://www.accesstoinsight.org/lib/authors/thanissaro/change.html (accessed March 21, 2018).

Blanchard, LInda. "Who Is The Ultimate Authority?" Secular Buddhist Association. July 23, 2012. http://secularbuddhism.org/2012/07/23/who-is-the-ultimate-authority/ (accessed March 13, 2018).

Bloom, A. "Buddhist Studies: Glossary of Terms." Buddha Dharma Education Association & BuddhaNet. 2018. https://www.buddhanet.net/e-learning/dharmadata/fdd29.htm (accessed March 19, 2018).

Blumenthal, David. "REPENTANCE AND FORGIVENESS." David Blumenthal's HomePage. n.d. http://www.js.emory.edu/BLUMENTHAL/Repentance.html (accessed January 29, 2019).

Boroditsky, Lera. "How language shapes the way we think." TED. May 2, 2018. https://www.youtube.com/watch?v=RKK7wGAYP6k (accessed November 19, 2018).

BrainyMedia, Inc. "Max Muller Quotes." Brainy Quote. n.d. https://www.brainyquote.com/quotes/max_muller_326659 (accessed December 10, 2018).

Brown, Raymond E. An Introdtion to the New Testament (abridged). New Haven & London: Yale University Press, 2016.

Bruckner, Pascal. "Condemned to Joy: The Western cult of happiness is a mirthless enterprise." City Journal. Winter 2011. https://www.city-journal.org/html/condemned-joy-13355.html (accessed February 8, 2019).

"Buddha." The Pursuit of Happiness - Bringing the science of happiness to life. n.d. http://www.pursuit-of-happiness.org/history-of-happiness/buddha/ (accessed March 27, 2018).

Burton, Tara Isabella. "This poll asked Americans if they believe in God. The answers were fascinating." Vox. April 26, 2018. https://www.vox.com/2018/4/26/17282284/pew-americans-god-religion-study-faith-identity (accessed April 27, 2018).

C.S.Lewis. God in the Dock (Essays on Theology and Ethics). Grand Rapids, Michigan/Cambridge, U.K.: William B. Erdmans Publishing company, 1970.

Caruso, Steve. "The Lord's Prayer in Galilean Aramaic." The Aramaic New Testament - Galilean New Testament in the Context of Early Christianity. n.d. http://aramaicnt.org/articles/the-lords-prayer-in-galilean-aramaic/ (accessed November 13, 2016).

Catron, Mandy Len. how to fall in love with anyone. New York, New York: Simon & Shuster, 2017.

Cavendish, Marshall. Islamic Beliefs, Practices, and Cultures. Malaysia: Marshall Cavendish Reference, 2011.

Chafer, Lewis Sperry. Systematic Theology Vol 1-8. Dallas, Texas: Dallas Seminary Press, 1947 Eleventh Edition 1973.

Chugh, Anmol. "As per Buddhism, what is the purpose of life?" Quroa. February 14, 2016. https://www.quora.com/As-per-Buddhism-what-is-the-purpose-of-life (accessed March 27, 2018).

Church of England. "Section XIV of Saving Faith." Center for Reformed Theology and Apologetics. 1646. http://www.reformed.org/documents/index.html?mainframe=http://www.reformed.org/documents/westminster_conf_of_faith.html (accessed March 14, 2018).

Clear, James. Atomic Habits: An Easy & Proven Way to Build Good Habits & Break Bad Ones. New York: Penguin Random House, 2018.

Cleveland Clinic. Female Reproductive System . February 5, 2019. https://my.clevelandclinic.org/health/articles/9118-female-reproductive-system (accessed March 27, 2019).

Cole, Wayne. "America First - The Battle Against Intervention 1940-1941." Amazon. November 4, 2008. America First - The Battle Against Intervention 1940-1941 (accessed April 13, 2019).

Conroy, Alec M. "File:Relationship between synoptic gospels.png." Wikimedia Commons. May 13, 2012. https://commons.wikimedia.org/wiki/File:Relationship_between_synoptic_gospels.png (accessed June 16, 2019).

—. "File:Synoptic problem two source colored.png." Wikimedia Commons. November 28, 2007. https://commons.wikimedia.org/wiki/File:Synoptic_problem_two_source_colored.png (accessed June 16, 2019).

Copyright: Freedom Studio. "Jesus knocking on the door, original oil painting on canvas; Image ID:264711281." Shutterstock. n.d. http://www.shutterstock.com/pic-264711281/stock-photo-jesus-knocking-on-the-door-original-oil-painting-on-canvas.html (accessed November 6, 2016).

Corey, Benjamin L. "To Those Christians Who Say, "God Doesn't Give Us More Than We Can Handle"." Patheos Progressive Christian. October 12, 2017. http://www.patheos.com/blogs/formerlyfundie/christians-say-god-doesnt-give-us-can-handle/#comment-3861255192 (accessed October 22, 2018).

Costa, Pam. "Reclaiming Female Sexual Desire." TedX Palo Alto. June 5, 2018. https://www.youtube.com/watch?v=0Sn_UhcXZm4 (accessed November 15, 2018).

Council of Nicea. "The Nicene Creed." creeds.net. 325 AD. https://www.creeds.net/ancient/nicene.htm (accessed March 14, 2018).

Dawkins, Richard. "The Genius of Charles Darwin." The Genius of Charles Darwin. Athena IWC Media Limited 2008, 2008.

Deepak, Chopra, and Leonard Mlodinow. War of the Worldviews - Science vs Spirituality. New York: Crown Publishing Group, a division of Random House, In, 2011.

Denning, Stephanie. "Dollar Shave Club Founder: Why Life Is Defined By Choices." Forbes. May 31, 2018. https://www.forbes.com/sites/stephaniedenning/2018/05/31/dollar-shave-club-founder-why-life-is-defined-by-choices/#419614495abd (accessed June 7, 2018).

Dhammika, Van S. "Nearly all religions have some kind of holy writings or Bible. What is the Buddhist holy book?" Good Questions With Good Answers. n.d. http://www.buddhanet.net/ans66.htm (accessed March 13, 018).

Drane, John. "The Bible." BBC - Religions. July 12, 2011. http://www.bbc.co.uk/religion/religions/christianity/texts/bible.shtml (accessed October 15, 2018).

Dubner, Stephen J, and Steven D Levitt. Think Like A Freak. New York: Harper Collins Publisher, 2014.

Duhigg, Charles. "Wealthy Successful and Miserable." The Future of Work - The New York Tmes Magazine. February 22, 2019. https://www.nytimes.com/interactive/2019/02/21/magazine/elite-professionals-jobs-happiness.html (accessed February 22, 2019).

Durant, Will and Ariel. The Story of Civilization. 11 vols. New York: Simon & Shuster, 1975.

Ehrenreich, Barbara. Natural Causes. New York Boston: Twelve, 2018.
Ehrman, Bart D. God's Problem, How the Bible Fails to Answer Our most Important Question - Why We Suffer. New York: Harper Collins, 2008.
Ehrman, Bart. God's Problem. New Hork: HarperCollins, 2008.
Encyclopedia Britannica. "Hinduism - Religion." Encyclopedia Britannica. February 7, 2018. https://www.britannica.com/topic/Hinduism/Introduction (accessed October 23, 2018).
Exstein, Ted. "What is the difference between the Talmud and the Torah?" Quora. July 16, 2015. https://www.quora.com/What-is-the-difference-between-the-Talmud-and-the-Torah (accessed October 15, 2018).
Fackenheim, Emil L. "Judaism & the Meaning of Life." Commentary. April 1, 1965. https://www.commentarymagazine.com/articles/judaism-the-meaning-of-life/ (accessed March 27, 2018).
Feddacheenee. "File:Annunciator.jpg." Wikimedia Commons. June 29, 2012. https://commons.wikimedia.org/wiki/File:Annunciator.jpg (accessed June 16, 2019).
Finkelstein, J. "File:Maslow's hierarchy of needs.svg." Wikimedia Commons. October 27, 2006. https://commons.wikimedia.org/wiki/File:Maslow%27s_hierarchy_of_needs.svg (accessed June 14, 2019).
Fish, Stanley. Winning Arguments, What works and Doesn't Work in Politics, The Bedroom, The Curtroom, and the Classroom. New York: Harper Collins, 2016.
Frea, Dick. "SS Jerimiah O'Brien." National Park Service - WWII In the San Francisco Bay Area. n.d. https://www.nps.gov/nr/travel/wwiibayarea/jer.HTM (accessed June 16, 2019).
Freeman, James Dill. The Household of Faith, Chapter XI, "Their Healing Work, "Heal the Sick" "". 1951. https://www.truthunity.net/books/the-household-of-faith-155-164 (accessed January 25, 2018).
Fritz, Robert. Corporate Tides. Oxford, England: Butterworth-Hinemann, 1994.
—. Creating. New York: Fawcett Columbine, 1991.
—. The Leader as Creator. Salem, Massachusetts: DMA, 1986.
—. The Path of Least Resistance - Learning to Become the Creative Force in Your Own Life. New York: Fawcett Columbine, 1989.
—. The Path of Least Resistance for Managers - Designing Organizations to Succeed. San Francisco: Berret-Koehler Publishers, 1999.
Funk, Ken. "Perspectives on Science and Christian Faith." American Scientific Affiliation. September 2007. http://www.asa3.org/ASA/PSCF/2007/PSCF9-07Funk.pdf (accessed March 7, 2018).
Gaylor, Annie Laurie. "Freethought of the Day." Freedom From Religion Foundation. Edited by Annie Laurie Gaylor. February 15, 2017. https://ffrf.org/news/day (accessed February 15, 2017).
Giovannoli, Joseph. The Biology of Belief - How Our Biology Biases Our Beliefs and Perceptions. Rosetta Press, Inc, 2000.
Goldhill, Olivia. "The person who's best at lying to you is you." Quartz. March 18, 2018. https://qz.com/1231534/the-person-whos-best-at-lying-to-you-is-you/ (accessed March 19, 2018).

Gray, Jason D. "Buddhist Views of the Afterlife." The Immortality Project, University of California, Riverside. n.d. http://www.sptimmortalityproject.com/background/buddhist-views-of-the-afterlife/ (accessed March 2, 2018).

Green, Khalil. "Love for God in Islam - The Highest Attribute of Spiritual Attainment." IslamiCity. March 15, 2015. http://www.islamicity.org/6526/love-for-god-in-islam-the-highest-attribute-of-spiritual-attainment/ (accessed March 1, 2018).

Gregorie, Rev. John. "Nazarene Lord's Prayer." The Tau. n.d. https://sites.google.com/site/thetaugbbo00/nazarene-lord-s-prayer (accessed April 12, 2019).

Grew, David. Paddy Points the Way. New York: Coward-McCann, 1950.

Guareschi, Giovannino. The Little World of Don Camilo. New York: Pellegrini and Cudahy, 1950.

Gunasekara, Dr V. A. "The Buddhist Attitude to God." BuddhaSasana. April 1997. https://www.budsas.org/ebud/ebdha068.htm (accessed February 26, 2018).

Hall, Douglas John. God & Human Suffering. Minneapollis: Augsburg Publishing House, 1986.

Hanh, Thich Nhat. "Buddhist Quotes." The Buddhist Center. n.d. http://www.thebuddhacenter.org/buddhism/buddhist-quotes/ (accessed March 20, 2018).

Hare, John Bruno. "Hinduism." Internet Sacred Text Archive. 2010. http://www.sacred-texts.com/hin/ (accessed October 17, 2018).

Harwell, Jaclyn. "Why Joy is More Important to Your Health than Food." The Family That Heals Together. May 22, 2016. https://www.thefamilythathealstogether.com/joy-important-health-food/ (accessed February 8, 2018).

"Having Hope in Allah The Almighty - I." Islamweb.net English. August 10, 2015. http://www.islamweb.net/en/article/178489/having-hope-in-allah-the-almighty-i (accessed March 20, 2019).

Hawkes, Brent. "Spirituality and sexuality. You can have both." TEDxToronto. December 7, 2015. https://www.youtube.com/watch?v=7NGB5rQKkpM (accessed December 20, 2018).

HealthCare Chaplaincy . ""Handbook of Patients' Spiritual and Cultural Values for Health Care Professionals" -Finding Meaning – Bringing Comfort." healthcarechaplaincy.org. 2013. http://www.healthcarechaplaincy.org/userimages/Cultural%20Sensitivity%20handbook%20from%20HealthCare%20Chaplaincy%20%20(3-12%202013).pdf (accessed November 6, 2018).

Hill, Napoleon. Think and Grow Rich. n.d.

Himilayan Academy, Saiva Siddhanta Theological Seminary at Kauai's Hindu Monastery. "Karma and Reincarnation." Himilayanacademy.com. n.d. https://www.himalayanacademy.com/readlearn/basics/karma-reincarnation (accessed March 21, 2018).

—. "TEACH HOW HINDUISM GRANTS EXPERIENCE OF GOD."

Raising Children As Good Hindus. n.d.
https://www.himalayanacademy.com/media/books/raising-children-as-good-hindus_ei/web/ch37_sec6.html (accessed March 1, 2018).

Hindu, The. "Experiencing God ." The Hindu. October 28, 2016.
http://www.thehindu.com/features/friday-review/religion/Experiencing-God/article12543677.ece (accessed March 1, 2018).

Hindupedia. "Ideals and Values/Forgiveness." Hindupedia. n.d.
http://www.hindupedia.com/en/Ideals_and_Values/Forgiveness (accessed February 19, 2018).

—. "Nature of God (This article was originally published in the April/May/June 2009 edition of "Hinduism Today"." Hindupedia. April 2009. http://www.hindupedia.com/en/Who_is_a_Hindu%3F#The_Nature_of_God (accessed Februry 27, 2018).

History, National Museum of American. "Ship Engine Order Telegraph." National Museum of American History. S. S. Leviathan Engine Order Telegraph. Currently not on view, n.d.

Hitchens, Christofer. the Portable Atheist. Philadelphia: Da Capo OPress, a member of th Perseus Books Group, 2007.

Hitchens, Christopher. "4 Clips of Our Greatly Missed Hitch." Youyube. n.d. https://www.youtube.com/watch?v=HKRonSOYBN8 (accessed October 4, 2018).

Horodysky, Daniel. "American Mariners in World War II: First to Go; Last to Return." Berkeley Daily Planet. December 6, 1999.
http://www.usmm.org/pearlharbor.html (accessed April 13, 2019).

International Planetarium Society, Incorporated. "The Age of the Earth and the Universe." n.d.
http://www.ips-planetarium.org/?age (accessed November 12, 2016).

Izquierdo, German. "What is the purpose of life according to Judaism?" Quora. January 19, 2017.
https://www.quora.com/What-is-the-purpose-of-life-according-to-Judaism (accessed March 27, 2018).

Jacoby, Susan. Freethinkers. New York : Metropolitan/Owl Book, Henry Holt and Company, 2004.

jannah.org. "The Attributes of God." Islam 101. February 26, 2018.
http://www.islam101.com/tauheed/AllahNames.htm (accessed February 26, 2018).

Jones, Robert. The End of White Christian America. New York: Simon & Schuster, 2016.

Judiasm 101. n.d.
http://www.jewfaq.org/613.htm (accessed November 6, 2017).

Kandell, Ellen. "Objectivity, Subjectivity, and the Known Unknows: Intentions vs. Assumptions in Conflict Resolution." Alternative Resolutions. June 3, 2016.
https://www.alternativeresolutions.net/2016/06/03/intentions-vs-assumptions/ (accessed June 16, 2019).

Karmapa, His Holiness the Gyalwang Karmapa. "Love and Compassion: Transforming our Relationships for the Better." The Karmapa. June 23, 2016. http://kagyuoffice.org/love-and-compassion-transforming-our-relationships-for-the-better/ (accessed February 16, 2019).

Keller, Timothy. Making Sense of GOD - An Invitation tothe Skeptical. New York: Penguin Random House LL, 375 Hudson Street, New York, 2016.

Khandavalli, Shankara Bharadwaj. "Karma." Hindupedia. n.d. http://www.hindupedia.com/en/Karma (accessed March 2, 2018).

Kivata. "What, according to Hinduism, is the purpose of life?" Quroa. December 16, 2016. https://www.quora.com/What-according-to-Hinduism-is-the-purpose-of-life (accessed March 27, 2018).

Kiyosaki, Robert. Rich Dad Poor Dad. New York: Warner Books, 2000.

Kiyosaki, Robert T. Rich Dad's CASHFLOW Quadrant: Rich Dad's Guide to Financial Freedom. New York: Warner Books, 2000.

Koch, Richard. The 80/20 Principle: The Secret to Achieving More with Less. New York: Currency Doubleday, 1998.

Kornfield, Jack. "Why Practice it? (Forgiveness)." Greater Good Magazine - Science Based Insights for a Meaningful Life. n.d. https://greatergood.berkeley.edu/topic/forgiveness/definition#why-practice (accessed October 4, 2018).

Kruger, J, and Dunning. D. "Unskilled and unaware of it: How difficulties in recognizing one's own incompetence lead to inflated self-assessments." Journal of Personality and Social Psychology, 77(6), 1121-1134. . Dec 1999. http://psycnet.apa.org/doiLanding?doi=10.1037%2F0022-3514.77.6.1121 (accessed March 19, 2018).

Kukkonen, Tuuli. "Still Going Strong: Sexuality in Older Adults." TEDxGuelphU. March 17, 2017.
 https://www.youtube.com/watch?v=pqLhPPOEJB4 (accessed December 19, 2018).

Kumar, Anjali. "My failed mission to find God — and what I found instead ." Ted Talks Worth Spreading. January 2018. https://www.ted.com/speakers/anjali_kumar (accessed February 1, 2018).

Lambert, Malcolm. God's Armies - Crusade and Jihad: Origins, History, Aftermath. New York London: Pegasus Books, 2016.

Lascola, Linda. "Our True Religion: Football, Firearms, and the American Flag." Patheos - Nonreligious. November 8, 2018. https://www.patheos.com/blogs/rationaldoubt/2018/11/our-true-religion-football-firearms-and-the-american-flag/?utm_medium=email&utm_source=BRSS&utm_campaign=Nonreligious&utm_content=456 (accessed November 8, 2018).

Leitch, Cliff. "What Does the Bible Say About Love?" The Christian Bible Reference Site. January 1, 2010.
   http://www.christianbiblereference.org/faq_love.htm (accessed February 12, 2018).
—. "What Does the Bible Say About the Old Testament Law?" Christian Bible Reference Site. 1996-2014.
   http://www.christianbiblereference.org/faq_OldTestamentLaw.htm (accessed February 2, 2018).
Lewis, C.S. Mere Christianity. New York: Harper Collins, 2004.
Linder, Doug. "Bishop James Ussher Sets the Date for Creation." 2004. http://law2.umkc.edu/faculty/projects/ftrials/scopes/ussher.html (accessed November 12, 2016).
Livni, Ephrat. "A Nobel Prize-winning psychologist says most people don't really want to be happy." Quartz - #Lifegoals. December 21, 2018.
   https://qz.com/1503207/a-nobel-prize-winning-psychologist-defines-happiness-versus-satisfaction/ (accessed December 21, 2018).
Lombard, Jay Dr. The Mind of God - Neuroscience, Faith, and a Search for the Soul. New York: Crown Publishing Group, a divisioin of Pengin Random House LLC, 2017.
Longenecker, Dwight. "Why Does God Allow Horrible Evil?" National Catholic Register. February 23, 2017.
   http://www.ncregister.com/blog/longenecker/why-does-god-allow-horrible-evil (accessed February 28, 2017).
Lumen Learning. "Introduction to Psychology - Humanistic Approaches." Lumen Learning Courses. n.d.
   https://courses.lumenlearning.com/waymaker-psychology/chapter/humanistic-approaches/ (accessed February 8, 2019).
Luskin, Fred. "What is Forgiveness?" Greater Good Magazine - Science Based Insights for a Meaningful Life. n.d.
   https://greatergood.berkeley.edu/topic/forgiveness/definition (accessed October 4, 2018).
Lyle, Kevin. "Helicopter Royal Air Force." Pixabay.com. May 26, 2014. https://pixabay.com/photos/helicopter-royal-air-force-chinook-354699/ (accessed June 16, 2019).
—. "kvnlyle." Pixabay. May 26, 2014.
   https://pixabay.com/photos/helicopter-royal-air-force-chinook-354699/ (accessed June 16, 2019).
"Making myths out of the Titanic (From Book, Titanic Lives, by Richard-Davenport Hines, Harper Press)." Church Times. April 11, 2012 (Picture taken on Titanic 1912).
   https://www.churchtimes.co.uk/articles/2012/13-april/comment/making-myths-out-of-the-titanic (accessed August 3, 2019).
Malaekah, Mostafa. "What is the Purpose of Life?" islam-guide.com. 2001. https://www.islam-guide.com/purpose-of-life.htm#s8 (accessed March 27, 2018).
Maltz, Maxwell. Psycho-Cybernetics. New York: Pocket Books a division of Simon & Schuster, 1989.

Manson, Mark. The Subtle Art of Not Giving a F*ck. New York: Harper One, 2016.
Marc Zvi Brettler, Peter Enns, Daniel J. Harrington. The Bible and the Believer. New York: Oxford University Press, 2012.
Maroof, Rabbi Joseph Maroof. "What does Judaism Say About Love." Ask the Rabiis. September/October 2010. Rabbi Joseph Maroof (accessed February 13, 2018).
Maroof, Rabbi Joseph. "What Does Judaism Say About Love pg 25." Ask the Rabbis. September-October 2010.
http://www.momentmag.com/wp-content/uploads/2013/02/What-Does-Judaism-Say-About-Love.pdf (accessed February 13, 2018).
McCandless, Jeremy R. "Experiencing God - Day By Day." Books.Google.com. 2012.
https://books.google.com/books?isbn=1471637093 (accessed March 1, 2018).
McCoy, Maxie. "Are you sabotaging everything you want? How to know." Ladders. March 7, 2019.
https://www.theladders.com/career-advice/are-you-sabotaging-everything-you-want-how-to-know (accessed March 7, 2019).
McGrath, James F. "Naming the Animals, Young-Earth Creationist Style." Patheos - Progressive Christiain. October 12, 2018.
http://www.patheos.com/blogs/religionprof/2018/10/naming-the-animals-young-earth-creationist-style.html?utm_source=Newsletter&utm_medium=email&utm_campaign=Progressive+Christian&utm_content=43 (accessed October 12, 2018).
McGrath, Maureen. "No Sex Marriage – Masturbation, Loneliness, Cheating and Shame." TEDxStanleyPark. July 6, 2016.
https://www.youtube.com/watch?v=LVgzOyHVcj4&t=206s (accessed December 20, 2018).
—. "No Sex Marriage – Masturbation, Loneliness, Cheating and Shame." TEDxStanleyPark. July 6, 2016.
https://www.youtube.com/watch?v=LVgzOyHVcj4 (accessed June 20, 2019).
McLeod, Ken. "Forgiveness Is Not Buddhist." Tricycle. 2017.
https://tricycle.org/magazine/forgiveness-not-buddhist/ (accessed February 19, 2018).
Merritt, Carol Howard. Healing Spiritual Wounds. New York, New York: HarperOne, 2017.
Meslier, Jean. "Superstition In All Ages (1732)." Gutenburg.org. January 25, 2013.
https://www.gutenberg.org/files/17607/17607-h/17607-h.htm#link2H_4_0013 (accessed March 23, 2018).
Meyers, Pamela. "How to spot a liar." TED Global 2011. October 11, 2011. https://www.youtube.com/watch?v=P_6vDLq64gE (accessed September 15, 2018).
Miles, Charles A. "In the Garden." Timeless Truths. 1913.
http://library.timelesstruths.org/music/In_the_Garden/ https://creativecommons.org/licenses/by-sa/3.0/ (accessed November 6, 2016).
Military Uniform Supply Company. "Genuine Vietnam-Era OG-107 Boonie Hat with Insect Net." Military Clothing.com. n.d.
https://www.militaryclothing.com/Genuine-Vietnam-Era-OG-107-Boonie-

Hat-with-Insect-Net.aspx?id=19818-60002-ABM-6&gclid=CjwKCAjwq-Tm-BRBdEiwAaO1enxH2qTnSAUwYdvXyRwa-XZYngKFu5FiHoipYZfTa4qNff-FUgkBOD1hoCZYYQAvD_BwE (accessed May 15, 2019).

MJL Staff. "Hatikvah, the National Anthem of Israel." My Jewish Learning. n.d. https://www.myjewishlearning.com/article/national-anthem-of-israel/ (accessed March 20, 2018).

—. "Is There A Jewish Afterlife?" My Jewish Learning. n.d. https://www.myjewishlearning.com/article/life-after-death/ (accessed March 2, 2018).

—. "Jewish Resurrection of the Dead." My Jewish Larning. n.d. https://www.myjewishlearning.com/article/jewish-resurrection-of-the-dead/ (accessed March 2, 2018).

—. "Judaism and Sex: Questions and Answers." My Jewish Learning. 2018. https://www.myjewishlearning.com/article/judaism-and-sex-questions-and-answers/ (accessed February 10, 2018).

—. "Tzitzit, the Fringes on the Prayer Shawl." My Jewish Learning. 2018. https://www.myjewishlearning.com/article/tzitzit/ (accessed February 10, 2018).

Mooney, Chris. The REPUBLICAN WAR on SCIENCE. New York: Basic Books, 2005.

Moran, Mark CEO. "Buddhist Sacred Texts: The Sutras." Finding Dulcinea. 2018? http://www.findingdulcinea.com/guides/Religion-and-Spirituality/Sacred-Texts.xa_1.html (accessed March 13, 2018).

—. "Hinduism: Understanding Sanatana Dharma." Finding Dulcinea. n.d. http://www.findingdulcinea.com/guides/Religion-and-Spirituality/Hinduism.pg_0.html#0 (accessed March 13, 2018).

Morehouse, Andrew R. Voltaire and Jean Meslier. New Haven: Yale University Press, 1936.

Moultman, Jurgend. "Theology of Hope by Jurgen Moltmann." On-line JournL OF Public Theology. n.d. http://www.pubtheo.com/theologians/moltmann/theology-of-hope-0b.htm (accessed March 19, 2018).

Muller, Richard A. Now - The Physics of Time. New York: W.W Norton & Company, 2016.

Murakami, Haruki. "Thailand." Granta - The Magazine of New Writing. 2011. https://granta.com/thailand/ (accessed February 8, 2019).

Murray, David. "8 Sources of Joy vs. 6 Thieves of It." Christianity.com. n.d. https://www.christianity.com/blogs/david-murray/8-sources-of-joy-vs-6-thieves-of-it.html (accessed March 22, 2018).

Nachman, Rabbi. "Experiencing the Presence of God." JewishOutlook.com. 2014. http://jewishoutlook.com/experiencing-the-presence-of-god/ (accessed March 1, 2018).

Neil, Herms. "Erika." Wikipedia. 1930's. https://en.wikipedia.org/wiki/Erika_(song) (accessed January 22, 2017).

Nelson, Jim, interview by Ivan Beggs. Willie Nelson Quote (Aug 9, 2019).

Newlyn, Emma. "Ganesh: The mudra, the meaning and the story of the elephant-headed god." Yoga Matters. March 6, 2017. https://www.yogamatters.com/blog/ganesh-mudra-meaning-story-elephant-headed-god/ (accessed October 8, 2018).

Nichols, Tom. "How America Lost Faith in Expertise (And Why Tgat's a Giant Problem)." Foreign Affairs, March/April 2017: 60-73.

Novella, Steven. Skptic's Guide to the Universe. New York: Grand Central Publishing, 2018.

Numrich, Paul. "Flow Chart of a Religious Ethical System." Self Published Paper, July 2018.

Nunez, Paul L. The New Science of Consciousness - Exploring the Complexity of Brain, Mind, and Self. Amerhest, New Yor: Prometheus Books, 2016.

Olivia, Keeley. "Masturbation is the New Meditation." TEDxLeamingtonSpa. November 28, 2018. https://www.youtube.com/watch?v=BUOzUTXFlQA&t=8s (accessed December 12, 2018).

O'Neill, Tim. "Jesus the Apocalyptic Prophet." History for Atheists. December 20, 2018. https://historyforatheists.com/2018/12/jesus-apocalyptic-prophet/ (accessed April 13, 2019).

Oshin, Mayo. "10 lessons from Benjamin Franklin's daily schedule that will double your productivity." Ladders - Productivity. February 11, 2019. 10 lessons from Benjamin Franklin's daily schedule that will double your productivity (accessed February 11, 2019).

—. "The Iron Mike rule: The one thing successful people do differently." Ladders. November 26, 2018. https://www.theladders.com/career-advice/the-iron-mike-rule-the-one-thing-successful-people-do-differently (accessed November 26, 2018).

Payne, Richard. "The Authority of the Buddha: ." Institute of Buddhist Studies, 2140 Durant Avenue, Berkeley CA 94704, U.S.A. n.d. http://www.zurnalai.vu.lt/acta-orientalia-vilnensia/article/viewFile/3660/5149 (accessed March 7, 018).

Peterson, Kay, and David A. Kolb. How You Learn is How You LIve. Oakland, California: Berrett_Koehler Publishers, Inc, 2017.

Peto, Alan. "Buddhism for Beginners (a Quick Intro)." Alan Peto. December 14, 2011. https://www.alanpeto.com/buddhism/buddhism-quick-intro/ (accessed October 22, 2018).

Pilgrim, Peace (aka Mildred Lisette Norman). Peace Pilgrim Her Life and Work In Her Own Words. Sante Fe, New Mexico, USA: Ocean Tree Books, 1983.

Piper, John. "What Is So Important About Christian Hope? ." desiring God. March 7, 2008. https://www.desiringgod.org/interviews/what-is-so-important-about-christian-hope (accessed March 20, 2018).

Pope, Msg Charles. "The Church Cannot Teach Error, Because She Was Founded by Jesus Christ, Who is God Himself." National Catholic Register. February 21, 2017. http://www.ncregister.com/blog/msgr-pope/the-church-cannot-teach-error-because-she-was-founded-by-jesus-christ-who-i (accessed February 28, 2017).

Prabhupada, Bhaktivedanta Swami. Bhagavad-Gita - As it is. Australia: McPherson's Printing Group, 2001.

Pratt, Ralph S. "I Was There! - I Was on the Bombed Steel Seafarer." The War Illustrated. September 30, 1941. I Was There! - I Was on the Bombed Steel Seafarer (accessed April 13, 2019).

"Pratyahara (Con't) – The Sense Organs." Discover-yoga-online.com. n.d. http://www.discover-yoga-online.com/sense-organs.html (accessed April 11, 2019).

Prothero, Stephen. Religious Literacy - What every American Needs to Know - and Doesn't. New York: Harper One - Harper Collins, 2008.

"Quotations on: Joy, Happiness ." A View on Buddhism. n.d. http://viewonbuddhism.org/dharma-quotes-quotations-buddhist/joy-happiness.htm (accessed March 26, 2018).

Rabbi. "Temple Ner Ami." http://templenerami.org/. November 2006. templenerami.org/.../Old/Nov%2006%20Good%20Evil%20and%20Freewill.pdf (accessed February 8, 2018).

Rasheta, Noah. "27 – Understanding Non-Attachment." Secular Buddhism. September 19, 2016. https://secularbuddhism.com/understanding-non-attachment/ (accessed October 31, 2018).

Raven. "File:Flammarion-color.png." Wikimedia. March 15, 2015. https://commons.wikimedia.org/w/index.php?curid=39827732 (accessed Auguest 1, 2019).

Reinke, Tony. 12 Ways Your Phone is Changing You. Wheaton, Illinois: Crossway, 2017.

Rich, Tracey R. "Beliefs." Judaism 101. 2011. http://www.jewfaq.org/defs/beliefs.htm (accessed March 13, 2018).

—. "Halakhah: Jewish Law." Judaism 101. 2011. http://www.jewfaq.org/halakhah.htm (accessed March 13, 2018).

—. "The Nature of G-d." Judaism 101. 2011. http://www.jewfaq.org/g-d.htm (accessed February 26, 2018).

—. "What Do Jews Believe?" Judaism 101. 2011. http://www.jewfaq.org/beliefs.htm (accessed March 18, 2018).

Rich, Tracy R. "Love and Brotherhood." Judaism 101. 1995-201). http://www.jewfaq.org/brother.htm (accessed February 13, 2018).

Rizvi, Sayyid Muhammad Rizvi. "Chapter Two: The Islamic Sexual Morality (1) Its Foundation." Al-Islam.org. Islamic Education & Information Center. 2018. https://www.al-islam.org/marriage-and-morals-islam-sayyid-muhammad-rizvi/chapter-two-islamic-sexual-morality-1-its-foundation (accessed February 10, 2018).

Robin. "The Buddhist Outlook on Hope." Buddhist Teachings. April 16, 2013. http://www.buddhistteachings.org/the-buddhist-outlook-on-hope (accessed November 19, 2018).

Roosevelt, Franklin. "On Maintaining Freedom of the Sea." FDR Library. September 11, 1941.
http://docs.fdrlibrary.marist.edu/091141.html (accessed April 13, 2019).

Rounds, Al. "Trial of Hope - Last Hill." Al Rounds - Fine Arts Studio. Trial of Hope - Last Hill. Salt Lake City, n.d.

S., Pangambam. "Maureen McGrath: No Sex Marriage – Masturbation, Loneliness, Cheating and Shame (Transcript)." The Singju Post. September 2, 2016.
https://singjupost.com/maureen-mcgrath-no-sex-marriage-masturbation-loneliness-cheating-and-shame-transcript/3/ (accessed June 20, 2019).

Sacks, Jonathan Rabbi. "Faith Lectures: Judaism, Justice and Tragedy – Confronting the problem of evil." http://rabbisacks.org/. April 6, 2000. http://rabbisacks.org/faith-lectures-judaism-justice-and-tragedy-confronting-the-problem-of-evil/ (accessed February 8, 2018).

—. "Future Tense – How The Jews Invented Hope." Rabbi Sachs. April 1, 2008.
http://rabbisacks.org/future-tense-how-the-jews-invented-hope-published-in-the-jewish-chronicle/ (accessed 2018 20, March).

—. "The Pursuit of Joy." Orthodox Union. n.d.
https://www.ou.org/torah/parsha/rabbi-sacks-on-parsha/the-pursuit-of-joy/ (accessed March 26, 2018).

Sallman, Warner. "Christ at Heart's Door." The Warner Sallman Collection. 1942.
http://www.warnersallman.com/collection/images/christ-at-hearts-door/ (accessed November 6, 2016).

Satlow, Michael. "How the Bible Became Holy." ReformJudaism.org. n.d. https://reformjudaism.org/jewish-life/arts-culture/literature/how-bible-became-holy (accessed March 7, 2018).

Schwartz, Gary E. PhD. The Aferlife Experiments. New York, NY: Atria Books, 2002.

Shade, Leah D. "I Want Jesus to Let Me Off the Hook: The Rich Young Man and Me." Patheos - Eco Preacher. October 10, 2018.
http://www.patheos.com/blogs/ecopreacher/2018/10/jesus-hook-rich-young-man-me/?utm_source=Newsletter&utm_medium=email&utm_campaign=Progressive+Christian&utm_content=43 (accessed October 12, 2018).

Shah, Zia, H. "Two Hundred Verses about Compassionate Living in the Quran." The Muslim Times . October 29, 2013.
https://themuslimtimes.info/2013/10/29/three-hundred-verses-about-compassionate-living-in-the-quran/ (accessed February 15, 2018).

Shakir, M.H. The Qur'an. Elmhurst, New York: Tahrike Tarsile Qur'an, Inc., 2004 9th U.S. Edition.

Shakya, Buddha. "Devotional Love in Hinduism." All You Need to KNow ABout Hinduism. n.d.
http://history-of-hinduism.blogspot.com/2010/10/devotioal-love-in-hinduism.html (accessed February 16, 2018).

Sheima. ""Love" in the Quran and Sunnah." How to Be a Happy Muslim. July 30, 2016.
http://howtobeahappymuslim.com/?p=946 (accessed February 15, 2018).

Shemtov, Rabbi Eliezer. "The Art of Forgiveness." Chabad.org. 2018 .
http://www.chabad.org/library/article_cdo/aid/1619314/jewish/The-Art-of-Forgiveness.htm (accessed February 19, 2018).
Shermer, Michael. Heavens on Earth - The Scientific Search for the Afterlife, Immortality, and Utopia. New York: Henry Holt, 2018.
Shoemaker, H. Stephen. "The Saving of Liberal Christianity." Shoemaker's Study - the Sermons and Writings of H. Stephen Shoemaker. n.d.
http://shoemakersstudy.com/2018/02/12/the-saving-of-liberal-christianity/ (accessed November 1, 2018).
Siddiqi, Dr. Muzammil H. "Why Does Allah Allow Suffering and Evil in the World?" Islam Online Archive. n.d.
https://archive.islamonline.net/?p=885 (accessed January 30, 2018).
Slick, Matt. "What is the meaning and purpose of life?" Christian Apologetics and Research Ministry (CARM). May 12, 2012.
https://carm.org/meaning-of-life (accessed March 27, 2018).
Smith, David Livingstone. Why We Lie - The Evolutionary Roots of Deception and the Unconscious Mind. New York: St. Martin's Press, 2004.
Spiritual Excellence. "Happiness in Islam: 5 Steps to a Life of Joy and Purpose." SpiritualExcellence. July 2013.
http://www.spiritualexcellence.com/blog/happiness-in-islam-5-steps-to-a-life-of-joy-and-purpose/ (accessed March 26, 2018).
Stewart, George. God and Pain. New York: Geroge H. Doran Company, 1927.
Story-Fund? "Dunning-Kruger Effect." Story.Fund. 2014.
http://story.fund/post/114093854037/dunning-kruger-effect (accessed March 19, 2018).
Stöwer, Willy. "Sinking of the RMS Titanic." Wekimedia Commons. 1912. By Willy Stöwer, died on 31st May 1931 - Magazine Die Gartenlaube, en:Die Gartenlaube and de:Die Gartenlaube, Public Domain,
https://commons.wikimedia.org/w/index.php?curid=97646 (accessed August 3, 2019).
"Student Dictionary." Merriam Webster - Word Central. 2007.
http://wordcentral.com/cgi-bin/student?faith (accessed December 29, 2018).
Subramuniyaswami, Satguru Sivaya. Dancing with Siva: Hinduism's Contemporary Catechism. IndiA: Himalayan Academy, 2003.
Sukel, Kayt. The Art of Risk - The New Science of Courage, Caution, & Chance. Washington, DC: National Geographic Society, 2016.

Svirsky, Rabbi Efim. "Feeling God's Presence." Aish.com. n.d.
http://www.aish.com/sp/pg/48894482.html (accessed March 1, 2018).
Taber, I. W. "Moby Dick final chase.jpg." Wikimedia Commons, the free media repository. Charles Scribner's Sons, New York. 1902.
https://commons.wikimedia.org/w/index.php?curid=11179929 (accessed August 1, 2019).
Thaler, Richard H., and Cass R. Sunstein. Nudge - Improving Decision Abou Health, Wealth, and Happiness. 375 Hudson Street, New York, New York 10014, USA: Penguin Group, 2009.

The Learning Network. "New York Woman Killed While Witnesses do Nothing." The Learning Network. March 13, 2012. https://learning.blogs.nytimes.com/2012/03/13/march-13-1964-new-york-woman-killed-while-witnesses-do-nothing/ (accessed June 19, 2019).

"The Meaning of Life in Buddhism ." ReligionFacts.com. November 19, 2016. http://www.religionfacts.com/buddhism/meaning-life (accessed March 27, 2018).

Thera, Nyanaponika. "Buddhism and the God-idea." Buddhist Publication Society - Access to Insight (BCBS Edition). November 10, 2013. http://www.accesstoinsight.org/lib/authors/nyanaponika/godidea.html (accessed March 1, 2018).

Turner, Laura Teddy. "Christian Beliefs on the Meaning of Life." Classroom. September 17, 2017. https://classroom.synonym.com/christian-beliefs-on-the-meaning-of-life-12087755.html (accessed March 27, 2018).

Tzadok, Ariel Bar. "Prayer for Receiving Divine Guidance (Torah)." KosherTorah.com. 2010. http://www.koshertorah.com/PDF/shavuotprayer.pdf (accessed February 9, 2018).

U.S. Department of Health and Human Services. "Leprosy." Genetics Home Reference. April 3, 2018. https://ghr.nlm.nih.gov/condition/leprosy (accessed April 9, 2018).

Unknown. "Sex." The Buddha's Advice to Laypeople (Guidelines for developing a happier life). February 8, 2018. https://buddhasadvice.wordpress.com/sex/ (accessed February 12, 2018).

US Government. All Types of STDs and STIs, STD Symptoms, STD Pictures, STD Treatment. July 20,, 2015. http://www.std-gov.org/blog/types-of-stds/ (accessed November 4, 2016).

V, Jayaram. "Ananda, the State of Bliss or Happiness." Hinduwebsite.com. n.d. http://www.hinduwebsite.com/hinduism/concepts/ananda.asp (accessed March 26, 2018).

—. "Death and Afterlife in Hinduism." Hinduwebsite.com. n.d. http://www.hinduwebsite.com/hinduism/h_death.asp (accessed March 2, 2018).

—. "Good and Evil in Hinduism." Hinduwebsite.com. n.d. http://www.hinduwebsite.com/hinduism/h_goodandevil.asp (accessed February 9, 2018).

—. Introduction to Hinduism. Pure LIfe Vision, 2012.

—. "The 24 Tattvas of Creation in Samkhya Darshana." Hinduwebsite.com. n.d. The 24 Tattvas of Creation in Samkhya Darshana (accessed March 19, 2018).

—. "The Abiding Principles of Hindu Dharma." Hinduwebsite.com. n.d. https://www.hinduwebsite.com/what-is-hindu-dharma.asp (accessed October 28, 2018).

—. "What is Faith? Faith in Hinduism." Induwebsite.com. n.d. http://www.hinduwebsite.com/faith.asp (accessed March 19, 2018).

Van Loon, Hendrik. Tolerance - The Story of Man's Struggle for the Right to Think. New York: Liveright Publishing Corp, 1927 Revised 1940.

Vance, J.D. Hillbilly Elegy - A Memoir of a Family and Culture in Crisis. New York: HarperCollins, 2016.

Vesconte, Pietro - British Library, Public Domain. "Early World Maps." Wikipedia. 1321. https://commons.wikimedia.org/w/index.php?curid=3595637 (accessed November 8, 2016).

Vidyamala. "Being here: A Buddhist approach to pain." Wildmind Buddhist Meditation. February 20, 2007.
https://www.wildmind.org/applied/pain/being-here (accessed January 30, 2018).

Vij, Rajiv. "Maslow's Hierarchy Revisited...the Eastern Way!" Personal Alchemy Blog. October 11, 2011.
https://rajivvij.com/2008/09/maslows-hierarchy-revisitedthe-eastern.html (accessed November 26, 2018).

Wakefield, Dan. How Do We Know When It's God? Boston, New York, London: Little, Brown and Company, 1999.

Waldinge, Robert. "What makes a good life? Lessons from the longest study on happiness." TED. January 25, 2016.
https://www.youtube.com/watch?v=8KkKuTCFvzI (accessed November 20, 2018).

Waldinger, Robert. "What makes a good life? Lessons from the longest study on happiness." TED. January 25, 2016.
https://www.youtube.com/watch?v=8KkKuTCFvzI (accessed December 13, 2018).

Watson, Peter. The Age of Atheists - How we have sought to live since the deth of God. New York: Simon & Schuster, 2014.

Weinberg, Rabbi Noah. "The Meaning Of Life." Aish.com. n.d.
http://www.aish.com/sp/f/48964356.html (accessed March 27, 2018).

Weiner-Davis, Michele. "The sex-starved marriage ." TEDxCU. April 14, 2014.
https://www.youtube.com/watch?v=Ep2MAx95m20 (accessed December 12, 2018).

Wellman, Jack. "Top 7 Bible Verses About Curiosity." Patheos. November 28, 2016.
http://www.patheos.com/blogs/christiancrier/2016/11/28/top-7-bible-verses-about-curiosity/ (accessed June 12, 2018).

Weston, Walter L. The Self-Healing Pocket Guide. Wadsworth, Ohio: Transitions Press, 1996.

"What is Islam?" Inspired by Mohammad.com. 2010?
http://www.inspiredbymuhammad.com/islam.php?&content_80=2#10 (accessed March 27, 2018).

"What is the Purpose of Life in Buddhism." Teachings of the Buddha. n.d. https://teachingsofthebuddha.com/what-is-the-purpose-of-life-in-buddhism/ (accessed March 27, 2018).

Wiesner, Irving. "A Jewish Psychiatrist's Views on the Meaning of Life." Jews for Jesus. April 1, 2006.
https://jewsforjesus.org/publications/issues/issues-v16-n06/a-jewish-psychiatrist-s-views-on-the-meaning-of-life/ (accessed March 27, 2018).

Wikipedia. "Buddhist vegetarianism." Wikipedia. November 29, 2018. https://en.wikipedia.org/wiki/Buddhist_vegetarianism (accessed February 5, 2019).

—. "Diet in Hinduism." Wikipedia. January 31, 2019.
https://en.wikipedia.org/wiki/Diet_in_Hinduism (accessed February 5, 2019).

—. "Eternal Sin." Wikipedia. August 17, 2018.
https://en.wikipedia.org/wiki/Eternal_sin (accessed September 27, 2018).

—. "List of Christian denominations by number of members." Wikipedia. August 20, 2018.
https://simple.wikipedia.org/wiki/List_of_Christian_denominations_by_number_of_members#Catholic_Church_-_1 (accessed December 28, 2018).

—. "List of religious populations." Wikipedia. February 5, 2018.
https://en.wikipedia.org/wiki/List_of_religious_populations (accessed February 13, 2018).

—. "Old Testament." Wikipedia. n.d.
https://en.wikipedia.org/wiki/Old_Testament (accessed October 15, 2018).

—. "Quran." Wikipedia. n.d.
https://en.wikipedia.org/wiki/Quran (accessed October 16 2018).

—. "Religous Views on Love." Wikpedia. November 10, 2017.
https://en.wikipedia.org/wiki/Religious_views_on_love#Hindu (accessed February 16, 2018).

—. "Synoptic Gospels - Wikipedia." Wikipedia. n.d.
https://www.google.com/imgres?imgurl=https://upload.wikimedia.org/wikipedia/commons/thumb/6/6f/Relationship_between_synoptic_gospels-en.svg/360px-Relationship_between_synoptic_gospels-en.svg.png&imgrefurl=https://en.wikipedia.org/wiki/Synoptic_Gospels&h=4 (accessed October 12, 2018).

—. "Tanmatras." Wikipedia. September 26, 2016.
https://en.wikipedia.org/wiki/Tanmatras (accessed April 11, 2019).

—. "Two Gospel Hypothesis." Wikipedia. n.d.
https://www.google.com/imgres?imgurl=https://upload.wikimedia.org/wikipedia/commons/thumb/e/ee/Synoptic_problem_two_source_colored.png/220px-Synoptic_problem_two_source_colored.png&imgrefurl=https://en.wikipedia.org/wiki/Two-source_hypothesis&h=257&w=220& (accessed November 11, 2016).

Wilber, Ken. The Religion of Tomorrow. Boulder: Shambhala Publications, 2018.

Wilder, Thornton. Our Town. 1938 Book 1940 Movie.

Willett, Sunder. "Evil and Theodicy in Hinduism." Denison Journal of Religion (Vol 14, Article 5). 2015.
https://digitalcommons.denison.edu/cgi/viewcontent.cgi?referer=https://www.google.com/&httpsredir=1&article=1095&context=religion (accessed February 9, 2018).

Winkler, Rabbi Gershon. "What Does Judaism Say About Love? pg 24." Ask the Rabbis. September-October 2010.
http://www.momentmag.com/wp-content/uploads/2013/02/What-Does-Judaism-Say-About-Love.pdf (accessed February 13, 2018).

Figure and Cover Permissions

Cover - SGCShutter @iStock by Getty Images. Cover – Five Religious Symbols Peter Hermes Furian, iStock by Getty Images,

Stock illustration ID:917069686, Upload date: February 12, 2018

1.1 Photograph by Albert Beggs. Reproduced by permission

1.2 Loading ships - File: Queens Wharf, Port Adelaide 31 December 1926, in the public domain

https://commons.wikimedia.org/wiki/File:Queens_Wharf,_Port_Adelaide,_before_1927.jpeg

1.3 El Oso Que no Era Oso Frank Tashlin, Permission granted courtesy by Penguin.

1.4 Bear in woods. Frank Tashlin, Permission granted courtesy by Penguin.

1.5 Bear sleeping Frank Tashlin, Permission granted courtesy by Penguin.

1.6 Ship Wheelhouse. Alamy permissions. Ivvoice number: IY01244302 Aug 5, 2019 Ship Wheelhouse

1.7 Ship Engine Order Telegraph of SS Leviathon. Courtesy of National Museum of American History - Smithsonian Institution,

https://americanhistory.si.edu/collections/search/object/nmah_1102378

1.8 Statue of Liberty. Courtesy of National Park Service

https://www.nps.gov/stli/learn/photosmultimedia/photogallery.htm

2.1 Photograph courtesy of Albert Beggs

2.2 Personal photograph collection by the author.

3.1 Photography with permission of Ingeborg Beggs.

3.2 Image courtesy of Book Fever. Used with permission. July 22, 2019 https://bookfever.com/book/69213/Grew-David-PADDY-POINTS-THE-WAY-first-edition/

3.3 Don Camillo talking with Jesus Stefan Kahlhammer, 2008, CC BY-SA 3.0 license.

https://commons.wikimedia.org/wiki/File:Don_camillo.jpg

3.4 Posillipo at IJmuiden, Port of Amsterdam, Alf van Beem, 2 September 2012, IMO 9410911, CC0 1.0 Universal Public Domain Dedication

3.5 Saturn Courtesy of JPL.

https://www.jpl.nasa.gov/spaceimages/images/wallpaper/PIA21046-1600x1200.jpg

4.1 Helicopter landing Image courtesy of the Australian War Memorial Photographer: Michael Coleridge. EKN/67/0130/VN.

4.2 Berm and immediate perimeter area of FSB Brown, 13 May 1970 Image by SP4 Peter Nagurny, 40th Public Information Office, US Army.

http://signal439.tripod.com/redcatcher199lib/cambodia.html

4.3 Berm and immediate perimeter area of FSB Brown 13 May 1970 Image by SP4 Peter Nagurny, 40th Public Information Office, US Army.

http://signal439.tripod.com/redcatcher199lib/cambodia.html

4.4 Chinook Helicopter. Image by Kevin Lyle courtesy from Pixabay.

https://pixabay.com/photos/helicopter-royal-air-force-chinook-354699/. I Inverted the picture for the manuscript.

4.5 Example of a boonie hat showing Lieutenant William Hatcher. Photograph courtesy by Lieutenant William Hatcher.

5.1 I felt Martin Luther attempting to dialogue with many people. Anton von Werner in the Public domain by Wikimedia Commons

https://commons.wikimedia.org/wiki/File:Luther_at_the_Diet_of_Worms.jpg

6.1 I felt like being cast out of the Garden of Eden Gustave Doré (1832–1883) for a new deluxe edition of the 1843 French translation of the Vulgate Bible. Common Domain.

https://upload.wikimedia.org/wikipedia/commons/1/13/Adam_and_Eve_Driven_out_of_Eden.png

6.2 My trying to understand religions felt like Captain Ahab pursuing Moby Dick the whale. By I. W. Taber - Moby Dick - edition: Charles Scribner's Sons, New York, Public Domain

https://commons.wikimedia.org/w/index.php?curid=11179929

6.3 Me at the beginning of an adventure seeing a new world. Flammerion Engraving - Permission in the Creative Commons: By Raven - Own work, CC BY-SA 4.0,

https://commons.wikimedia.org/w/index.php?curid=39827732   https://commons.wikimedia.org/wiki/File:Flammarion-color.png

7.1 The Scream – an example of suffering. Edvard Munch (1863–1944), 1910. Work in the public domain.

https://commons.wikimedia.org/wiki/File:Edvard_Munch_-_The_Scream_-_Google_Art_Project.jpg

7.2 An example of personal and corporate suffering. Mathew Brady (1822–1896), Gordon, scourged back, NPG, 1863.jpg. Public domain.

FIGURE AND COVER PERMISSIONS 417

7.3 Warlord With Pencils instead of guns. Permission granted by Omaid Sharifi July 31, 2019

8.1 Individual and Societal Sin The Protectors of Our Industries, Puck Magazine, 7 February 1883. This work is in the public domain.

https://commons.wikimedia.org/wiki/File:The_protectors_of_our_industries.jpg

9.1 An example of forgiveness. After leaving the family the child returns and is forgiven. Rembrandt Harmensz van Rijn, Return of the Prodigal Son. This work is in the public domain.

https://commons.wikimedia.org/wiki/File:Rembrandt_Harmensz_van_Rijn_-_Return_of_the_Prodigal_Son_-_Google_Art_Project.jpg

10.1 Ships in a Storm on a Rocky Coast. Jan Porcellis. This work is in the public domain.

https://upload.wikimedia.org/wikipedia/commons/5/5b/Jan_Porcellis_-_Ships_in_a_Storm_on_a_Rocky_Coast_-_Google_Art_Project.jpg

11.1 Trial of Hope – The Last Hill Permission granted by artist Al Rounds, Al Rounds Studio, Salt Lake City, Utah August 29, 2019.

12.1 Perhaps an example of peace and joy. Dietmar Rabich (1962–), Sunset at the Oedlerteich (Heubachniederung) near Hausdülmen, Dülmen, North Rhine-Westphalia, Germany, 21 April 2016. Dietmar Rabich / Wikimedia Commons / "Dülmen, Kirchspiel, Oedlerteich -- 2016 -- 1929-35" / CC BY-SA 4.0 (https://commons.wikimedia.org/wiki/File:Dülmen,_Kirchspiel,_Oedlerteich_--_2016_--_1929-35.jpg).

13.1 Perhaps an example of love: Romeo and Juliet Frank Dicksee (1853–1928). This work is in the public domain in the United States.

https://commons.wikimedia.org/wiki/File:DickseeRomeoandJuliet.jpg
https://upload.wikimedia.org/wikipedia/commons/a/a3/DickseeRomeoandJuliet.jpg

14.1 Warm, tender, loving sex. Salvador Viniegra (1862–1915), The First Kiss of Adam and Eve. This work is in the public domain

https://commons.wikimedia.org/wiki/File:El_primer_beso_Salvador_Viniegra_y_Lasso_de_la_Vega_(1891).jpg

15.1 God creating Adam and the universe. Michelangelo (1475–1564), The Creation of Adam. This work is in the public domain.

https://commons.wikimedia.org/wiki/File:Michelangelo_-_Creation_of_Adam_(cropped).jpg

16.1 People experience God in many ways. Fuzzypiggy, St Michaels Mount, Marazion in Cornwall UK, 20 August 2014 CC BY-SA 3.0 This image was awarded First Prize by the UK judges in the 2014 Wiki Loves Monuments competition https://commons.wikimedia.org/wiki/File:St_Michael%27s_Mount_II5302_x_2982.jpg

16.2 Many people experience God or the Devine knocking at the door to their heart. It is a gentle warm knocking to enter one's life. "I stand at the door and knock" by Paul Geissler (1802-1872).

https://upload.wikimedia.org/wikipedia/commons/c/cf/Jesus_Christ_%28German_steel_engraving%29.jpg

17.1 The five religions have similar and different views of the afterlife. Louis Janmot (1814–1892), 1854, Courtesy of Musée des beaux-arts de Lyon. This work is in the public domain.

https://upload.wikimedia.org/wikipedia/commons/e/e6/Le_poeme_de_lAme-16-Louis_Janmot-MBA_Lyon-IMG_0499.jpg https://commons.wikimedia.org/wiki/File:Le_poeme_de_lAme-16-Louis_Janmot-MBA_Lyon-IMG_0499.jpg

18.1 Devotees in the five faith study their scriptures. Thomas Waterman Wood (1823–1903), Reading the Scriptures, 1874. This file was donated to Wikimedia Commons as part of a project by the Metropolitan Museum of Art. See the Image and Data Resources Open Access Policy.

https://upload.wikimedia.org/wikipedia/commons/c/c7/Reading_the_Scriptures_MET_APS2558.jpg https://www.metmuseum.org/art/collection/search/13347

18.2 Two Source Hypothesis for three New Testament books. Alec M. Conroy, GNU Free Documentation License, Version 1.2 or any later version published by the Free Software Foundation; with no Invariant Sections, no Front-Cover Texts, and no Back-Cover Texts.

https://commons.wikimedia.org/wiki/File:Synoptic_problem_two_source_colored.png

18.3 More detailed view of the Two Source Hypothesis. Alec M. Conroy, Relationships Between the Synoptic Gospels, November 27, 2007. Author placed it in the Creative Commons.

https://commons.wikimedia.org/wiki/File:Relationship_between_synoptic_gospels.png

19.1 Pope Pius VII (1742-1823) Thomas Lawrence (1769–1830), 1819, This work is in the public domain.

https://commons.wikimedia.org/wiki/File:Sir_Thomas_Lawrence_-_Pope_Pius_VII_(1742-1823)_-_Google_Art_Project.jpg

19.2 Jews Praying in the Synagogue on Yom Kippur Maurycy Gottlieb (1856–1879), 1878. This work is in the public domain.

https://upload.wikimedia.org/wikipedia/commons/1/1e/Maurycy_Gottlieb_-_Jews_Praying_in_the_Synagogue_on_Yom_Kippur.jpg

19.3 An Iman T. Jefferys, Habit of the Iman of the great mosque in 1749. Iman de la grande mosque, 1749. NYPL The Miriam and Ira D. Wallach Division of Art, Prints and Photographs: Art & Architecture Collection. https://commons.wikimedia.org/wiki/File:Habit_of_the_iman_of_the_great_mosque_in_1749._Iman_de_la_grande_mosquee_(NYPL_b14140320-1638036).jpg

19.4 Buddha Otgo Otgonbayar Ershuu, Buddha, GNU Free Documentation License, Version 1.2 or any later version published by the Free Software Foundation; with no Invariant Sections, no Front-Cover Texts, and no Back-Cover Texts. This file is licensed under the Creative Commons Attribution 3.0 Unported license.

https://commons.wikimedia.org/wiki/File:Buddha-painting.jpg http://www.mongolian-art.de/galerie_buddha_goetter/index.htm

19.5 Lakshmi, an example of one of many Hindu gods. Unknown author, Lakshmi, 1894. Purchase, Gift of Mrs. William J. Calhoun and Bequest of Nina Bunshaft, by exchange, 2013.

http://commons.wikimedia.org/wiki/File:Lakshmi_Print.jpg https://www.metmuseum.org/Collections/search-the-collections/78264?rpp=60&pg=18&ao=on&ft=india&pos=1079

This work is in the public domain. The Indian Copyright Act applies in India, to works first published in India.

20.1 One example of the meaning of life: being considerate neighbors. Jan Wijnants (1632–1684), Parable of the Good Samaritan, 1670. This work is in the public domain.

https://upload.wikimedia.org/wikipedia/commons/f/f2/Jan_Wijnants_-_Parable_of_the_Good_Samaritan.jpg

21.1. The heart, a universal symbol of love.(Bubinator), 11-05-2007, A red love heart. The copyright holder of this work, releases this work into the public domain.

https://upload.wikimedia.org/wikipedia/commons/4/42/Love_Heart_SVG.svg
https://commons.wikimedia.org/wiki/File:Love_Heart_SVG.svg

21.2 A universal symbol for work. Duesentrieb, "Construction Site" (European), 11 September 2005. The copyright holder of this work, releases this work into the public domain.

https://commons.wikimedia.org/wiki/File:Baustelle.svg

22.1 Smiley face – a symbol for happiness. Pumbaa80, A Smiley, 1 April 2006. The copyright holder of this work, release this work into the public domain.

https://commons.wikimedia.org/wiki/File:Smiley.svg

22.2 Runner – a symbol for being healthy Free onlinewebfonts.com, Person Running Free Icon

https://www.onlinewebfonts.com/icon/425986 http://www.onlinewebfonts.com/icon" Icon Fonts is licensed by CC BY 3.0

22.3 Gold, a symbol for wealth Stevebidmead, A pile of stacked gold bars, 17 June 2018

https://commons.wikimedia.org/wiki/File:Gold_bullion_bars.jpg

https://pixabay.com/en/gold-ingots-golden-treasure-513062/ archive copy at the Wayback Machine (archived on 8 November 2014) Courtesy of Pixabay, where the creator has released it explicitly under the license

22.4 Owl – a symbol for being wise. Cornelis Bloemaert (circa 1603 –1692), Uil met bril en boeken, 1625, This work is in the public domain.

23.1 Maslow's Hierarchy of Needs FireflySixtySeven, Pyramid showing Maslow's hierarchy of needs, 2 November 2014. Licensed under the Creative Commons Attribution-Share Alike 4.0 International license. https://commons.wikimedia.org/wiki/File:MaslowsHierarchyOfNeeds.svg

23.2 Maslow Hierarchy of Needs chart J. Finkelstein, Maslow Hierarchy of Needs chart, 27 October 2006. Released under the terms of the GFDL. https://upload.wikimedia.org/wikipedia/commons/thumb/5/58/Maslow%27s_hierarchy_of_needs.svg/1000px-Maslow%27s_hierarchy_of_needs.svg.png

23.3 Johari Window. Creative Commons Attribution-Share Alike 4.0 International license.

https://nursingcrib.com/wp-content/uploads/2010/10/Johari-Window.jpeg http://www.theinnovationcenter.org/files/doc/A4/CLW%20pp%20120%20Building%20Deeper%20Relationships%20with%20the%20Johari%20Window.pdf

23.4 Permission granted by Omaid Sharifi July 31, 2019

24.1 Paper money – a symbol of finance, economics, and sometimes psychology. Hohum, Obverse of United States one dollar bill, series 2003, 23:01, 3 August 2019. This image is in the public domain.

https://commons.wikimedia.org/wiki/File:United_States_one_dollar_bill,_obverse.jpg

25.1 Being creative."Black Man Getting an Idea Cartoon Vector.svg from Wikimedia Commons by Videoplasty.com, CC-BY-SA 4.0.

https://commons.wikimedia.org/wiki/File:Black_Man_Getting_an_Idea_Cartoon_Vector.svg

26.1 Inviting guest into our lives. Jean Leon Gerome Ferris (1863–1930), The First Thanksgiving, 1621, painted between circa 1912 and circa 1915. This work is in the public domain.

https://commons.wikimedia.org/wiki/File:The_First_Thanksgiving_cph.3g04961.jpg

27.1 Is sex really this complicated? Justin Gummer, Sex, Gender, Sexuality bases and precepts interlace a 3-circled venn diagram, 2 December 2017, I. Creative Commons Attribution-Share Alike 4.0 International license. https://commons.wikimedia.org/wiki/File:Sex,_Gender,_Sexuality_Interlace.png

28.1 Question mark – no matter what we want nor try, it might not happen. Stannered, Question mark; originally by Neutrality, inverted by AngryParsley, SVGed by Stannered,. 9 March 2007. In the public domain because it consists entirely of information that is common property and contains no original authorship.

https://commons.wikimedia.org/wiki/File:Question_mark_alternate.svg

28.2 Even with the best made plans, disasters happen like the sining of the Titanic. Willy Stöwer, Sinking of the Titanic (Der Untergang der Titanic), 1912. Public Doman.

https://commons.wikimedia.org/wiki/Category:Sinking_of_the_RMS_Titanic#/media/File:St%C3%B6wer_Titanic.jpg

28.3 When faced with a crisis like the sinking of the Titanic, many people rearrange the deck chairs instead of facing the crisis. Unknown photographer, 1912. In the public domain.

https://www.churchtimes.co.uk/articles/2012/13-april/comment/making-myths-out-of-the-titanic

29.1 Creating your meaning of life includes making decisions and monitoring progress. Just like directing a ship at sea, especially during a storm. Winslow Homer (1836–1910), Eight Bells,1886. This work is in the public domain

https://commons.wikimedia.org/wiki/File:WinslowHomer-Eight_Bells_1886.jpg

29.2 We live on the earth. It is, "Our Town."Augiasstallputzer, The earth. The copyright holder of this work, releases this work into the public domain https://commons.wikimedia.org/wiki/File:Globe.svg

Rec 1 War Lord with Pencils Permission granted by Omaid Sharifi July 31, 2019

Rec 2 Paddy Points the Way Image courtesy of Book Fever.

Rec 3 Trial of Hope – The Last Hill Permission granted by artist Al Rounds Al Rounds Studio, Salt Lake City, Utah August 29, 2019.

Figure List

Figure 1.1 Ivan as a one-year in Peru

Figure 1.2 Typical scene where I would play and run while the cargo was loaded and unloaded from ships. Great fun

Figure 1.3 Cover of my favorite book the babysitter would read to me.

Figure 1.4. The bear thinking about who he is

Figure 1.5 He knows he is a bear

Figure 1.6. Alone in the wheelhouse, I steered the freighter all by myself hoping it would go like a speedboat.

Figure 1.7 Then I moved the handle to full astern, then to full ahead, then full astern, then full ahead, then left the wheelhouse.

Figure 1.8 My first memory of the US.

Figure 2.1 Ivan as seven-year-old

Figure 2.2 My friends at the home

Figure 3.1 Back with mother in our new home.

Figure 3.2 My first book - it is till precious to me. After reading it, I knew in my bones that I could read.

Figure 3.3 Like Father Don Camillio, I imagined conversations with Jesus

Figure 3.4 Looking through a telescope for the first time and seeing Saturn. "There are other worlds out there!"

Figure 3.5 I alone or with others would swim in front of the oil tankers. The thrill was hearing the propeller and feeling the undertow pulling us backwards. Great fun.

Figure 4.1 Engineer units built

Figure 4.2 The result of operations in which I did not participate but indirectly supported.

Figure 4.3 Seeing the dead along some roads or fields was a nearly a daily occurrence.

Figure 4.4 Type of Chinook Helicopter that broke apart above me.

Figure 4.5 Lt William Hatcher with M79 Grenade Launcher and wearing a boonie hat.

Figure 5.1 I talked individually with almost every student and faculty member of the seminary about faith and God questions.

Figure 6.1 I was shunned but unlike Adam and Eve, I was not cast out of seminary

Figure 6.2 Similar to Captain Ahab pursuit of Moby Dick the whale, I was determined to pursue faith and God questions.

Figure 6.3 Similar to the traveler on the left, I was about to poke into new realities.

Figure 7.2 Individual pain, suffering and evil.

Figure 7.2 Corporate pain, suffering, and evil

Figure 7.3 "Warlords instead of weapons, use pencils and dialogue."

Figure 8.1 The five religions have strong beliefs on individual sin or karma and some beliefs on societal sin. Healthy people and corporations create a better world.

Figure 9 1Individual and corporate forgiveness are fundamental in the five religions

Figure 10.1 Faith is trust or confidence that one can do something like keep away from the rocks

Figure 11.1 Hope is an expectation or desire like this is the last hill

Figure 12.1 Joy is a deep sense that life is satisfying and meaningful

Figure 13.1 Love is the most important activity of life

Figure 14.1 Sexual desire is one of the most basic, misunderstood, and manipulated drives of life

Figure 15.1 God's character is enigmatic and debated for millennia

Figure 16.1 People experience their God in nature, meditation, groups, and many other ways.

Figure 16.2 I stand at your door and knock.

Figure 17.1 The five religions have similar and different views of the afterlife

Figure 18.1 Scriptures are crucial to all five religions

Figure 18.2 Two source hypothesis of the three Gospels

Figure 18.3 Percentage relationship between three Gospels

Figure 19.1 Muslim, Buddhist, Hindu, Jewish, Christian

Figure 20.1 The five religions are concerned about people in this life. While some are more concerned about the afterlife. Here the Good Samaritan is concerned about a person. Does he care about the afterlife?

Figure 21.1 Love gives the ultimate meaning to life

Figure 21.2 Work is a contribution to society, family, and oneself

Figure 22.1 Wise,.Wealthy, Happy, Healthy

Figure 23.1 Simplistic view of how Maslow viewed human needs in life

Figure 23.2 More detailed view of Maslow's hierarchy

Figure 23.3 Four quadrants of the Johari Window

Figure 23.4 Let's use honest dialogue and pencils instead of war

Figure 24.1 Understanding household finances and basic economics helps to do pretty much what you want.

Figure 25.1 Freewill is one of the most contentious issues in the five faiths and life. How much freewill do you have?

Figure 26.1 We are all guests in other people's lives

They too are guests in our lives.

Figure 27.1 Sex can't be this complicated! Can it?

Figure 28.1 Will what we want happen? It might..it might not

Figure 28.2 No one planned for the Titanic to sink. Stuff happens in life.

Figure 28.3 When a problem is about to happen, people arrange the deck chairs on the Titanic instead of addressing the problem.

Figure 29.1 Life is filled with choices. Decide which choices will you make.

Figure 29.2 The world is like the play "Our Town"

Figure 30.1 Support ArtLord's efforts in Afghanistan and around the world

Figure 30.2 Find out of print and rare books at Book Fever

Figure 30.3 Trial of Hope - The Last Hill

Acknowledgments

Many thanks to each guest in my life, for shaping my life, and in different ways contributing to this book. You were guests in my life as I was a guest in your life. Thank you.

Particular thanks to Jim Nelson for about 2,000 grammar improvements,. and editing improvements to the book and to Phyllis Barnard for dogged determinism in designing the book.

Mrs Sweeney, Mrs Adler, Mrs Olson, Miss Hansen, Mrs Charette, Mrs Ida Powell, and Mr Richmond, all who gave an outstanding grammar school education along with the many high school teachers whose names I have unfortunately long forgotten but not their faces.

Rose and Billy Shaw, Erin Hayes, Rev Henry Cornish, Robert Kopp, Betty Jean Lohwasser, Gail Fingado, Lauren Fingado, and Lloyd Schloen, for childhood and adolescent discussions.

Richard Dubsky, Ken Crawford, Jim Wendell, Eric Durling, Bruce Hillson, Al Berg, Helen Hickey, Kris Gill, Elaine Johnson, and Beth Axelson, for the many conversations and encouragement in college.

Major General Razz Waff, Major General John Tindall, Major General James Hughes, Brigadier General James Caldwell, Colonel Jim Ashenhurst, Colonel Melvyn Remus, Colonel Henry J. Thayer, Colonel Michael Bendas, Command Sergeant Major Paul & Lynn Walby, Captain Roger T. Heiman, Captain Richard Hillier, First Lieutenant Charles Stewart, First Lieutenant Ken Ament, First Lieutenant Donald Scholtz, and especially Bob Hollyfield, LTC Edward Guthrie, Chaplains Wright and Ammerman. Each in their own way gave me valuable counsel, advice, and direction in the military.

Dr Kenneth Funk for a listening ear while challenging for growth in s:tatistics and engineering . Dr Edward Dudewicz, Dr Walter Giffin, and the many other engineering professors who taught rigorous logic and testing of science and engineering.

Paul Crites, Glenn Crites, Dan Yeager, Ron Saxvik, Don Bianchamano, Holly Gardner, Dave Werve, Jim Griffith, Art Schneider, Dave Hoecker, Florian Scarlatescu, Marian Marinescu, Bogdan Scarlatescu-rafu, Catalin Savu, Christine Lecoq, Maggie Zhang, Jifu Xu, Shi Yong, Joe Berecek, Warren Waldorf, Chris Howes, Michael Ott, Parminder Singh, Paul & Wanda Peterson, Kim and Zhen Ridgway, Russ Bilowich, Roger Lee, Gary Smith, George Cunningham, Viji Vaijayanthi, Jim Griffith, and Tim Timken for their support and discussions.

Pat Chanterelle and Jim Carter for their meaningful guidance and discussions.

Dr Gilbert Rowley, Mike Jones, Robert Capestrain, Scott & Nicki Archer, Dr Julia Villasenor, Rev Mark Sherwindt, Brad Yoder, for their discussions and assistance.

Many ministers and professors: Rev Davis, Rev Charles Bergstrom, Rev Paul Kennedy, Rev Mark Scherwindt, Chaplain Ammerman, Chaplain James Wright, and Rev Henry Cornish. The Rev Professors Ron Hals, Hans Schwarz, Walter Bowman, Art Becker, Leland Elhard, Frank Seilhammer, and of course, the Unknown Priest who started me on this path. In varying ways, they all guided, stimulated, changed, and challenged my life.

Rev Jack Koch, Rev Robert Mylod, Rev Leon Appel, Rev Professors Allen Sager, Walter Bowman, Leland Elhard all of whom stayed with me in my tumultuous seminary days and afterwards.

Irene Baltes, Lutz Kliche, Wolfgang & Inge Kliche, Gerhard & Margot Kliche, Carmen Uspenski-Berghofer, Karen & Eduardo Pereira, Joan & Herb Beggs, Andy & Keiko Beggs, Amy Strombotne, David Beggs, Bobby & Tim Sargent, Steven Beggs, and Ian Beggs.

The Asheville Writers Group: Ray Russell (Chairman and President), Mike Hopping, Arlene Duane Hemmingway, Brooks Gibson, Harry Bryan, Judy

Floyd, John Waterman, Sam Bedinger, and Anne S. Cunningham for their patience, encouragement, and improving my writing.

The Unity of Blue Ridge Men's Group: Robert DeBrecht (Facilitator), Rev Morgan Barclay, Bruce Roth, Lynn Van Aiken, Milam Wall, and Evan Ruiz for patience and encouragement in listening.

The Hendersonville Humanist Group – Ken Schmidt (President), Al Worrell, Cliff Smithers, Judy and Dennis Berman, Frank Prazma, Ron Hollmeirer, Bobby Roland for the enlightening and open discussions.

The Writers' Guild of Western North Carolina led by John Waterman for giving me the courage to publish this book. Particular thanks to Steve Zaley for his advice.

The authors of thousands of books and articles that I studied, skimmed, or scanned. Particularly Bart Ehrman, John Spong, Karen Armstrong, Will & Ariel Durant, Marcus Aurelius, Hendrik Van Loon, Lewis Chafer, Joachim Jeremias, Francis Schaefer, Lewis Sperry Chafer, Josh McDowell, Soren Kierkegaard, Jean Meslier, Reinhold Niebuhr, Gerhard von Rad, Josh McDowell, Edward Gibbon, Abraham Maslow, Ernest Holmes, Mildred Norman (aka Peace Pilgrim), and Robert Fritz. Carlos Gaivar, Bob & Debbie Wood, Jim & Jane Nelson.

Most of all to my wife Marlene and my children for the patience and stamina to put up with so much pondering, questioning, and studying. It was not easy for them to put up with my mania. Last and not least for my mother being a tiger mom by teaching me the skills to read, write, arithmetic, work, persistence, and loyalty. I became her life.

Some people commented that the acknowledgments should only be a few people. However, the above communities helped form this book. So, to the people in this apparently extensive list, "Thank you."

Recommendations

Figure 30.1 Support ArtLord's efforts in Afghanistan and around the world for peace through pencils and dialogue. Reference figure 7.3

Warlord with Pencils
Available at https://www.artlords.co
https://www.facebook.com/ArtlordsofAfghanistan/
ArtLords are Afghan artists and volunteers using art and culture for social transformation and behavioral change.
Omaid Sharifi Co-Founder; President ArtLords
ArtLords.co Publisher; Kabul Diplomat Magazine
Cell. 0093700232441 | Skype. omaid.lima
@OmaidSharifi https://www.facebook.com/ArtlordsofAfghanistan/

Figure 30.2 Find out of print and rare books at Book Fever Reference figure 3.2

Book Fever, where you can find thousands of rare, used, signed, first editions and out of print books. Check it out. Great children's story.
https://bookfever.com/ heyyou@bookfever.com (209) 274-6960
https://bookfever.com/book/69213/Grew-David-PADDY-POINTS-THE-WAY-first-edition/

Figure 30.3 Trial of Hope - The Last Hill
Reference figure 11.1

""Trial of Hope – The Last Hill" by Al Rounds Al Rounds Studio, Salt Lake City, Utah https://www.alrounds.com

About the Author

Ivan Beggs has lived, worked, and traveled in the US, Europe, India, China, Vietnam, and South America. He retired from The Timken Company with the position of Program Manager and from the US Army Reserves with the rank of Colonel, two Bronze Stars and a Legion of Merit.

He tries to understand why people believe what they do.

So, he is open to conversation about the book and is willing to change the statements. Feel free to contact him as guests in each other's lives at: quest4a@protonmail.com

Education:

- Brooklyn Technical High School
- BS, Mathematics, Worcester Polytechnic Institute
- MA, Theology, Trinity Lutheran Seminary
- MS, Industrial Engineering, Ohio State University
- MBA, Business, Ohio State University
- Graduate US Army War College.
- Married with four children, four grandchildren.
- Lives in Hendersonville, North Carolina.

www.ingramcontent.com/pod-product-compliance
Lightning Source LLC
Chambersburg PA
CBHW061213070526
44584CB00029B/3817